The Polish Short Story in English

Winner of
the Kosciuszko Foundation's
Doctoral Dissertation Award
for 1967

The Polish Short Story in English

A Guide and Critical Bibliography

by

Jerzy (George) J. Maciuszko

Cleveland Public Library and Case Western Reserve University

With a Foreword by
Professor William J. Rose

Wayne State University Press, Detroit

1968

Library of Congress Catalog Card Number 68–12253

Published with financial assistance from the Polish American
Academic Association, secured through the Kosciuszko Foundation

To My Mother

Contents

Preface

The Officers and Trustees of The Kosciuszko Foundation are pleased to bestow their Doctoral Dissertation Award for 1967 upon Dr. Jerzy Maciuszko's THE POLISH SHORT STORY IN ENGLISH. This award, initiated in 1964 as part of the Foundation's programs to commemorate the Millennium of Poland's Conversion to Christianity, is granted annually to assist in the publication of that doctoral dissertation which, in the opinion of the Foundation, has made the most significant contribution to the development of Polish studies in any given year.

The Foundation congratulates Dr. Maciuszko for his painstaking attention to the details required in this important work, confident that it will play a part in making Polish literature in general and Polish short stories in particular better known to the English speaking world.

It thanks the National Executive Committee of the Polish American Academic Association and its Chapters in Chicago, Cleveland, and Detroit for their truly enlightencd commemoration of Poland's Millennium by raising the funds which have made this award possible.

Stephen P. Mizwa
President
The Kosciuszko Foundation

New York, 1967

Acknowledgments

With all its probable faults and errors of commission and omission, for which the compiler alone is responsible, this bibliography is truly a cooperative venture with help coming from so many sources that space allows only a few to be mentioned here.

First I wish to express warm thanks to my Dissertation Committee consisting of Professor Helen M. Focke, School of Library Science, Dr. John S. Diekhoff, at that time Dean, Cleveland College, and the chairman Dr. Jesse H. Shera, Dean, School of Library Science, Case Western Reserve University, for their wise counsel, valuable aid, and encouragement. (The work is based on the doctoral dissertation presented to the School of Library Science, Western Reserve University, in 1962.)

I am equally grateful for the counsel and guidance of Professor Edmund Ordon of Wayne State University, and the uncounted volumes from his private library which, as the work was progressing, kept flowing from Detroit to Cleveland. His "Tentative Bibliography of the Polish Short Story in English Translation," published in 1956 in *The Polish Review,* was very helpful. I am also in debt, for several items, to Mrs. Marion Moore Coleman and her POLISH LITERATURE IN ENGLISH TRANSLATION (1963). I share her admiration for Mrs. Eleanor Edwards Ledbetter whose pioneering work in this area was also a source of inspiration to me.

I am happy to acknowledge the assistance and cooperation of the following persons and institutions: Mrs. Huldah F. Kraemer; Miss Marion Vosburgh, at that time Librarian at Bard College; Mrs. Maria Danilewicz and her staff at the Polish Library in London; the Bibliographic Center in the Library of the University of

Warsaw; the Polish National Library in Warsaw; Dr. Alphonse S. Wolanin of the Buffalo and Erie County Public Library, New York; Dr. Józef Jasnowski of the Polish Research Centre in London. Last but not least, at the Cleveland Public Library: Miss Myrtle Graves and her staff of the Broadway Branch (at the time of writing the Polish collection was located there); Mrs. Anna Bage and her staff of the Interlibrary Loan Office; and Miss Edith Wirt, then Head of the Foreign Literature Department.

Most authors were very helpful. In that connection, the name which comes to my mind first is that of Teodozya Lisiewicz of London who, through her close association with the International P.E.N. Club Centre for Writers in Exile, has become an important link with the authors residing in England.

The Kościuszko Foundation has been a source of much help and encouragement. I wish to thank Dr. Stephen P. Mizwa, President of the Foundation, for his Preface. I am very much indebted to Professor F. Kusielewicz, Vice President, whose unfailing interest in this bibliographic venture led to securing financial assistance from the Polish American Academic Association. My grateful acknowledgment is due to the P.A.A.A. and to all the persons and institutions who helped raise the funds involved. Of the latter, one that is known to me is the Polish Veterans in Exile Association in Cleveland.

I am grateful to the staff of Wayne State University Press for their keen interest, sympathetic understanding, and many valuable suggestions which have greatly improved this work.

I wish to thank Professor William J. Rose, former Director of the School of Slavonic Studies, University of London, for his gracious Foreword.

Finally, I sincerely appreciate the skilled and determined efforts of Mrs. Hertha Kemmler in typing the manuscript.

J.J.M.

Cleveland, Ohio, 1967

Foreword

It is an honour to be asked to contribute a Foreword to this important (I should like to say "encyclopaedic") study of the Polish Short Story in English Translation. My chief difficulty is that the author has dealt so finely in his Introduction with both the art of translation and the fruits of its practice that I can add nothing of value on that score. I can, however, say something about the man who has written this book; and about the satisfaction I feel in my old age at the appearance of his work in print.*

In the autumn of 1946 a young Pole walked into my office at the School of Slavonic Studies in London. I had known him from pre-war days, having met him both in London and in Warsaw. He spoke fluent English. He had been taken prisoner of war in the Nazi campaign against Poland in 1939 and had spent almost the whole period of the war in various P.O.W. camps in Germany—an ordeal that was made less terrible by the possession of his violin. Born in Warsaw, he had won his degree at the University in English Literature, and he was now taking up the duties of In-spector of the Polish Secondary Schools in the United Kingdom. His newly wedded bride soon joined him, and we saw one another from time to time until I left London four years later. In 1951 the young couple came to the New World, and after a year on the Staff of Alliance College in Cambridge Springs, Jerzy became a student in Library Science at Western Reserve University in

---

* Fate deprived the author of these words from seeing this work in print. Professor William John Rose passed away in Vancouver, B.C., Canada on March 10, 1968. The acknowledgment of this Foreword, written while Professor Rose was still living, has been left unchanged.

Cleveland. A year later he became an Assistant in the Cleveland Public Library.

Nearly twenty-five years earlier, while teaching at Dartmouth College I had corresponded with, and come to know personally, a lady who was to do much for Polish Studies in the New World, Miss Eleanor Ledbetter (born a Texan), who was Head of Broadway Branch of the Public Library in Cleveland, and published in 1932 a valuable study on POLISH LITERATURE IN ENGLISH TRANSLATION. This was only one of a number of services done to the cause of the "melting pot" in the New World; and Dr. Maciuszko could be said to have taken up and greatly advanced the work she began.

From 1954 he was registered as an aspirant to the Doctorate in Library Science at Western Reserve, and the dissertation that won him this degree eight years later provided the sum and substance of the present volume. Already in 1958 he had been a contributor to 10 CONTEMPORARY POLISH STORIES (in English), edited by Prof. Ordon of Wayne State University in Detroit, so it is not surprising that the Press of that institution has undertaken to publish the work now completed.

Story telling must be nearly as old as human speech. It was already a "calling" or profession twenty-five hundred years ago in both of the cultural traditions that have given us our Christian civilization—that of the Semites (more precisely the Hebrews), and that of Greece. Three "short stories" are to be found in the Old Testament; and the "Rhapsodists" of early Greece, of whom Homer is the supreme example, were to leave behind them a priceless, though as yet unwritten, heritage. In view of all this, to which the achievements of the mediaeval troubadors must be added, it is perhaps surprising that the *art* of the short story, as we use the term today, is quite modern. It can be said to have been born about the middle of the nineteenth century with the work of Edgar Allan Poe and his Russian contemporary, Nicolai Gogol. The next generation produced Turgeniev, Daudet, and Maupassant; and close at their heels came two immortal Poles, Henryk Sienkiewicz and Bolesław Prus.

Our own century has seen short story writing become a profession *per se,* making acute demands on those who attempt it. What concerns us here, however, is the "lifting" of a work of art like this from one language into another, the faithful reproducing of the thought and the style of the original. On all this, in my view, Dr. Maciuszko says as nearly as possible the last word, given the space at his disposal.

One further remark. When I was growing up at the turn of the century, Poland was only a name. The land was *terre inconnue.* The people were subject to foreign powers and were discouraged from having any close converse with the rest of the world. Nevertheless, in those years three Poles—one of them a woman—won world-wide fame and distinction in quite different fields: Maria (Skłodowska) Curie, Ignacy Paderewski, and Joseph Conrad Korzeniowski. A moment's reflection on the pre-eminence of these masters should suffice to dispel any doubts in regard to Poland's distinctive contribution to the cultural pattern of Western civilization. In my view the book now to be published can well be a landmark in that process to all who take the trouble to read it.

William John Rose
University of British Columbia
Vancouver, British Columbia, 1967

15

How To Use This Bibliography

The arrangement of this work is clear and simple. Any story may be located in four different ways.

A. Suppose you have an *English* title of a story, and you want to check whether it is included in this bibliography. Your steps are as follows:
  1. Check Appendix IVa for its Polish title and the author.
  2. Then turn to the main body of the bibliography for the entry under the author; the arrangement is alphabetical. The story is listed under the author in alphabetical order by the Polish title.

B. Suppose you have only the *Polish* title.
  1. Check Appendix IVb to find the author.
  2. Turn to the main body of the work for the entry under the author as directed in A–2.

C. If all you have is the name of the *translator,* and you want to know whether any stories in his (or her) translation have been included in this work:
  1. Turn first to Appendix III. Under the name of the translator find titles of the stories in English.
  2. Proceed as directed in A.

D. If you have the *author,* and want to know which of his stories have been translated into English, you simply turn to the Index of Authors which will give you the specific page reference.
  Stories are arranged alphabetically by the original title under

17

the author. Various editions of the same translation are listed chronologically, beginning with the earliest.

Throughout the volume short story titles are italicized, while book titles are distinguished by the use of small capitals.

In bibliographic entries the use or omission of diacritical marks in the authors' names follows precisely the form used in the English translation. It is Hlasko (and not Hłasko) whenever the diacritical mark is omitted in the translation.

Diacritical marks are disregarded in the alphabetical order of letters. Thus Żeromski precedes Zieliński, etc.

Introduction

The purpose of this bibliography is threefold:

1. To provide a scholar, a publisher, or anyone interested in the subject, with a handy tool, enabling him to determine quickly which Polish stories have appeared in English translation.
2. To inform a translator contemplating a new translation as to which stories have already been rendered from Polish into English.
3. To assist a compiler of an anthology in English by supplying him with information as to what Polish stories could be considered for inclusion in the contemplated anthology. The résumés supplied for stories published in book form are designed to indicate the subject and, whenever possible, to give the flavor of the original story.

The work lists analytically all Polish stories translated into English and known to the compiler which have appeared in book form, and it includes some stories published in various periodicals. The task of attempting to include all Polish short stories appearing in English translations in periodical literature would be impractical as well as impossible. However, all the stories in *The Slavonic and East European Review* and in *Poland* (of New York) have been included. Most of the stories from *Poland* currently being published in Warsaw have been listed also. In addition, it is hoped that no items of historical importance, published in periodicals in the early period of translations, have been omitted. Although some titles from the periodicals listed in Appendix II have found their way into this bibliography, the claim to a certain completeness within reason is made only for the stories published in book form. No résumés are offered for the stories which appeared in periodicals only, or for self-contained fragments from novels frequently included in anthologies, or for those we may consider to be border-line cases, such as novellas.

The Supplement does not claim to be either comprehensive or critically selective. Its purpose is to give a reader interested in folk tales, legends, fairy tales, fables, and children's stories an idea where some of those stories in English translation can be found. Ten résumés included in the Supplement are given as random samples. The titles in this list do not belong to the genre of the short story proper, and they are offered as a supplementary material, strictly speaking outside the scope of this bibliography.

It is, moreover, not only in the Supplement that this compilation extends beyond the boundaries of the short story, as defined later on in the Introduction. Listing fragments from novels, and including such titles as Hłasko's *Ósmy dzień tygodnia* (*The Eighth Day of the Week,* a novella, i.e., a border-line case with the novel) or Fiedler's stories on the border of the reportage, may expose this compiler to a charge that he has occasionally stepped outside his marked boundaries. However, no fragments from novels are included in this bibliography without being clearly identified as such and without an indication of the title of the novel from which they have been taken. All border-line cases have been marked as have the adaptations.

Chronologically this bibliography ends with the last day of 1960. Later years may be mentioned occasionally in this Introduction or in the bio-bibliographic notes, but in the analytical entries and in the List of Anthologies and Collections (Appendix I) the end of 1960 was taken as the terminal date.

As to the subject of the stories in general, the longing for Poland's independence after the three partitions of the country at the end of the eighteenth century accounts, to a great extent, for the fact that matters related to the collective aspects of Polish life are a dominant theme of early stories. As a result of two World Wars which deeply affected practically every Polish family, war topics, including P.O.W. and concentration camps, seem to prevail in the more recent ones.

Appendix I lists primarily the titles of collections and anthologies analyzed in the main body of this bibliography (including the Supplement). But it goes beyond this. It also lists some related titles, such as collections of legends, collections of reportages bordering on the short story which have not been summarized or, in some cases, neither summarized nor analyzed. Each title in this last category has been marked as such.

The form of entries follows roughly the rules for descriptive cataloging in the Library of Congress. In many instances it has been found necessary to modify the rules in order to adapt them to the bibliography in a specialized field.

It is not the aim of this Introduction to deal at length with the art of translation. The theory of translation is a complex matter which cannot be given justice in a few lines. The brief remarks that follow stress only those problems of translating from Polish into English which are particularly relevant to this bibliography. The compiler allowed himself to indicate those specific problems with a few quotations and some observations of his own, fully aware that they do not even begin to exhaust the subject.

First there are some problems of language. Polish, like Latin, has a highly developed morphology. The Polish noun is highly inflected and has a grammatical gender; relative pronouns and participles are also inflected. It is this highly inflected noun and a broader use of participles at the beginning of subordinate clauses which permit Stefan Żeromski, Cyprian Kamil Norwid, and many other Polish writers to build long sentences without the danger of ambiguity. It allows them to build around the principal clause a number of subordinate clauses which clearly show their hierarchy and logical connection. The same feature permits placing emphasis on a word by means of word order. In the English language, where the accusative case both sounds and is written exactly like its nominative form, the function of a noun depends on its position in the clause. This excludes, in many instances, the possibility of placing emphasis by changing the word order. Where a relative pronoun is necessary to carry the principal clause to the subordinate one, the whole sentence, to avoid becoming cumbersome or ambiguous, is likely to be shorter.[1]

Another problem facing a translator from Polish into English is that of articles. There are no articles, definite or indefinite, in Polish. This poses questions in translation which go beyond the choice of a right article or a decision to omit one in English. In some instances a noun accompanied by an adjective in its superlative form in Polish can be rendered by a noun with the definite article and no adjective in English. There are cases in which the lack of articles in Polish leaves the meaning of nouns vague; this vagueness has to be conveyed in English by some other means than just the use (or omission) of an article.

There is yet another problem which affects a translation from English into Polish much more than vice versa. It is the basic difference in forms of addressing other persons in the two languages. The English pronoun "you" can be rendered in manifold ways in its Polish equivalents. In Polish for all social classes, except the peasants who still may use the second person plural corresponding to the English "you," the form *pan* (Mr. or Sir) and *pani* (Mrs. or Madam) plus a verb in the third person singular is in general use.[2]

---

[1] Discussing the difficulty of translating Żeromski into English, Olga Scherer-Virski makes these apt observations which will exemplify our theoretical deliberations.

A serious difficulty in translating Żeromski, especially into English, is found in the realm of his style. At least one of the difficulties results from the length of his sentences. While being long and compound, they are, like poetic sentences, compact, free of wordiness. Where in Polish one active word suffices to carry the main clause to the dependent without any break, feeling of wordiness or verbal fatigue, a relative pronoun must be placed in English and sometimes in French. Breaking the rhythm of the sentences it spoils Żeromski's stylistic effects. Naturally, this particular difficulty is always felt in the translation of literary texts from Slavic languages into tongues with a less inflected noun.

Olga Scherer-Virski, THE MODERN POLISH SHORT STORY ('s-Gravenhage: Mouton and company, 1955), p. 183.

[2] The Communist regime in post-war Poland made an attempt to replace *pan* with *obywatel* (citizen) and *pani* with *obywatelka* (woman-citizen), the toned

A student in the *gimnazjum* or at the university will address his instructor *panie profesorze* (the vocative) which will correspond to the American or English "sir." The employee in addressing his supervisor will use the form *Proszę pana* or *pani* (the genitive), and he may add the person's title to the phrase. The problem was still more complicated earlier in the history of Poland, when many varied forms of address were in use among the higher gentry. This requires more than a linguistic knowledge from the translator of historical fiction.

Then there is the problem of the dialect. Can, for instance, the dialect of the Polish mountaineers be successfully rendered into English? Although the following lines will be meaningful only to a Polish speaking person, a specific example is being used to make our point. Let us take as an illustration the opening lines of *Jak umarł Jakób Zych* (*The Departure of Jacob Zych*) from Kazimierz Przerwa-Tetmajer's TALES OF THE TATRAS.[3] In the Polish text the author's own words are in literary Polish, while the conversation between Zych and his wife is in dialect:

Pewnego pogodnego rana w grudniu Jakób Zych rzekł do swojej żony Katarzyny z Zeglenіów od Janika:
—Do dziśkak zył, a dzisiak umrem.
Działo się we Witowie.
Kiedy tak rzekł do żony, ona odpowiedziała:
—Ej nieboze, nieboze!
I wcstchnęła.
—Kaśka—rzekł znowu Jakób Zych—Wyzyłek godnie więcyl, jako dziewięćdziesiąt roków, moze trzi, abo pieńć.
Ona westchnęła znowu.
—A tobie bedzie blizko osiemdziesieńci. Nie bęło ci jak

---

down counterparts of the Soviet Russian *tovarishch*. In general practice the experiment failed, but it has been retained in official usage at party meetings, in government offices, etc.

3 Kazimierz Przerwa-Tetmajer, TALES OF THE TATRAS, trans. H. E. Kennedy and Zofia Umińska, foreword by William John Rose (London: Minerva Publishing Company, 1941).
Also published by Roy in New York in 1943 with a foreword by Carl Carmer. Most of these translations had appeared earlier in *The Slavonic Review*.

siedemnaście, kiek cie brał. A mnie béło pono trzidzieści, abo
mało co mniéj, abo mało co wyséj.

—Ej nieboze, nieboze! . . .

—Nie fciałaś sie wydać za mnie, zek stary.

—Hej, hej! Boze!

—Ale cie prziniewolili, zek béł bogaty.

The same in the translation of Kennedy and Umińska:

One fine morning in December Jacob Zych said to his wife
Katherine, maiden name Zeglen, of the Janik clan:

"Till today I've lived and today I shall die."

That was at Vitov.

When he said that to his wife, she replied, "Oh, poor soul,
poor soul!"

And she sighed.

"Kate," continued Jacob Zych, "I've lived a good deal more
than ninety years—perhaps three or five more."

She sighed again.

"And you must be nearly eighty. You were but seventeen
when I married you and I was thirty—not much less or more."

"Oh, poor soul, poor soul!"

"You didn't want to be my wife, for I was old."

"Dear, dear, Lord!"

"But they made you, because I was rich."

The translators faced the decision whether they should attempt to
render the dialect of Polish mountaineers into some kind of dialect
in English. *Mutatis mutandis*, translating dialect into literary English can be likened to the translation of poetry into prose. Just as
it is better, whenever possible, to translate verse into verse, so
whenever a corresponding dialect can be found and successfully
applied in the translation, it may and, perhaps with proper caution,
should be used. In this instance the decision was made against using
it; thus the dialogue between Zych and his wife is presented in
literary English. To retain to some extent the flavor of the conversation of the original and give roughly the same effect, the
translators purposely oversimplified the language. What is the
result of this method? Clearly, although some of the flavor of the
original may be retained, a great deal of it is lost in the process.
Suppose one tried to replace "more" with *mair* in the dialect of the

Scotch Highlanders, or "today" with *dhu-day,* "five" with *fiiv,* etc. At best one would have produced in the English or American reader associations with Scotland, but not with the Polish Tatra Mountains.[4] In the final analysis, one is bound to conclude that with, perhaps, a few exceptions when a satisfactory way out can be found, dialect, as a rule, is untranslatable.

Apart from any special difficulties such as those mentioned above, the complexity of the problem of translation as a whole may, to some extent, be indicated by reproducing here the six contrasting pairs arranged by Savory as twelve principles of the theory of translation. The translator, depending on the theory he follows, has to make his choice within each contrasting pair:

1. A translation must give the words of the original.
2. A translation must give the ideas of the original.
3. A translation should read like an original work.
4. A translation should read like a translation.
5. A translation should reflect the style of the original.
6. A translation should possess the style of the translator.
7. A translation should read as a contemporary of the original.
8. A translation should read as a contemporary of the translator.
9. A translation may add to or omit from the original.
10. A translation may never add to or omit from the original.
11. A translation of verse should be in prose.
12. A translation of verse should be in verse.[5]

We cannot allow ourselves to be drawn into a lengthy discussion

---

4 Olgierd Wojtasiewicz, WSTĘP DO TEORII TŁUMACZENIA (Wrocław: Zakład imienia Ossolińskich, 1957), pp. 90–91.

Although that author does not recommend translating Tetmajer's dialect of Polish Podhale into the dialect of Scotch Highlanders, he asserts that an occasional use of a word from the Scotch dialect may remind the reader that the conversation is going on in the local dialect of mountaineers, and thus produce, at least partly, an intended effect. According to Wojtasiewicz, the dialect is untranslatable.

5 Theodore Savory, THE ART OF TRANSLATION (London: Jonathan Cape, 1959), p. 49.

of this complex matter. Suffice it to say that a thorough knowledge of the two languages is not an end but only a modest beginning of the required qualifications of the translator. It is obvious that the art of translation calls for a thorough knowledge not only of the languages but also of the cultures of the peoples involved. The problem of addressing others which has already been touched upon may serve as an illustration of this point. To us the translator emerges in the role of a creator. "Like the original author he is ordering and expressing experience in dramatic and rhythmic speech."[6] The translator in the field of art should never be merely an interpreter. Even though *stricto sensu* he may not create, he does *re-create*.

> In scholastic terms, both original and translation deal with a single substance, differentiated into two unique, and incommensurable, accidents. It is this oddity, or quiddity, that changes the translator from a decorator into a re-creator, that turns him into an author or a poet, a lesser or a minor poet, to be sure, but still a genuine one. From this viewpoint he stands at the opposite pole from the performing artist, whether musician, singer, or actor. . . .[7]

The translator does not work with words alone. If he did, he would not deserve the name of "translator"; he would have stayed at the lower, interpretative level. If he is to rise above interpretation at all, he has to "transpose an alien aesthetic personality into the key of his own."[8] In other words, what comes from under the pen of the translator belongs, in a sense, to the original author, but it is *also* the translator's own creation. His task may be equally difficult when the original author lived a thousand years ago as when both the author and the translator belong to the same generation.

The art of translation is not a new art; it is unfairly taken for granted. It pays so few dividends that only too often superior minds stay away from this pursuit with the obvious result that many

---

[6] Reuben A. Brower, ed., ON TRANSLATION (Cambridge, Mass.: Harvard University Press, 1959), p. 7.

[7] Renato Poggioli, "The Added Artificer," in Brower, *op. cit.*, p. 138.

[8] *Ibid.*, p. 139.

inferior translations have been produced. We may remind ourselves
in this connection of John Dryden's words: "It seems to me that
the true reason why we have so few versions that are tolerable, is
not from the too close pursuing of the Author's Sense, but because
there are so few who have all the Talents requisite for Translations,
and that there is so little Praise and so small Encouragement for
so considerable a part of Learning."[9]

Neglected at times, and only too often looked down upon
(*traduttore–traditore*), the art of translation goes back to antiquity.
Livius Andronicus was the first who was recorded as practicing that
art in Europe; in about 240 B.C. he translated the ODYSSEY from
Greek into Latin verse. Euripides' works as well as other Greek
plays were translated into Latin by Naevius and Ennius. Cicero
and Catullus were among the many translators who translated
from Greek into Latin. In the other direction some translations
from Latin to Greek, though on a smaller scale, were also produced
during that period.

In the Middle Ages, Arabian scholars continued the classical
tradition. In the eighth and ninth centuries the works of Greek
authors were translated in Bagdad by a group of Syrian scholars.
Bagdad became the center of scholarship which was based on translating. It was the first great center and a school of translation. The
works of Aristotle, Plato, Hippocrates, and others were translated
from the original Greek into Arabic. It may well pay to say "from
the original Greek," because later on when the "college of translators" was moved to Toledo in Spain, these Arabic versions were
converted into Latin. Savory makes an apt observation when he
notes that "when a writer in the twelfth century refers to an author
like Aristotle, he may in fact be thinking of a Latin translation of
an Arabic translation of a Syriac translation of the Greek."[10]

Without venturing into a lengthy history of translation, these
few lines should be enough to indicate that the translator has a

---

9 "The Preface to Ovid's Epistles," quoted from THE POETICAL WORKS OF DRYDEN,
  a new ed. rev. by George R. Noyes (Cambridge ed.; Boston: Houghton Mifflin
  Company, 1950), p. 92.
10 Savory, *op. cit.,* p. 38.

respectable history behind him. In our times the awareness of importance of the role of the translator has been growing. His name figures more prominently on the title-page. It is less frequently that the translator remains unacknowledged altogether. The UNESCO quite rightly looks to translations as a means leading to more understanding between the peoples of the world.[11] The same faith in the translator's mission is manifested in postwar international conferences of translators of which the earliest was the First International Meeting of Literary Translators in 1958 in Warsaw, organized by the Polish P.E.N. Club, which was attended by authors and translators from all over the world, including the U.S.A. As the proceedings, published in the form of a bulletin,[12] indicate, the delegates to the Meeting were not only interested in solving their many practical problems, but they were also justly concerned about raising the prestige of the translator.

Before we proceed further let us turn our attention briefly to the short story as a genre.

In the English language brevity is implied in the very term "short story."[13] Outward brevity is unquestionably an important characteristic of this genre. It is, however, not the only one. A very short novel does not simply become a short story. Between a novel and a short story there is a distinct difference in kind.

To give but one example of differences between the two genres, the necessity for economy of means compels the short-story writer to avoid overburdening his story with dialogue. If dialogue is used,

---

11 The INDEX TRANSLATIONUM is the case in point. Although it dates back to 1932, it did not assume a serious role as a key to the literatures of the world in translation until after World War Two. It is published annually. INDEX TRANSLATIONUM. Repertoire International des Traductions. International Bibliography of Translations (Paris: International Institute of Intellectual Cooperation, 1932–1941; United Nations Educational, Scientific and Cultural Organization, 1947–).

12 Michał Rusinek, ed., P.E.N.: BULLETIN DU CENTRE POLONAIS (Warsaw, 1959).

13 This is not necessarily true of the corresponding terms in other languages. The Polish nowela, German Novelle, French nouvelle, Italian novella, suggest novelty rather than brevity.

it has to perform more than one function: it not only narrates, but also describes and characterizes (e.g. Hemingway's *The Killers*). Thus the dialogue of the short story differs essentially from that of the novel. It is not only more compact and used more sparingly; by performing multiple functions it is charged with more meaning.

A Polish novelist, Eliza Orzeszkowa (1841–1910), herself an author of excellent short stories, makes an interesting and an illuminating comparison between the two genres. Her approach is that of an artist rather than of a critic, and her definitions are given as metaphors.

> If we compare the novel to the sun, whose sparkling robe falls upon the whole world, illuminating it together with everything on it, then the short story should be compared to a burst of lightning, which briefly, yet superbly, throws light upon one corner of the world or one object in it.
>
> If the novel is a mirror, in which man, generation, humanity may be reflected from outside and from within, then the short story may be considered as a fragment of a mirror, in which only one glance, one smile, one tear, one facial expression, or one movement of the soul is reflected.[14]

Let us note that brevity is stressed in the first part of Orzeszkowa's statement. In the second part, her insistence on *"one* glance, *one* smile, *one* tear, *one* facial expression, or *one* movement of the soul" leads us to what we consider, along with brevity, as another important trait of the genre the singleness of effect.

The following quotations (not necessarily inclusive or representative of the current critical approach to the subject) suggest some emphases and characteristics attributed to the genre.

For Canby and Dashiell, for instance, the term "short story" suggests "a brief narrative, all of whose constituent parts unite to make a single impression upon the mind of the reader."[15] According to Brander Matthews (he spells Short-story with a capital S and

---

14 Konstanty Wojciechowski, "Powieść a Nowela," PAMIĘTNIK LITERACKI (Lwów, XII, 1913), pp. 204-205. Cited in Olga Scherer-Virski, *op. cit.*, p. 5.
15 Henry Seidel Canby and Alfred Dashiell, A STUDY OF THE SHORT STORY, rev. ed. (New York: Henry Holt and Company, 1935), p. 1.

insists on a hyphen) "a Short-story deals with a single character, a single event, a single emotion, or the series of emotions called forth by a single situation. . . ."[16] For Clayton Hamilton the singleness of effect in the short story is so important that he insists that the number of characters and incidents be reduced to the bare minimum, and the range of place and time be as narrow as possible. He asserts that if the author of the story can get along with two characters, he should not use three. If a single event will suffice for his effect, he should confine himself to that. If his story can pass in one place at one time, he must not disperse it over several times and places. It is equally important that this conciseness should lead to producing effect "with the utmost emphasis."[17] In his theoretical investigations, Edgar Allan Poe has also emphasized in the short story the essential unity of impression, effect, and economy.[18]

Summarizing, then, we may suggest that, apart from *external brevity,* it is *the singleness of effect leading to the unity of the structure* that is at the heart of the short story.[19]

In common with drama and the novel, the short story has plot. If the story centers on atmosphere rather than on action, the plot will be very slight, but thin as it may be, whatever happens in the story will still be called its plot. The necessary simplicity of the plot follows from the prerequisite of the singleness of effect.

---

16 Brander Matthews, "The Philosophy of the Short-Story," PEN AND INK, 3rd ed. (New York: Charles Scribner's Sons, 1902), pp. 76–77.

17 Clayton Hamilton, MATERIALS AND METHODS OF FICTION (New York: The Baker and Taylor Company, 1908), p. 175.

18 "It is only with the denouement constantly in view that we can give a plot its indispensable air of consequence, or causation, by making the incidents, and especially the tone at all points, tend to the development of intention."

Edgar Allan Poe, "Philosophy of Composition," in his POEMS . . . WITH A SELECTION OF ESSAYS, Everyman's Library ed. (London: J. M. Dent, 1927), p. 164.

19 For a more exhaustive discussion of the subject the reader is referred to the studies listed in the bibliography at the end of this volume, such as Olga Scherer-Virski's, *op. cit.*

A preconceived single effect can hardly result from a complicated plot, while external brevity is yet another factor compelling the author to simplicity.

The short story plot will, by its very nature, be less realistic and more abstracted than that of a novel. In a sense it substitutes *pars pro toto:* it is fragmentary through its external limitations, but more important still, through its tendency to the unity of the narrative structure. Hence it depends more on the imagination of the reader than the plot of a novel. Because of the possibility of supplying more details, the novel becomes more realistic, more down-to-earth, and hence better adapted to credulity than any short story.

Three types may be distinguished within the short story proper: the short story of action, of character, and of atmosphere or setting.[20] Action comes to the fore—as the term indicates—in the short story of action. The plot and the setting are dominated by the significance of character in the short story of character, whereas both the plot and the character are subordinated to atmosphere in the story of setting. Boccaccio's DECAMERON may be considered as the prototype of the short story of action. On the pages that follow Goetel's *Samson and Delilah,* Sieroszewski's *The Chukchee,* and *The Real End of the Great War* by Jerzy Zawieyski are in this category. Choynowski's *Boarding House,* Szymański's *Kowalski the Carpenter,* and *Chawa Ruby* by Świętochowski may serve as examples of the short story of character. Characterization may sometimes constitute the whole story, as is the case with *Banasiowa* by Maria Konopnicka. Stories in this category are subdivided into dynamic or dramatic stories of character (such as *Jerzy* by Grubiński) and static stories of character (Orzeszkowa's *Miss Antonina*). The former attempt to catch a significant moment in the formation of a character, the latter describe the development of a characteristic trait. Stories of character in general are, but do not necessarily have to be, biographical. The story of setting is essentially descriptive. Its plot is practically non-existent; atmos-

---

[20] In this classification the compiler follows Olga Scherer-Virski. *Op. cit.,* p. 28 ff.

phere prevails. It has no *pointe;* it dissolves into atmosphere. "Dissolution is its solution."[21] Sienkiewicz's *Sielanka* and *The New Philosophical School* by Tadeusz Różewicz are classic examples of this type.

There is one specifically Polish form which deserves our special attention. We refer to what in Polish is called *gawęda*. The author who first used this form was Henryk Rzewuski (1791–1866). This is how it is defined by Scherer-Virski:

> It narrates events and presents characters, which are usually historical, subordinating them to a coherent work; devoid of a continuous line of action or any salient characteristics capable of defining a given "gawęda" within a certain type of short story, each piece nevertheless possesses a certain unity which produces a single effect. One of the outstanding characteristics of the "gawęda" is that its structure is completely subordinated to its narrative tone.[22]

Historically *gawęda* is an early form of the Polish short story. Its classic example is Rzewuski's PAMIĄTKI SOPLICY (THE MEMOIRS OF SOPLICA, written in 1830, published 1839). In twenty-five stories Mr. Soplica, the imaginary narrator, speaks about life of the gentry in Polish Lithuania in the second half of the eighteenth century. Many of them are character sketches approaching the type of the short story of character, e.g. *Father Marek* or *King Stanisław*. Although *gawęda* may be claimed as a literary phenomenon characteristic of the early Polish short-story writing, it does not follow that traces of it are absent from other literatures. Early stories of Gogol and Pushkin have certain similarities with the Polish *gawęda*.

The short story proper, as we understand it, may often be on the border-line with a novelette, a reportage, an anecdote, etc. Any distinction between the classical short story and related genres, important as it is, has remained, so far as this bibliography is concerned, in the sphere of theory. The paramount problem in

---

21 *Ibid.,* p. 30.
22 *Ibid.,* p. 70.

this compilation has been making practical decisions which of the borderline cases to include, with full awareness that they were outside the strict definition of the classical short story. As pointed out earlier in this Introduction, the practical consideration of making this work as useful as possible has prompted the compiler to include even fragments of novels (which only too often appear in anthologies as translations of short stories) or reportages, such as those by Arkady Fiedler. It is the compiler's hope that his judgment in allowing pure theory to give way to practicality will be fully justified in the eyes of a considerate reader.

It is not our purpose in this space to present an evaluation of the short stories in the Polish original. Our emphasis is on translations. Consideration of the artistic value of the stories in the original would necessitate a discussion concerning the place of these stories in the larger context of the creative output of their authors. Any such attempt would extend this Introduction out of proportion.[23] The few remarks that follow should thus be viewed as nothing more than marginal notes which only touch the subject. Their only purpose is to give an American reader entirely unfamiliar with Polish literature some notion about the stories in the original.[24]

A repetition of the same story in various anthologies should not necessarily lead one to conclude that it is the merit of the story or the quality of translation which accounts for its recurrence. It is only too often that a compiler of an anthology encompassing literatures of various nations reaches out for what is readily available in English. Once the story has been reprinted, there is a tendency to take its literary merit for granted, especially if the author's name is big enough to appear to a compiler treading unfamiliar ground as a "safe" selection. *Zevila* by Adam Mickiewicz could be considered as a case in point. The author's greatness as

---

[23] An interested reader is referred to Olga Scherer-Virski, *op. cit.*
[24] Brief information on the subject can also be found in some bio-bibliographic notes on the authors.

a poet is undisputed. This does not change the fact that *Zevila*, judged as a short story on its own merits, is an inferior one. It is comparatively little known in Poland. What has been said of Mickiewicz could also apply to Zygmunt Krasiński and his *Legend*. The analogy cannot, however, be extended to Cyprian Kamil Norwid. Norwid's stories have their unique quality of style and imagination and they do deserve the attention of a literary critic. Norwid seems to be an exception to the rule that a great poet does not necessarily make a good short-story writer. This may—or may not—be true of a great novelist or a playwright. Stefan Żeromski, to take only one instance, is a great novelist, but, with a few exceptions, he does not reach the heights of his talent in his short stories. Henryk Sienkiewicz could be cited as an author excelling in the genre of the novel as well as the short story. However, to point out the obvious, even in dealing with such a "standard" author, one has to exercise one's judgment. Some of Sienkiewicz's novels are good and some are inferior, and the same is true of his short stories. His *Is He the Dearest One?* may be considered an interesting example of an allegorical story, but artistically it is far below the level of such masterpieces as *The Lighthouse Keeper* or *Janko the Musician*.

From the practical point of view (and this is our prime consideration), it may be of interest to the reader who is not familiar with the stories in the original to know first which of them are now considered minor classics. At the risk of oversimplification, and consciously drawing our picture with very rough lines, we may make the following generalizations: With some exceptions, all the stories by Henryk Sienkiewicz, Eliza Orzeszkowa, Bolesław Prus (pseudonym of Aleksander Głowacki), Władysław Stanisław Reymont, and Maria Konopnicka have attained the status of classics or semi-classics. The following should also be mentioned in the same breath: *The Stronger Sex, Forest Echoes,* and *Twilight,* by Stefan Żeromski; *Father Peter,* by Kazimierz Przerwa-Tetmajer; *Srul from Lubartow,* by Adam Szymański; *A Sacrifice to the Gods* and *In Autumn,* by Wacław Sieroszewski. Finally, to this list may be added the name of Adolf Dygasiński, popular author of animal stories, such as *The Just Hare.*

Among the more recent stories, some of the best are: *The Sons,* by Jerzy Andrzejewski, *The President Calls,* by Jerzy Zawieyski, and the early stories of Marek Hłasko. Tadeusz Borowski's *Ladies and Gentlemen, to the Gas Chamber* and the collection, ASCENT TO HEAVEN, by Adolf Rudnicki are representative of the best among the modern Polish documentary stories. An example of a good psychological story with philosophical overtones is *The Thimble,* written by the émigré author, Wacław Grubiński. A good detective story written in the form of a short story is Witold Gombrowicz's *Premeditated Crime.*

Calf Time, by Kornel Makuszyński could serve as a good sample of this author's humorous vein, typical of his output between the wars. Another example of a good humorous story, written in exile (after World War Two) by Mieczysław J. Lisiewicz is his *Life of a Drunkard.*[25]

The most avant-garde story which anticipated in short-story writing the style typical in France today of the so called anti-novel novels (see bio-bibliographic note on the author) is *My Father Joins the Fire Brigade,* by Bruno Schulz. Very few Polish authors have restricted themselves to the exclusive writing of short stories. Zygmunt Niedźwiecki is the one lonely soul on the Polish scene whose two hundred and fifty stories were all his literary output. (His only novel was never published.)

While some second-rate stories have been translated, printed, and reprinted, there are still some first-rate Polish stories which await translation into English. *Stara szkapa (An Old Mare)* by Maria Konopnicka or a collection of stories by Maria Dąbrowska, LUDZIE STAMTĄD (People from Yonder, 1925) could serve as an illustration of this point.

This final section of the Introduction will present, briefly, an historical survey of the Polish short story in English. The first at-

---

25 Sławomir Mrożek's excellent stories represent a satirical humorous trend in present-day Poland.

tempt to categorize the genre in English translation by dividing it into periods was made by Edmund Ordon in 1957 in his article in *The Polish Review*.[26] Each phase or stage is marked by some special characteristics distinguishing it from the preceding and the following period.

For Ordon the first stage in the spread of the Polish short story in English begins in 1884, when the first of Sienkiewicz's stories was published in English translation, and ends in 1915. This is the period dominated totally by Henryk Sienkiewicz. The second stage beginning in 1915 terminates in 1924. This is the period when the authors other than Sienkiewicz enter the scene, mainly through the able efforts of Else C. M. Benecke and Marie Busch. Translations in various periodicals and anthologies are for Edmund Ordon the characteristic feature of the next, the third stage in the spread of the Polish short story in English, between 1924 and World War Two. The fourth stage includes the years of World War Two and those immediately following. His final stage begins with the publication of Scherer-Virski's THE MODERN POLISH SHORT STORY in 1955.

This compiler has introduced into this division some modifications. His first period (1884–1915) coincides with that of Edmund Ordon. The second stage, beginning in 1915, extends over Ordon's second and third periods, making World War Two its upper boundary mark. It includes both World War One and the period between the world wars. Its distinguishing feature is a variety of authors, as contrasted to Sienkiewicz's monopoly during the first stage, as well as a variety of means, with translations appearing in periodicals, anthologies, collections, etc. The third stage begins for this compiler with World War Two and includes the postwar period ending roughly in 1955. This is the period which clearly bears the mark of the war as its distinguishing feature. Finally, the present stage beginning about 1955 brings us up to date.

Henryk Sienkiewicz was the exclusive representative of the Polish short story in English from 1884, when his *Z pamiętnika*

---

[26] Edmund Ordon, "The Reception of the Polish Short Story in English; Reflections on a Bibliography," *The Polish Review*, II (1957), 127.

poznańskiego nauczyciela was translated by W. R. Thompson under the title *Paul,* until 1915, when Else C. M. Benecke published her anthology of translations of Polish short stories, which for the first time included some other Polish authors. Thus Sienkiewicz alone dominated the scene for the period of over thirty years, during which time a total of thirty-two of his stories was translated into English, and of that number twenty-three appeared in more than one translation.[27] One story (*Za chlebem*) appeared in print in six different translations under six different titles. The story *Paul,* printed in a monthly, *The Catholic World,* in 1884, is noteworthy as the first recorded translation of the genre from Polish into English. It has, however, to be treated as an isolated case; no other translations by W. R. Thompson are known to us. It is Jeremiah Curtin to whom credit is due for introducing the Polish short story to the English-speaking reader.

Polish literature was not entirely unknown in English at that time. In England, an anthology of Polish verse, SPECIMENS OF POLISH POETS, was prepared as early as 1827 by a disciple of Jeremy Bentham and a famous polyglot, John Bowring (1792–1872), with the aid of Christian Lach Szyrma, a Pole residing in Edinburgh.[28] It was the great Polish romantic poet, Adam Mickiewicz who first attracted attention in America. It seems that James Gates Percival (1795–1856), the New England poet, was the first to translate his poetry when he rendered into English Mickiewicz's Crimean sonnet XVII, "Ruiny zamku w Bałakławic" ("The Ruins of the Castle at Balaclava"), and published it in the *New England Magazine* in April, 1835.[29] Percival's interest in Mickiewicz con-

---

27 This figure does not include fragments from the author's larger works, published in the form of a short story; see, for example, *The Escape,* a fragment from the novel WITH FIRE AND SWORD (OGNIEM I MIECZEM), in Alfred Brant and Frederick Houk Law, eds., WAR OR PEACE (New York and London: Harper & Brothers, 1938).

28 Marion Moore Coleman, ADAM MICKIEWICZ IN ENGLISH (Cambridge Springs, Penna.: Alliance College, 1954), p. 1.

29 This free translation is called an "imitation of." *New England Magazine,* VIII (1835), 291. Reprinted in James Gates Percival, DREAM OF A DAY (New Haven, 1843), pp. 139–40.

tinued, and he later translated a number of his poems.[30]

Curtin began his work as a translator of Polish literature with the historical novel, OGNIEM I MIECZEM (WITH FIRE AND SWORD) in 1888. It was so well received that he continued with seven other novels by the same author, and also rendered into English most of Sienkiewicz's short stories.

This serious activity of the prolific translator has all the appearances of a carefully planned action. There are, however, no grounds for such an assumption. According to the translator himself it was by mere chance that he undertook the work. Born in 1840[31] in Wisconsin of Irish parents, Jeremiah Curtin was educated at Harvard. He was later sent as a member of the diplomatic corps to various European and Asiatic countries.[32] While in the service of the United States government, he developed a taste for ethnology and comparative mythology. This led to linguistic studies, and Curtin mastered about seventy languages and dialects. One day while on a streetcar in Washington, D.C., Curtin noticed

---

It is not claimed that this is the earliest instance of any literary translation from Polish published in this country. The compiler is indebted for the data relating to early Mickiewicz translations to Marion Moore Coleman, *op. cit.*, p. 70.

[30] A proof that interest in Mickiewicz has been more than a passing vogue can be seen in the fact that new translations of his epic, PAN TADEUSZ, have been offered in English:

Adam Mickiewicz, PAN TADEUSZ OR THE LAST FORAY IN LITHUANIA, translated by Watson Kirkconnel, with an introductory essay by Dr. William J. Rose and notes by Professor Harold B. Segel (New York: The Polish Institute of Arts and Sciences in America, 1962).

Adam Mickiewicz, PAN TADEUSZ OR THE LAST FORAY IN LITHUANIA . . . translated into English verse with an introduction by Kenneth Mackenzie (London: The Polish Cultural Foundation, 1964).

[31] Or 1838. The date of Curtin's birth is uncertain.

[32] For some data on the early translations of Sienkiewicz and for the biographical information on Jeremiah Curtin we are indebted to the Rev. Professor Joseph Swastek. His "Pierwsi amerykańscy tłumacze Sienkiewicza" appeared in *Sodalis*, XXXVII (April–May 1956), 100–101. (*Sodalis* is published monthly by the SS. Cyril and Methodius Seminary, St. Mary's College and St. Mary's High School, Orchard Lake, Michigan.)

a passenger reading a Polish paper. He sat next to him and began a conversation in Polish. When the owner of the paper enthusiastically praised the novel printed as a serial in the paper, Curtin grew so interested that he wrote for it to Poland. This was WITH FIRE AND SWORD, the initial volume of the trilogy later translated by Curtin in full. In the summer of 1888, Curtin had the first two chapters ready, and the novel appeared in print in 1890, published by Little, Brown and Company in Boston.

Curtin's interest in the novels of Sienkiewicz inevitably led him to the short stories. The first collection of Sienkiewicz's short stories in Curtin's translation was published by the same house in 1893, under the title, YANKO THE MUSICIAN, AND OTHER STORIES, followed by LILLIAN MORRIS, AND OTHER STORIES (1894). The long list of Curtin's translations ended in 1904 with LIFE AND DEATH, AND OTHER LEGENDS AND STORIES (same publisher). Jeremiah Curtin died two years later, in 1906.

Another early translator of Polish short stories ("Polish" in this period means "Sienkiewicz's" stories) was Charlotte O'Conor-Eccles, a member of the faculty of the University of Notre Dame, Indiana. As early as 1892, she translated in the *Ave Maria*, a Catholic magazine, *Za chlebem* and *Janko Muzykant* (*Little Janko*). The first one was given the title *For Daily Bread*, and was issued in 1898 in book form as PEASANTS IN EXILE. In the period around the turn of the century many other translators appeared on the scene. Among them were: Vatslaf A. Hlasko and Thomas H. Bullick who collaborated as joint translators, Iza Young, J. Christian Bay, Casimir Gonski, Casimir W. Dyniewicz, and S. C. de Soissons. The choice of the stories was in a large measure dictated by the personal taste of the translator. The frequent selection by early translators of *Za chlebem* can easily be accounted for by the factor of locale: it is a story of the Polish immigrants in America.[33]

The period of the Polish short story in English dominated en-

---

[33] See Appendix V. The analysis of the various translations of Sienkiewicz's *Za chlebem* also throws light on the quality of translations of the period.

tirely by Henryk Sienkiewicz came to an end in 1915.[34] It was in 1915 that TALES BY POLISH AUTHORS, edited and translated by Else C. M. Benecke, appeared in English.[35] Sienkiewicz was represented in this volume by one story, *Bartek the Conqueror*, twice translated before. *Bartek the Conqueror* fitted very well into a volume dealing in part with Poles thrown by fate outside their native country. "Of the contemporary Polish authors represented in this volume, only Henryk Sienkiewicz is well known in England," writes Miss Benecke in her Translator's Note to the volume. "Although the works of Stefan Żeromski, Adam Szymański, and Wacław Sieroszewski are widely read in Poland, none have as yet appeared in English, so far as the present translator is aware."

Two stories by Żeromski were included, one by Szymański, and two by Sieroszewski. Miss Benecke considered *Srul—from Lubartow* as "the most striking of Adam Szymański's Siberian 'Sketches.'" Miss Benecke's choice of Sieroszewski's stories, which had been based on the author's studies of native Siberian tribes while he was a political exile in Siberia, was probably influenced by her belief that they would have a universal appeal.

The following year Else Benecke joined forces with Marie Busch, and the two as joint translators published MORE TALES BY POLISH AUTHORS.[36] There were new welcome names in this volume: another Polish Nobel Prize winning author, Władysław Stanisław Reymont (Sienkiewicz was absent from this collection), and Bolesław Prus (the pseudonym of Aleksander Głowacki). There were two more stories by Adam Szymański, and one by W. Sieroszewski.

This collection marks the peak of the period. It is the volume in which Benecke and Busch were actively and most fruitfully

---

[34] The reader will recall that E. Ordon has suggested this date as the beginning of the "second stage" in the spread of the Polish short story in English translation. It coincides with the beginning of this compiler's second period.

[35] Else C. M. Benecke, ed. & trans., TALES BY POLISH AUTHORS (Oxford: B. H. Blackwell, 1915).

[36] Else C. M. Benecke and Marie Busch, trans., MORE TALES BY POLISH AUTHORS (New York: Longmans, Green and Company, 1916).

collaborating.[37] From the point of view of the quality of translations, it is the best volume of the three in which Benecke had
a hand. (Of the third collection, SELECTED POLISH TALES, we shall
speak later.) As to the selection, it gives more stories by the
writers already known in English translation, but it also introduces
good new names. The stories selected are representative of their
authors. So far as subject matter is concerned, Edmund Ordon
remarks that "it is difficult to escape the conclusion that Miss
Benecke and Miss Busch intentionally chose stories which portrayed both German and Russian occupied Poland."[38]

The Benecke-Busch text is, no doubt, superior when compared
to the early translations of Sienkiewicz's stories. The two anthologies (TALES BY POLISH AUTHORS and MORE TALES BY POLISH AUTHORS)
are a big step forward in presenting the Polish short story to the
English-speaking public. Their importance can hardly be over-
rated. "They proved," as E. Ordon has pointed out, "that even
unknown Polish authors could be presented successfully to readers
of English and they set a new standard of excellence for future
translators."[39]

It was during this period that P. Selver produced the ANTHOLOGY
OF MODERN SLAVONIC LITERATURE.[40] It is divided into two parts:
prose and verse. The prose part contains selections from Russian,
Ukrainian, Polish, Czech, and Serbian authors. It includes Wiktor
Gomulicki's *The Ploughman* (*Oracz*), Bolesław Prus's *From the
Legends of Ancient Egypt* (*Z legend dawnego Egiptu*), an essay by
Stanisław Przybyszewski, *Chopin*, and a fragment from Władysław
Stanisław Reymont's ZIEMIA OBIECANA (THE PROMISED LAND). Al-
though the quality of translation in this volume is, on the whole,

---

[37] Although Marie Busch claims (in the preface to SELECTED POLISH TALES) that
she also had a hand in it, the first of the three volumes was officially published by Benecke alone. The last one, SELECTED POLISH TALES (1921) appeared
in print after Benecke's death.

[38] Ordon, *op. cit.*, p. 129.

[39] *Ibid.*

[40] P. Selver, ANTHOLOGY OF MODERN SLAVONIC LITERATURE (London: Kegan, Paul,
Trench, Trubner and Company, 1919).

satisfactory, with only four authors representing Polish prose, the matter of selection would seem open to criticism. "My aim," writes Selver in his Preface (p. v), "has been to include what is most typically racial . . ." If this was the basis of selection, then it would be difficult to account for the inclusion of *From the Legends of Ancient Egypt* by Bolesław Prus. One also might question *The Ploughman* which is not Gomulicki's most representative story, while the author himself can hardly be graded first rate.

Four years after Else Benecke's death in 1917, the final volume, titled SELECTED POLISH TALES,[41] still bearing the names of both Benecke and Busch, appeared. Miss Busch continued working on the rough drafts left by her friend, and prepared the volume for print.[42] It included authors already known, viz., Szymański, Żeromski, and Reymont, but it also introduced new authors, such as J. Kaden-Bandrowski and Zofia Nałkowska. Kaden-Bandrowski had to translate his story, *The Sentence,* into French before it could be rendered into English by Marie Busch, giving us grounds for the suspicion that Miss Busch did not know Polish, and suggesting that in the work of collaboration on the volumes published jointly with Else Benecke, she depended on the latter's knowledge of the language. Not surprisingly the quality of translation in this collection falls below the standard set by the two ladies in the previous volume.

There does not seem to be a need for singling out the period between 1924 and World War Two as a separate stage marked by

---

[41] Else C. M. Benecke and Marie Busch, trans., SELECTED POLISH TALES (London: H. Milford, 1921).

On several occasions, this compiler came across a reference to yet another title in the translation of Benecke and Busch, viz., POLISH TALES BY MODERN AUTHORS. The title is quoted by such a respectable source as A HANDBOOK OF SLAVIC STUDIES, edited by Leonid I. Strakhovsky (Cambridge, Mass.: Harvard University Press, 1949), p. 478. No such book could be found, and the compiler has a strong suspicion that it is a ghost title which has crept into bibliographies through somebody's error.

[42] "My friend the late Miss Else C. M. Benecke left a number of Polish stories in rough translation, and I am carrying out her wishes in editing them and handing them over to English readers." Preface, p. vii.

a number of translations appearing in various periodicals and anthologies. Apart from anthologies devoted entirely to Polish short stories, some stories appeared singly in periodicals and in general anthologies during this period as well as before and after. As early as 1916 Reymont's *At Twilight* (*O zmierzchu*) appeared in *The Pagan; a Magazine for Eudaemonists*. We remember that some of Sienkiewicz's stories had appeared in periodicals much earlier. As pointed out at the very outset of this survey, for this compiler the second period, beginning in 1915, continues until World War Two. It would be impossible to trace all the single short stories scattered throughout general anthologies and various periodicals. This compilation, we repeat, does not attempt to include the stories in all periodicals. But two periodical publications cannot, at this point, go unmentioned. *The Slavonic and East European Review*, published in London,[43] and *Poland* published in New York.[44]

In the very first volume of *The Slavonic Review*, 1922–23, there appeared two fragments of CHŁOPI (THE PEASANTS) by Reymont, translated by Professor Roman Dyboski under the title *The Polish Peasants*. This was only a good beginning. In 1924 *The Slavonic Review* printed another fragment from CHŁOPI, titled *The Sowers*, in the translation of S. Żółtowska. Until the end of 1960, when this bibliography closes, twenty-two stories and fragments from larger works were published in this esteemed journal. Twelve authors represented, in the chronological order of their appearance, were as follows: Władysław Stanisław Reymont, Stefan Żeromski, Bolesław Prus, Maria Konopnicka, Kazimierz Przerwa-Tetmajer, Cyprian Kamil Norwid, Gustaw Morcinek, Henryk Sienkiewicz, Ewa Łuskina, Adolf Dygasiński, Magdalena Samo-

---

43 *The Slavonic and East European Review; a Survey of the Slavonic Peoples, Their History, Economics, Philology and Literature.* Published for the University of London, School of Slavonic and East European Studies. (London: 1922–   ).

44 *Poland; a Publication and a Service.* A monthly magazine for those seeking facts, figures, and information regarding any phase of Polish life, business, current conditions . . . (New York: 1920–33).

zwaniec, and Józef Ignacy Kraszewski. As the appearance of stories was spread over a number of years, and Polish was only one of the many literatures of the Slavic peoples represented, one could hardly expect the selection of the Polish stories to follow a strictly balanced program. Yet, surprisingly, there is hardly any ground for criticism of the selection. The high quality of translations was assured by such able hands as W. J. Rose, N. B. Jopson, Roman Dyboski, Monica M. Gardner, H. E. Kennedy, and Zofia Umińska, to name but a few.

It was different with *Poland*. Most of the numerous translations which appeared in that magazine were the work of one person, Mrs. K. Żuk-Skarszewska. Ten stories by six authors were published in *Poland* in 1926 alone. The broad principle of selection was to bring in a variety of good new authors, never translated before. Translations of some outstanding authors, who had already been introduced to the English speaking public, such as Reymont, were, however, not excluded. Three translations of Sienkiewicz's stories found their way to the pages of *Poland*. (Virgilia Peterson's translation of *Jamioł*[45] was one of them.) Such authors as Piotr Choynowski, Julian Ejsmond, Ferdynand Goetel, Kornel Makuszyński, and Maria Rodziewiczówna were only a few of the newly introduced.

With regard to the quality of Żuk-Skarszewska's translations this compiler agrees with E. Ordon that "though her translations are at least satisfactory, it must be said that the speed with which she published is evident in them."[46] There is every indication that if she had taken the time, she could have improved her texts considerably. For instance, in Tetmajer's *Father Peter*[47] she renders the Polish *człowiek strzela, Pan Bóg kule nosi* by a literal word-for-word "man shoots, but God guides the bullets," when "Man

---

[45] *The Angel, Poland-America* XII (1931), 418–21.

[46] *Op. cit.*, p. 130.

[47] Reprinted in Joseph Weyssenhof *et al.*, POLISH SHORT STORIES (London: Minerva Publishing Company, 1943), p. 81. The entry in Appendix I is under the title.

proposes, God disposes" is the obvious idiomatic equivalent of this universal proverb. Although Żuk-Skarszewska's translations may be criticized, it does not follow that this should diminish our gratitude to her. There is no doubt that without her, the Polish short story would have been much less known in this country than it is.

The Slavonic and East European Review, New York's *Poland* as well as another *Poland* which was published later in Warsaw, provide excellent examples of the fact that, apart from short poems, it is the genre of the short story which is best suited to publication in magazine form. It should be stressed that this refers not only to translations, but, and perhaps primarily, to original stories. The development of the short story genre was largely due to the fact that in their compact form short stories could easily be accommodated not only in periodicals, but also in some newspapers. Many short story collections saw the light of day in book form only because they had been printed in periodicals first.

We are now ready to pass on to the third stage in the history of the Polish short story in English translation, the period of World War Two and the years immediately following the war (roughly until 1955). Four anthologies devoted exclusively to the Polish story and one collection of TALES FROM HENRYK SIENKIEWICZ[48] were published during this period. Two of the anthologies were edited by Wanda Dynowska (Umadevi) in India,[49] one by Minerva Publishing Company in London,[50] and one by Irena Morska in New York.[51]

The Monica Gardner collection of Sienkiewicz's *Tales* testifies

---

[48] Monica Gardner, ed., TALES FROM HENRY SIENKIEWICZ (London: J. M. Dent and Sons, 1946).

[49] [Wanda Dynowska] ed., POLISH SHORT STORIES; ed. Umadevi [pseud.] (Bombay: Indo-Polish Library, c1946).

[Wanda Dynowska] ed., THE WINTER MAIDENS AND OTHER STORIES; ed. Umadevi [pseud.] (Bombay: Indo-Polish Library, 1947).

[50] Weyssenhof, *op. cit.*

[51] Irena Morska, ed., POLISH AUTHORS OF TODAY AND YESTERDAY (New York: S. F. Vanni, c1947).

to the fact that interest in this author's stories in translation did not, by any means, end at the close of the first period under review. Sienkiewicz no longer held the attention of the English and American reader exclusively, but the interest in his stories never died.

The less said about the POLISH SHORT STORIES, published with the Minerva imprint in 1943 in London, the better. Not a single translation in the anthology has been acknowledged. Of twelve titles (except for two stories of Włodzimierz Perzyński and Wacław Grubiński which this compiler was unable to trace) ten translations are the unacknowledged work of Mrs. K. Żuk-Skarszewska. There is no introduction to the book, no preface, and no name on the title page of a person responsible for the selection of the stories.

We should deplore showing ingratitude for the noble efforts of Wanda Dynowska in the spread of the Polish short story in India. Her two volumes were offered to the Indian readers not merely as a means of acquainting them with some specimens of Polish literature, but also in order to promote a better understanding between the Polish and the Indian peoples. The POLISH SHORT STORIES was meant to be part of a bridge thrown between the peoples of the two nations. "In helping to build such [a] bridge every one of us can be active," writes Dynowska in the Introduction. "As a small brick in the arch of such a bridge this volume of Polish short stories is offered to the Indian public. In its three parts three different aspects and periods of Polish life are presented.[52] In view of such undeniably noble intentions, it seems petty but necessary to point to such typographical errors as "Stafan" for "Stefan" (Żeromski), or "Raymont" for "Reymont." An equally small matter is the use of such forms of names as Kazimir, which is neither Polish nor English. Much more serious is the fact that both volumes are made up of unacknowledged translations. If the editor, due to undeniable difficulties, was unable to establish the names of some translators, she at least could

---

[52] [Dynowska], ed., POLISH SHORT STORIES, *op. cit.*, p. viii.

have stated so in the preface or the introduction. Granting that some of the obstacles in publishing these volumes in India might have been insurmountable, such facts as these cast a big shadow on this venture. This compiler purposely refrains from any criticism concerning selection, which was probably limited to materials available at that time in India, and could have been hampered by restrictions imposed by the copyright.

Almost as if by design, Irena Morska seemed to follow suit in preparation of her anthology. She acknowledges some translations, notably her own, but leaves the translations of Benecke or joint translations of Benecke and Busch and some others unacknowledged. The volume was designed for the American reader, and the authors presented ranged from the turn of the nineteenth century up to the present. On the assumption that "the historical and social conditions of Poland are reflected in the literature of this period," the collection was offered "to provide an insight into the forces that created modern Poland, and thereby lead to a greater understanding of that nation."[53] Side by side with such classics as Sienkiewicz, Żeromski, Reymont, Orzeszkowa, and Prus, the collection presents some comparatively new names, e.g., Sydor Rey.

The picture becomes brighter when we pass on to three volumes of stories by single authors published during the same period. The first one chronologically is Tetmajer's TALES OF THE TATRAS, already referred to in connection with the problem of translation of the dialect. Most of the original TALES were written in the dialect of the Polish mountaineers. The translators have approached the problem cautiously and sensibly. As has already been pointed out, they decided against an attempt of rendering the Polish dialect into a comparable dialect in English. The purposeful oversimplification of the dialogue to give some effect of the use of the dialect in the original has produced good results. The translation of the TALES by Kennedy and Umińska is, on the whole, successful.

The other two collections of stories by single authors are

[53] Morska, *op. cit.*, Preface, p. vii.

47

Kazimierz Wierzyński's THE FORGOTTEN BATTLEFIELD (POBOJO-WISKO)[54] and ASCENT TO HEAVEN[55] by Adolf Rudnicki. Wierzyński's book is a collection of reportages on front-line events during World War Two. Although according to the author it is factual, it is stylized to such an extent that it can be taken as a collection of short stories. The subject of Rudnicki's stories centers on the fate of Jews in Poland during the last war. Both collections have been presented in good translations: the first by Edmund Ordon, the latter by H. C. Stevens.

Such works as Arkady Fiedler's THE RIVER OF SINGING FISH or THANK YOU, CAPTAIN, THANK YOU and Janusz Meissner's G FOR GENEVIEVE or L FOR LUCY are border-line cases, bordering on reportage. Although for the convenience of the readers who may look for them in this bibliography they have been listed, résumés of the stories have not been presented.

This brings us to our final division in the history of the trans-lations under discussion—the present period. Arbitrarily we have taken the year 1955 as its beginning, but we cannot draw the line too sharply as, for instance, we would like to include in it the first volume of THE PEN IN EXILE, edited by Paul Tabori and published in London in 1954.

The beginning of that phase coincides with the appearance in 1955 of the work, previously cited, by Olga Scherer-Virski. It is the first study of its kind in English. It contains a thorough dis-cussion of the genre, classifying short stories beginning with Rzewuski's *gawędas* and ending with the stories of Iwaszkiewicz.

---

54 Kazimierz Wierzyński, THE FORGOTTEN BATTLEFIELD, trans. Edmund Ordon; illus. Zdzislaw Czermanski (New York: Roy Publishers, c1944).

55 Adolf Rudnicki, ASCENT TO HEAVEN, trans. H. C. Stevens (New York: Roy Publishers, c1951).

    The compiler regrets that another important collection by the same author, viz., THE DEAD AND THE LIVING SEA AND OTHER STORIES, was not at hand when this Introduction was being written. Although not discussed in the Intro-duction, all the stories of that volume have been examined and included in the main body of the bibliography and in the appendices. The reader will note that three stories forming part of the ASCENT TO HEAVEN appear also in THE DEAD AND THE LIVING SEA AND OTHER STORIES.

It contains a bibliography of the subject, and includes four stories rendered into English by the author. For the first time the Polish short story is presented to the English reader in a manner as comprehensive as the materials available to the exiled author would allow.

No general anthologies have been discussed in the Introduction. An exception has to be made for two volumes of THE PEN IN EXILE, published in London in 1954 and 1956 under the editorship of Paul Tabori.[56] They contain an unusual number of Polish authors, some of whom are presented in English for the first time. A total of fifteen stories by Polish authors has appeared in those two volumes, presenting such new names as Adolf Fierla, Roman Orwid-Bulicz, Tadeusz Wittlin, Helena Heinsdorf, Janusz Kowalewski, Teodozya Lisiewicz, and Stefan Legeżyński. Unfortunately many translations remain unacknowledged; their quality is uneven.

In 1958 there appeared in this country a collection edited by Edmund Ordon, entitled 10 CONTEMPORARY POLISH STORIES.[57] The editor followed the best tradition in selection of the stories; he brought in new stories by authors already known in translation, such as Maria Dąbrowska and Kazimierz Wierzyński, and he also introduced some new authors, such as Marek Hłasko. The basis of the selection was broad; authors in exile as well as writers living in Poland were included. The volume was furnished with an excellent introduction by Olga Scherer-Virski. It is not only the conscientious editing and the good introduction which make this volume important. It is the approach to the translator which raises this collection almost to a model of editing. No fuller recognition could be given to a translator. The translations are not only acknowledged in a manner as complete as possible, but each story

---

[56] Paul Tabori, ed. THE PEN IN EXILE; AN ANTHOLOGY (London: The International P.E.N. Club Centre for Writers in Exile, 1954).

Paul Tabori, ed., THE PEN IN EXILE; A SECOND ANTHOLOGY (London: The International P.E.N. Club Centre for Writers in Exile, 1956).

[57] Edmund Ordon, ed. 10 CONTEMPORARY POLISH STORIES; trans. by various hands and with an introd. by Olga Scherer-Virski (Detroit: Wayne State University Press, 1958).

is also preceded by a brief note, first about the author, then about the translator. Although this anthology was widely reviewed, none of the reviewers expressed any reservations with regard to the quality of translations. Undoubtedly, good editorship has assured a high artistic level of the translations throughout the volume.

During the same year (1958), and also in this country, there appeared a collection of writings from contemporary Poland under the editorship of Paweł Mayewski, entitled THE BROKEN MIRROR.[58] It contained translations of short stories by Tadeusz Różewicz and Kazimierz Brandys. Różewicz's *Nowa szkoła filozoficzna* (*The New Philosophical School*) was translated by the editor of the volume, while the translation of Brandys' *Obrona Grenady* (*The Defense of Granada*) was the competent work of Norbert Guterman. We have nothing but praise for both translations.

The volumes of short stories published by the Polonia Publishing House in Warsaw bring us to the close of this brief and fragmentary survey. The first is a collection by a single author, Maria Dąbrowska, under the title of A VILLAGE WEDDING AND OTHER STORIES (GWIAZDA ZARANNA).[59] It is a collection of nine stories of unacknowledged translations. Judging by the uneven quality of the translations, this compiler believes that it is a work of various hands with the possibility that some of the texts have been prepared jointly. The next two volumes of the Polonia series require more of our attention. We are referring to POLISH SHORT STORIES[60] and CONTEMPORARY POLISH SHORT STORIES,[61] both published in

---

58 Pawel Mayewski, ed. THE BROKEN MIRROR; A COLLECTION OF WRITINGS FROM CONTEMPORARY POLAND; introd. by Lionel Trilling (New York: Random House, 1958).

59 Maria Dąbrowska, A VILLAGE WEDDING AND OTHER STORIES (Warsaw: Polonia Publishing House, 1957).
   THE DEAD AND LIVING SEA AND OTHER STORIES, by Adolf Rudnicki, published the same year by the same house, has not been discussed in this Introduction. See footnote 55, page 48.

60 Zbigniew Żabicki, comp. POLISH SHORT STORIES (Warsaw: Polonia Publishing House, 1960).

61 Andrzej Kijowski, comp. CONTEMPORARY POLISH SHORT STORIES (Warsaw: Polonia Publishing House, 1960).

1960. The first selection was prepared by Zbigniew Żabicki, the other by Andrzej Kijowski. The volumes taken together are an important milestone in the spread of the Polish short story in English. The latter two volumes are well edited, attractively presented, and are distinguished by such features as good introductions and bio-bibliographic notes about the authors. The POLISH SHORT STORIES volume also includes an interesting, though not scholarly and far from comprehensive "Bibliography of Translations."

Fourteen stories by as many authors have been selected by Zbigniew Żabicki. He begins with stories by Cyprian Kamil Norwid and Henryk Sienkiewicz, includes Orzeszkowa, Konopnicka, Prus, and Reymont, and closes with Stefan Żeromski and Andrzej Strug. Considering that no selection, however thoughtfully and impartially done, can ever satisfy everybody, this one should not raise any serious objections. The question still remains whether the stories selected are those most representative of the authors. Should, for instance, *Na trumienkę* (*For a Coffin*) be considered as the most representative story of Adolf Dygasiński? Have other than literary considerations influenced the editor's judgment? Or, is it fair to represent Konopnicka, if only one story of hers is offered, by the lesser-known and comparatively inferior *Miłosierdzie gminy* (*Community Welfare Service*)? So far as translation into English is concerned, their quality is uneven, but on the whole quite satisfactory.

Certainly valuable, but the less interesting of the two, is the collection of CONTEMPORARY POLISH SHORT STORIES. Very prudently Andrzej Kijowski has written in the preface to the volume:

> The dozen or so short stories and tales collected in this volume give a full picture neither of contemporary Polish literature nor of contemporary Polish history. Nor does the collection give an idea of the literary hierarchy and the trends within the Polish artistic environment. Eminent writers like Maria Dąbrowska, Zofia Nałkowska, Jarosław Iwaszkiewicz, who have written some of our best prose and drama, are here represented by lesser works of small significance in comparison to their full, rich output. A number of other excellent prose-writers have been left out of the

present collection simply because their literary activity does not lie within the particular genre represented here. Many a writer is shown through a work not at all characteristic of his artistic achievements.

The main purpose of this selection of Polish stories is to give a brief but full record of the experiences of the Polish people over the last twenty years. This book depicts neither the literature nor the history of the Polish nation, but it does attempt to give an outline of the psychological and moral problems involved. (p. 7)

It would be pointless to make any serious criticism of the principle of this selection after such a statement. Tadeusz Borowski (who died tragically in 1951), Bohdan Czeszko, Kornel Filipowicz, Stanisław Zieliński, and Wojciech Żukrowski are among the newly introduced authors, to name only a few. It is still difficult to understand why the story chosen to represent Maria Dąbrowska should be the same and in the same anonymous translation (*A Change Came O'er the Scenes of my Dream*) as the one already included in the volume published by the same house a few years earlier (A VILLAGE WEDDING AND OTHER STORIES). The long story by Kazimierz Brandys which took about fifty-nine pages of the text of the collection had already been published outside Poland in English in 1958 in THE BROKEN MIRROR, mentioned earlier. Jadwiga Zwolska is the translator of the story in the Polonia collection. It would not be particularly useful to indicate which of the two translations is the better one, that of Norbert Guterman (in THE BROKEN MIRROR) or of Zwolska, as, apart from everything else, the very inclusion of the story was likely to have been guided by other than strictly literary considerations.

This discussion would be incomplete without mentioning a periodical publication which has made it a routine practice to include short stories in its Polish, English, and now also American editions. We are referring to *Poland*[62] published in Warsaw. Besides its Polish and English editions, it appears also in French,

---

[62] *Poland; Illustrated Magazine.* A monthly published in Polish, English, French, German, Spanish, and Swedish (Warsaw: Polonia Publishing House, 1954–).

German, Spanish, and Swedish. Its short story feature reminds one of the *Poland* of New York. Among the obvious differences is the fact that *Poland* of Warsaw is a government publication.

Concluding this cursory survey, one is bound to note that it would be pointless to seek any form of concerted or coordinated efforts in the spread of the Polish short story in English translation. On the other hand, we could not help noticing that not only one or two periodical publications, such as *The Slavonic and East European Review* or *Poland* of New York or Warsaw, but that periodicals in general have considerably helped in the spread of the Polish short story in English. For instance, many stories which appeared later in book form had been previously printed in the magazine *Poland* (of New York) in the translation of Mrs. K. Żuk-Skarszewska, just as many stories later included in the Polonia book publications (of Warsaw) had appeared before in various periodicals such as *Twórczość* in Polish. This phenomenon is not specifically Polish. Periodicals in general help promote not only short stories in translation, but the genre of the short story as such.

We have observed a variety of situations. The development in this country and in England (many volumes of short stories were reprinted in Canada) has been noted; relevant anthologies published in India have not been overlooked. The scene dominated for a long time by one single author came to our notice at the initial period in this country. As more authors subsequently appeared on the scene, we noted a steady improvement in the quality of translations. We have focussed our attention on good collections and bad. We have often noticed translations unacknowledged, but we have also seen due attention paid to the translator. We happily note the trend today towards recognition by publisher and public alike of the translator's creative task. We have witnessed, on occasion, the printing and reprinting of inferior stories while better works passed unnoticed.

All things considered, we deem ourselves justified to end this survey on an optimistic note. Speaking of recent events, we recall an anthology devoted exclusively to Polish short stories in English which appeared in this country in 1958, followed by another anthology of Polish writings with the inclusion of short stories also published in the United States during the same year. We recall two more collections devoted entirely to short stories published in Warsaw two years later,[63] and a special short story feature in *Poland; Illustrated Magazine*. Thus it seems safe to conclude that there is a growing interest among English-speaking readers in the Polish short story. This unassuming work may, perhaps, play a small part in promoting this growth.

---

[63] As has been stated, the terminal date in the analytical entries of this bibliography is the end of December, 1960.

Bibliography of Translations

Explanatory Notes.

As has been pointed out before, this list is alphabetical by author, and by the Polish title within the author. Editions of stories by the same title are arranged chronologically, beginning with the earliest.

Most authors have been introduced by brief bio-bibliographic notes. There are no such notes in the Supplement. With, perhaps, one or two exceptions no bio-bibliographic notes have been offered for the authors whose stories in English translation have appeared in periodicals only or who are represented by fragments from larger works rather than stricto sensu *short stories. The importance of the author has no direct bearing on the length of the note. In some cases more space has been given to the authors about whom no information was readily available in print. Polish works quoted in the notes have been followed in parentheses with a more or less literal translation into English of their titles. Those which have been translated into English are indicated by use of the same type as in the original title.*

All stories which have appeared in translation in book form have been summarized. The résumé always follows the Polish title of the story with its English equivalent, and precedes the analytical entries. Stories which have appeared in periodicals only have not been summarized, and with one exception, no résumés have been included in the Supplement. Ten stories from one volume, summarized in the Supplement, are to serve as samples only. As a rule, no résumés have been given of fragments from novels or other border-line cases. In a few instances, when such a résumé is offered, the fragment has been clearly identified as such, and its source indicated.

In the proper nouns appearing in the résumés, the general rule has been to retain the Polish form whenever possible and practical. When an anglicized form of a Polish name had to be used, e.g. Yan for Jan (John), or Vavron for Wawrzon, the form suggested by the translator has been adopted. Whenever several forms were used by different translators, the compiler followed what he thought was the most sensible course to take, without adhering blindly to any hard and fast rule. On the whole, difficult Polish names were avoided. To reduce the number of footnotes, a glossary dealing with various forms of Polish names and their English equivalents has been included in the Appendices.

Two periodicals, one formerly published in New York and the other currently appearing in Warsaw, bear the same title, Poland. *The New York periodical has been identified by the place of its publication spelled out in parentheses. The periodical published in Warsaw will be recognized by its subtitle:* Illustrated Magazine, *italicized for this purpose.*

Whenever the translation was unacknowledged, the translator's name, as established by the compiler, was placed in brackets at the beginning of the analytical entry immediately following the title of the story before In *or* In his.

To avoid repetition, in a succession of analytical entries from the same book, a shorter form of entry was used, and the illustrator was usually omitted. When identical tables of contents for two different editions of the same title were to appear in close proximity, they were listed only once with the edition appearing first.

Andrzejewski, Jerzy (1909–   )

The author made his literary debut in 1932 with a volume of short stories, DROGI NIEUNIKNIONE (Inevitable Roads). In 1938 his novel, ŁAD SERCA (The Harmony of Heart), was awarded The Young Writers' Prize by the Polish Academy of

Literature. Among Andrzejewski's most important post-war works are a collection of stories, NOC (Night, 1945) and a novel which has also been made into a motion picture, POPIÓŁ I DIAMENT (Ashes and Diamonds, 1948), a keen analysis of the Polish post-war generation. His novel about late fifteenth century Spain, CIEMNOŚCI KRYJĄ ZIEMIĘ (1957) was published in 1960 in English as THE INQUISITORS. The author's short stories written between 1933 and 1958 were collected in one volume under the title NIBY GAJ (A Would-Be Grove, 1959). His most recent novel, IDZIE, SKACZĄC PO GÓRACH (1963), appeared in London as HE COMETH LEAPING UPON THE MOUNTAINS and in New York as A SITTER FOR A SATYR (the imprint of both editions in English is 1965).

Apel. Translated as *Roll Call.*
From his NOC (Night).

Roll Call. Translation anonymous. In *Poland; Illustrated Magazine*, No. 7 (71) 1960. (Am. ed.) p.13–16, 25–28.
Preceded by a brief note about the author, by Jacek Bocheński.

Mój chłopięcy ideał. Translated as *My Boyhood Hero.*

My Boyhood Hero. Translated by Krzysztof Klinger. In *Polish Perspectives; Monthly Review*, III, No. 10, 1960. p.34–37.
Preceded by an article on the author by Ryszard Matuszewski. p.30–33.
From his NIBY GAJ (A Would-be Grove), 1959.
First printed in *Nowa Kultura*, 1955.

Synowie. Translated as *The Sons.*

Résumé. The Grodzickis' only son, nineteen-year-old Janek, was killed in the Warsaw Uprising. Soon afterwards the house in which the Grodzickis were living was bombed and destroyed. They were among the few survivors. After the surrender they were shipped to one of the camps in Saxony. They were liberated in the spring of 1945 by the advancing Soviet Army. The Grodzickis decided to return to Warsaw; they wanted to find Janek's grave and transfer his body to the cemetery.

After many days of hardship, the Grodzickis reached Warsaw at the end of May. It was a bright, warm day. Hoping to find Janek's grave before dark, Helena Grodzicka was quickening her pace.

Hardly able to drag his feet, Adam remained behind. Half-way down Grójecka Street Grodzicki was suddenly seized by a violent pain in his stomach. He dragged himself into the nearest court-yard. Helena was impatient. "It's getting late," she kept saying. "Does it hurt a lot?" After a while he continued, but the attack came back four or five times. It was too late to look for the grave that day.

They decided to go by way of Śniadeckich Street where Helena's sister, Maria Olszewska, had lived. Miraculously one room of her apartment remained habitable among the rubble and ruins, and Maria was there. The Grodzickis stopped overnight. Maria asked about Janek. When she learned that he was dead, Maria confided that her son, Zbyszek, was also killed in the Uprising. She had no hope of finding his grave. (They knew that her older son had been shot by the Germans in one of the street executions.)

Early next morning Helena got up first; she was getting ready to go to look for Janek's grave by herself. There was an exchange of bitter words between her and her husband when Adam noticed she was leaving him behind. Late in the afternoon she returned tired and hunched up, her hands blackened with earth. She had searched the place where Janek's grave was supposed to be, but had found nothing.

After a moment's silence Adam whispered that he was sorry for what he had said that morning. She, in turn, insisted that it was her fault. "Now we should be very good to each other," Helena said soothingly.

From his NOC (Night).

The Sons. Translated by Edward Rothert. In CONTEMPORARY POLISH SHORT STORIES, selected by Andrzej Kijowski. Warsaw, Polonia Publishing House, 1960. p.[13]-36.

Baliński, Stanisław (1898–   )

This poet and short story writer studied law, literature and music in Poland, France and Italy. From 1925 to 1945 he served the Polish Foreign Office in Brazil, Iran, China and

Denmark. Besides his original writing, Baliński also translated English, French, Russian and Czech poetry into Polish.
The odes of John Keats appeared in London in his translation into Polish as ODY [JOHNA KEATSA] (1951). The author's
first collection of short stories was published in Warsaw in
1924 under the title MIASTO KSIĘŻYCÓW (City of the Moons).
WIELKA PODRÓŻ (A Long Journey, 1941) and TAMTEN BRZEG
NOCY (The Other Side of the Night, 1943) are examples of
his volumes of poetry which appeared in exile. His WIERSZE
ZEBRANE, 1927–1947 (Collected Poems, 1927–1947) were published in London by the Polish Writers Association in 1948.
Stanisław Baliński has settled in London.

Tak odlatują ptaki. Translated as *The Migration of the Birds.*

The Migration of the Birds, by Stanislaw Balinski. Translated
from the Polish by Frances Notley. In *New Writing and Daylight,*
Autumn 1944, p.98–104.

The Migration of the Birds, by Stanislaw Balinski. Translated
from the Polish by Frances Notley. In *The Penguin New Writing.*
[No.] 29, Autumn 1946, p.177–186.

Migration of the Birds, by Stanislaw Balinski. Translated from
the Polish by Frances Notley. In *Argosy.* September, 1946, p.35–40.
"By permission of 'New writing and Daylight' . . ."

Uśmiech losu. Translated as *The Smile of Destiny.*

Résumé. In the autumn of 1932 the narrator was sent as a
member of the Polish diplomatic corps in China from Harbin to
Pekin for some weeks. The Japanese had just occupied Manchuria,
and from the north they were drawing near to the Great Wall,
threatening the capital.

In Pekin the narrator had a friend, an old Chinese painter.
Li Chang was leaving Pekin for the South, supposedly for the
sake of its warmer climate, but his real reason was the Japanese
threat to the capital. Li Chang had destroyed his pictures. He
said he doubted whether he had a real talent. Instead of one of
his own pictures he offered the narrator a little statuette of a
smiling Buddha.

It was once a genuine object of worship in one of the temples
of Jehol. Its most important characteristic was that it brought to

its owner good or bad fortune. Should it bring misfortune the owner must not throw it away, for the ill luck would remain. He must give it as a free gift to someone else.

The narrator accepted the gift without hesitation. On his return trip to Harbin his train was derailed near Mukden. All his luggage was burnt. The ill luck continued upon his arrival in Harbin until he gave the statuette to the secretary of the Consulate.

A chain of misfortunes was now transferred to the new owner until she implored a friend of hers to take the smiling god. That very same evening the new owner fell, breaking her ankle. And so it continued.

The narrator saw his statuette again in London during the blitz, in the autumn of 1940. He went to visit his friend Stanwood. The Englishman confided that he was not in the habit of taking shelter, as he had a talisman which brought him good luck. This was the smiling Buddha. At this moment there came the sound of sirens. Fearful of Buddha's spell, the narrator insisted that they go down to the shelter. It was with great reluctance that Stanwood finally agreed. At dawn they discovered that the whole third floor, where Stanwood lived, had vanished.

Even then the Englishman asserted that the incident, taken as a whole, was a miracle of good fortune. But the narrator did not want to see the smiling face of Buddha again.

The Smile of Destiny, by Stanislas [Stanislav, in the table of contents] Balinski. Translated by Francis Notley. In THE PEN IN EXILE; a Second Anthology. Edited by Paul Tabori. [London] The International P.E.N. Club Centre for Writers in Exile, 1956. p.106–115.

Bandrowski, Juliusz Kaden (1885–1944)

In his development as a writer, Juliusz Kaden-Bandrowski made a conscious effort to rise against the commonplace. He never failed to remain an original artist even when presenting most common people in their everyday life. In his first novel, NIEZGUŁA (1911), the author portrayed a weakling led by his weakness to an inevitable degradation. As though to counterbalance it, in a most original manner he displayed strength as demonstrated in work in his second novel, ZAWODY (Contests, 1911). His most popular works include GENERAŁ BARCZ (General Barcz, 1923), WAKACJE MOICH DZIECI (My Children's Vacation, 1924) and, above all, MIASTO MOJEJ MATKI (My Mother's Town, 1924) and W CIENIU ZAPOMNIANEJ OLSZYNY (In the Shade of the Forgotten Alder-tree, 1926). Bandrowski was a member of the Polish Academy of Literature. He was killed during the Warsaw Uprising.

Wyrok. Translated as *The Sentence.*

Résumé. (A story from World War One.)

Jakób had been sitting in the chimney-corner in the straw and dust, covered with his frozen rags. He noticed something approaching from the mountains. Soon Cossacks, hairy like bears, filled his hut; the yard was full of their shaggy ponies. They ate and drank, but Jakób, hungry as he was, refused all the invitations to join in the feast. One of them put a sausage between his teeth. The old man tried to clench his teeth in refusal, but in doing so he bit the sausage. Soon he found himself eating and, when offered a drink, he accepted it. They gave him a muffler and a pair of breeches. Jakób put them on.

When the detachment was leaving, the captain asked the way to the village. Jakób explained, but the captain did not understand. To make sure that they would not return Jakób thought he had better accompany them as far as the crossroads. He felt the effect of the whiskey. At the crossroads they made him go on. First, the Cossacks took cover and then they advanced. Jakób wanted to withdraw, but the captain hit him across the head. Suddenly Jakób found himself in the midst of the fighting and the next moment he was surrounded by the Polish soldiers who were attacking the Cossacks. He threw himself at the soldiers' feet and wept. He was happy. His fear miraculously disappeared.

He was led under guard to the officer in command. Yes, he had shown the Cossacks the way. Taken to the general, he repeated the same story. A small detachment unwillingly took him back to the crossroads, and in single file down the path. They sat down by the side of a ditch. Jakób hid his head between his knees; his heart was breaking. Shots rang out. He sprang up, and then fell like a branch.

Translated into English by Marie Busch from the French text prepared for that purpose by the author.

The Sentence. In SELECTED POLISH TALES. Translated by Else C. M. Benecke and Marie Busch. London. New York [etc.] H. Milford, Oxford University Press [1921] p.307–338.

Bartkiewicz, Zygmunt (1870–1944)

Interested in old Polish traditions, village and animal life, Bartkiewicz published many of his stories first in periodicals. His early stories remind us of Dygasiński. His works include SŁABE SERCA (Weak Hearts, 1907), KRWIĄ I ATRAMENTEM (With Blood and Ink, 1919), HISTORIA JEDNEGO PODWÓRZA (The Story of a House-Yard, 1922), and POLITYKA W LESIE (Politics in the Woods, 1925).

Nudził się Pan. Translated as *The Pan was Bored.*

Résumé. His Lordship had spent the night in a spacious hotel dining room with his guests: a gentleman and two French women who were cabaret singers. He was bored, because throwing money around thoughtlessly started to get on his nerves. The Pan[1] decided to return to his estate; he took the cabaret girls with him.

After breakfast his Lordship went out to inspect the stables. While looking at the fine horses he felt an awakening interest. He asked which of the horses was not yet broken, and ordered a half-wild black stallion to be saddled. He mounted, the horse jumped violently forward and fell to the ground, throwing off the magnate. In a flash he got to his feet, jumped astride the horse and galloped away.

It was almost dark when the Pan returned home and made the black horse circle the courtyard at an even trot. He turned to his old servant, and pointing to the girls said, "Outside the gates."

The guests were politely shown the way out.

---

1 "Pan" means Mister or Sir. Here it replaces the title of nobility.

"The Pan was Bored." Translated by Irena Morska. In POLISH AUTHORS OF TODAY AND YESTERDAY . . . Selected by Irena Morska. New York, S. F. Vanni [c1947] p.1–10.

Borowski, Tadeusz (1922–1951)

The author's first volume of short stories, POŻEGNANIE Z MARIĄ (Farewell to Maria, 1947), put him in the forefront of the young writers in Poland. Borowski was entrusted with the editorship of the weekly, *Pokolenie* (Generation). He died tragically in 1951, leaving several volumes of short stories, feuilletons, political articles, and a collection of verses.

Koniec wojny. Translated as *The End of the War.*

The End of the War. Translated by Krzysztof Klinger. In *Polish Perspectives;* Monthly Review, III, No. 6, 1960. p.37–39.
First printed in *Nowiny literackie,* 1948.

Matura na Targowej. Translated as *Exams on Targowa.*

Exams on Targowa. Translated by Edward Rothert. In *Polish Perspectives;* Monthly Review, III, No. 6, 1960. p.31–35.
From his PEWIN ŻOŁNIERZ; OPOWIEŚCI SZKOLNE (A Certain Soldier; School Tales), 1947.
At head of title: Three stories by Tadeusz Borowski.
Preceded by an article on the author by Wiktor Woroszylski, "The Prosecutor Within." p.27–30.

Proszę państwa do gazu. Translated as *Ladies and Gentlemen, To the Gas Chamber.*

Résumé. (The story is told in the first person.)
The narrator was invited by a Frenchman to join the crew unloading transports at the Nazi Concentration Camp at Birkenau. He knew the "kapo" (block leader); they were short of men anyway. They marched to a typical rural station which, bordered by tall green trees, looked almost idyllic. They were posted on the platform where "goods" were unloaded for Birkenau: material for the expansion of the camp and people for the gas chambers.
The transport arrived. Freight cars were packed tight with

people. When the train stopped there began a seething and pounding inside the wooden walls of the cars. There were dull, despairing shrieks for air and water. To silence the noise the guard took aim and fired from his automatic a round at the railway cars. It was a transport of Jewish men, women and children from Sosnowiec and Będzin.

The cars were opened. The human swarm was ordered to get out with all their belongings. But as soon as their feet touched the platform, their baggage was torn from their hands. Soon the suitcases, bundles, all kinds of banknotes, gold, watches, piles of bread, ham and sausages formed a big pyramid. Again there were shrieks of women, separated from their children. No one knew his fate. The young and healthy were ordered to the right. They would not escape gassing, but first they would be put to work. The trucks drove away packed to capacity with the human cargo and returned continuously. The Red Cross ambulance travelled tirelessly; it carried the gas for poisoning the people.

Then came the order to clean the cars out. The crew jumped inside. Babies with huge heads and bloated bellies lay scattered about amidst human excrement and lost watches. The narrator carried them out, while the women were running away from them in terror. The dead bodies, the crippled and the paralyzed were unloaded and directed straight to the crematorium. The living were to be cremated alive with the dead.

Soon after the first came another transport, then still another. When the narrator, tired and sick with disgust, returned to the camp, columns of smoke rose from the crematoria. The Sosnowiec transport was already being cremated.

From his POŻEGNANIE Z MARIĄ (*Farewell to Maria*), *1947.*

Ladies and Gentlemen, To the Gas Chamber. Translated by Jadwiga Zwolska. In *Poland; Illustrated Magazine*, No. 3 (55) 1959. p.13–16.

Preceded by a brief note about the author, by Wiktor Woroszylski.

Ladies and Gentlemen, To the Gas Chamber. Translated by Jadwiga Zwolska. In CONTEMPORARY POLISH SHORT STORIES, selected by Andrzej Kijowski. Warsaw, Polonia Publishing House, 1960. p.[39]–66.

Śmierć Schillingera. Translated as *Schillinger's Death.*

Schillinger's Death. Translated by Jerzy Łowiński. In *Polish Perspectives; Monthly Review,* III, No. 6, 1960. p. 35–37.
First printed in *Nowiny literackie,* 1948.

Brandys, Kazimierz (1916–   )

In his tetralogy, MIĘDZY WOJNAMI (Between the Wars, 1947–1951), the author tackles the ideological conflict between communism and what he defines as capitalism. Brandys paints a picture of a socialist society in his novel, OBYWATELE (Citizens, 1954). He is preoccupied with the same problem of building a socialist society in a collection of stories, entitled WSPOMNIENIA Z TERAŹNIEJSZOŚCI (Recollections of the Present). A history of a proletarian family is presented in his MATKA KRÓLÓW (Mother of Kings, 1957) which was published in English under the title SONS AND COMRADES (c1960).

Obrona Grenady. Translated as *The Defence of the "Granada"/ The Defense of Granada.*

Résumé. The Granada Theater was founded by young enthusiasts who did not believe in a gentle revolution. They wanted to "kick the petty bourgeoisie in the groin." The theater was on Polna Street. Piotr Sławski was one of the founding "three," and he was the spirit of the venture. The play in rehearsal in the summer of 1949 to be presented in the fall was Mayakowski's *The Bath.* Firmly they consolidated their ideological unity. Jacek Woynar, another one of the "three," was made to separate from his wife who worked at the Swedish Embassy. Yust was the third. In September administration of the Granada was taken over by the I.O.K. (the Institute for Cultural Organizations), and Swatkowski and Miernik came to one of the rehearsals. These two were closest collaborators of Doctor Faul of the I.O.K.

The Doctor stopped the rehearsals of *The Bath,* and suggested that it be replaced with the *Shock Brigade,* a play which in simple

65

terms and in a naive plot extolled two Chmar brothers who organized a shock brigade for the better production of coal.

At first the Granada refused to put on the recommended play. It was too stupid, they said. But finally they were convinced by the Doctor's arguments. *Shock Brigade* went into rehearsal late in November. This was required of them, and this they would do.

Julka Glińska, whose husband had been arrested, and who had been dismissed from the I.O.K., was given by Piotr a vacancy on the Granada staff. Piotr paid her a great deal of attention.

Shock Brigade was a success. The victory seemed complete. Then, after a month, Swatkowski and Miernik felt that it was necessary to "organize the audience." At first their plan was rejected with contempt, but ten days later it was accepted. Routine performances followed. When Julka's husband was released from jail, Piotr had a talk with him. Soon after Piotr tried to commit suicide. He was saved, but he left the Granada. Yust and Woynar carried on.

Five years after its founding the Granada was to be transformed into a musical comedy. It seemed that the company did its duty. But, despite everything, the flame of the initial enthusiasm was not yet extinguished. Rehearsals had now begun for *The Bath*.

> *Written in Warsaw, September–October 1955.*
> *First published in Twórczość, Warsaw, January, 1956.*

The Defence of the "Granada." Translated by Jadwiga Zwolska. In CONTEMPORARY POLISH SHORT STORIES, selected by Andrzej Kijowski. Warsaw, Polonia Publishing House, 1960. p.[69]–127.

The Defense of Granada. Translated by Norbert Guterman. In THE BROKEN MIRROR; A COLLECTION OF WRITINGS FROM CONTEMPORARY POLAND, edited by Pawel Mayewski . . . Introduction by Lionel Trilling. New York, Random House [1958] p.30–75.

Brandys, Marian

Ostatnia bitwa. Translated as *The Last Battle.*

The Last Battle. Translated by Hilda Andrews. In *Polish Perspectives;* Monthly Review [II], No. 8–9 (16–17), 1958. p.41–54.

From his O KRÓLACH I KAPUŚCIE (About Kings and Cabbage), 1959.
Preceded by a note about the author, p. 41.
A border-line with a reportage.

Buczkowski, Marian Ruth (1910–)

Łącznik. Translated as *The Liaison Man.*
The Liaison Man. Translation anonymous. In *Poland; Illustrated Magazine,* No. 9 (37) 1957. p.24–27.

Bulicz, Roman Orwid, *see* Orwid-Bulicz, Roman

Bunikiewicz, Witold (1885–1946)

Żałosny żywot djabła Hejdasza. Translated as *The Sad History of Heydasz the Devil.*
The Sad History of Heydasz the Devil. Translated by K. Żuk-Skarszewska. In *Poland* (New York), XII, 1931. p.19–23.

Choromański, Michał (1904–)

The most celebrated and at the same time the most characteristic work of this author is his novel, ZAZDROŚĆ I MEDYCYNA (JEALOUSY AND MEDICINE, 1932). It won the prize of the Polish Academy of Literature. Its plot is centered on the history of love and jealousy of a provincial doctor. It was, however, not the theme but the composition of the book which made it a literary event. The action is treated retrogressively, while a great variety of methods is used to present the flashbacks. Knitting those loose fragments into an artistic entity has been the successful achievement of the author. Choromański now lives in exile.

Opowieść cyniczna. Translated as *A Cynical Tale.*

Résumé. A strange story of a marital triangle. An account of the love affair of Tykiewicz's wife, Eva, with her husband's friend, engineer Vavrzecki, is told in the first person by a witness of all events, who happens to live in a closely neighboring villa in the Polish mountains. To build tension, the reader is reminded time and again that something extraordinary is going to happen.

The climax comes when the slow-witted servant, Richie, also in love with Eva, almost strangles her in the belief that he is killing Vavrzecki when he finds her in the latter's bed. Richie stops his attempt as soon as he discovers his mistake. Eva leaves her husband.

In the train compartment the narrator himself reveals his love for Eva. The door of the compartment shuts, they kiss, and the tale closes with our heroine's words justifying the title of the story: "Of course, you won't believe the gossip that I terrorized my husband."

A Cynical Tale. Translated by Thad Kowalski. In 10 CONTEMPORARY POLISH STORIES . . . Edited by Edmund Ordon; with an introduction by Olga Scherer-Virski. Detroit, Wayne State University Press, 1958. p.53–115.

Preceded by a note about the author and the translator.

Choynowski, Piotr (1885–1935)

Choynowski is one of the few Polish authors who successfully concentrated on short story writing. His first stories bear the stamp of Maupassant. Through their precision and economy of means, his later stories were fulfilling the precepts of Edgar Allan Poe. On the other hand O PIĘCIU PANACH SULERZYCKICH (The Five Sulerzycki Gentlemen, 1928) reminds us very strongly of the early Polish "gawęda." His collections of stories include ZDARZENIE (An Event, 1911), HISTORIA NAIWNA (A Naive Story, 1913) and POKUSA (Temptation, 1918). KIJ W MROWISKU (A Stick in the Antheap, 1922) contains the same stories as ZDARZENIE with an addition of the title story. KUŹNIA (A Forge, 1926) is an historical novel of the period 1861–1863. One of Choynowski's popular novels was MŁODOŚĆ, MIŁOŚĆ, AWANTURA (Youth, Love, and Adventure, 1926).

Na stancji. Translated as *Boarding House.*

Résumé. (The scene is the professor's boarding house in Kielce. The time—Saturday afternoon. The characters: Wróblewski of the third class, Turowicz of the second, and little Chet of the first.)

Chet has been in the boarding house only a month and a half, and has earned the nickname "Mama's boy." Fourteen years old and now for his second year in the third class, "Mister" Wróblewski bullies little Chet. During his first shave with cold water in an attempt to shave off two blond hairs from a wart on his upper lip, "Mister" Wróblewski cuts his ear.

The boldness of Chet in securing the necessary alum for his tormentor transforms the "Mama's boy" into an altogether new boy who drops the "Mister" in addressing Wróblewski, and dares call him now—just as the others do—"Sparrow."[2]

Boarding House. Translated by Helen Jankowska. In 10 CONTEMPORARY POLISH STORIES . . . Edited by Edmund Ordon; with an introduction by Olga Scherer-Virski. Detroit, Wayne State University Press, 1958. p.127–133.

Preceded by a note about the author and the translator.

Pokusa. Translated as *Temptation.*

Résumé. The story is told in the first person.

A boy was sent to a Russian school in Russian-occupied Poland before World War One. His patriotic uncle and aunt had instilled in him a fervent love for his country which, at the time, had been erased from the map of Europe.

The boy earned a nickname, "the spitfire Pole," for his quick reactions whenever he felt that his forlorn country was not referred to respectfully by any of his colleagues. To the best of his ability he came to the defense of Poland against the attacks by a Russian captain of the Lancers, a cousin of the widow in whose house the boy was rooming.

---

[2] The root "wróbel" in the name "Wróblewski" means a sparrow.

He arrived in a happy mood in his uncle's and aunt's house for the Easter holiday. In this stronghold of Polish patriotism, before he knew what he was saying, the boy inadvertently suggested that in order to avert interminable questions from the Russian guests, the word "Alleluja!" in icing letters on the traditional Easter cake be inscribed in the Russian instead of in the Polish letters. This was the boy's "temptation" which his aunt considered a serious and dangerous matter. The boy's bliss was suddenly interrupted. On his aunt's orders in the midst of the happy Easter holidays, the boy was confined to his room and made, as it were, an outcast in the house.

After the punishment, accompanied by the aunt's loving tears, came the boy's reconciliation with the family.

Temptation. Translated by K. Żuk-Skarszewska. In *Poland* (New York), VII, 1926. p.350–52, 380, 382.

Temptation, by Piotr Choynowski. [Translated by K. Żuk-Skarszewska.] In POLISH SHORT STORIES, by Joseph Weyssenhof, Piotr Choynowski, Kornel Makuszynski [and others] . . . London, Minerva Publishing Company [1943] p.16–25.

Temptation. Translated by K. Żuk-Skarszewska. In THE WINTER MAIDENS AND OTHER SHORT STORIES. Edited by Umadevi. [Bombay] The Indo-Polish Library, 1947. p.42–[54].

Straszny dzień Janka. Translated as *Janek's Ordeal.*

Janek's Ordeal. Translated by K. Żuk-Skarszewska. In *Poland* (New York), VIII, 1927. p.14–17, 34–40.

Wigilja Wojewody. Translated as *The Voyevoda's Christmas Eve.*

The Voyevoda's Christmas Eve. Translated by K. Żuk-Skarszewska. In *Poland* (New York), XI, 1930. p.716–722.

Czeszko, Bohdan (1922–)

The author is one of the postwar generation of prose writers in Poland. His short story, *Początek edukacji* (*The Beginning of Education,* 1949) and the novel, POKOLENIE

(Generation, 1951), deal with the process of "ideological development" of young Communists. His more recent collection of short stories, EDUKACJA NIESENTYMENTALNA (An Unsentimental Education) and a novel, PRZYGODA W KOLORACH (An Adventure in Color) were published in 1959.

Kłopoty władzy. Translated as *Vexations of Power.*

Résumé. (The story is told in the first person.)

Four days of maintaining public order after withdrawal of the German army were for the narrator days of testing his ability to exercise power. He believed that he had failed. He lost faith in himself. Then only twenty years old, he took his problem to the secretary of the City Committee.

The secretary was bustling between two telephones. He looked very tired, but asked the narrator to go on talking while he left his desk and walked diagonally up and down the room with the measured step of a prisoner.

The narrator spoke rapidly. He told about meeting Zacharias Zaltsman, a tailor, one of the Jews liberated from the Lowa-Werke concentration camp, wrapped in a genuine Bokhara carpet which obviously had been stolen. When questioned, Zacharias replied that he felt he was entitled to it. The narrator did not take the carpet away from him. The reply of the Jew had astonished him and made him sad. Was a person subject to such astonishment capable of keeping order? asked the narrator.

Or the barracks. There were twenty new barracks on the land beyond the "Lowa" concentration camp, just as the Todt Organization had left them. They were to be sent to Warsaw with the first transport. But the Jews released from behind the barbed wire moved into some of the barracks, and started tearing down the empty ones for firewood. Despite all his power of persuasion the narrator was helpless. When he posted two guards to stop anyone carrying an axe, he caught two offenders. He could hardly stand the deadly sorrow in their eyes. . . .

He did give orders to take the hat and carbine away from one of his militiamen for terrorizing a citizen and assaulting his daughter. But when he asked his men to surrender all small arms, no one paid any attention to him. This was stumbling from one defeat to another.

The secretary's only advice was that he should call a big meeting of the workers in the district. He added that he kept walking not because he wanted to play a boss, but because he was afraid that otherwise he would fall asleep. It dawned upon the narrator that he might have been asleep anyway. And again he felt shame welling up in his chest.

From his KRZEWY KORALOWE (*Coral Reefs*), 1953.

Vexations of Power. Translated by Ilona Ralf Sues. In CONTEMPORARY POLISH SHORT STORIES, selected by Andrzej Kijowski. Warsaw, Polonia Publishing House, 1960. p.[131]-139.

Kukułka. Translated as *The Cuckoo*.

The Cuckoo. Translated by Agnieszka Glinczanka. In *Polish Perspectives; Monthly Review* [II], No. 5 (13), 1959. p.39-40.

Słonecznik. Translated as *The Sunflower*.

Sunflower. Translated by Christopher J. Klinger. In *Polish Perspectives; Monthly Review*, [II], No. 5 (13), 1959. p.36-39.

At head of title: Two stories from the collection EDUKACJA NIESENTYMENTALNA (An Unsentimental Education) by Bogdan Czeszko.

Preceded by a note about the author, p.36.

The Sunflower. Translation anonymous. In *Poland; Illustrated Magazine*, No. 6 (10) 1955. p.14.

Preceded by a brief note about the author.

From his KRZEWY KORALOWE (Coral Reefs).

Dąbrowska, Maria (1889–1965)

Dąbrowska belongs to the generation of older writers, and was one of the most distinguished authors now living in Poland. Her most important work, a novel in four volumes, NOCE I DNIE (Nights and Days, 1932–1943), is an epic of life and customs of the Polish gentry. She has shown keen insight into the life of village people in a volume of short stories, entitled LUDZIE STAMTĄD (People from Yonder, 1925). Her collection of more recent stories, GWIAZDA ZARANNA, was translated into English and published in Warsaw as A VILLAGE WEDDING AND OTHER STORIES (1957).

Dziecko. Translated as *The Child.*

Résumé. One evening, instead of discussing lofty subjects, the author (the story is autobiographical) listened to the dialogue between little Dot and her nurse. From among her toys Dot selected as her favorite that evening a big plush Teddy.

The little girl had a wonderful time and prattled that her giant Teddy insisted on eating rubbish and throwing away food. He would go to church but he did not pray; he switched the light on in the daytime and never when it was dark.

The nurse's comment was that the child was "contrary." Even at play she would have everything topsy-turvy.

The author tried to explain the phenomenon to the nurse. Dot was unconsciously following the rules of some folk songs. She was inventing what the popular songs say, for instance, about John who "carried water in a sieve, was belted with a stick and leaned on a sackcloth."

The author saw in the prattling of the child the very history of folk art.

The Child. Translation anonymous. In her A VILLAGE WEDDING AND OTHER STORIES. Warsaw, Polonia Publishing House, 1957. p.31 [34].

Jesionka. Translated as *The Winter Coat.*

Résumé. Frances, the author's housekeeper, had a way of standing at the table and talking while the others were eating. She liked telling stories.

A man was deported to Germany after the Warsaw Uprising. When the war was over, he found himself in one of the American or British Displaced Persons' Camps. He did not return to Poland for fear of being exiled to Siberia. He volunteered for work, and was sent to a post in a tropical jungle where monkeys kept throwing coconuts at him. The man was overcome by such terrible despair that he soon hanged himself. Frances' point was that "he was afraid of people and died among monkeys."

This story led to another.

After the end of war, in July, she sat on a hillock of rubble in Mokotów Fields. She met a woman who sat there with a winter coat over her arm. Questioned by Frances, the woman explained that in September 1939 her home was destroyed and burnt to cinders, while the whole family was at the funeral of her husband's mother. Again, during the Warsaw Uprising, when both she and her husband were out, their home with two children was turned into a heap of ruins.

Her most valuable possession now was her winter coat. She was so afraid of losing it that she never went anywhere without it. She always had the feeling that she would lose everything again. When she had her coat with her she thought that perhaps there would be no more wars.

"That's how that terrible war bedevilled the heads of some people," concluded Frances.

Written in 1948.

The Winter Coat. Translation anonymous. In her A VILLAGE WEDDING AND OTHER STORIES. Warsaw, Polonia Publishing House, 1957. p.25–[29].

The Winter Coat. Translation anonymous. In *Polish Perspectives;* Monthly Review, [II], No. 7 (15), 1959. p.26–28.

Preceded by "A Visit to Maria Dąbrowska," [by Lesław M. Bartelski]. p.19–25.

Ksiądz Filip. Translated as *Father Philip.*

Résumé. Father Philip had taken holy orders to please his parents. He himself had no calling for the priesthood. Both his parents, however, had died before he arrived as rector in the parish church. Doubts tormented his soul though he performed his duties well.

One day a young girl, Verosia, came in distress asking for the rector's help. She had been adopted by his parents at the time when he was leaving for the seminary. Father Philip let her stay, and love soon possessed them. The rector took to drinking heavily; his prestige among the parishioners sank low.

Shaken by a tragic incident indirectly caused by his decree after a man's confession, Father Philip suffered a stroke and died only a few minutes before his sacristan, Anthony, walked in with a letter from the bishop summoning him to appear before the diocesan curia.

Father Philip. Translated by Edmund Ordon. In 10 CONTEMPO-RARY POLISH STORIES. Translated by various hands and edited by Edmund Ordon; with an introduction by Olga Scherer-Virski. Detroit, Wayne State University Press, 1958. p.3–36.

Preceded by a note about the author and the translator.

Na wsi wesele. Translated as *A Village Wedding.*

Résumé. (This story of a postwar village wedding dramatizes the clash between the "new ideas" and the traditional village customs. It is a detailed treatment of the whole ceremony from the time the guests arrive until the moment when they start departing. Against the background of the wedding folklore, the author proceeds with a keen analysis not only of the chief characters of the wedding party, the bride, Susie Jasnota, and the bridegroom, Czesiek Ruciński, but also of their whole families and the next of kin participating in the reception.)

Although not one person from the village co-op, which represents socialistic trends, comes to the wedding, the shadow of the new order hangs over the whole ceremony. At one point a quasi-ideological quarrel between two young boys almost leads to a fight. The drunken proponent of communism displays a complete ignorance of the part played in the revolution by Marx and Lenin.

The young couple is wed in church. Susie is only seventeen, and she has to wait another year before she can give an oath at the registry. When the priest pays a brief visit to the reception, he cannot make himself at home in the atmosphere prevailing among the guests. His appearance, bringing the point of the story clearly into focus, is almost symbolic. Representing the traditional order, he is not sure whether he is welcome when he comes, and he leaves quickly to avoid uncomfortable questions about the Pope. His position in the parish is extremely difficult. No matter what he does and how much courage he shows, he always leaves somebody dissatisfied.

Michael Boguski, Susie's maternal uncle, is the first to leave. What he tells his sister Margaret in farewell seems to sum up the story. ". . . And where are you going to on this road of life? Into the future. That's why you must be careful . . . not to lose yourself out of fear, not to destroy your future. . . ."

Written in 1954.

A Village Wedding. Translation anonymous. In her A VILLAGE WEDDING AND OTHER STORIES. Warsaw, Polonia Publishing House, 1957. p.133–[216].

Nocne spotkanie. Translated as *Night Encounter.*

Résumé. (The story centers on hardships of wartime travelling, and is autobiographical.)

At a small railway station at Błonie, the author was waiting for a train to Łowicz. The station building had been burned down; the whole station was unusually quiet.

A lone railwayman explained that "civilian" trains for Łowicz did not pass that way. He invited the narrator to a tiny wooden hut temporarily serving as a station office. There was a chance that a passing military transport train might stop there.

The train did arrive and stopped. On the way to the train, the author met a young woman on her way to Sochaczew.

The Soviet commanding officer of the train refused to take the women at first; it was against orders. But as they walked off in disappointment the women were recalled; they were allowed to travel at the rear of the train on an unheated platform.

Alexey, a Soviet officer or soldier, accompanied them. He climbed with them to the top of the car, and although he could not speak Polish and the young woman knew no Russian, he began flirting with her despite the bitterly cold night wind. The cold was chilling to the marrow.

Another young Red Army man joined the group. Fedia, though only eighteen, was well-read and eager and able to discuss Russian classics with the author, who could speak the language and knew Russian literature well. He quoted by heart passages from Nekrassov.

In the middle of nowhere the train stopped for an hour. The author was almost frozen stiff; due to Alexey's intervention the commanding officer allowed her to get into the heated carriage. Alexey remained with the young woman.

When the train stopped at Sochaczew, Alexey reappeared in the carriage. He was taciturn and preoccupied, or embarrassed.

In the morning the train rolled into Łowicz.

Written in 1949.

Night Encounter. Translation anonymous. In her A VILLAGE WEDDING AND OTHER STORIES. Warsaw, Polonia Publishing House, 1957. p.41–[53].

Pani Zosia. Translated as *Madame Sophie.*

Résumé.√ Paying a visit to the "Secretariat of such and such a ministry" the author met Mrs. Turska, a widow who had lost three sons. One had perished in prison during the occupation, the other two in the Warsaw Uprising. The fourth son, a pianist, had lost a hand.

In the course of the conversation there came up the subject of Mrs. Sophie Latoska, their common acquaintance. Madame Sophie's husband was an army major who "passed" the war years in a P.O.W. camp. Mrs. Latoska had her hands full bringing up on her own their two children, Charlie and Mary. Mary, then only thirteen, was a resolute and sensible girl beyond her years. Sixteen-year-old Charlie was a partisan fighting the Nazis, who as a liaison scout took part in attacks on bridges and trains.

The author had spent two weeks at Madame Sophie's place, when she was hiding from the Nazi informers spying on her home. Madame Sophie's house was recommended to her as "exceptionally safe." Hardly had she moved in when she discovered that there was a radio hidden there, monitored by a Jewish person, and there were weapons in the garden.

Madame Latoska with her children left Warsaw in July 1944 for a month in the country. They were enjoying their first vacation on the bank of the Pilica river. Her only worry was whether she would be able to return to Warsaw in time, before what she called "important developments."

She left her vacation spot in haste. She could not get a train, so she hired a truck. They arrived in Warsaw the night before the Warsaw Uprising.

Charlie was killed the very next day in the attack on the Mokotów stronghold. A month later in Kazimierzowska Street Madame Sophie's head was torn off by a shell, when she was serving the soldiers dinner.

Major Latoski never returned to Poland. He was in France or in England, and he married again. Mary joined them, but she was not happy.

When the author left Mrs. Turska, the square she walked through was flooded with sunshine. She thought of life at grips with death which survived in the memories of those who do not forget.

Written in 1950.

Madame Sophie. Translation anonymous. In her A VILLAGE WEDDING AND OTHER STORIES. Warsaw, Polonia Publishing House, 1957. p.55–[63].

Pielgrzymka do Warszawy. Translated as *A Pilgrimage to Warsaw.*

Résumé. This is an autobiographical description of Warsaw and the hardships of travelling in this region in the period toward the end of World War Two, when the civilian population began to pour back to the city. The war was still going on, but the Soviet army had already passed through the Polish capital and pushed westward toward Berlin.

The author's journey from Dąbrowa Zduńska near Łowicz to Warsaw, and the hardships which she shared with other faithfully returning Varsovians in the bitter cold of February 1945, are described in detail. She finds her home looted but still habitable, and obtains permission (an "occupation order") from the Housing Office to move into her own apartment.

She visits the grave of her sister, Jadwiga, killed in the Warsaw Uprising and buried in the garden of a house in Mokotowska Street.

Due to illness of friends or relatives in Dąbrowa, the author decides to make the trip back, and goes through another agonizing experience of wartime travelling.

>*Written in 1945.*

A Pilgrimage to Warsaw. Translation anonymous. In her A VILLAGE WEDDING AND OTHER STORIES. Warsaw, Polonia Publishing House, 1957. p.7–[24].

Poranek w ogrodzie zoologicznym. Translated as *A Morning at the Zoo.*

Résumé. Early in the morning the author, other adults, and a little girl, Dot, went to visit the part of the Wrocław Zoo which had been newly reconstructed after the war.

The author sees a justification for living, caged animals in the Zoo. The all-too-modern idea of watching the same animals free— on a cinema screen—does not appeal to her.

Some birds and animals seen in the Zoo are described.

Beyond pavilions hidden behind scaffoldings, the group discovers a children's slide. The adults take a seat on a bench, while little Dot keeps sliding down unassisted, to her heart's delight. She is setting an example of bravery to some boys who are older than herself.

It was a bucolic and wonderfully carefree morning.

>*Written in 1949.*

A Morning at the Zoo. Translation anonymous. In her A VILLAGE WEDDING AND OTHER STORIES. Warsaw, Polonia Publishing House, 1957. p.35–[40].

Trzecia jesień. Translated as *The Third Autumn.*

Résumé. (The story deals with postwar life in Warsaw.)

Clement Łohojski lived in a low bungalow which used to be part of the outbuildings of a suburban garden residence. He occupied just one room with a diminutive hall. Surrounded by splendid modern blocks of flats, the bungalow survived for the time being. Besides the simplest, most basic furniture, Łohojski had collected in his room practically anything that any of his neighbors might ever want. "Go and ask Łohojski. He is sure to have it," had become a proverbial saying.

Łohojski's dream was to have a small allotment of his own. While others were able to cultivate their own flowers and garden vegetables, he was refused on the ground that he had no regular employment and allegedly his papers were not in order. He could not produce his birth certificate.

Clement had just completed his first year at the St. Petersburg Agricultural Institute when his father died. He had to give up his studies and go to work to support himself, his sister and his mother. Life was too expensive in the Russian capital. They moved to a small provincial town in the Urals. His next post was that of a private tutor in a residence of a Polish landowner in the Ukraine. The October Revolution had found him as a second lieutenant, convalescing in a hospital in a West Russian town. When the Bolsheviks captured the town, the nurses of the hospital burned all the officers' documents.

Finally, through the help of a carpenter neighbor, Strojny, his dream came partially true. Łohojski was given permission to work on the allotment of a Mrs. Mielczarek whose husband was an habitual alcoholic, and who was unable to do any work on it herself. It turned out that Łohojski had once called an ambulance when he found Mielczarek lying in the street early one morning.

Łohojski turned his allotment into a miniature agricultural experiment station. Even then he seemed to be working more on the neighboring allotments than on his own. In the third autumn suddenly and unexpectedly the news came that for his allotment Łohojski was awarded a prize.

Never discouraged and always ready to help others, Łohojski fought against adversities all his life. It was at the very end of it that a bright streak of light crossed his path.

Written in 1954.

The Third Autumn. Translation anonymous. In her A VILLAGE WEDDING AND OTHER STORIES. Warsaw, Polonia Publishing House, 1957. p.77–[132].

Tu zaszła zmiana. Translated as *"A Change Came o'er the Scenes of My Dream."*

Résumé. (The title paraphrases Byron's refrain in *The Dream*.[3] In Polish, the title follows the adaptation by Mickiewicz.) The changing scene as observed by the author from the windows of her study for the past thirty-four years, far from being monotonous, symbolizes the recent history not only of Warsaw, but, to a certain extent, of the whole country. Each section ends with the same refrain which gives the story its title.

Before the war the author could see from her window a typical, old-fashioned building of Warsaw suburbs, in the style built at the beginning of the century. It was squeezed between a school on Polna Street and the end of Jaworzyńska Street. From that house right up to her windows there stretched a luxurious garden. It was almost a rustic retreat. The calm aspect of the garden stood in sharp contrast to the swarming and noisy school next door.

In September 1939 the horses of the cavalry detachment tore at the leaves of the trees. The cavalrymen soon left. Other soldiers came. They cut down several trees, and a battery of light guns was brought into the garden. They too departed. Then came the night of the occupation.

In May 1943 during an air raid, a bomb fell in the middle of the garden, and made a huge crater in the lawn. The next bomb was a half-tonner. It killed and buried alive many people.

August 1944. The Warsaw Uprising. A barricade went up between the school and the house in which the author lived.

When the Germans left Warsaw in 1945, there were about twenty graves in the garden-cemetery. Not a trace remained of the out-buildings. The school building was hurriedly repaired, and the former garden became a provisional playground for the school children of all age groups. At the instigation of the author's

---

[3] "A change came o'er the spirit of my dream."

81

nephew, the school children, who had been tramping over the graves, cleared the garden of weeds and meticulously adorned every grave. One December night there came an exhumation brigade. Soon after the garden was turned into a regular school playground.

The work of reconstruction to build new Poland had begun.

Written in 1951.

"*A Change Came o'er the Scenes of My Dream.*" Translation anonymous. In her A VILLAGE WEDDING AND OTHER STORIES. Warsaw, Polonia Publishing House, 1957. p.65–[75].

A Change Came o'er the Scenes of My Dream. Translation anonymous. In CONTEMPORARY POLISH SHORT STORIES, selected by Andrzej Kijowski. Warsaw, Polonia Publishing House, 1960. p.[143]–154.

W piękny letni poranek. Translated as *On a Beautiful Summer Morning.*

On a Beautiful Summer Morning. Translation anonymous. In *Poland: Illustrated Magazine,* No. 4 (56) 1959. p.16. 25–28.

A note about the author, by Wilhelm Mach: p.14.

Dygasiński, Adolf (1839–1902)

One of the most prominent representatives of the Polish naturalist school in literature, Dygasiński was an educator as well as an author of novels and short stories. He was equally successful in painting the life of the manor, as he was in the description of the small town or village. Gifted with the ability to pierce the secrets of the animal soul, Dygasiński became famous for his stories of animal life. His works include NOWELE (Short Stories, 1884–1886), NA PAŃSKIM DWORZE (On the Master's Estate, 1884) and WŁAŚCICIELE (Proprietors, 1887). GODY ŻYCIA (Feast of Life, 1902) is his most popular novel.

The Fern Flower of Happiness. From his GODY ŻYCIA (*Feast of Life*).

The Fern Flower of Happiness. Translated and adapted by Florence Wassell. In THE WAYSIDE WILLOW: Prose and Verse. Edited by Marion Moore Coleman. Student editor: Loretta M. Bielawska.

[Trenton. Printed by the White Eagle Publishing Company, 1945]. p.5–6.

Na trumienkę. Translated as *For a Coffin.*

Résumé. An old man threw himself into the powerful current of the Bug river to get possession of a plank. He safely fished it out. Asked by a passer-by why he needed the plank, he explained that he meant to use it as—a lid for a coffin.

He was sixty-seven years old. He worked for the distillery, and surely would have been dismissed if it had not been for his daughter Marysia, who carried heavy sacks of potatoes to be mashed at the distillery for him. She hurt herself and died. She would have been nineteen on St. Mary's day.

The old man had asked for planks for the coffin at the estate, but he was refused. He tried to sneak into the barn, and was caught by the guard, who took away his cap and his coat. He tried another estate, but the master was away on a journey.

While talking to the narrator, he saw more planks in the water. Not hearing the narrator's shouted offer to get some planks for him, he jumped into the river again. This time the powerful current swept him into a whirlpool. There his life and his grief came to an end.

First published in 1889.

For a Coffin. Translated by Ilona Ralf Sues. In POLISH SHORT STORIES, selected by Zbigniew Żabicki. Warsaw, Polonia Publishing House, 1960. p.183–[187].

Sprawiedliwy zając. Translated as *The Just Hare.*

Résumé. Once upon a time there lived in a certain village a peasant called Matthias who was a very good man. One day he was collecting dry wood in a forest and was making it into a pile, when he caught a sound of something groaning nearby. An enormous spruce tree had fallen and crushed a bear. The bear begged the peasant to have pity on him and save his life. Matthias was seized with compassion and saved the bear.

Some time passed. Matthias went again to the forest for firewood. The first thing he saw there was the bear who asked him if he was the man who once saved his life. When Matthias assented, the bear said that he owed him a debt of gratitude, and therefore he must . . . eat him up. The bear insisted that everybody in this world paid back good with evil. The peasant was indignant. He firmly believed that justice and gratitude have existed and will go on existing in this world. The bear agreed that he would admit that Matthias was right only if he could find a judge who would decide the case between them.

Matthias first called a fellow peasant. The man suggested that Matthias pay him if he is to decide in his favor. Matthias called an ox. The ox called both of them butchers, and stated frankly that he should be glad if the devil took at least one of them. In turn, the peasant called a ram, a dog, a horse, a fox, and a wolf, with the same results. A swallow chirped that only those know justice who have themselves experienced injustice. Just then a hare tumbled out from under the bush, and told Matthias that he had heard about his adventure with the bear. The hare asserted that although created beings were often ungrateful, justice proceeds from God Himself, and it would never pass away.

The hearing began. The hare insisted that he had to see for himself how the bear looked when he was under the tree trunk. When the bear had lain down, the hare winked, and the peasant quickly pulled out the supporting logs. The trunk crushed the bear. The hare told the bear that now things were as they had been at the beginning. If there was no gratitude in the world, justice had overtaken him. Then he turned to Matthias and asked him to keep gratitude and justice in his heart whether or not he might be the only man in the world who possessed them.

The Just Hare. Translated by D. F. Tait. In *The Slavonic Yearbook,* being Volume XIX of the *Slavonic and East European Review,* n.d. p.29–33.

The Just Hare. Translated by D. F. Tait. In WORLD LITERATURE; an Anthology of Human Experience, edited by Arthur E. Christy and Henry W. Wells. New York, American Book Company [c1947]. p.99–101.

Dygat, Stanisław (1914–   )

Dygat is one of the more talented among the postwar generation of writers in Poland. He is the author of the collections of stories, POLA ELIZEJSKIE (Elysian Fields, 1949), SŁOTNE WIECZORY (Rainy Evenings) and RÓŻOWY KAJECIK (A Pink Notebook). A selection from them was later published in a volume, NA PIĘĆ MINUT PRZED ZAŚNIĘCIEM (Five Minutes Before Falling Asleep, 1960). JEZIORO BODEŃSKIE (Lake Constance) is the best known of his novels.

Bardzo ciasny punkt widzenia. Translated as *A Rather Narrow Point of View.*

A Rather Narrow Point of View. Translation anonymous. Drawings by T. Bogdański. In *Poland; Illustrated Magazine,* No. 7 (35) 1957. p.27.
Preceded by a brief note about the author.

Dalekie podróże. Translated as *Long Journey.*

Résumé. Marion sighed. Terrible things were happening behind his back. His children fought and hurled vulgar words at each other. His wife was peeling potatoes, shouting at the children.

He thought, "One more step, perhaps two, and old age will get me by the neck." Girls dressed in brightly colored skirts walked by in the street. His children began asking questions which he was unable to answer. His wife put a pot full of potatoes on the stove. She began asking him commonplace questions, and became angry when he answered her in monosyllables. He had time for everything except her. The children continued to fight. Marion put aside his paper, and thought, "I still have the night. I still own my dreams. Nobody has the right to invade my dreams." At night his wife nagged at him. She wept. When he said nothing and only sighed now and then, she bit him on the nose.

On his way from the office, Marion met Alfred. Alfred was leaving for Brussels, for a conference. Marion made an envious remark about Alfred's life full of adventure. Suddenly he thought of something. He asked Alfred for the keys to his apartment. Marion clutched the keys in his hand; he felt strange and shivered slightly.

When he told his wife of a meeting that night, and that he was going to be late, his voice sounded foreign and unpleasant to him. As he opened the door of Alfred's apartment, his hands trembled and his throat was dry. Quickly he took off his coat, ran smiling into the room, flung out his arms and took a deep whiff of air. The room was quiet. A scent of lavender and English cigarettes still lingered in it. Gaily, he began to dance until, exhausted, he sat down in an armchair. He reached for the phone, and speaking into the humming emptiness pretended that he, Director Jack Brown of Alabama, was reserving two seats on a plane to Rome tomorrow. In another call to nobody he ordered supper for two: whisky, champagne, lobsters . . . He fell silent and began to stare at the wall. He walked toward the window. Girls dressed in brightly colored skirts walked by in the street. He hid his face in his hands, and began to cry.

> *First published in* Przegląd Kulturalny, *Warsaw, September 9, 1956.*

Long Journey, by Stanislaw Dygat. Translation anonymous. In *East Europe; a Monthly Review of East European Affairs, VI, No. 3, 1957. p.29.*

Long Journey, by Stanislaw Dygat. Translation anonymous. In BITTER HARVEST; the Intellectual Revolt Behind the Iron Curtain. Edited by Edmund Stillman; introduction by François Bondy. London, Thames and Hudson [1959]. p.42–44.

Reprinted from *East Europe.*

Filozof Panteleon. Translated as *The Philosopher Panteleon.*

The Philosopher Panteleon, by Stanislaw Dygat. Translation anonymous. In *Poland of Today,* III, No. 11, 1948. p.12, 20.

From his POLA ELIZEJSKIE (Elysian Fields).

Stary profesor. Translated as *The Old Professor.*

The Old Professor. Translation anonymous. Drawings by T.

Bogdański. In *Poland; Illustrated Magazine*. No. 7 (35) 1957. p. 26–27.

From his POLA ELIZEJSKIE (Elysian Fields).

Ejsmond, Julian (1892–1930)

Akademik smorgoński. Translated as *The Graduate of Smorgonie*.

The Graduate of Smorgonie. Translated by K. Żuk-Skarszewska. In *Poland* (New York), XI, 1930. p.346–349.

Dwie moce. Translated as *The Strongest*.

The Strongest. Translated by K. Żuk-Skarszewska. In *Poland* (New York), XI, 1930. p.468–471.

From his W PUSZCZY; OPOWIEŚCI O SERCU ZWIERZĘCEM (In the Wilderness; Tales about the Animal Heart), 1927.

Dzieje dębu. Translated as *The Story of an Oak*.

The Story of an Oak. Translated by K. Żuk-Skarszewska. In *Poland* (New York), XI, 1930. p.471–472.

From his ŻYWOTY DRZEW (The Lives of Trees), 1929.

Matka. Translated as *Within a Red Circle*.

Within a Red Circle; a Tale of a Lynx-Hunt in the Polesie Wilderness. Translated by K. Żuk-Skarszewska. In *Poland* (New York), XI, 1930. p.273–276.

From his W PUSZCZY; OPOWIEŚCI O SERCU ZWIERZĘCEM (In the Wilderness; Tales About the Animal Heart), 1927.

Miłość i śmierć. Translated as *Love and Death*.

Love and Death; a Tale of the Carpathians. Translated by K. Żuk-Skarszewska. In *Pologne litteraire*, No. 46, 1930. p.2.

Falkowski, Edward (1901–   )

Falkowski has published nothing in Polish. His play about immigrant coal miners, QUITTIN' TIME, was produced by the

Hedgerow Theater in Moylan Rose Valley, Pa. Several of his poems have found their way into anthologies.

Our Fathers and We (Three Generations). Written originally in English.

(This is neither a short story nor a translation from the Polish. It has been included in the collection of Polish stories because of the affinity of the subject matter and the similarity of form. The author, an American of Polish descent, is a typical example of the third generation.)

Résumé. His grandfather, a Polish peasant, emigrated to America. For him, America was a strange land of new opportunities. His father was fourteen when he arrived with his parents in Shenandoah. He represents the generation of adjustment to the new country for whom the ties with the country of his fathers are still strong. His loyalties are divided.

The author got his first job in a coal-breaker at fifteen and gained what education he could by self-directed study at night. He feels that he has some ties with Poland, and even visited the country of his grandfathers, but his home is America. And—he has only one home.

Our Fathers and We (Three Generations). In POLISH AUTHORS OF TODAY AND YESTERDAY . . . Selected by Irena Morska. New York, S. F. Vanni [c1947]. p.11–27.

Fiedler, Arkady (1894–   )

The most popular author-traveller now living in Poland, Fiedler began his career in 1927, when he was sent to the northern regions of Norway to collect samples of the fauna for the Polish zoological museums. Since that time he travelled extensively all over the world. World War Two caught him on the island of Tahiti; he went to France to join the Polish forces which were later transferred to Great Britain. His DYWIZJON 303 (London, 1942, translated as SQUADRON 303) commemorates the heroic stand of the Polish airmen in the Battle of Britain. Fiedler's books, based on his travels, include KANADA PACHNĄCA ŻYWICĄ (Resin Fragrant Canada, 1936) and ŻARLIWA WYSPA BENIOWSKIEGO (London, 1944), in English, THE MADAGASCAR I LOVE (London, 1946).

Czarna struga śmierci. Translated as *A Black Stream of Death.*

A Black Stream of Death. In his THE RIVER OF SINGING FISH. [Translated by H. C. Stevens.] London, Hodder and Stoughton [1948]. p.91–96.

Gorące miasto. Translated as *A Hot-Bed of Racial Rivalry.*

A Hot-Bed of Racial Rivalry. In his THE RIVER OF SINGING FISH. [Translated by H. C. Stevens.] London, Hodder and Stoughton [1948]. p.30–33.

Gorąco!! Translated as *Heat!*

Heat! In his THE RIVER OF SINGING FISH. [Translated by H. C. Stevens.] London, Hodder and Stoughton [1948]. p.175–180.

Ich bitwa. Translated as *Their Battle.*

Their Battle. In his THANK YOU, CAPTAIN, THANK YOU! Translated by Celina Wieniewska. London, MaxLove Publishing Company [1945]. p.125–[146].

Indjanie, pogardzający białymi ludźmi i małpami. Translated as *Contempt for Whites and Monkeys.*

Contempt for Whites and Monkeys. In his THE RIVER OF SINGING FISH. [Translated by H. C. Stevens.] London, Hodder and Stoughton [1948]. p.118–124.

Kolibry. Translated as *Living Sunbeams.*

Living Sunbeams. In his THE RIVER OF SINGING FISH. [Translated by H. C. Stevens.] London, Hodder and Stoughton [1948]. p.130–135.

Kwiaty, które poruszyły Anglików. Translated as *Flowers Which Moved Britons.*

Flowers Which Moved Britons. In his THE RIVER OF SINGING FISH. [Translated by H. C. Stevens.] London, Hodder and Stoughton [1948]. p.69–74.

"La France est morte!"—krzyknął Murzyn i dostał kopniaka. Translated as *"La France est morte."*

"La France est morte." In his THANK YOU, CAPTAIN, THANK YOU! Translated by Celina Wieniewska. London, MaxLove Publishing Company [1945]. p.27–42.

Mały Czikinjo i wielka Amazonka. Translated as *Little Chicinho and the Great Big Amazon.*

Little Chicinho and the Great Big Amazon. In his THE RIVER OF SINGING FISH. [Translated by H. C. Stevens.] London, Hodder and Stoughton [1948]. p.15–17.

Motyle. Translated as *Butterflies.*

Butterflies. In his THE RIVER OF SINGING FISH. [Translated by H. C. Stevens.] London, Hodder and Stoughton [1948]. p.152–157.

Niewolnictwo nad Ukajali. Translated as *Slavery on the Ucayali.*

Slavery on the Ucayali. In his THE RIVER OF SINGING FISH. [Translated by H. C. Stevens.] London, Hodder and Stoughton [1948]. p.158–164.

Odwiedzają mnie czole. Translated as *Embarrassing Visitors.*

Embarrassing Visitors. In his THE RIVER OF SINGING FISH. [Translated by H. C. Stevens.] London, Hodder and Stoughton [1948]. p.34–38.

Okrucieństwo. Translated as *A Chapter on Cruelty.*

A Chapter on Cruelty. In his THE RIVER OF SINGING FISH. [Translated by H. C. Stevens.] London, Hodder and Stoughton [1948]. p.65–68.

Pająki. Translated as *Spiders.*

Spiders. In his THE RIVER OF SINGING FISH. [Translated by H. C. Stevens.] London, Hodder and Stoughton [1948]. p.53–58.

Papugi nad Iquitos. Translated as *The Ants and Parrots of Iquitos.*

The Ants and Parrots of Iquitos. In his THE RIVER OF SINGING FISH. [Translated by H. C. Stevens.] London, Hodder and Stoughton [1948]. p.26–29.

Papugi zielone i arary szkarłatne. Translated as *Green Parrots and Crimson Macaws.*

Green Parrots and Crimson Macaws. In his THE RIVER OF SINGING FISH. [Translated by H. C. Stevens.] London, Hodder and Stoughton [1948]. p.187–191.

Pięćdziesiąt kroków cywilizacji. Translated as *Fifty Yards of Civilization.*

Fifty Yards of Civilization. In his THE RIVER OF SINGING FISH. [Translated by H. C. Stevens.] London, Hodder and Stoughton [1948]. p.44–48.

Polujemy na Binuji. Translated as *Europe versus Snake.*

Europe versus Snake. In his THE RIVER OF SINGING FISH. [Translated by H. C. Stevens.] London, Hodder and Stoughton [1948]. p.59–64.

Puszcza nad Amazonką. Translated and adapted as *The Personal "Great Adventure."*

The Personal "Great Adventure." In his THE RIVER OF SINGING FISH. [Translated by H. C. Stevens.] London, Hodder and Stoughton [1948]. p.18–20.

Roch płata figle. Translated as *Roch, the Practical Joker.*

Roch, the Practical Joker. In his THANK YOU, CAPTAIN, THANK YOU! Translated by Celina Wieniewska. London, MaxLove Publishing Company [1945]. p.43–51.

Romantyczni pasażerowie. Translated as *Romantic Passengers.*

Romantic Passengers. In his THE RIVER OF SINGING FISH. [Translated by H. C. Stevens.] London, Hodder and Stoughton [1948]. p.9–14.

S.S. Bielsk, statek z charakterem. Translated as *S.S. Bielsk, a Ship with Character.*

S.S. Bielsk, a Ship with Character. In his THANK YOU, CAPTAIN, THANK YOU! Translated by Celina Wieniewska. London, MaxLove Publishing Company [1945]. p.52–63.

Smarownik Łoza chce jeść. Translated as *Greaser Loza Is Hungry.*

Greaser Loza Is Hungry. In his THANK YOU, CAPTAIN, THANK YOU! Translated by Celina Wieniewska. London, MaxLove Publishing Company [1945]. p.64–75.

Sny na Ukajali. Translated as *Dreaming on the Ucayali.*

Dreaming on the Ucayali. In his THE RIVER OF SINGING FISH. [Translated by H. C. Stevens.] London, Hodder and Stoughton [1948]. p.49–52.

Starzy, dobrzy przyjaciele. Translated as *Good Old Friends.*

Good Old Friends. In his THE RIVER OF SINGING FISH. [Translated by H. C. Stevens.] London, Hodder and Stoughton [1948]. p.80–83.

Szalejąca przyroda. Translated as *Where Nature Runs Wild.*

Where Nature Runs Wild. In his THE RIVER OF SINGING FISH. [Translated by H. C. Stevens.] London, Hodder and Stoughton [1948]. p.102–106.

"Thank You, Capt'n, Thank You!" Translated as *Thank You, Captain, Thank You!*

Thank You, Captain, Thank You! In his THANK YOU, CAPTAIN, THANK YOU! Translated by Celina Wieniewska. London, MaxLove Publishing Company [1945]. p.7–25.

Tragedia kauczukowa. Translated as *An India-Rubber Tragedy.*

An India-Rubber Tragedy. In his THE RIVER OF SINGING FISH. [Translated by H. C. Stevens.] London, Hodder and Stoughton [1948]. p.21–25.

Wiele hałasu o . . . Letycję. Translated as *Much Ado about— Leticia.*

Much Ado about—Leticia. In his THE RIVER OF SINGING FISH. [Translated by H. C. Stevens.] London, Hodder and Stoughton [1948]. p.39–43.

Woda, woda, woda . . . Translated as *Water, Water Everywhere.*

Water, Water Everywhere. In his THE RIVER OF SINGING FISH.

[Translated by H. C. Stevens.] London, Hodder and Stoughton [1948]. p.136–140.

Wspaniały kapitan i niezłomny statek. Translated as *A Gallant Captain and a Dauntless Ship.*

A Gallant Captain and a Dauntless Ship. In his THANK YOU, CAPTAIN, THANK YOU! Translated by Celina Wieniewska. London, MaxLove Publishing Company [1945]. p.76–124.

Znów padają deszcze. Translated as *More Rain.*

More Rain. In his THE RIVER OF SINGING FISH. [Translated by H. C. Stevens.] London, Hodder and Stoughton [1948]. p.141–146.

Fierla, Adolf (1908–1967)

The poet was born at Orłowa in Silesia. He studied at the universities of Cracow and Prague. During the war he was imprisoned in the concentration camps of Dachau and Mauthausen. From 1946 on he lived in England. PRZY-DROŻNE KWIATY (Flowers by the Road) was his first collection of poetry published in 1928, soon followed by a collection of short stories descriptive of the life of Silesian miners, HAŁDY (1929) and a novel about the Silesian Robin Hood, ONDRASZEK (1930). More collections of poetry followed: CIENIE I BLASKI (Lights and Shadows, 1931), DZIWY NA GRONIACH (The Miraculous Mountains, 1932), KOPALNIA SŁONECZNA (The Mine in the Sunshine, 1933), and KOLĘDY BESKIDZKIE (The Beskid Carols, 1935). Another collection of short stories, KAMIEŃ W POLU (A Stone in the Field), was published in 1937. Some of his works have been translated into other languages, mostly Slavic. The author was a member of the International P.E.N. Club Centre for Writers in Exile.

Chleb na dłoni. Translated as *Their Everyday Bread.*

Résumé. The concentration camp bread thief in the block under the charge of the trusty, a Viennese bandit, was always punished ruthlessly. If the trusty was in a pleasant mood, he would grip the man by the neck and rain blows with his fist upon head, ears and mouth. But if the devil possessed him, as often happened, he would tie the victim's hands behind his back with a stout rope, the other end of which he would throw over the crossbeam of the hut, and tug at it with all his might. The bread thief's body would then writhe in agony.

This time bread had been stolen from the man known as "Butcher," a loathsome fellow. "Some son of a bitch has stolen my bread," he roared. One man came running, offering his own piece of bread in an effort to quell the storm. To no avail. "I want my bread," "Butcher" kept shouting.

Everyone froze to silence as the trusty, suddenly appearing on the scene, yelled angrily, "Was ist los?" In an all-pervading silence came "Butcher's" unexpected answer that it was nothing. He had lost his cap, but he had it now. The trusty knocked him down, raining blows and kicks upon his head and chest. "Where's the rope?"

Then the unbelievable happened. Franek, a small boy, frail, and paler than usual, forced his way into the madman's path and grabbed him by the arm. Trusty should not punish "Butcher," he said. It was not the cap which had been lost. It was bread—and it was he, Franek, who had stolen it. He did not steal for himself; he did it for his brother who was dying in another block. He had thought more bread would keep his brother alive. But now his brother was dead, and Franek had brought back the bread. He wanted to return it—this was the bread.

Puny Franek seemed great and mighty—almost holy. "Butcher" broke the silence crying plaintively, "O Lord . . ."

"Idiots," mumbled the trusty under his breath.

> *First published in the London literary weekly,* Wiadomości, *1947.*

Their Everyday Bread. Translated by Karol Lewicki. In THE PEN IN EXILE; a Second Anthology. Edited by Paul Tabori. [London] The International P.E.N. Club Centre for Writers in Exile, 1956. p.140–145.

Filipowicz, Kornel (1913–   )

Before the war this author restricted himself to writing poetry. His first volume of short stories, KRAJOBRAZ NIE-WZRUSZONY (A Still Landscape), was not published until 1947, to be followed later by PROFILE MOICH PRZYJACIÓŁ (Profiles of My Friends, 1954). In the collections of stories, KSIĘŻYC NAD NIDĄ (The Moon over the Nida River, 1950) and BŁĘKITNY ZESZYT (The Blue Notebook, 1955), Filipowicz is mainly concerned with the struggles of Polish partisans against the Nazi occupant. Life of students in prewar Poland is the subject of his cycle of novels. NIEPOKÓJ MŁODEGO SERCA (Anxieties of a Young Heart). His latest volume of short stories was published in 1959 under the title, CIEMNOŚĆ I ŚWIATŁO (Darkness and Light).

Zwycięstwo. Translated as *Victory.*

Résumé. John was thrown into a prison cell at night. There was already one occupant there, a Cracovian worker. He put a cigarette into John's mouth and lit it. John asked about the window. It was sealed with armor plate.

A little later a third man joined the two in the darkness. Unlike the first two, he was not from Cracow. When he struck the bench in the dark and sat down, John asked if he smoked. No, he did not. John cautiously offered him wise words as the only medicine at his disposal. "You can't break the wall with your head," he said.

The reply from the Jewish newcomer was unexpected. For him —in this Gestapo prison—the only chance was to break the wall with his head. If he had a murder on his conscience or some political act like the other two, he would be happy. Dying, he would feel victorious. But they were not going to ask him anything. He was marked, branded.

After daybreak an SS-man, the same who had arrested John, opened the door. John was led into an interrogating room.

He said that he didn't know German, and would give his evidence in Polish. At one point of the questioning, they suddenly put a gas mask on his face with the inhaler plugged up, and they all began to whip him with whips of plaited fibre. Before he suffocated, they took the mask off. "Did he know Gertych?" "No." "Jaskólski?" "Yes." Then came the question concerning the organization, which he answered in the negative. They put the mask on him again. He felt the first blows but soon lost consciousness.

When he opened his eyes only two Germans sat in the room. He was in a state of joyous dazzlement. He recalled the words of the Jew that if he had something to conceal, he would be happy. And John smiled at his victory.

From his KRAJOBRAZ NIEWZRUSZONY (*A Still Landscape*), *1947.*

Victory. Translated by Jadwiga Zwolska. In CONTEMPORARY POLISH SHORT STORIES, selected by Andrzej Kijowski. Warsaw, Polonia Publishing House, 1960. p.[157]–167.

Gałecki, Tadeusz, *see* Strug, Andrzej, pseud.
Giertych, Jędrzej (1903–   )

The author has made himself known as an historian, publicist, fiction writer, and an essayist. By 1939 he had published eight historical and political works. KAJAKIEM PO NIEMCZECH (In a Canoe through Germany, 1937) was one of his three travel books of the pre-war period. As a Navy reserve officer, the author was taken prisoner of war by the Nazis in 1939. After six attempts to escape, he was sent to Colditz Castle. Four novels were written by Giertych during the war; all were destroyed. Since the war the author, who now lives in London, has published twelve books. W POLSCE MIĘDZY WOJNAMI (In Poland between the Wars, 1951) is his three-volume novel. His historical and political works include POLITYKA POLSKA W DZIEJACH EUROPY (The Place of Polish Politics in European History, 2v., London, 1947–1953) and U ŹRÓDEŁ KATASTROFY DZIEJOWEJ POLSKI; JAN AMOS KOMENSKY (The Sources of Poland's Historical Disaster; Jan Amos Comenius, 1964). Giertych is co-editor and a regular contributor to the Polish political monthly, published in Paris, *Horyzonty* (Horizons).

Hania z międzymorza. Translated as *Hannah.*

Résumé. In Gdańsk the coach in which Casimir sat huddled in a corner seat was attached to a local train bound for Wejherowo. Only yesterday he thought that he was no longer in love with Clara. When he saw her on the day of her vows, he had a feeling that he could recover from that love as one recovers from an illness. During the whole period of her novitiate he used to send flowers to the cloister.

There had been a distant kinship between them. He had seen her once as a little girl, but later, during his university studies in Cracow and during the war (i.e. World War I) he lost sight of her entirely. They met when he took a few days' furlough from the army to see his mother. Their home was in Kiev, but his mother came to her sister's estate near Kamieniec Podolski in Podolia. Clara came for a visit. He fell in love with her at first sight. During the Russian revolution, Clara's estate mansion was burnt and her father killed, while Clara and her mother escaped and took refuge in one of the huts in the village. Her mother fell ill and died. When, as a result of the Treaty of Riga, Podolia was ceded to the Russians, Clara decided to stay with her people. It was only when the peasants themselves begged her to leave that she escaped and crossed the border. Instead of marrying Casimir, she decided to enter the cloister.

Casimir took a local train to Puck. Wandering about the place, he walked into a church. A young woman was earnestly praying. He decided to join her in her prayers for her cause. When he left the church, he saw her again on a cutter bound for Jastarnia. Driven by a sudden impulse, he got on the same boat. In the course of the conversation, it appeared that she (her name was Hannah) was a fisherman's daughter, and that her parents had a room for rent. Casimir, now a teacher of Polish literature in a Warsaw *gimnazjum* on vacation for about two months, decided to take the room. Hannah was a simple girl, but, although strongly built, she was beautiful, sensitive, and had a deep appreciation of poetry and music.

The rest of the story is devoted to the ripening of their love, and Casimir's decision to marry Hannah. The author takes every opportunity to expound his political philosophy. For him Poland's attachment to the Roman Catholic Church is the country's strength. It was the same faith, with different degrees of awareness, which formed a bond between the two.

Written originally in 1928. When the manuscript was burnt by the SS in 1944, it was rewritten in 1953–54.

Hannah. In his BALTIC TALES. [Translation anonymous.] Preface by Patrick R. Reid . . . London, Jędrzej Giertych [1955]. p.[147]–243.

Morze żywi, morze zabija. Translated as *The Sea Nourishes, the Sea Destroys.*

Résumé. A fisherman's widow, Miotkowa, dressed in the dark. It was two o'clock in the morning. Her only son was to go fishing. She fixed her eyes lovingly on the young face, the same way she had looked at her husband before waking him on that memorable day when he had gone fishing never to return. She delicately touched his arm, and softly asked him to get up.

Jank opened his eyes and with a smile thanked his mother for waking him. When Jank left the hut, she ran after him to the gate, embraced him and kissed him again, gripped by a sudden feeling of sadness and fear. The night was beautiful, the stars shone brightly, and there was a steady wind from northwest. Miotkowa went back to bed. In the morning she went to Mrs. Schultze's to buy wool for socks for her son. Before she left the store, Mrs. Schultze told her of a telephone call from Pozew about the coming storm. Filled with anxiety for her son, instead of going home, Miotkowa walked to the shore. The sea was calm and the sky clear. She went home. Before she had finished cooking her meal, Miotkowa's anxiety grew again, and she returned to the shore.

It came suddenly. In the raging storm only one boat reached the land, but the fishermen in it were from another village. In the dark and in the torrential rain Miotkowa lay on the ground, praying for her son, all she had in the world. She was almost unconscious, when Hannah (Jank was in love with her) gently embraced her. In the lightning's flash, Hannah saw another boat. This again was one from another village. Miotkowa took a young fisherman from the boat home with her for the night. She dressed the wound on his head. His name was also Jank.

Miotkowa's Jank never returned from the sea. Now she prayed that his body be found, so that she could bury him. On the eighth day after the storm, the village mayor informed her that two bodies had been found on the far away coast near Jastarnia. Miotkowa made the trip there by train. The first body she looked at was that of the fisherman who was on the boat with Jank. She knew that the other one was her son's. She pulled the cloth. His face was calm, his eyes closed as in sleep. Miotkowa sank to her knees and wept. She began to pray. When she left the shed she was no longer angry with the sea.

> *Written originally in 1927 as* Z nad morza. *It was published in a new version in a Poznań magazine,* Tęcza, *under the title,* Morze, żywiciel i morderca. *It appears in the collection with a changed title, but no change in the text.*

The Sea Nourishes, the Sea Destroys. In his BALTIC TALES. [Translation anonymous.] Preface by Patrick R. Reid . . . London, Jędrzej Giertych [1955]. p.[117]–146.

Różaniec. Translated as *The Rosary.*

Résumé. A story of World War I. The hero, a Pole from Kaszuby, drafted in the German navy, serves on a German trawler.

He awoke in the darkness of the night. The ship had a dangerous tilt, and he felt a feverish tremor going through her. The instinct of a man in danger told him that the ship was sinking. He grabbed from under his pillow his life-jacket, put it on, and moved to the exit. Passing the beds of his mates he tried to wake them, but found the beds empty. Probably everyone was already on deck. When he got to the deck he did not find a soul there. The life boat was gone. They had left him alone on a sinking ship.

Had they struck a mine? Did they encounter the British? He realized that he had to get away from the ship fast. He crossed himself and slid into the cold water. He was chilled to the bone. He swam as fast as he could. When the high wave caught up with him, he understood that the ship had sunk and that he was saved. Dawn brought with it a hope of survival. Then came daylight and the sight of a ship on the horizon. After several hours it disappeared. He felt deserted not only by man but by God. He cursed his mother that she bore him, and he cursed God. There was no God. All there was was the emptiness which frightened him. Again came the night. The setting sun dissipated all his hope. In the depths of despair he became aware of a hard object in the pocket of his trousers. It was a rosary, the gift of his mother. He felt as though the hand of his mother touched him, and he heard her plea that he should pray. He began to pray. "Our Father . . ." "Thy will be done" were his last words.

The dawn revealed the body of a sailor drifting in a life jacket. It was not the body of an animal. It was the body of Man whose immortal soul was on the way to God.

> *Written originally in 1929. When the manuscript of the story was burnt with the rest of the author's library by the SS in 1944, it was rewritten in 1953–54.*

The Rosary. [Translation anonymous.] London, Published by the author, 1954. 16 p.

"Published by the author, 16 Belmont Road, London N.15."

The Rosary. In his BALTIC TALES. [Translation anonymous.] Preface by Patrick R. Reid . . . London, Jędrzej Giertych [1955]. p.[98]–116.

Szczur z Dalekiego Wschodu. Translated as *A Rat from the Far East.*

Résumé. Michael Ostrowski was a Pole born in Siberia. When his father remarried, he could not get along with his step-mother, and he left his home as a boy of sixteen. His father and step-mother were murdered by peasants in 1919, but he never learned the fate of his then six-year-old half-sister, Jadwisia.

In Vladivostok he joined the crew of a Russian cargo boat. In Shanghai he worked first as a servant in a hotel, then as a shoreman in the port, finally as a hand in a foundry. He returned to the sea to serve on a British boat, then he moved to the Dutch Indies and became a Dutch seaman. He learned to speak Dutch, and was promoted to the rank of a bossman. After many years of service, he was suddenly struck with the idea that he could return to Poland. He enlisted as a simple sailor on the first boat bound to Europe and landed in Gdynia.

There he joined the crew of a cargo ship, "Tarnów," sailing between Gdynia and the ports of Sweden. One day he met in a street of Gdynia a beautiful young girl. He made her acquaintance when he helped her pick up her papers strewn around by the wind. She too was born in Siberia, and she knew Vladivostok. Her name was Jadwiga Mrozowska. The next day they spent together in Gdańsk. During a walk in the evening, he kissed her. A day later, Michael rented a yacht, and together they sailed to Hel. Without landing they decided to change their course for Puck. Their instinctive love for each other suddenly became apparent. Their kisses and caresses came as naturally as though they had known each other for a long time. Fishermen's nets all around them compelled Michael to lower an anchor. During the night, when Michael began unbuttoning her dress, he found on her neck a medallion which proved to him that she was his sister. Quickly he went up to the deck. In the morning Jadwiga left the yacht without a word.

From Sweden Michael sent her a telegram confessing that he was her half-brother. Upon his return to Gdynia he went straight to her, and showed her an old family photograph. She was now convinced of the truth. The two were happily reunited as brother and sister.

> *Written originally in 1928, in a new version in 1939. After the loss of the manuscript in the war, the story was rewritten in 1953–54.*

A Rat from the Far East. In his BALTIC TALES. [Translation anonymous.] Preface by Patrick R. Reid . . . London, Jędrzej Giertych [1955]. p.[9]–97.

Głowacki, Aleksander, *see* Prus, Bolesław, pseud.

Goetel, Ferdynand (1890–1960)

Born at Sucha in the Tatra Mountains, the author studied architecture in Vienna, but abandoned it for literature. He became associated with the "Młoda Polska" (Young Poland) literary group. Interned by the Russians at the beginning of World War One, Goetel was deported to Turkestan, where he worked as a common laborer and later as a highway engineer. His escape through Iran and India as well as his experiences in Turkestan provided him with colorful subjects for his literary output. The author's most popular collection of short stories, PĄTNIK KARAPETA (Karapet's Pilgrim) was published in 1924, while his widely read novel, Z DNIA NA DZIEŃ (From Day to Day) appeared in print in 1927. His SERCE LODÓW (1929), which was awarded a State Literary Prize, was published in English as THE MESSENGER OF THE SNOW (1931) with a preface by G. K. Chesterton. A former president of the Polish P.E.N. (1925–1930), Goetel spent World War Two in Poland. He died in London.

Kos na Pamirze. Translated as *Back to Civilization.*

Back to Civilization: Reminiscences of an Adventurer. Translated by K. Żuk-Skarszewska. In *Poland* (New York), VIII, 1927. p.654–657, 681–687, 720–729.

From his PĄTNIK KARAPETA (Karapet's Pilgrim), 1924.

Samson i Dalila; fragment skończony. Translated as *Samson and Delilah.*

Résumé. Pan Józef, hero of the factories and savior of the besieged citadel, had earned the fame of the greatest hero of the revolution in Tashkent. For the last few days, during the unsuccessful attack of the Whites, he had been completely in his element. The chaotic firing reminded him of Wola in 1905.

Felka went wild over the presents he brought her every evening. Now she wanted a beaver collar. Strolling at night in the street, he stepped inside a church. A man wearing a fur collar was kneeling. It might have been of beaver. Pan Józef slipped out of the church. When the "collar" appeared, he took aim and the man fell. He threw the collar at Felka, but when she complained that it was nothing but rubbish, he gave her a look that made her cower with fright.

Out in the street again, he saw a young schoolgirl hunting for bread. He followed her into a store and terrorized the shopkeeper. She slipped out and ran blindly. He accompanied her to the house. The girl called her brother Janek, a boy of about ten. Hardly had Pan Józef got inside when a detachment of revolutionary soldiers entered the house. Pan Józef brutally turned them out. At night a desperate chase after the girl began. It was during that chase that he found the rest of the coat from which he had severed the collar. It belonged to the girl's father. He stopped the chase.

Upon his return to Felka, Pan Józef took to drinking. Then he went back to the house of the "collar." The boy showed him full confidence. The girl said that "they" had been there again, and in desperation timidly asked him for protection. Pan Józef left, promising to watch out for them from the street.

He took refuge in a little deserted shop at the corner of the street, from which he watched the house. One night he overheard a conversation between two soldiers who were after the girl. When one of them went in to gag her, quick as lightning Pan Józef followed. Two shots killed the men, but they also brought the rest of the soldiers. Pan Józef lifted the boy and the girl over the garden wall to safety. He fought against the detachment singlehandedly; for two days and two nights he defended himself like a lion. On the third day, twice wounded, he was taken and thrown into prison. When the guns pointed at him cracked, he strove to resuscitate the image of his dearest girl.

From his PĄTNIK KARAPETA (Karapet's Pilgrim), 1924.

Samson and Delilah. Translated by K. Żuk-Skarszewska. In *Poland* (New York), VIII, 1927, p.78–81, 106–110, 112, 114, 116, 118, 143–146, 167–170, 172, 174, 176, 178, 180.

Samson and Delilah, by Ferdynand Goetel. [Translated by K. Żuk-Skarszewska.] In POLISH SHORT STORIES, by Joseph Weyssenhof,

Piotr Choynowski, Kornel Makuszynski [and others] . . . London, Minerva Publishing Company [1943]. p.118–157.

Zemsta (?) Translated as *Vengeance*.

Résumé. (The theme of the story is woven around the Polish underground movement during the German occupation of Poland during World War Two.)

An emissary of the Polish underground was sent on a mission from Warsaw to the Tatra Mountains region. Lost in the mountain forests, he met a girl tending cows high up in the Grey Upland Pasturage. It had been raining for four days, so Aniela invited the stranger to her hut. Pressed by the girl to tell his story, he found himself telling her the true story of the underground. Before he realized what was happening, they were both gripped by a sudden passion, and she was lying naked at his side, gathering him to herself with her strong arms.

The next morning he agreed to take Aniela as his assistant. She was to go down to the village with the cows, and he was to return to his unit and come back for her. But drawn immediately into hard and pressing work in his unit, he did not send a messenger for her until the tenth day. The messenger found no trace of Aniela; her hut was burned to ashes.

Swift (his underground pseudonym) met an emissary from London, and was called to Warsaw. Upon returning he was told that a strange girl, roving the forests, kept asking for him. She soon came to see him. Aniela was now in the service of a smuggler, Kite. Swift told her that his orders now were to go abroad. He did not know when he would return.

Kite, assisted by Aniela, was to smuggle Swift through the border to the railway in Hungary. On the way, tired and worn out, Swift caused an unscheduled stop. Kite lost contact with Aniela, who had gone ahead carrying the secret papers. Next morning the two men found her frozen to death, clutching the papers. The only way to destroy the papers was to burn the sitting statue of the girl.

The smuggler found his way to the western armies and bravely fought in the Italian mountains. Swift returned to his underground comrades, and was killed in a fight with the Germans.

Vengeance. Translated by H. C. Stevens. In THE PEN IN EXILE; an Anthology. Edited by Paul Tabori. [London] The International P.E.N. Club Centre for Writers in Exile, 1954. p.60–74.

Gojawiczyńska, Pola (1896–1963)

The author belonged to the group of young writers, organized in the thirties, called "Przedmieście" (Suburbia). Their purpose was to portray life of the less respectable suburbs with their factories, neglected children, etc. Among others, Zofia Nałkowska and Kazimiera Muszałówna were members of this literary group. ZIEMIA ELŻBIETY (Elizabeth's Land), which deals with Silesia, RAJSKA JABŁOŃ (A Crab-Apple Tree) and, above all, DZIEWCZĘTA Z NOWOLIPEK (The Girls of Nowolipki Street) are Gojawiczyńska's most important novels. One of her more recent works is a reportage on postwar Warsaw, entitled STOLICA (The Capital).

Lipa. Translated as *The Linden Tree.*

The Linden Tree. Translation anonymous. In *Poland: Illustrated Magazine,* No. 12 (28) 1956. p.19–20.
"A story from a collection published in 1956."
Preceded by a brief note about the author.

Powszedni dzień. Translated as *Just Another Day.*

Résumé. (A story of tragic love.)
Marie read in the paper the announcement that "Mr. Kazimierz Smoleński was joined in holy matrimony to Mrs. Vera Kozłowska." He had tried to justify his action to Marie by pointing to his financial situation and complicated circumstances. When he talked, her image of him crumbled to dust. So far as she was concerned, this was the end.

The pangs of suffering were beyond her endurance. Marie rented a room from Mrs. Gertrude Golombek in a strange smoky town. She had her first night's rest.

All the tenants in Mrs. Golombek's apartment house lived a hard life. Some details of their lives are described. One of the tenants, Mrs. Fiolka, dies.

As Mrs. Golombek is getting ready to go to the funeral, a gentleman in a light travel coat enters. She points without a word to Marie's apartment and pushes the door open. Kazimierz and Marie stand facing each other. Marie opens the window and the two silently watch the funeral ceremony in the barren cemetery. Marie turns her head to Kazimierz. She looks into his face, and shakes her head in an inaudible "No."

Just Another Day. Translated by Irena Morska. In POLISH AUTHORS OF TODAY AND YESTERDAY . . . Selected by Irena Morska. New York, S. F. Vanni [c1947]. p.28–43.

Gombrowicz, Witold (1904–   )

This eminent author happened to reach Buenos Aires a week before the beginning of World War Two, and had remained in Argentina as a Polish émigré. Gombrowicz published some volumes of short stories before the war. His PAMIĘTNIK Z OKRESU DOJRZEWANIA (The Diary of an Adolescent) is best described as "a mixture of the macabre and the burlesque." Perhaps the most characteristic of Gombrowicz's works is his fantastic novel FERDYDURKE (1937), recently translated under the same title into English (1961). Within his cleverly knit story the author analyzes such concepts as the traditional and modern education, "modernism" in general, liberalism and traditionalism. Ten years after its first publication, it was translated into Spanish by the author in cooperation with a Committee of South American writers. When the French translation appeared in 1959, FERDYDURKE was compared to Sartre's LA NAUSÉE.

Zbrodnia z premedytacją. Translated as *Premeditated Crime.*

Résumé. An examining magistrate visits the home of a country gentleman, Mr. Ignace K., in order to help him settle some questions of property.

There are no horses waiting for him at the station, although the magistrate had wired Mr. K., and the telegram had been duly delivered. More surprises await the official on arrival. No one seems to expect him, and he is made to feel unwelcome by every member of the household. Finally Mrs. K. comes forward with an explanation of it all: her husband died suddenly last night of a heart attack.

The magistrate is led to see the dead man's body. A suspicion creeps into his mind that "something is not in order." Once conceived, the suspicion grows, together with the mounting tension in the house until in the climax Mr. K.'s son is forced to a confession that he had strangled his father.

Solution and denouement follow. Crushed by the irresistible force of the magistrate's logic when he asserts that Mr. K.'s neck shows no signs of violence, the tormented young man only now leaves the marks of his fingers upon the neck of the corpse.

Premeditated Crime. Translated by Olga Scherer-Virski. In 10 CONTEMPORARY POLISH STORIES. Translated by various hands and edited by Edmund Ordon; with an introduction by Olga Scherer-Virski. Detroit, Wayne State University Press, 1958. p.147–186.
Preceded by a note about the author and the translator.

Gomulicki, Wiktor (1850–1919)

This poet and novelist has also left ten volumes of short stories. Gomulicki is remembered as a poet of Warsaw and a popular author of tales about The Old Town (Stare Miasto) of Warsaw. His muse is light, the form of his verse exquisite, his prose carefully chiselled, but his thought is never deep. His works include POEZJE (Poems, 1887), NOWELE (Short Stories, 1890), WARSZAWIANKA (The Warsaw Girl, 1900), PIEŚŃ O GDAŃSKU (A Song of Gdańsk, 1900) and OPOWIADANIA O STAREJ WARSZAWIE (Tales about Old Warsaw, 1900–1909).

Oracz. Translated as *The Ploughman.*

Résumé. The ploughman reminded the narrator of one of Holbein's immortal sketches of the cycle "The Dance of Death." Only the landscape was different. There was no curving line of a mountain chain; the crinkled waves of the Mazurian plain stretched in a grey mass of clods to the horizon.

The back of the old ploughman was arched, his head drooped

toward the ground. He looked so feeble that the earth seemed to be waiting impatiently for him. His eyes and cheeks were hollow. Every moment that the horses stopped, the plough stopped also, and the old man struggled with an evil-sounding cough. When following the plough, the old man was reciting the litany of the dying.

A week before, the narrator had seen the ploughman trying to seek advice from the district doctor. From the window of his carriage the surly doctor had only remarked, "To your coffin, gaffer, to your coffin . . ."

Now the narrator asked the ploughman if his health had improved. No, he was only ploughing the last two ridges. Did he hope to see the harvest? By all means, no. He was sure to be buried in the holy soil within a week. So, why was he ploughing the field if he did not expect the harvest? To this the old man replied, "Not for myself, of course, but for those who will come after me."

The narrator took leave of the old man, but his words sank deep into his soul. Death seemed to him as elusive as the merging of one color with another in a rainbow.

The Ploughman, by W. Gomulicki. In ANTHOLOGY OF MODERN SLAVONIC LITERATURE IN PROSE AND VERSE. Translated by P. Selver. With an introduction and literary notes. London, Kegan Paul, Trench, Trubner and company; New York, E. P. Dutton and company, 1919. p.71–76.

Górecki, Juliusz, pseud., *see* Kamiński, Aleksander

Grubiński, Wacław (1883–)

Playwright, novelist and short-story writer, Grubiński shows in his first play, NA RUBIEŻY (On the Border, 1906) a marked influence of Stanisław Przybyszewski who wrote an introduction to this and some other of his plays. In his literary output Grubiński presents himself as an intellectual with talent, but without a great message. His works include such plays as KOCHANKOWIE (The Lovers, 1915), LENIN (1921), KSIĘŻNICZKA ŻYDOWSKA (A Jewish Princess, 1927), and a collection of short stories, CZŁOWIEK Z KLARNETEM (The Man with a Clarinet, 1927). MIĘDZY MŁOTEM A SIERPEM (Between the Hammer and the Sickle, 1948) and a novel, PANI SAPOWSKA (Mrs. Sapowska, 1953) are examples of Grubiński's more recent publications. Since 1939 the author has lived in exile.

Dajmonion-Bib. Translated as *Daimonion Bib.*

Résumé. The old man had been ill. At the foot of the bed slept a young woman. For Nathalie it was the fourteenth night at the bedside of her husband. The doctor had assured her that the sick man would die before midnight.

Nata ground her teeth in anger when she thought of the years passed in the embraces of this old man, a hypocrite and a miser. She could hear her mother's words, meant as encouragement: "He will die after a while and you will be free, rich and still young."

During the first years of their married life he forgot his passion for gold and burned with a fruitless ardor. He devoted himself entirely to Nata. She remained indifferent and cold. He began to waste away under the strain of his love, and started to torture her, trying to wrest from her her thoughts.

Suddenly Nata felt her husband's gaze fixed upon her. He asked for a cigarette. Nata lighted a cigar for him. He tried to take it but it fell upon his chest. He began to cough. Feebly he asked about his dog, Bib, which had been shut up in the kitchen.

Nathalie fell asleep. When she woke, she realized that her husband was dead. She brought in her mother, who kissed her and whispered: "You are free, my little Nata!" Nathalie did not return the kiss.

She sat down and fell asleep again. She was awakened by a loud noise. It was Bib that entered the room, jumped on the bed, horror-stricken when he discovered his master's death. The dog trembled, licked the old man's face, uttering a plaintive cry. Tears streamed from the animal's eyes.

An overwhelming impulse drove Nathalie towards the bedside of her husband. She burst into sobs and threw her arms about her husband's lifeless body.

Daimonion Bib. Translation anonymous. In THE BEST CONTINENTAL SHORT STORIES OF 1926, AND THE YEARBOOK OF THE CONTINENTAL SHORT STORY; edited by Richard Eaton. New York, Dodd, Mead, and company, 1927. p.148–159.

Jerzy. Translated as *Jerzy.*

Résumé. At the railway station Jerzy saw his father and mother off. For the first time in his life, though for a few days only, he was to be on his own. He was thrilled with the idea of being independent.

Walking home, he stopped at a large café. It was overcrowded. Jerzy made his way out to the street and jumped into a cab. When he arrived home the janitor told the boy that someone had brought him a cake. The boy commanded him to bring it upstairs. On the second floor Jerzy proudly took out his key, and for the first time in his life opened the door of the apartment. He gave the janitor a tip.

Eating the cake, Jerzy entered his father's bedroom; he decided to sleep in his father's bed. Trembling he opened the safe. He was haunted by the idea that he could do anything he wanted. In the dining room he found a bottle of wine; he filled his glass many times to the brim. He returned feverishly to the safe, and began to take its contents out. His eyes glowed with an unnatural passion; his hands perspired, his body trembled.

He wandered through the other rooms. He went to the rear stairway. When he coughed, the door opened across the hall, and a young girl appeared in the doorway. She was their neighbors' maid. The boy said he was not well, and she, hesitating because of the lateness of the hour, offered to make him tea.

He treated her to a glass of wine. They went into his father's room, and Jerzy took all the jewelry out of the safe. "They are for you," he whispered hoarsely. He seized her in his arms. She struggled, then fell in a sort of semi-coma. Her life lay in his hands.

He began slowly to strangle the girl. They fell to the floor. After moments of writhing she finally succeeded in getting up, but when the boy threatened her again, she fainted once more.

Frightened, the boy screamed, "Get up!" Her body began to grow stiff. Half conscious, he pushed open the window. Was she now crawling toward him, or was she lying still? He felt her hands creeping towards his neck. Jerzy leaned farther out of the window. He began to fall into the still darkness below.

Jerzy. Translation anonymous. In THE BEST CONTINENTAL SHORT STORIES OF 1924–1925, AND THE YEARBOOK OF THE CONTINENTAL SHORT STORY; edited by Richard Eaton. Boston, Small, Maynard [c1925]. p.333–345.

Kochane nic. Translated as *The Beloved "Nothing."*

The Beloved "Nothing"; a Christmas Story. Translated by K. Żuk-Skarszewska. In *Poland* (New York), IX, 1928, p.14–15.

From his BAJ-BAJU-BAJ (Incredible Stories), 1920.

Kremowe róże. Translated as *The Cream-Colored Roses*.

The Cream-Colored Roses. Translated by K. Żuk-Skarszewska. In *Poland* (New York), IX, 1928. p.406–408, 410–411.

The story is written in the form of a dialogue.

From his CZŁOWIEK Z KLARNETEM (The Man with a Clarinet), 1927.

Naparstek. Translated as *The Thimble*.

Résumé.   Three friends George, Antony, and Charles were drinking wine. George made an emphatic statement that he did not want to have any children. He was young, healthy, rich, and had a lovely wife. When questioned, he answered that he loved life too well. For him love of life was synonymous with hatred of death. It was painful for him to think that life must end. For him, having children also meant condemning them to the inevitable death.

Charles maintained that children had no consciousness. Children did not think. Antony was sure that thoughts were born in children, but they had no sense of the irrevocable. George insisted

111

that he had seen a five-year-old boy whose childish heart, when he was faced with the irrevocable, turned to stone.

It was in Thomas Wolski's house. George was spending a few days with the Wolskis in the country. Thomas had gone to the stable. Pani[4] Wolska was sitting in a wicker chair embroidering a cushion. Five-year-old Kaspar was building houses on the carpet with the aromatic boxes which had once held his father's Havanas. Suddenly there came the faint tap of a thimble which had fallen from Pani Wolska's finger, and rolled on the carpet close to Kaspar. The boy glanced at the thimble and continued to play with his boxes. George picked it up and handed it back to Pani Wolska. Kaspar took his mother's mild reproach so much to heart that Pani Wolska, pretending awkwardness, dropped the thimble again to give her son another chance. But no, Kaspar would not pick it up this time. Sobbing, he explained that he had wanted to pick up the thimble *the other time.*

The friends had more wine. In the conversation that followed Charles remarked that if children really had a sense of the irrevocable, then there was no joy in this world. Jokingly the friends drank to womankind, who, as creatures of inconsequence, surely must have known nothing of the irrevocable.

The Thimble, by Waclaw Grubinski. Translation anonymous. In POLISH SHORT STORIES, by Joseph Weyssenhof, Piotr Choynowski, Kornel Makuszynski [and others] . . . London, Minerva Publishing Company [1943]. p.56–62.

The Scream of a Peacock. [Original title not established.]

The Scream of a Peacock. Translated by K. Żuk-Skarszewska. In *Poland* (New York), XI, 1930. p.591–595.

Straszny pajac Stasia. Translated as *The Terrible Puppet.*

The Terrible Puppet; Another Christmas Story. Translated by K. Żuk-Skarszewska. In *Poland* (New York), IX, 1928. p.17–19.

From his BAJ-BAJU-BAJ (Incredible Stories), 1920.

---

4 Equivalent of Madame.

Gwiżdż, Feliks (1885–1952)

Himself close to the life of peasants, the author brought into his stories a fresh breeze from the countryside. The folklore elements in Gwiżdż's literary works have the ring of a genuine product. He was the first editor of *Gazeta Podhalańska* (The Podhale Journal) established at Nowy Targ in 1912. Between 1927 and 1937 the author was editor-in-chief of *Gospodarz Polski* (The Polish Farmer). Gwiżdż began his literary career with a drama, PODCIĘTY DĄB (The Undercut Oak) in 1906. FALE (The Waves, 1907) and KOŚBA (The Mowing, 1931) were his collections of poetry. His short stories were published in the volumes DOBRZY LUDZIE (The Good People, 1912) and OBRAZY NA SZKLE (Pictures on the Glass, 1926).

O żołnierzu błędowcu. Translated as *The Revenant/The Visitor.*

Résumé. Two years before, when their son came home from the war for Christmas, the Jasieńs' ancient hut was alive with joy and merriment. Last year, towards autumn, their boy was killed. His father was sent only the eagle's feather from his cap. Jasień and his wife became suddenly bent and old. The fine farm buildings seemed to sink into the soil.

On Christmas Eve, after they had partaken of a tearful meal, a few of the older neighbors dropped in for a chat. The visitors sat down in a row on the bench, lit their pipes, and began to rack their brains for a word that might bring comfort to the old people.

Neighbor Bieniaś turned his thoughts to the Great War.[5] "There's talk of a ghost—a soldier . . ." he remarked. Jasień put in that he had had such a visit tonight. Then Bieniaś continued.

"A plain, simple peasant was ordered to fight, and he fought. In a battle near some great city, he fell, torn with bullets. He had been murdering and fighting—so he set out for Hell. The older devil there looked through the papers and could not find his name. He was advised to try Purgatory. But he was not inscribed in the books of Purgatory either. The souls there told him to go to

---

[5] World War One, 1914–1918.

113

Heaven. The guardian opened the heavenly gates, looked among the papers, but there was no trace of the soldier's name.

"On his way out he saw a hut. The Child lay inside on a wisp of hay. The Child smiled at the soldier, and the Mother of Mercy said, 'He will find you all and will take you to His bosom.' The soldier came to Poland and he saw whole regiments of such wanderers as himself.

"And this one who came tonight to neighbor Jasień—he must have been one of them," concluded Bieniaś.

"Maybe my son," sobbed the father.

The Revenant. Translated by K. Żuk-Skarszewska. In *Poland* (New York), VII, 1926. p.732–734.

The Visitor, by Feliks Gwiżdż. [Translated by K. Żuk-Skarszewska.] In POLISH SHORT STORIES, by Joseph Weyssenhof, Piotr Choynowski, Kornel Makuszynski [and others] . . . London, Minerva Publishing Company [1943]. p.52–55.

The Visitor, by Feliks Gwiżdż. [Translated by K. Żuk-Skarszewska.] In THE POLISH SHORT STORIES. Edited by Umadevi. [Bombay] Indo-Polish Library. No.35 [c1946]. p.52–56.

Urlop. Translated as *The Furlough.*

The Furlough. Translated by K. Żuk-Skarszewska. In *Poland* (New York), VII, 1926. p.668–670, 698–700, 746–748, 764–766, 768, 770.

Wróble. Translated as *Sparrows.*

Sparrows. Translated by K. Żuk-Skarszewska. In *Poland* (New York), IX, 1928. p.140–142, 144–145.

Heinsdorf, Helena

Helena Heinsdorf is a graduate of the University of Warsaw in German Literature and History of Art. A journalist with headquarters in Berlin, she was arrested by the Gestapo and expelled from Germany in June 1939. The author was assigned to the Polish Ministry of Information in London from 1940 to 1944. Her works include "Der Eingang der russischen Literatur in Deutschland" (unpublished doctoral dissertation, 1931), MŁODZIEŻ NIEMIECKA, DZIŚ I JUTRO (German Youth, Today and Tomorrow, 1945), and "Zygmunt Łempicki" in STRATY KULTURY POLSKIEJ 1939–1944 (Glasgow, 1945), a biographical study of this outstanding Professor of German Literature at the University of Warsaw. A regular contributor to the *Dziennik Polski* in London (*The Polish Daily*), since 1945 Helena Heinsdorf has been a free-lance writer.

The Skies Opened. Written originally in English.

Résumé. Katherine was nine. She was ill and bedridden. When her brother Matt had made a shawm,[6] he promised that he would take Katherine to church to let her hear how he played it. But Matt did not take her . . . He said he would carry her to church for the Midnight Mass on Christmas Eve.

Matt brought some presents for his little sister. In two hours they were to sit down to their Christmas Eve dinner; Katherine began to comb her hair and to dress, constantly wiping the sweat from her forehead. If only her mother was still alive. A fit of coughing overcame her; blood welled from her mouth. With one leap old Matthew, her father, was at the bed. He sat with her on the wooden bench, while young Matthew got a towel to wipe her mouth.

Matthew Puhala had been a widower since the previous April; his neighbor, Konarek, had been killed in the war. So it was only natural that Magda Konarek with her two small boys would come in to cook the dinner. Katherine did not like Magda's dark, piercing and cunning eyes.

Katherine pleaded with her father to be allowed to sit at the table. When the first star was out, the traditional meal followed. The clock struck eleven; it was time to start off for the Midnight Mass. Katherine was put back in bed. This time Matt promised to take her to church on Epiphany—she should have completely recovered by then.

Alone, Katherine suddenly remembered the story her father had

---

6 An obsolete wind instrument similar to the oboe.

told her—that at midnight all beasts could speak with human voices. She remembered her mother's words that at the hour of our Lord's birth the skies opened and whoever was without sin could see God and His Son and all the saints. She dressed herself and struggled to the stable. The cow licked the girl's face, wet with tears. The skies opened for Kate. She saw God the Father, and to His right there was—her mother.

"Mamma! Mamma!" she cried, "It's me, Kate. . . ."

The Skies Opened, by Helena Heinsdorf. In THE PEN IN EXILE; a Second Anthology. Edited by Paul Tabori. [London] The International P.E.N. Club Centre for Writers in Exile, 1956. p.156–161.

Hen, Józef

Krzyż walecznych. Translated as *The Cross of Valor.*

The Cross of Valor. Translated by Maria Paczyńska. In *Poland; Illustrated Magazine,* No. 10 (74) 1960. (Am. ed.) p.15–16.

Preceded by a brief note about the author.

From his collection KRZYŻ WALECZNYCH.

Herbert, Flight-Lieutenant, *see* Meissner, Janusz

Herbert, J. M., *see* Meissner, Janusz

Hłasko, Marek (1931–   )

One of the ablest writers of the new generation, an angry young man, Hłasko made headlines in 1959, when after seven months in Western Europe, he decided to ask for asylum in West Germany. His two short novels, CMENTARZE and NASTĘPNY DO RAJU, originally published in a single volume in Paris in 1958, have now been translated into English as THE GRAVEYARD (1959) and NEXT STOP—PARADISE (1960). Both represent a courageous indictment of communism, and were written and published when the author was still in Poland. To the compiler's best knowledge Hłasko resides now in Israel.

Cmentarze. Translated as *The Graveyard.*

The Graveyard. Translated from the Polish by Norbert Guterman. New York, Dutton, 1959.

126 p.

First edition.

Border-line with a novel.

Kancik czyli wszystko się zmieniło. Translated as *"A Point, Mister?" or, Everything Has Changed.*

Résumé. A journalist got off the train at a small station. His next train was not due for a few hours. He asked the stationmaster how far was it to town. He had not slept for two nights, and badly needed a shave. The stationmaster's son lived in Warsaw; he worked for the Supply Department. The journalist also lived in Warsaw, but he did not know him. The stationmaster invited the traveler for a glass of vodka. He declined the invitation. His comment was that nothing had changed in those lousy small towns. He was born in one exactly like that.

Fifteen minutes later, he was in town. A few carts were idling in the market place; the horses stood dozing, their heads drooping over the fodder bags. This was market day. It was raining and the pedestrians shivered with cold.

The barber was an old man. He had a bald head with funny, withered ears, and a sharp look in his beady black eyes. The old man asked if he wanted a shampoo. No, he wanted just a shave and a haircut. No shampoo. Will he have a point cut? Heaven forbid, no. He wanted a regular cut.

Nobody nowadays wanted a point cut, complained the barber. Before, people used to like it. Mostly the tough guys. Everything has changed, sighed the barber. There was a man in town who repaired organs, and drank himself to death. He had his hair cut here. He liked a nice point. Did Mister want a point? A regular cut, repeated the journalist. The mirror in front of him was dotted with flies.

In the past, said the barber, women in this town had lovers. There was a certain Barcikowski, a harness maker, who once caught his wife with a lover. He threw the lover down the stairs and beat his wife for a week, asking if the last child was his or not. After a week she died. Her last words to him were, "The fifth one is yours, but the other four—they aren't yours." Barcikowski drank a bottle of vodka, took an ax—and that was the end of the five of them. That's how it was. But now it's different. Everything has changed. People have no time for fooling around.

When he reached the station, the stationmaster renewed his invitation. This time the journalist accepted. The stationmaster filled two glasses. He knew the barber. He was a good chap. "Everything has changed, hasn't it?" said the journalist. He looked in the mirror. He drew nearer and saw that his hair was cut in a hideous point.

From his PIERWSZY KROK W CHMURACH, 1956.

"*A Point, Mister?*" *or, Everything Has Changed,* by Marek Hlasko. Translation anonymous. In *East Europe:* a Monthly Review of East European Affairs, VI, No. 9, 1957. p.10, 12–14.

"Notes about the author": p.11.

"*A Point, Mister?*" *or, Everything Has Changed,* by Marek Hlasko. Translation anonymous. In BITTER HARVEST; the Intellectual Revolt Behind the Iron Curtain. Edited by Edmund Stillman; introduction by François Bondy. London, Thames and Hudson [1959]. p.78–85.

Reprinted from *East Europe.*

Najświętsze słowa naszego życia. Translated as *The Most Sacred Words of Our Life.*

Résumé. A young man spent the first night with his beloved. In the morning he is so overwhelmed with almost heavenly pleasure that, putting his clothes on, he does not dare touch his body. She compares him to a little puppy which smells of milk, and asserts that she had never been so happy with any man. The boy must not be late for work, and leaves in a hurry. She does not want to say good-bye to him; she does not want to part with him even for a moment.

On the way to work the lover meets his friends: Gene, Fanfan, and Joe. In the course of casual conversation it comes out that all these men had had exactly the same experience with Barbara as had our hero, including the little puppy smelling of milk, and not wanting to say good-bye in the morning.

The boy turns around, and saying only that he has "some business to settle," he is now headed back where he started from.

From his PIERWSZY KROK W CHMURACH, 1956.

The Most Sacred Words of Our Life. Translated by Wojciech Gniatczyński and Adam Czerniawski. In 10 CONTEMPORARY POLISH STORIES. Edited by Edmund Ordon; with an introduction by Olga Scherer-Virski. Detroit, Wayne State University Press, 1958. p.243–252.

Preceded by a note about the author and the translators.

Następny do raju. Translated as *Next Stop—Paradise.*

Next Stop—Paradise. Translated from the Polish by Norbert Guterman. New York, Dutton, 1960.

250 p.

First edition.

Border-line with a novel.

Ósmy dzień tygodnia. Translated as *The Eighth Day of the Week.*

The Eighth Day of the Week, by Marek Hlasko. Translated from the Polish by Norbert Guterman. New York, E. P. Dutton and company, 1958.

128 p.

Border-line with a novel.

The Eighth Day of the Week, by Marek Hlasko. Translated from the Polish by Norbert Guterman. London, George Allen and Unwin [1959].

127 p.

Pierwszy krok w chmurach. Translated as *A First Step into the Clouds/We Take off for Heaven.*

Résumé. On Saturdays people in all parts of the country have a shorter workday. In anticipation of the pleasures of Sunday everyone becomes better on Saturday afternoon. Only the transportation depots do not share the general satisfaction. On Saturday afternoons drivers wash and polish their trucks and look into the defects of their motors.

It is different on payday. On one payday, a warm, fair Saturday afternoon in June, driver Tadeusz Jabłoński returned to his base at about two o'clock. He received his pay from Mr. Konopka, the dispatcher, who wanted to talk to him. Tadeusz would not be detained, he had something important to do. Just then the loudspeakers announced a Popular Science lecture at 16:30 about the possibilities of a flight to the moon.

Tadeusz heard somebody's comment about flying to the stars. He turned and saw Zawadzki, a short, stout man with a nervous face. Zawadzki had returned two hours earlier and had been waiting for Tadeusz. Tadeusz' face grew darker; he anticipated a quarrel. They passed through the gate. Zawadzki was calm and collected. They were going to the field; Zawadzki's brother-in-law was waiting there. They left the street and cut across the ugly and littered field. The loudspeakers roared about the lecture. At the far end of the fence a man was lying on the grass. He jumped up and wanted to take a collection for a bottle. Tadeusz' heart was beating heavily and painfully. "When did she tell you?" he asked. "Today," Zawadzki replied. "You can both do what you want." Tadeusz spoke now of his love for Zawadzki's wife. He would rather kill himself than live without her. Zawadzki's face was perspiring but he replied quietly. For him this woman and the child were all he had in the world. And where would Tadeusz go with her? Would he take her to a hostel where drunkards come home with whores every night? The day would come when she would look at Tadeusz with hatred, and he would hit her, his wife. "How about a bottle?" Zawadzki's brother-in-law asked. Again came the announcement over the air. Never hitting Tadeusz, Zawadzki spoke of the wretchedness and hopelessness of such a life, those bottles, those lines for meat, those girls at the hostels. Suddenly Tadeusz understood that because of all the wretched things this man had mentioned, his own love, his desires and all that he held as sacred came to nothing.

A red mist rose before his eyes. He started to run. Falling and getting up, he kept on. A crowd began to chase him. Once again he heard the announcement, "The lecture will be . . ." He heard no more, for the people had caught up with him and knocked him down.

From his collection PIERWSZY KROK W CHMURACH, 1956.

A First Step into the Clouds. Translation anonymous. Illustrated by J. Ćwiertnia. In *Poland; Illustrated Magazine,* No. 3 (43) 1958. p. 24–25.
Preceded by a brief note about the author.

We Take Off for Heaven, by Marek Hlasko. Translation anonymous. Drawings by Jerzy Cwierinia [i.e. Ćwiertnia]. In *East Europe; a Monthly Review of East European Affairs,* VI, No. 10, 1957. p.31–35.

We Take Off for Heaven, by Marek Hlasko. Translation anonymous. In BITTER HARVEST; the Intellectual Revolt Behind the Iron Curtain. Edited by Edmund Stillman; introduction by François Bondy. London, Thames and Hudson [1959]. p.3–11.
Reprinted from *East Europe.*

Iwaszkiewicz, Jarosław (1894–   )

In the 1930's the author was associated with the so-called Skamander group of poets which was distinguished by such names as Jan Lechoń, Julian Tuwim, Antoni Słonimski and Kazimierz Wierzyński. Iwaszkiewicz has published over ten volumes of poetry. Before the war there appeared his collection of short stories, PANNY Z WILKA (The Young

Ladies from Wilk, 1933) and an historical novel, CZERWONE TARCZE (Red Shields, 1934). In the postwar years the author has become engaged in writing a cycle of novels under the title SŁAWA I CHWAŁA (Fame and Glory) which deals with the decline of morals and culture of the European intelligentsia between the two world wars.

Borsuk. Translated as *The Badger.*

Résumé. The narrator happened to be in a strange city just before Christmas. There were such crowds in the vicinity of the railway station that people of all ages overflowed the sidewalks and moved along the pavement.

His attention was drawn to two men. The one marching in front was tall and wore grey prisoner's garb. His movements were self-assured, his step steady. He and the short soldier following him with an outsize gun walked in rhythm with the rest of the people. The narrator walked in the same direction.

Near the middle of the block was a sports-goods shop. Guns, game bags, cartridges, and such were displayed in the window. In the center sat an attractively posed, stuffed badger. The convict and his soldier escort suddenly caught sight of the stuffed animal and stopped in common accord. The narrator posted himself behind their backs.

Gazing at the animal, the soldier forgot his duties as an escort, and a leisurely conversation about badgers ensued between him and the convict. It started quite spontaneously. They were then just two human beings with a common interest. The convict had been a forest guard near Radom in the time of the occupation, and there were plenty of badgers around there. He used to shoot them. The guard had been a peasant near Leszno in the Poznań province. He had had no gun. The snares he used to set were not sturdy enough for a hare, not to speak of a badger.

Suddenly the soldier noticed the narrator's curious gaze reflected in the window-pane. Immediately he resumed his authority and changed his tone. Within a few moments they had disappeared in the crowd.

From his OPOWIEŚCI ZASŁYSZANE *(Stories Once Heard), 1954.*

The Badger. [Translated by Ilona Ralf Sues.] Drawings by Aleksander Wejchert. In *Poland; Illustrated Magazine,* No. 11 (39) 1957. p.29.

The Badger. Translated by Ilona Ralf Sues. In CONTEMPORARY POLISH SHORT STORIES, selected by Andrzej Kijowski. Warsaw, Polonia Publishing House, 1960. p.[171]–177.

Ikar. Translated as *Icarus.*

Icarus. Translation anonymous. Drawings by Aleksander Wejchert. In *Poland; Illustrated Magazine,* No. 11 (39) 1957. p.28.
Preceded by a brief note about the author.

Jadwinia (Dzień kwietniowy). Translated as *Jadwinia (A Day in April).*

Jadwinia (A Day in April). Translated by Edward Rothert. In *Polish Perspectives; Monthly Review,* [II], No. 10 (18), 1959. p.27–47.
From his TATARAK I INNE OPOWIADANIA (Sweet Rush and Other Tales), 1960.
Preceded by a note about the author, p.27.
First published *in Twórczość,* July 1959.

Kaden-Bandrowski, Juliusz, *see* Bandrowski, Juliusz Kaden

Kamiński, Aleksander

Aleksander Kamiński, known also under the pseudonym of J[uliusz] Górecki, has published books on scouting for the Polish Boy Scouts and Girl Guides Association, such as ZUCHY: THE POLISH WOLF CUBS (1944).

Kamienie na szaniec. Translated as *Stones for the Rampart.*

Stones for the Rampart; the Story of Two Lads in the Polish Underground Movement, by J. Gorecki [pseud.] [Translation anonymous.] With a foreword by Percy Hugh Beverley Lyon.

Cover and illustrations by A. Horowicz. London, Polish Boy Scouts' and Girl Guides' Association, 1945.

68 p. illus.

At head of title: Polish Boy Scouts' and Girl Guides' Library. Volume 12.

"Translated from the 1st edition of Kamienie na szaniec, published by the Underground Movement—T.Z.W.W.–K.O.P.R., Warsaw, 1943."

The story of Wojtek and Czarny, two boy scouts in the Warsaw Uprising of 1944.

Karski, Jan (1914–   )

Torture. Chapter from his STORY OF A SECRET STATE, 1944.

Torture, by J. Karski. Translation anonymous. In THE WINTER MAIDENS AND OTHER SHORT STORIES. Edited by Umadevi. [Bombay] The Indo-Polish Library, 1947. p.144–182.

STORY OF A SECRET STATE is the author's personal account. Although included in this collection of short stories, *Torture* can be more properly classified as a fragment of personal reminiscences.

Konopnicka, Maria (1842–1910)

A poet and author of short stories, Konopnicka née Wasiłowska also wrote under the pseudonym, Jan Sawa. She is the author of the great patriotic song, "Rota." As a promoter of social reforms and a fervent patriot, she was persecuted by the Russians (then occupying a part of Poland), and compelled to live in Italy, Switzerland, and Germany. She composed an epic, PAN BALCER W BRAZYLII (Mr. Balcer in Brazil, 1910), but she is now best remembered for her shorter poems and short stories. Among her collections of stories, the best known are NOWELE (Short Stories, 1897), LUDZIE I RZECZY (People and Things, 1898), and NA NORMANDZKIM BRZEGU (On the Shores of Normandy, 1904). Her charming fairy-tale for children, O KRASNOLUD-

KACH I SIEROTCE MARYSI, has been translated into English by
K. Żuk-Skarszewska under the title, THE BROWNIE SCOUTS.

Banasiowa. Translated as *Banasiowa/Banasyova.*

Résumé. On a hot and sultry day at noon the narrator sat on
a bench in a park. A little old woman in a snow-white cap, bent
almost double, approached. She had a basket on her arm, and was
hobbling along with the aid of a small stick.

Her name was Banasiowa, and she did not know how old she
was—"it's all written down in the [parish] papers." She thought
she was eighty—or maybe more. She was from Wadowice; everybody knew old Banasiowa there. When she felt that her time was
drawing near, she had come to Lwów to her daughter, married to
a nailsmith.

She came to her children to die, and there she was, still living
on and on . . . She waited a month, two months, and nothing
happened. Then, one Sunday the janitor came to her son-in-law,
Pete, demanding two florins for a residence card. Pete gave him a
few groshes, and the janitor went off. Banasiowa felt it was a waste
of money, and so did her daughter.

One quarter passed, then another, and old Banasiowa was still
alive. The old woman was ashamed of herself, and began to fast
two days a week. Her son-in-law protested, but she would not be
dissuaded. The janitor had come again, and again he left with a
few groshes.

The third week of her fasting, when she had grown very feeble
and was just getting ready for the end, the janitor returned again.
Peter was not in. The old woman was summoned to the police
station.

Banasiowa had to pay five florins. She had to use all the money
saved for her burial, and even then Peter had to lend her an
extra florin. She sold the pillow she had made.

"If I don't die, I may have to pay for this year as well," she
concluded her story, and gazed before her with shaking head.

Banasiowa. Translated by K. Żuk-Skarszewska. In *Poland* (New
York), IX, 1928. p.212–215.

Banasiowa. Translated by N. B. Jopson. In *The Slavonic and East European Review,* X, 1931–32. p.252–259.

Banasiowa, by Marja Konopnicka [Translated by K. Żuk-Skarszewska.] In POLISH SHORT STORIES, by Joseph Weyssenhof, Piotr Choynowski, Kornel Makuszynski [and others] . . . London, Minerva Publishing Company [1943]. p.63–69.

Banasiowa, by Marja Konopnicka [Translated by K. Żuk-Skarszewska.] In INTERNATIONAL SHORT STORIES (first series). Edited by Denys Val Baker. London, W. H. Allen and company, 1944. p.63–69.

Banasiowa, by Maria Konopnicka. Translated by N. B. Jopson. In WORLD LITERATURE; an Anthology of Human Experience, edited by Arthur E. Christy and Henry H. Wells. New York, American Book Company [c1947]. p.902–906.

Banasyova. [Translated by K. Żuk-Skarszewska.] In THE POLISH SHORT STORIES. Edited by Umadevi. [Bombay] Indo-Polish Library, No. 35 [c1946]. p.12–20.

Martwa natura. Translated as *Still Life.*

Still Life. Translated by Ilona Ralf Sues; drawings by Tadeusz Michaluk. In *Poland; Illustrated Magazine,* No. 10 (74) 1960. (Am. ed.) p.25–28.
Preceded by a note about the author, by S. R. Dobrowolski.

Miłosierdzie gminy. Translated as *Community Welfare Service.*

Résumé. (The story is a biting satire against hypocrisy in the disguise of lofty humanitarianism.)
Old Kuntz Wunderli, eighty-two though pretending to be seventy-four years old, weak and decrepit, is presented by a very "humane" councillor of the Community Welfare Service to a group of men and women. According to law and the local custom, someone from those present may take such an indigent individual home, with an agreed remuneration from the Welfare Service, and with a hope of making a profit on the deal by squeezing out of the old person as much work as he is capable of rendering. Bids are made for the amount of remuneration. To cover his frail structure and

his poverty, Kuntz is presented to the public with a scarf and in an overcoat lent to him by the caretaker. Later, to Kuntz's misfortune, this trick is exposed.

What is supposed to be a humane action for the benefit of the aged soon appears in a truer light as an auction for cheap labor. Old Kuntz's son makes a bid too, but, unable to stand his ground, quits and leaves his father to the mercy of others.

Toward the end of the session Probst walks in. His manner is that of a master. Probst has a fine herd of cows and needs help in the delivery of milk. He knows how to squeeze enough work out of those old fellows. Hänzli, whom Probst got from the community not long ago, hanged himself in the attic three months later. Probst quickly and successfully outbids the others by accepting one hundred and twenty-five francs for the old man's keeping.

A little later Kuntz Wunderli is standing in the shafts of the milk wagon, trying with shaking hands to put the harness strap over his shoulders.

First printed 1891.

Community Welfare Service, Pages from Hottingen. Translated by Ilona Ralf Sues. In POLISH SHORT STORIES, selected by Zbigniew Żabicki. Warsaw, Polonia Publishing House, 1960. p.151–[180].

Na drodze; obrazek grecki. Translated as *On the Road.*

On the Road; a Greek Picture. Translated by Ilona Ralf Sues; drawings by Tadeusz Michaluk. In *Poland; Illustrated Magazine.* No. 10 (74) 1960. (Am. ed.) p.28.

Konwicki, Tadeusz (1926–)

Kapral Koziołek i ja. Translated as *Corporal Kid and I.*

Corporal Kid and I. Translation anonymous. Drawings by Jan Młodożeniec. In *Poland; Illustrated Magazine,* No. 12 (64) 1959. p.[24]–27.

Korzeniowski, Józef (1797–1863)

A Mysterious Visit. Fragment from his TADEUSZ BEZIMIENNY.

A Mysterious Visit; An Episode from THADDEUS NAMELESS, a Novel by the Great Uncle of Josef Conrad. Translated by K. Żuk-Skarszewska. In *Poland* (New York), VII, 1926. p.416–419, 443–446, 448.

Kossak, Zofia, *see* Kossak-Szczucka, Zofia

Kossak-Szczucka, Zofia (1890–1968)

Her first novel, which showed great artistic maturity, POŻOGA (THE BLAZE, 1922), had as its background the Bolshevik invasion of Poland in 1917, when the writer's quiet and cultured life on a country estate in Volhynia came to an abrupt end. The novel was translated into English in 1927. (Although he never did, Joseph Conrad seriously planned to translate it himself.) Silesia soon (in 1922) became Kossak-Szczucka's adopted land, and historical fiction became her means of artistic expression. Two cycles of Silesian tales, WIELCY I MALI (The Great and the Small, 1927) and NIEZNANY KRAJ (The Unknown Land, 1932) dealt with the history of the land from the eleventh century until modern times. ZŁOTA WOLNOŚĆ (The Golden Freedom, 1928) was her most important historical novel, displaying the whole panorama of Poland under Sigismund III. Designed on the same grand scale is her historical trilogy beginning with the volume KRZYŻOWCY (The Crusaders), published in English as THE CRUSADERS, THE LEPER KING, and BLESSED ARE THE MEEK. Kossak-Szczucka is also the author of a delightful children's book, KŁOPOTY KACPERKA, GÓRECKIEGO SKRZATA (1926), translated by Monica M. Gardner as THE TROUBLES OF A GNOME (1928).

Widzę Go. Translated as "*I See Him.*"

Résumé. Balaam, son of Beor, ordered his camels to be halted and an ass to be brought. He sent his servants to tell Balak, the king of Moab, that he, the prophet, who had been sent for, had now arrived. He would ride on an ass and talk with the gods seeking counsel and strength in order to overcome Israel.

Riding alone, the wise prophet reflected on how to gain time and get out of the delicate situation. Suddenly the ass dug its forefeet into the ground. He began to lash the animal, but Sahor flung itself sideways in terror. Balaam was enraged. He beat the creature as he had never done before. Sahor dropped to its knees. Suddenly Balaam heard the animal speak to him in intelligible words, "Master! Why are you beating me?"

From wayside wall to wayside wall there rose a column of great brightness. Balaam thought that in the heart of that light he saw the shape of a man in scarlet robes. Balaam was possessed with fear such as he had never known before. He recognized that it was the Lord of Heaven and Earth who had led His people dry-shod through the sea. "Lord, what dost Thou desire me to do?" he asked. "Go to Balak; but speak only the words that I shall put into thy mouth." The vision vanished.

Balaam now demanded that he be led to a place whence he could survey the camping Israel. Instead of hurling a curse, he began praising the God of Israel. The king was enraged; the prophet wanted to be led to yet another hill. He declared that God was with Israel. The kings of Moab shall die, but Israel shall stand for ever.

In great anger the king and his retinue had departed. Balaam was returning to Pethor. He realized that his days were numbered; those that remained were of no consequence to him.

"I See Him," by Zofia Kossak. Translated by H. C. Stevens. In THE PEN IN EXILE; an Anthology. Edited by Paul Tabori. [London] The International P.E.N. Club Centre for Writers in Exile, 1954. p. 83–89.

Kossowski, Jerzy

Powroty. Translated as *The Return.*

The Return. Translated by K. Żuk-Skarszewska. In *Poland* (New York), XI, 1930. p.666–671, 674.

Kotowska, Monika (1942–   )

Podróż do wnętrza muszli. Translated as *Journey into a Sea-Shell.*

Journey into a Sea-Shell. Translated by Krzysztof Klinger. In *Polish Perspectives; Monthly Review,* III, No. 3, 1960. p.32–35.
Preceded by a brief note about the author.

Kowalewski, Janusz (1910–   )

Born in Warsaw, the author now lives in London. Kowalewski wrote for Warsaw newspapers and periodicals until 1939. Arrested by NKWD at the beginning of World War Two, the author was deported to Russia. Released to join the Polish Forces in the Middle East, he took part in the Italian campaign with General Anders' Army, and participated in the taking of Monte Cassino. The author now contributes to émigré periodicals in London. In 1955 Kowalewski published a collection of stories with a common theme, O ŻOŁNIERZU CIUŁACZU (About a Soldier Hoarder).

Twardy chleb and *Tragarz John.* Translated and adapted as *Mutton-Fat.*

Résumé. Mrs. Brownhill tried to discourage John (the narrator of the story) from taking on that heavy work. He would have to carry 140-lb. sacks. Besides, she would have to see how he would get on with the twenty girls employed there. She decided to let him try the job for a week.

The place was the kitchen headquarters which supplied the diners of the British Restaurant and the Meals Service points of the L.C.C.[7] John carried the sacks expertly, and he did get along with the girls—all except one, Elsie.

Elsie was in charge of the kitchen. She had shapely breasts, almost masculine arms, and her head turned sharply on its short neck. Then there was the stout-thighed, tubby Maud—a splendid advertisement for the unending joy of life. For her the people were all lovely and nice. Her companions in the kitchen were the nicest girls in the world—all except Elsie, whom she called a "bloody nuisance."

Carrie was in charge of the potato-peeling machine. Four sacks an hour passed through the machine, and then through her hands. Carrie was fanatically conscientious in her work. But her fanaticism blended well with her English habit of getting on with the surrounding world.

Orders to John were given by all the girls, including Mrs. Brownhill, in a pleasant, friendly manner. Elsie's brusque orders reminded him of the English in the colonies. On one occasion she felt she had hurt John. To make up for it she offered to bring him some butter to replace the mutton-fat on his bread. She had heard that Poles did not care for mutton-fat. Then John could not help remarking, "You'd be a very good woman, Elsie, if . . you didn't suffer from a certain disease which has already been the death of lots of people and even nations. . . . ."

"And what disease is that?"

"The lust for power, Elsie."

> *Adapted from his* O ŻOŁNIERZU CIUŁACZU (*About a Soldier Hoarder*), *1955.*

Mutton-Fat, by J. Kowalevski. [Translated by Jerzy Iranek-Osmecki.] In THE PEN IN EXILE; a Second Anthology. Edited by Paul Tabori. [London] The International P.E.N. Club Centre for Writers in Exile, 1956. p.167–171.

---

7 London County Council.

Krasiński, Zygmunt (1812–1859)

The third of the Polish trio of the great Romantic poets (with Mickiewicz and Słowacki), Krasiński began to create early in his life. His masterpieces include a drama in four parts, NIEBOSKA KOMEDIA (THE UNDIVINE COMEDY, 1833), a dramatic poem IRYDION (1835), and a poem PRZEDŚWIT (Before Dawn, 1843). In THE UNDIVINE COMEDY, probably for the first time in world literature, the class struggle between the propertied class of aristocrats and the "democrats" was presented as a struggle between two cultures, representing ideologies so different that they could not exist side by side. The poet, himself an aristocrat, rose above his personal feelings and detached himself from his prejudices. In IRYDION Krasiński deals with the Polish problem by analogy, when a Greek patriot takes revenge on the Romans for conquering his country. Humanity as consisting of free and independent nations is the theme of PRZEDŚWIT. THE UNDIVINE COMEDY was translated into English by Martha Walker Cook and published in 1875 (J. B. Lippincott); it also appeared in the translation of H. E. Kennedy and Zofia Umińska in 1924 (London, G. G. Harrap). IRIDION, translated by Florence Noyes, was published by Oxford University Press in 1927.

Cholera. Translated as *Cholera.*

Résumé. A young man was looking at the monument of Carrara marble erected by Canova to the memory of an Austrian archduchess in the Church of the Augustines in Vienna. It represented the archduchess, a lion and an angel. The contradiction between the chosen and the damned was a terrible thing to see as it was a foreglimpse of the Last Judgment. He raced through the door and leaped down the granite steps. Two gentlemen in perukes passed him. One of them recognized in the young man Don Antonio del . . . The clatter of a passing equipage drowned his voice.

In the midst of loud merry-making at the Prater sat Don Antonio, alone at a small table with a half-emptied glass of alicante before him. Suddenly, opposite him, he noticed an old man at whose sight he remained motionless for a moment. The old man led Don Antonio to the topmost deck of the pavilion. "Young man, you have committed a crime" he said. "Is it your wish to atone for this crime?"

Don Antonio replied that it was impossible. He had tried everything, God and humankind. The passionate consolations of mistresses and the sober consolations of priests—all had failed. The old man bid him come tomorrow at midnight, and wait on the fifth step leading to the Capuchin Chapel.

At the last stroke of midnight Don Antonio was led blindfold from the steps of the Chapel. When he was allowed to look, he saw a tribunal. All earlier centuries were easily discernible in the judges of the court. On a throne, surrounded by a fiery mist, sat the High Priest of Isis. The tableau was constantly shifting. It appeared that some great action against the nations was before the court. One great city was sentenced to atone by suffering a visitation of the plague. From the group a human form detached itself. Don Antonio recognized the old man. He bore a flagon filled with fine dust, and commanded Don Antonio to go forth and strew death. By Divine Mercy the masses were to expiate their guilt through the atonement of the individual.

Don Antonio took the flagon, and in the morning all Vienna found itself in the grip of terror. Cholera was spreading everywhere. Before the flagon was empty, the old man bid Don Antonio to make his greatest sacrifice—to destroy her whom he truly loved. Don Antonio entered the house of his beautiful beloved, and when, in response to her entreaties of love he had strewn the dust over her, he fell lifeless at her side.

Written in 1831.

Cholera. Translated by Lola Gay-Tifft. In THE BLUE FLOWER. Edited by Hermann Kesten, illustrated by Z. Czermanski. New York, Roy Publishers [c1946]. p.493–509.

Legenda. Translated as *A Legend*.

Résumé. (The story is allegorical, and told in the first person.)

133

It seemed to the narrator that during the vigil at the Birth of Christ he walked along the Campanile outside the gates of Rome. He walked all day long. Standing on the highest summit of the earth, he saw a great black ship, without sails or masts, advancing toward the land. A voice from the deck asked if this was the last night of the vigil of the Birth of our Lord? The narrator answered, "Today is the vigil." The ship stopped at the edge, and figures in crimson caps and white cloaks came out rushing toward the narrator. They asked him to lead them to Rome. They were what was left of the Polish nobility. An angel with a mourning veil over his brow appeared to them, and directed them hither. They had been sailing through gales and storms for a long time. At midnight they should arrive at the basilica of St. Peter. The narrator asked them to follow. As he advanced, he saw a great body of pilgrims passing over the Campanile with torches in their hands. The light glistened on the tall crosses, pictures of saints and on the flags of various nations. The narrator beheld the melancholy features of those who followed him. They carried swords on which they leaned as did the other pilgrims upon their staffs. At first they marched unrecognized, but then all the bands of pilgrims suddenly cried out, "We know you—you are the last heroes of the earth." He led them across the Forum; they entered the court of St. Peter's. The doors of the cathedral stood open and within there was a blazing brightness. The crowds closed up the way. A cardinal in royal purple appeared high above the heads of the people and commanded them to yield passageway to the Polish nobles who for the Catholic faith ransomed another from death, and later for that faith perished themselves. The Polish nobles moved to the tomb of Peter, unfastened their white capes and worshipped, holding their unsheathed weapons in hand.

When the procession arrived at the main altar, an aged man walked slowly forward, wearing on his head a triple crown and a white vestment over his golden surplice. When the Pope ascended the steps of the main altar, the cardinal announced, "Christ is born." The cardinal assisting the Pope at the mass uttered the words, "Ite, missa est!" And then, "The times are fulfilled." He extended his hand toward the grave of Peter, saying, "Awake and speak." A body arose with hands upstretched to the dome, and shrieked, "Woe!" The cardinal asked if Peter recognized him. The body answered, "Your head rested on the bosom of the Master at the last supper, and you have never perished from the earth." With a cry, "Woe be unto me!" the body fell with a terrible crash back into its grave. The vaulted arches began to shiver and break. The Romans began to flee, but the Pope remained at the altar. The departing cardinal asked the Polish nobles to follow him. They refused. When they advanced to offer a hand to the kneeling Pope, the entire white cupola fell to the ground.

The narrator followed the cardinal who now ascended the mountain of ruins of the basilica. The narrator asked if it was true that Christ was born for the last time in that church which was now no more. And he responded, "From the time of Christ none are born and none die on this earth." And about the Polish nobles, he said, "Fear not for them. Because they performed the last service for Him, God will reward them . . ."

The narrator understood and rejoiced.

- *A Legend.* Translated by Šarka B. Hrbkova. In GREAT STORIES OF ALL NATIONS; One Hundred Sixty Complete Short Stories from the Literatures of All Periods and Countries. Edited by Maxim Lieber and Blanche Colton Williams . . . New York, Brentano's Publishers, 1927. p.801–808.
Preceded by a note about the author.

A Legend. [Translated by Šarka B. Hrbkova.] In TREASURY OF WORLD LITERATURE, edited by Dagobert D. Runes. New York, Philosophical Library [c1956]. p.735–744.
Preceded by a brief note about the author.

Kraszewski, Józef Ignacy (1812–1887)

One of the most prolific Polish writers, Kraszewski has left close to two hundred novels. Some of his works deal with contemporary life in Poland, as e.g., DZIECIĘ STAREGO MIASTA

(The Child of the Old Town Square), written under the pseudonym "Bolesławita" during the Polish Uprising against the Russians in 1863, but he is best remembered for his historical novels. One cycle of his novels traces the history of Poland from prehistoric times to the nineteenth century. The best known of this cycle is his STARA BAŚŃ (Old Fable). In a large measure Kraszewski takes credit for replacing the French novel, then very popular among Polish readers, with the native product. HRABINA COSEL (Countess Cosel, 1874) and BRÜHL (1874) are just two examples of his tremendous output.

Jak się dawniej listy pisało. Translated as *Letter Writing of Long Ago.*

Letter Writing of Long Ago. Translated from the Polish of J. I. Kraszewski by N. B. Jopson. In *The Slavonic (and East European) Review,* XXIV, 1946. p.36–46.

Kuncewicz, Marja (Szczepańska), *see* Kuncewiczowa, Maria

Kuncewiczowa, Maria (1897–   )

Born in Samara, on the middle Volga, Kuncewiczowa is the descendant of a Polish legionary who had fled to San Domingo after the uprising of 1863. She has been active as a writer since the publication of her PRZYMIERZE Z DZIECKIEM (The Pact with a Child) in 1926. An interesting cycle of her short stories DWA KSIĘŻYCE (Two Moons) was published in 1933. Many of her novels were translated into English. CUDZOZIEMKA (1936) is the counterpart of THE STRANGER (1945), ZMOWA NIEOBECNYCH was published as THE CONSPIRACY OF THE ABSENT (1950), while THE FORESTER (1954) is the English translation of LEŚNIK (Paris, 1952). Kuncewiczowa was the founder of the International P.E.N. Club Centre for Writers in Exile in London. When the volumes of THE PEN IN EXILE were being published by the Centre (1954, 1956), the author was its President. She has edited and brought about the publication of THE MODERN POLISH MIND; an Anthology (Boston and Toronto, Little, Brown and company, 1962).

Turban i dzika. Translated as *A Turban.*

Résumé. Simon, a Jewish painter, is on vacation with a colony of artists in a small town on the Vistula. His Jewish appearance makes it difficult for him to conquer his dream, a pale and blonde and fairy-like Madzia.

Struck with a brilliant idea, he conceals his Jewishness under a turban which gives him the appearance of an Arab. Now he succeeds in making a date with Madzia. When he comes dressed in his turban and drunk with anticipation of the awaiting bliss, he finds Madzia transformed into a dark, wild woman. Through black lids, thick with mascara, her eyes were boring rapaciously into Simon, as he looked in astonishment, his desire suddenly leaving him.

Finally he broke into laughter. All he managed to utter was, "A terrific wild couple . . . Shouldn't we go to have a picture taken? It would be a fine vacation souvenir!"

From her DWA KSIĘŻYCE (*Two Moons*).

A Turban. Translated by George J. Maciuszko. In 10 CONTEMPORARY POLISH STORIES. Edited by Edmund Ordon; with an introduction by Olga Scherer-Virski. Detroit, Wayne State University Press, 1958. p. 135–144.
Preceded by a note about the author and the translator.

Legeżyński, Stefan (1912–   )

Born in Lwów, the author now lives in London. A journalist and film critic, Legeżyński was on active service with the Polish Forces from 1942 to 1948 in Iran, Irak, Palestine, and finally in England. He is a former President of the Polish literary group called "Rytm," founded in Jerusalem in 1944, and author of the following volumes of poetry: SYDRIA (in Polish, Jerusalem, 1944), ZŁOTA BRAMA (Golden

Gate, London, 1953), STUDNIA W NAZARECIE (The Well in Nazareth, Paris, 1957), and POEMAT O SEKWANIE (Poem on the Seine, London, 1960). Legeżyński has also published WCZORAJ—DZIŚ—JUTRO SREBRNEGO EKRANU (A Study of Yesterday, Today and Tomorrow of the Silver Screen, 1955). He is a member of the International P.E.N. Club Centre for Writers in Exile.

An Odd Story. Written originally in English.

Résumé. The air from the sea was bitterly cold. The Captain, the judge, had lent the narrator a very odd diary to read. The narrator knew that in a few minutes its author would die before a firing squad as a German spy. It was in part the contents of this diary that had convicted him. The prisoner spoke only once during the trial. "I am not guilty," he said.

The diary was written very illegibly. The prisoner was a Polish officer. The war pushed him around. Wherever he went, sooner or later there emerged an Austrian girl, Marlene, the one who kissed him in the tunnel when the train was passing under a mountain chain in Austria.

When, as a prisoner in Russian hands, he was summoned before a judge, the girl who showed up as the interpreter was his Marlene. Thanks to her interpreting he was set free. Next morning Marlene visited him in his apartment, and gave him some names and addresses together with maps of the mountains on the frontier. The former prisoner left hurriedly, and crossed to Hungary.

After more adventures he was arrested in Syria as a German spy, and spent three months in prison. As a result of his appeal to the International Red Cross, he was released, given a few pounds and permission to live in Palestine. He rented a small room in Tel-Aviv.

Again he caught sight of Marlene, talking with a Greek officer in an alien officers' club. They climbed into a jeep and slowly drove away. As the Polish diarist ran after the jeep something fell from the car. It was a portfolio, with a message scrawled on it in lipstick: "Take it to my room." The last entry in the diary read: "Now I am in my room waiting for her."

The portfolio obviously contained important military secrets.

The narrator put the diary on his desk, and opened the door. There was beautiful Anne O'Hara, the very best of the Allied intelligence staff. She had heard of the diary, and came in the nick of time to save its author. She was Marlene. The Greek officer was a German spy. The author of the diary was innocent.

An Odd Story, by Stefan Legeżynski. In THE PEN IN EXILE; a Second Anthology. Edited by Paul Tabori. [London] The International P.E.N. Club Centre for Writers in Exile, 1956. p.238–241.

Ligocki, Michał

Pies sierota (?) Translated as *"Sierota" the Dog*.

"Sierota" the Dog. Translation anonymous. In *Poland America*, XIV, 1933. p.123–126.

Lisiewicz, Mieczysław J. (1897–   )

This poet and novelist, born in Lwów, now resides in London. He fought in both World Wars. Before 1939 the author was a member of the editorial board of *Czas* (The Times) in Cracow. His collection of poetry, SUITA LOTNICZA (The Aviation Suite, 1932), was reprinted during the last war by the Polish Underground Press. The play *Nocne loty* (Night Flights), written with the collaboration of his wife Aleksandra, was successfully produced in Lwów in 1935. His volumes of poetry, U 33 (1931), LEGENDY I BALLADY (Legends and Ballads, 1933) and CORONEL (1934), all dealing with the sea, show originality, ingenuity and a wealth of imagination. More recent among Lisiewicz's works are memoirs of General Sikorski's aide-de-camp in 1918–1920, Z PAMIĘTNYCH DNI; WSPOMNIENIA ADJUTANTA (An Adjutant's Diary, 1944), and a thematically connected cycle of stories, KRONIKI NAROCZAŃSKIE (1943), published in English as THE CHRONICLE OF LAKE NAROCZ (1945). The author was editor and principal contributor of the history of the Polish Air Force, published in English under the title DESTINY CAN WAIT; THE POLISH AIR FORCE IN THE SECOND WORLD WAR

(London, 1949). His later works include the novel GDZIE
GORĘCEJ BIJĄ SERCA (Where the Hearts Beat Faster), published in London by Veritas in 1954.

Śmierć Azy. Translated as *The Death of Aza*.

Résumé. Aza, the mother bitch, was dying on the sand on the
edge of the green swamp. She had dug a shallow hole in the sand
in which she rolled herself in a ball. She watched.

She was a hunting dog, and not long ago she had proudly led her
two pups into the forest to hunt. The inexperienced pups, wandering near the lake, found a lizard sleeping in the sun. Playing with
it they bit it, and smeared their muzzles and paws with the lizard's
blood. Aza had smelt the fatal scent from far off. She had spent a
long time licking the puppies, and had rolled on the ground,
rubbing her muzzle with her paws and wiping her nose in the sand
to get rid of the evil smell. All in vain.

The puppies began to grow thin and to shrivel. Their master
had stuck black tar patches on their noses, but to no avail. Aza,
already sick herself, had bidden each of her puppies farewell, licking their faces interminably, as they went into the loneliness of
the woods.

Then Aza herself felt that her time had come. At night she bit
through the leash. Dragging it she circled the house, bidding farewell to happy memories. Then she turned straight into the forest.

She had been looking on the world for many hours now. Flies
and gnats settled thickly on her muzzle. She no longer felt pain.

It grew dark. With the moon came from far off the echo of the
baying of hounds in chase. Aza pricked her ears. She felt that the
pain and fear were leaving her. She rose. Obedient to her instinct
she ran to the forest. She saw the forms of the hunting pack. She
threw out a loud song of the joy of hunting. She was now in the
midst of the pack, and she ran . . .

> *From his* KRONIKI NAROCZAŃSKIE (THE CHRONICLE OF LAKE
> NAROCZ).

The Death of Aza, by Mieczyslav Lisiewicz. Translated by Ann
Maitland-Chuwen. In THE PEN IN EXILE; an Anthology. Edited by

Paul Tabori. [London] The International P.E.N. Club Centre for Writers in Exile, 1954. p.93–95.

Żywot pijaka. Translated as *Life of a Drunkard*.

Résumé. On the verge of the forest not far from Podhorce Castle in southeast Poland, was once the lair of a savage, foul-mouthed creature, a brigand, an inveterate drunkard. Simon, more generally known as Bloody Simon, because of the sadistic delight he would take in seizing an unsuspecting victim's finger in his beak, was a starling. He did not spare even the Right Reverend Canon of Podhorce. Simon drank to excess, particularly when the wine was sweet.

He did not like strangers. Whenever the servants began to arrange various shining things on the white tablecloth in the dining room, a sure sign of expected visitors, he would swoop down upon the table and toss all he could to the ground. Simon had his likes and dislikes. He bestowed a special sentiment on Flash, a golden cocker-spaniel. Flash permitted Simon to perch on his head.

It happened once that Flash went off into the forest and did not return. For two days Flash could not be found. The head forester went about his duties in gloom and worry. Even Simon was mute. Finally he flew out of the house.

All hope had been lost when Simon returned to the house uttering great cries. He began to fly in and out of the window, time after time. At last Aslan, the head forester, went out and followed Simon, who led him to poor Flash who lay unconscious from loss of blood, his paw caught in a fox trap. On that happy occasion both Simon and the forester were drunk.

A month or two later Simon got at some cherries soaking in pure alcohol. He drank himself to death.

Life of a Drunkard, by H[i.e. M.] J. Lisiewicz. Translated by A. Truscoe. In THE PEN IN EXILE; a Second Anthology. Edited by Paul Tabori. [London] The International P.E.N. Club Centre for Writers in Exile, 1956. p.178–181.

Lisiewicz, Teodozya (1903–   )

Novelist, playwright and actress, Teodozya Lisiewicz was on the staff of the Polish Radio in Lwów from 1930 to 1939. Arrested by the Soviet occupation authorities in 1940, she was sentenced to eight years in prison. The author spent two years in various Russian concentration camps. She served with the Polish w.a.a.f. in Great Britain from 1943 to 1945. The memoirs of her life in Soviet Russia were granted the first prize in a Polish literary contest in 1945. Her first play, *Manon Lescaut,* was performed at the Festival of Slavonic Art at Brno, Czechoslovakia, in 1935. Of her plays written in exile, *Dom* (Home) received a Polish award in London in 1945, *Wejście tylko dla służby* (Staff Entrance) was awarded a prize in 1949, *Madame Iksow* (Madame X-ov) and *Jaworowe buty* (The Maple-tree Boots) were granted a Polish award in the U.S.A. in 1951. Her latest publications include a collection of short stories, DZIURA W DACHU (A Hole in the Roof, London, 1962) and a widely reviewed novel, CHLEB (Bread, London, 1966). Active in the International P.E.N. Club Centre for Writers in Exile, the author now resides in London.

Solitude. Fragment from her SIOSTRA IKARA.

Résumé. WAAF Corporal Janka walked along the promenade toward the south side of the town. She felt happy and thoroughly pleased with life. She had just had tea in the canteen. She started on her way, because her boy-friend would be waiting. Janka liked to go out for an hour or two to escape the monotony of the daily routine. Could one be alone and feel happy? When was it that she had understood the real meaning of solitude for the first time?

The Russian guard called out six women from the group waiting in the camp yard. Five Russian women and Janka, a Pole, followed him to the kitchen. He pushed a dilapidated and leaky bucket at each of the women. "You'll go to the woods and gather berries," he announced.

They followed the guard. Janka's legs and hands were in rags, rotten with pus. The ragged group of prisoners was hardly fit for any physical or mental effort. There was one subject which brought them to life—sex. If there was no outlet for desire, at least they could talk of it. It was a degenerated subconscious instinct of the reproduction of the species. Obscene jokes did not affect Janka. She managed to separate herself from the surroundings, and not allow her mind to be polluted.

They stopped at the wide river. The guard whistled for a boat and ordered the women in. He himself remained on the shore. He let them go to the woods on the other side alone with the prisoner-boatman. Soon Janka was surrounded by a strange, dim silence. She walked for a while hardly realizing what had happened. For the first time in two years she was alone. What a joy! She sat down. Then she slowly stretched herself on the ground and pressed her body close to the velvety couch of moss. At that moment she discovered that life's strong pulse could be felt only in solitude.

From her SIOSTRA IKARA (*Icarus' Sister*).

Solitude, by Teodozya Lisiewicz. Translation anonymous. In THE PEN IN EXILE; a Second Anthology. Edited by Paul Tabori. [London] The International P.E.N. Club Centre for Writers in Exile, 1956, p.182–186.

Łuskina, Ewa

Mistyczna róża (?) Translated as *The Mystic Rose*.

The Mystic Rose. Translated from the Polish of Ewa Łuskina by Dorothy F. Tait. In *The Slavonic (and East European) Review*, XVII, 1938–39. p.272–281.

Mackiewicz, Józef (1902–   )

The author was born near Wilno. Before World War Two he published a volume of short stories and, in collaboration with Kazimierz Leczycki, wrote a play, *Pan poseł i Julia* (The Deputy and Julia). From 1935 to 1940 Mackiewicz was editor of the daily, *Gazeta codzienna*, in Wilno. He moved to Warsaw to publish an underground anti-Nazi newspaper. In 1945 he escaped to Italy and later settled in England. His documentary KATYN—UNGESÜHNTES VERBRECHEN (Zürich, 1949, and München, 1958) appeared in English with a foreword by Arthur Bliss Lane under the title THE KATYN WOOD MURDERS (London, 1951; New York, 1952). Mackiewicz's novel DROGA DO NIKĄD, translated also into German and French, was published in English as THE ROAD TO NOWHERE (London, 1962; Chicago, 1964). Another novel, KONTRA (Counter Blow, 1957), denounces bitterly the British for the way they handed over anti-Communist Cossacks to the Soviet Army at the end of World War Two. His most recent titles include ZWYCIĘSTWO PROWOKACJI (The Victory of Provocation, Monachium, 1962), POD KAŻDYM NIEBEM (Under Every Sky, London, 1964) and the novels SPRAWA PUŁKOWNIKA MIASOJEDOWA (Colonel Miasojedow's Affair, London, 1962) and LEWA WOLNA (Keep to the Right, London, 1965).

Morderstwo w dolinie rzeki Waki. Translated as *Murder on the Waka.*

Résumé. The Bołtuszkos worked for the narrator barely a year, up to the outbreak of war in 1939. Antoni Bołtuszko was a man of old peasant stock. His wife, Aquilina, had this strange kind of beauty which comes from the admixture of Tartar blood. (Five centuries before, the Grand Duke Witold of Lithuania had settled Tartar prisoners in the valley of the river Waka.) Bołtuszko married her in 1937. In 1938 the narrator hired him as a watchman for the orchard.

At the beginning of the war the Bołtuszkos moved to the other end of the village. During the Soviet occupation Bołtuszko went about the district building and repairing stoves and chimneys. Aquilina was hardly suitable for any kind of work. Dropping her long eyelashes, she carried her child about, wrapped in a shawl. She was always poorly dressed.

Stocky and tough Bołtuszko never beat his wife. But soon he turned to easy money: the illicit distillation of vodka. Before long every third cottage was making its own vodka, and the price began to fall sharply. Bołtuszko began to drink heavily. In December, 1940, he had nothing left with which to celebrate even a most wretched Christmas. It was then that Monica, his sister-in-law, made an intrusion into the Bołtuszkos' marriage.

Then the Germans came. Seven months after, some people found in a forest the body of a Jewish woman, stripped, violated, robbed, and hanged by a trouser strap from a pine branch. Suspicion was cast upon Bołtuszko, but it proved unjustified. For a month past he had been away from home. When he returned, he was rolling in wealth. He drank heavily and ran wild.

Bołtuszko's fixed idea now was to go to Święciany and open a shop there. He wanted Monica to go with him. When she refused, Bołtuszko pulled out a pistol and fired three times. Did he want to kill Monica or Aquilina's semblance in her?

The police were informed. On the third day they rounded up Bołtuszko. He must have tried to escape, as he was shot in his tracks.

Murder on the Waka, by Josef Mackiewicz. Translated by H. C. Stevens. In THE PEN IN EXILE; an Anthology. Edited by Paul Tabori. [London] The International P.E.N. Club Centre for Writers in Exile, 1954. p.96–103.

Przygody małego diabełka. Translated as *The Adventures of an Imp.*

Résumé. (A satire on human beings wittily shown through the activities of a Devil family.)

The young Little Nick, an imp, is hired by another Devil to tempt children of a manufacturer's family to actions bad from the human point of view. "Good" and "bad" are human concepts foreign to the language commonly used in Hell. Both Heaven and Hell are only different points of view enclosed in different circles.

Discouraged by his lack of success, the imp goes on revolt, tries to materialize by breaking out of his circle. Taken back to Hell and punished, Little Nick quite accidentally causes the clerk of a store to commit suicide, thus capturing for Hell his first soul.

The Adventures of an Imp. Translated by Bronislas de Leval Jezierski. In 10 CONTEMPORARY POLISH STORIES. Edited by Edmund

Ordon; with an introduction by Olga Scherer-Virski. Detroit, Wayne State University Press, 1958. p.189–211.
Preceded by a note about the author and the translator.

The red flag. Fragment from his DROGA DO NIKĄD.

The Red Flag, by Josef Mackiewicz. Translated by Lew Sapieha. In THE PEN IN EXILE; a Second Anthology. Edited by Paul Tabori. [London] The International P.E.N. Club Centre for Writers in Exile, 1956. p.187–189.
From his DROGA DO NIKĄD (ROAD TO NOWHERE), 1955.

Majewski, Witold, pseud.

Kolporter. Translated as *Jack the Distributor/Yanek the Distributor.*

Résumé. Mrs. Wanda's husband was a lawyer and an officer in the reserve; he had been called up at the last moment before the outbreak of war with Germany in September 1939. He had gone straight from the office. Mrs. Wanda received no news of him.

She lived in a state of continuous anxiety. When her son Yanek was late returning home, every moment brought a new tormenting supposition. She had to leave her apartment and rented one large room which sufficed for herself and her son. She sold her jewelry, and visited relatives and friends in the country from time to time, bringing back stocks of food sufficient for long periods. All Warsaw took to trade; so did Yanek. But Mrs. Wanda could not believe her ears, when she heard the familiar voice in the street, calling: "Cigarettes, lighters, flints. . . ."

One night Yanek put his clothes on a chair as usual, but shifted the chair close to his bed. His mother distinctly heard the rustling of paper. Tormented by suspicions, when Yanek had fallen asleep Mrs. Wanda went through her son's clothes. Her trembling fingers touched a large Colt revolver and a yellow patch of papers, copies of the "Political Weekly of the Defenders of Poland." Clearly Yanek was the distributor of the paper. Mrs. Wanda locked her son's secret deep in her heart.

The narrator was Yanek's former teacher. He was to meet the boy in a quiet coffee-shop, and get from him copies of the illegal newspaper for distribution in the provinces. On his way to meet Yanek he heard shots ringing out in the street. There was a crowd gathered opposite the coffee-shop. Yanek was lying on the pavement. The newspapers were scattered in the mud. His Colt was gripped tightly in his hand.

Jack the Distributor, by W. Majewski. Translated by H. C. Stevens; illustrations by A. Horowicz. London [c1942].

23 p. illus.

"Wydane staraniem Ministerstwa Spraw Wewnętrznych Rządu Polskiego."

"From the story-cycle: Thorns and blood [Ciernie i krew]."

Yanek the Distributor, by W. Majewski. Translated by H. C. Stevens. In THE POLISH SHORT STORIES. Edited by Umadevi. [Bombay] Indo-Polish Library. No. 35 [c1946]. p.122–129.

Makuszyński, Kornel (1884–1953)

A popular author of humorous stories, Makuszyński also wrote a few novels which reflect the same smile through the tears that is evident in most of his works. His RZECZY WESOŁE (Humorous Tales, 1909), not much more than clever feuilletons made up into stories, was published at the beginning of his literary career. His first novel, SŁOŃCE W HERBIE (Sunshine in the Coat-of-Arms, begun in 1914, but not published until 1918) raised him to a higher level which the author was still to surpass in his PO MLECZNEJ DRODZE (Along the Milky Way, 1917). Full of gentle humor and replete with poetic scenes, this novel describes the lives of a painter and a poet who escape to an attic from the platitude, tedium and misery of everyday existence. Other popular titles include AWANTURY ARABSKIE (Arabian Adventures, 1914) and PERŁY I WIEPRZE (Pearls and Swine, 1920). Makuszyński continued writing between the wars and after World War Two.

Cielęcy żywot. Translated as *Calf Time.*

Résumé. Calf time was for the author-narrator the time of "The Spirit of the Wilderness" and of "The Mysterious Valley." There were many Red Indian camps in the marshes along the river, and constant warfare was carried on between the different tribes.

The most terrible of the chiefs was a boy who in ordinary life was called Staszek, but who on the warpath was known as "Fighting Bull." He commanded a band of seven ten-year-old, savage and ruthless Comanches. Fighting Bull threatened to exterminate all refractory tribes to the last man. The narrator, looked upon as an authority on all Indian customs and languages, belonged to another tribe whose chief was "Flying Stag." His main qualifications for command were that he was terribly cross-eyed and freckled.

One day a rumor reached Flying Stag that Fighting Bull had sworn to kill him. He planned to take him captive and then scalp him. Pressed by danger the narrator's tribe looked for alliances, and persuaded four other tribes to join them. Among those who joined was a policeman's son, "Grumbling Thunder," who promised to bring to battle a wonderful weapon, his father's drum.

When the tribe of savage Comanches, in anticipation of victory, was enjoying two pots of strawberry jam, it was suddenly overrun, to the sound of the drum, by the allied tribes commanded by Flying Stag. Fighting Bull was seized and bound securely to an alder tree. His warriors surrendered and went over to the enemy. But instead of asking for mercy, Fighting Bull jeered at his enemies in accordance with the best Indian traditions.

Suddenly somebody somehow lit a pile of dry leaves and twigs that reached to the prisoner's armpits. When the crowd of Indians withdrew in terror, it was Flying Stag who rushed to the prisoner's rescue and brought him to safety. Blissfully happy the tribes watched how Fighting Bull stretched out his hand to his savior, and assured his red brother that if he should ever need help, he should call with the cry of the vulture, and Fighting Bull would come were it a hundred miles.

From his BEZGRZESZNE LATA (*The Years Without Sin*), *1925.*

Calf Time. Translated by K. Żuk-Skarszewska. In *Poland* (New York), VIII, 1927. p.398–400, 425–430, 432, 434.

Calf Time, by Kornel Makuszynski. [Translated by K. Żuk-Skarszewska.] In POLISH SHORT STORIES, by Joseph Weyssenhof, Piotr Choynowski, Kornel Makuszynski [and others] . . . [London] Minerva Publishing Company [1943]. p. 26–42.

Duch zapomniany. Translated and adapted as *The Forgotten Ghost.*

Résumé. Mr. Valentine Zieba bore the name of a bird (Zięba —a finch), but he did not look like one. Mr. Zieba was thin, bald, and absent-minded. His wife was fat and ill-tempered. They had a daughter, Helusia, who had a lily-white complexion and was always elegantly dressed.

Mr. Zieba decided that he should get rid of his wife. But by no illegal means. He would do it in a gentle and polite manner. To secure a divorce he would have to acquire wealth.[8] A plan occurred to him: he would be a ghost. His seances during which he conjured up all sorts of spirits were such a success that Mr. Zieba became known, much to Madame Zieba's annoyance, as "The Devil's Brother."

The day after one such successful seance at which the spirit of Alexander the Great had appeared, Mr. Zieba sat alone in his room. He lit a cigar, and in the smoke he espied a ghost. Mr. Zieba was frightened. The spirit pretended at first that he was Alexander the Great, but he later divulged that he had been a university professor who died three years ago. The spirit took pleasure in inhaling Mr. Zieba's cigar smoke and in smelling his brandy. At one of his successive visits, the ghost asked him to peep through a keyhole into Helusia's room. To his horror, Mr. Zieba beheld his daughter in the arms of a handsome artillery lieutenant. Then the spirit led Mr. Zieba to his wife. Her head tied up in a towel, Madame Zieba lay on her bed. The ghost glided towards her and spoke in such a frightful voice that Mr. Zieba nearly fainted. Some-

---

8 This and some other statements in this translation have no basis in the Polish text. The résumé reflects the English text.

one ran out of Helusia's room and disappeared into the night. Madame spoke incomprehensible words, her lips moving quickly. The ghost assured Mr. Zieba that she would remain ill for about an hour. Jeeringly the spirit suggested that they go now and smoke a cigar. Mr. Zieba tried to catch the ghost, but all he caught was a peg of the hat-stand that had seemed just in the middle of the ghost's figure.

The Forgotten Ghost. Translation and adaptation anonymous. In THE BEST CONTINENTAL SHORT STORIES OF 1923–1924, AND THE YEARBOOK OF THE CONTINENTAL SHORT STORY; edited by Richard Eaton. Boston, Small, Maynard and company [c1924]. p.259–270.

Dziecinne argumenty słonecznego promienia. Translated as *The Childish Arguments of a Sunbeam.*

The Childish Arguments of a Sunbeam. Translated by K. Żuk-Skarszewska. In *Poland* (New York), VI, 1925. p.594–596, 619–620. *From his* BEZGRZESZNE LATA (*The Years Without Sin*).

Pan z kozią bródką. Translated as *Another "Paradise" Lost and Regained.*

Another "Paradise" Lost and Regained. Translated by K. Żuk-Skarszewska. In *Poland* (New York), VIII, 1927. p.526–529, 558–562, 590–593, 621–622, 624, 626, 628.

Małaczewski, Eugeniusz (1895–1922)

The author is one of the noblest soldier-poets in Polish literature. After having fought in many far-away front-lines, Małaczewski returned to the Poland of his dreams only to die there at the age of twenty-seven. His poetry was strongly influenced by Słowacki and Tetmajer, while his prose bears traces of Sienkiewicz and Żeromski. The well-known collection of his stories, KOŃ NA WZGÓRZU (A Horse on the Hill, 1921) was written, above all, in the spirit of service to his country. His only volume of poetry, POD LAZUROWĄ STRZECHĄ (Under the Azure Thatch, 1922) is also full of patriotic overtones. "*O Wiośnie I Słowikach*" (About Spring and Nightingales) is the most representative and, perhaps, the most beautiful poem in this collection.

"Tam gdzie ostatnia świeci szubienica." Translated as *"There, where the Last Gaunt Gallows Stands and Beckons."*

Résumé. In the summer of 1918 the headquarters of the Polish Military Organization sent several thousand officers and soldiers to Murmansk. Of these only a few hundred reached their destination. News was received of numerous executions of Polish soldiers in the prisons of revolutionary Russia.

The author tells the story of the last two days of two Legionnaires, brothers Jan and Jerzy Zwada, corporals of Haller's Iron Brigade and formerly students at Kraków University.

After the battle of Kaniów they were to proceed to France. But they never reached the coast. Through their ignorance of the Russian language and lack of proper documents, they were thrown into the prison of Trotsky's Russia, and executed in July 1918, in the town of Vologda in the Far North of Russia.

Several times the two brothers had been summoned to stand before the Tcheka.[9] During the final hearing they appeared before Vasha whose secretary and mistress, Zosia, was a Polish girl from Łódź. She resolved to save the prisoners. But the more she insisted that they were innocent, the more determined was Vasha that they should die.

The two brothers spent their last night in their cell deliberating their mission for Poland. Their thoughts rose high above death, and their souls joined in Holy Communion with the immortal soul of their beloved country. Jan, the elder, found true greatness in his poet-brother.

Vasha came to command the execution in person. He ordered Jerzy before the death squadron first, made Jan watch the execution, and then carry his brother's corpse behind the prison wall, near the rubbish-heap where a shallow hole had been prepared. Jan carried his brother's body as carefully as though it were a sleeping child.

After a time, Jan saw the muzzles pointed straight at his breast. . . .

---

[9] Soviet Secret Police; what is now N.K.W.D.

From his KOŃ NA WZGÓRZU *(A Horse on the Hill), 1921.*

"*There, where the Last Gaunt Gallows Stands and Beckons.*" Translated by K. Żuk-Skarszewska. In *Poland* (New York), IX, 1928. p.470–478, 608–612. X, 1929. p.57–60.

"*There where the Last Gaunt Gallows Stands and Beckons,*" by Eugeniusz Malaczewski. [Translated by K. Żuk-Skarszewska.] In POLISH SHORT STORIES, by Joseph Weyssenhof, Piotr Choynowski, Kornel Makuszynski [and others] . . . [London] Minerva Publishing Company [1943]. p.92–117.

"*There, where the Last Gaunt Gallows Stands and Beckon [i.e., Beckons],*" by Eugeniusz Malaczewski. [Translated by K. Żuk-Skarszewska.] In THE POLISH SHORT STORIES. Edited by Umadevi. [Bombay] Indo-Polish Library. No. 35 [c1946]. p.70–103.

Meissner, Janusz (1901–   )

A pilot himself, Janusz Meissner has made flying an exciting subject from the very beginning of his literary career. Under his pen, aircraft acquire traits of individuality. His first collection of short stories, HANGAR NO. 7 (1927), and the novels ESKADRA (A Squadron, 1928) and SKOK PRZEZ ATLANTYK (A Leap over the Atlantic, 1928) were all very promising. Then the line of Meissner's development seemed to have stopped, and the author continued with popular books for young people (e.g., SZKOŁA ORLĄT, The School for Young Eagles, 1930). He also wrote one historical novel, CZARNA BANDERA (The Black Banner, 1957). Meissner's wartime volumes have brought him a new wave of popularity. Published originally in England, they were re-issued in Poland.

A - jak ciocia Andzia. Translated as "*A for Aunt Annie.*"

"*A for Aunt Annie.*" In his "L FOR LUCY," by Flight-Lieutenant Herbert. [Translation anonymous. Illustrated by A. Horowicz.] Edinburgh, Składnica Księgarska, 1945. p.101–113.

Bujak "nawala." Translated as *Buyak Fails.*

Buyak Fails. In his "G FOR GENEVIEVE," by Flight-Lieutenant Herbert. [Translation anonymous.] Edinburgh, Polish Book Depot, 1944. p.142–156.

Dowód niezbity. Translated as *Conclusive Proof.*

Conclusive Proof. In his "L FOR LUCY," by Flight-Lieutenant Herbert. [Translation anonymous. Illustrated by A. Horowicz.] Edinburgh, Składnica Księgarska, 1945. p.49–63.

Ewakuacja. Translated as *Evacuation.*

Evacuation. In his "G FOR GENEVIEVE," by Flight-Lieutenant Herbert. [Translation anonymous.] Edinburgh, Polish Book Depot, 1944. p.17–25.

Flying control. Translated as *Flying Control.*

Flying Control. In his "L FOR LUCY," by Flight-Lieutenant Herbert. [Translation anonymous. Illustrated by A. Horowicz.] Edinburgh, Składnica Księgarska, 1945. p.113–139.

"G" – jak Genowefa; "L" – jak . . . Translated as *"G for Genevieve"; "L for . . ."*

"G for Genevieve"; "L for . . ." In his "G FOR GENEVIEVE," by Flight-Lieutenant Herbert. [Translation anonymous.] Edinburgh, Polish Book Depot, 1944. p.174–185.

Góra Ojca. Translated as *"The Father's Mountain."*

"The Father's Mountain." In his "G FOR GENEVIEVE," by Flight-Lieutenant Herbert. [Translation anonymous.] Edinburgh, Polish Book Depot, 1944. p.59–64.

Inny gatunek. Translated as *A Different Species.*

A Different Species. In his "G FOR GENEVIEVE," by Flight-Lieutenant Herbert. [Translation anonymous.] Edinburgh, Polish Book Depot, 1944. p.133–142.

La douce France. Translated as *La douce France.*

La douce France. In his "G FOR GENEVIEVE," by Flight-Lieutenant

Herbert. [Translation anonymous.] Edinburgh, Polish Book Depot, 1944. p.97–100.

"Lucy" wraca do bazy. Translated as *"Lucy" Returns to Base.*

"Lucy" Returns to Base. In his "L FOR LUCY," by Flight-Lieutenant Herbert. [Translation anonymous. Illustrated by A. Horowicz.] Edinburgh, Składnica Księgarska, 1945. p.9–19.

Missing. Translated as *Missing.*

Missing. In his "L FOR LUCY," by Flight-Lieutenant Herbert. [Translation anonymous. Illustrated by A. Horowicz.] Edinburgh, Składnica Księgarska, 1945. p.35–49.

Na pułapie. Translated as *On the Ceiling.*

On the Ceiling. In his "G FOR GENEVIEVE," by Flight-Lieutenant Herbert. [Translation anonymous.] Edinburgh, Polish Book Depot, 1944. p.9–17.

Niezapominajki. Translated as *Forget-Me-Nots.*

Forget-Me-Nots. In his "G FOR GENEVIEVE," by Flight-Lieutenant Herbert. [Translation anonymous.] Edinburgh, Polish Book Depot, 1944. p.25–31.

O kilka mil od brzegu. Translated as *A Few Miles from the Shore.*

A Few Miles from the Shore. In his "L FOR LUCY," by Flight-Lieutenant Herbert. [Translation anonymous. Illustrated by A. Horowicz.] Edinburgh, Składnica Księgarska, 1945. p.25–34.

Obóz w Dobrudży. Translated as *The Camp in Dobrudja.*

The Camp in Dobrudja. In his "G FOR GENEVIEVE," by Flight-Lieutenant Herbert. [Translation anonymous.] Edinburgh, Polish Book Depot, 1944. p.46–59.

Odwrót. Translated as *The Retreat.*

The Retreat. In his "G FOR GENEVIEVE," by Flight-Lieutenant Herbert. [Translation anonymous.] Edinburgh, Polish Book Depot, 1944. p.32–37.

Plama na morzu! Translated as *A Stain on the Sea.*

A Stain on the 'Sea. In his "G FOR GENEVIEVE," by Flight-Lieutenant Herbert. [Translation anonymous.] Edinburgh, Polish Book Depot, 1944. p.168–174.

Pryszczyk wieje. Translated as *Pryszczyk Escapes.*

Pryszczyk Escapes. In his "G FOR GENEVIEVE," by Flight-Lieutenant Herbert. [Translation anonymous.] Edinburgh, Polish Book Depot, 1944. p.38–46.

Pryszczyk wieje po raz drugi. Translated as *How to Escape?/ Pryszczyk Escapes Again.*

How To Escape? by J. M. Herbert, pseud. Translation anonymous. In THE WINTER MAIDENS AND OTHER SHORT STORIES. Edited by Umadevi. [Bombay] The Indo-Polish Library, 1947. p.115–132.
From his ŻĄDŁO GENOWEFY ("G FOR GENEVIEVE").
Same as *Pryszczyk Escapes Again.*

Pryszczyk Escapes Again. In his "G FOR GENEVIEVE," by Flight-Lieutenant Herbert. [Translation anonymous.] Edinburgh, Polish Book Depot, 1944. p.71–85.

Sierżant Prot, nocny myśliwiec. Translated as *Sergeant Prot, Night Fighter.*

Sergeant Prot, Night Fighter. In his "G FOR GENEVIEVE," by Flight-Lieutenant Herbert. [Translation anonymous.] Edinburgh, Polish Book Depot, 1944. p.115–123.

Sergeant Prot, Night Fighter, by J. M. Herbert, pseud. Translation anonymous. In THE WINTER MAIDENS AND OTHER SHORT STORIES. Edited by Umadevi. [Bombay] The Indo-Polish Library, 1947. p.133–143.
From his ŻĄDŁO GENOWEFY ("G FOR GENEVIEVE").

Święte bomby. Translated as *Sacred Bombs.*

Sacred Bombs. In his "G FOR GENEVIEVE," by Flight-Lieutenant Herbert. [Translation anonymous.] Edinburgh, Polish Book Depot, 1944. p.157–168.

"Świńska sprawa." Translated as *Pryszczyk's Adventures.*

Pryszczyk's Adventures. In his "L FOR LUCY," by Flight-Lieutenant

Herbert. [Translation anonymous. Illustrated by A. Horowicz.] Edinburgh, Składnica Księgarska, 1945. p.85–101.

Targu-jiu. Translated as *Targu-Jiu.*

Targu-Jiu. In his "G FOR GENEVIEVE," by Flight-Lieutenant Herbert. [Translation anonymous.] Edinburgh, Polish Book Depot, 1944. p.64–71.

Trzynasta wyprawa: Osnabrück. Translated as *Thirteenth Operation: Osnabrück.*

Thirteenth Operation: Osnabrück. In his "G FOR GENEVIEVE," by Flight-Lieutenant Herbert. [Translation anonymous.] Edinburgh, Polish Book Depot, 1944. p.124–132.

Turyn. Translated as *Turin.*

Turin. In his "L FOR LUCY," by Flight-Lieutenant Herbert. [Translation anonymous. Illustrated by A. Horowicz.] Edinburgh, Składnica Księgarska, 1945. p.19–25.

W drodze do Francji. Translated as *On the Way to France.*

On the Way to France. In his "G FOR GENEVIEVE," by Flight-Lieutenant Herbert. [Translation anonymous.] Edinburgh, Polish Book Depot, 1944. p.85–96.

Wyspa Ostatniej Nadziei. Translated as *The Island of Last Hope.*

The Island of Last Hope. In his "G FOR GENEVIEVE," by Flight-Lieutenant Herbert. [Translation anonymous.] Edinburgh, Polish Book Depot, 1944. p.100–103.

Żądło Genowefy. Translated as *"Genevieve's" Sting.*

"Genevieve's" Sting. In his "G FOR GENEVIEVE," by Flight-Lieutenant Herbert. [Translation anonymous.] Edinburgh, Polish Book Depot, 1944. p.103–114.

Zestrzelili nas nad Francją. Translated as *Just Prejudice.*

Just Prejudice. In his "L FOR LUCY," by Flight-Lieutenant Herbert. [Translation anonymous. Illustrated by A. Horowicz.] Edinburgh, Składnica Księgarska, 1945. p.64–85.

Mickiewicz, Adam (1798–1855)

This great Polish Romantic poet is still comparatively little known to the Western world. His mystical drama DZIADY (FOREFATHERS), derived from the poet's own experiences in the trial by the Russians of university students in Wilno in 1823, contains scenes of martyrdom which place it among the greatest masterpieces of world literature. The poet's great epic, PAN TADEUSZ (1834), first translated by George Rapall Noyes and published in London in 1949, is now offered in two new translations, one by Watson Kirkconnel as PAN TADEUSZ, OR THE LAST FORAY IN LITHUANIA (New York, 1962), the other by Kenneth Mackenzie (same English title, London, 1964). Among recent attempts on a smaller scale, a modest selection of his poetry under the title ADAM MICKIEWICZ; SELECTED POEMS, edited by Clark Mills, was published in 1956 (The Noonday Press). M. M. Coleman's ADAM MICKIEWICZ IN ENGLISH (1954) is the best bibliographic guide to English translations of the works of the poet.

Żywila. Translated as *Zevila*.

Résumé. (An old Lithuanian legend.)

About the year 1400, powerful Prince Koryat reigned over the land of Novogródek. He had a beautiful daughter, Zevila, who secretly loved Knight Poray. She shook her head when princes and great barons from distant lands sent their ambassadors requesting her hand.

It happened that when Prince Koryat returned from the wars, he was grieved to see a change in his beloved daughter. Her cheeks were ashen, her voice trembled. He ordered her from his eyes and threatened that the man who had brought her to dishonor would die a hard death together with her. But Zevila refused to disclose the identity of her lover, and no one throughout the city would name him. The angry prince commanded that his only daughter be put in chains and cast into a dungeon to await her death.

While Zevila was in prison a Russian kniaź,[10] Ivan, very swiftly

---

[10] Title comparable to prince or duke.

attacked the city on the day before the Great Feast, the morning of which Princess Zevila was to die.

Prince Koryat prayed Poray to ride forth with a company of knights and engage the foe in battle while the prince strengthened the walls of his city. Prince Poray dealt the kniaź such a mighty blow that the assailants ran back to their Cossack camp.

When Poray returned to the city, the people made merry, and Koryat called him the defender of the city and bade him to the castle for a mighty feast. But when Poray asked him to save his daughter from death, the Prince angrily refused.

In despair Poray returned to kniaź Ivan, and offered to deliver the city to him in exchange for the promise that he would not harm the folk with fire or sword, and would grant him the imprisoned princess as wife.

When Poray returned with the Russians and broke open the prison, and his beloved saw him, she fell in a swoon. For a long time she did not open her eyes. Suddenly Zevila drew Poray's sword and smote him in the breast with such might that the blade sank deep. "Traitor!" she cried. So saying Zevila struck out with the sword at the foemen. Now all the people fell upon the unsuspecting Russians, and again they freed the city.

Zevila hastened to the place where Prince Koryat stood fettered to the barricade. "My father," she cried, and fell dead at his feet.

She was buried at the foot of the mountain Mendoga.

Written in 1819.

Zevila. Translated by Lola Gay-Tifft. In THE BLUE FLOWER. Edited by Hermann Kesten, illustrated by Z. Czermanski. New York, Roy Publishers [c1946]. p.488–492.

Zevila; a Short Story. Translated by Lola Gay-Tifft. In *The Polish Review,* bi-weekly magazine. (New York), VII, No. 1, 1947. p.8–9.

Reprinted from THE BLUE FLOWER.

Preceded by a brief note about the Polish translations in THE BLUE FLOWER anthology. Concluded with an excerpt from Hermann Kesten's Introduction to this anthology.

Zevila. [Translated by Lola Gay-Tifft.] In TREASURY OF WORLD

LITERATURE, edited by Dagobert D. Runes. New York, Philosophical Library [c1956]. p.892–896.
Preceded by a brief note about the author.

Morcinek, Gustaw (1891–   )

Cisza. Translated as *Silence.*

Silence. Translated by Monica M. Gardner. In *The Slavonic (and East European) Review,* XII, 1933–34. p.273–281.

Wiara. Translated as *Faith.*

Faith. Translated by Monica M. Gardner. In *The Slavonic (and East European) Review,* XIII, 1934–35. p.506–521.

Morska, Irena (1895–ca.1958)

Born in Warsaw, Irena Morska graduated from the University of Geneva. She also studied in Paris and at San Francisco State College. Morska was interested in the workers' theaters. She wrote and translated some short stories, poems, and one-act plays. Very little of her work has been published.

Kajdany (?) Translated as *The Chains.*

Résumé. (The story is told in the first person.) The narrator left the well-to-do home of her parents still as a young girl to live an independent life, and "to join efforts with the courageous dreamers of our country."

One snowy night in December she was visited by a small outfit of soldiers, guards and detectives who came accompanied by the janitor. Her room was searched; she was taken to the railway station and put into jail in another town. The prison was overcrowded with men and women, criminals as well as political prisoners. Most of them wore heavy chains. At times groups of prisoners ready for transport crowded outside her cell. They were to be sent to Eastern parts of Russia or cold Siberia—from jail to jail.

Once such a chain-clinking group became aggressive, and the narrator saved herself by singing the Polish Marseillaise, "Warszawianka." She was then eighteen.

After about a year in prison, she was suddenly released without any explanation. Drunk with the joy of freedom, she returned to the home of her parents musing about those left behind the prison gates.

The story might have been written originally in English.

The Chains (a Reminiscence). In POLISH AUTHORS OF TODAY AND YESTERDAY . . . Selected by Irena Morska. New York, S. F. Vanni [c1947]. p.44–51.

Mrożek, Sławomir (1930–   )

Chcę być koniem. Translated as *I Want To Be a Horse.*

I Want To Be a Horse. Translation anonymous. In *Poland; Illustrated Magazine,* No. 2 (42) 1958. p.27.

I Want To Be a Horse. (Written in the Darkness VIII.) Translated by Norbert Guterman. Illustrated by Daniel Mróz. In *Portfolio; Including Art News Annual,* No. 1, 1959. p.68–69.

From his collection SŁOŃ (THE ELEPHANT), 1957.[11]

Cichy współpracownik. Translated as *Quiet Collaborator.*

Quiet Collaborator. Translation anonymous. [Illustrated by Daniel Mróz.] In *East Europe; a Monthly Review of East European Affairs,* VIII, No. 1, 1959. p.26–27.

From his collection SŁOŃ (THE ELEPHANT), 1957.

At head of title: Three Polish Fables, by Sławomir Mrożek.

Preceded by a brief note about the author and his work.

Dzieci. Translated as *The Children.*

The Children. (Written in the Darkness I.) Translated by Louise

---

[11] *Written in the Darkness* in *Portfolio* (p.[56]–71) contains nine stories. A complete collection of stories in SŁOŃ was published in the English translation of Konrad Syrop as THE ELEPHANT (New York: Grove Press, [1963, c1962]).

Varèse. Illustrated by Daniel Mróz. In *Portfolio; Including Art News Annual,* No. 1, 1959. p.59–60.
From his collection słoń.
Preceded by a brief note about the author and the illustrator [p.56].

Fakt. Translated as *Fact.*

Fact. (Written in the Darkness IV.) Translated by Louise Varèse. In *Portfolio; Including Art News Annual,* No. 1, 1959. p.63–64.
From his collection słoń.

Imieniny. Translated as *Birthday Party.*

Birthday Party. (Written in the Darkness VII.) Translated by Louise Varèse. In *Portfolio; Including Art News Annual,* No. 1, 1959. p.67–68.
From his collection słoń.

Lew. Translated as *The Lion.*

The Lion. (Written in the Darkness VI.) Translated by Louise Varèse. Illustrated by Daniel Mróz. In *Portfolio; Including Art News Annual,* No. 1, 1959. p.66–67.
From his collection słoń.

The Lion. Translated by Christopher J. Klinger. [Illustrated by Daniel Mróz.] In *Polish Perspectives;* Monthly Review, [II], No. 3 (11), 1959. p.38–39.

The Lion. Translation anonymous. [Illustrated by Daniel Mróz.] In *East Europe;* a Monthly Review of East European Affairs, VIII, No. 1, 1959. p.27.

Losy hrabiego N. Translated as *The Fortunes of Count N.*

The Fortunes of Count N. Translation anonymous. Illustrated by Daniel Mróz. In *Poland; Illustrated Magazine,* No. 8 (72) 1960. (Am. ed.) p.25–26.
Preceded by a brief note about the author, by Tadeusz Drewnowski.

Peer Gynt. Translated as *Peer Gynt.*

Peer Gynt. Translation anonymous. In *Poland; Illustrated Magazine,* No. 2 (42) 1958. p.26–27.

Peer Gynt. (Written in the Darkness IX.) Translated by Louise Varèse. In *Portfolio; Including Art News Annual,* No. 1, 1959. p.69–71.

From his collection słoń.

Proces. Translated as *The Trial/Trial.*

The Trial. (Written in the Darkness III.) Translated by Louise Varèse. Illustrated by Daniel Mróz. In *Portfolio; Including Art News Annual,* No. 1, 1959. p.61–63.

From his collection słoń.

Trial. Translation anonymous. [Illustrated by Daniel Mróz.] In *East Europe; a Monthly Review of East European Affairs,* VIII, No. 1, 1959. p.28–29.

Przejażdżka. Translated as *The Ride.*

The Ride. Translation anonymous. Illustrated by Daniel Mróz. In *Poland; Illustrated Magazine,* No. 8 (72) 1960. (Am. ed.) p.26–27.

Przypowieść o cudownym ocaleniu. Translated as *The Man Saved by a Miracle/The Parable of the Miraculous Salvation.*

A Man Saved by a Miracle. (Written in the Darkness II.) Translated by Louise Varèse. Illustrated by Daniel Mróz. In *Portfolio; Including Art News Annual,* No. 1, 1959. p.60–61.

From his collection słoń.

The Parable of the Miraculous Salvation. Translated by Cecylia Wojewoda and Neil Morris. In *Polish Perspectives; Monthly Review,* [II], No. 3 (11), 1959. p.36–37.

At head of title: Two stories from the collection słoń (THE ELEPHANT).

Słoń. Translated as *The Elephant.*

The Elephant. Translation anonymous. In *Poland; Illustrated Magazine,* No. 2 (42) 1958. p.26.

Wesele w Atomicach. Translated as *A Wedding in Atomville.*

A Wedding in Atomville. Translation anonymous. Illustrated by Daniel Mróz. In *Poland; Illustrated Magazine,* No. 8 (72) 1960. p.27.

Z ciemności. Translated as *Written in the Darkness.*

Written in the Darkness. (Title story of *Written in the Darkness V.*) Translated by Louise Varèse. Illustrated by Daniel Mróz. In *Portfolio; Including Art News Annual,* No. 1, 1959. p.64–66. From his collection SŁOŃ.

Muszal, Kazimiera, *see* Muszałówna, Kazimiera

Muszałówna, Kazimiera (1902–   )

Muszałówna was a member of the literary group of the thirties, "Przedmieście" (Suburbia). She contributes articles and short stories to such periodicals as *Kobieta współczesna* (The Contemporary Woman). *Bluszcz* (The Ivy), *Epoka* (The Epoch) and *Start.* The author's publications include POD OLIMPIJSKIM SZTANDAREM (Under the Olympic Banner) and ZIMOWI OLIMPIJCZYCY (The Winter Olympians).

Klimontów. Translated as *The Pit.*

Résumé. The miners descended in the elevator cage into the shaft a thousand feet underground to protest against the company's order to flood the mine.

On the third day the bell signals sounded an emergency. Crowds gathered by the fence and watched as the stiffened body of an unconscious rebel was brought up. Women wept. More alarms, and more unconscious bodies were carried to the first-aid station. The police tried in vain to follow the order, "Disperse the crowd."

The miners refused any contact with the living. The telephone was silent. The priest refused to take the money to say a Mass for those locked in the pit. At the altar his face was wet with tears. The miners stopped the hunger strike, but remained in the pit.

When at last the day of the victory came for the miners, their wives had no more tears left for their joy.

From PRZEDMIEŚCIE (*Suburbia*), *1934*.

The Pit, by Kazimiera Muszal. Translated by Irena Morska. In POLISH AUTHORS OF TODAY AND YESTERDAY . . . Selected by Irena Morska. New York, S. F. Vanni [c1947]. p.52–56.

Naglerowa, Herminia (1892–1957)

This novelist and short story writer studied history at the University of Lwów, where she received her Ph.D. Her first collection of short stories won the Zapolska prize in Lwów. The next two volumes of short stories and her first novel ZAWALIDROGA (1930) were published in Warsaw. Naglerowa is the author of a three-volume novel KRAUZOWIE I INNI (The Krauzes, 1946), the first volume of which appeared in English under the title LOVES AND AMBITIONS (1954). Arrested by the N.K.W.D. at the beginning of World War Two, the author spent some time in Soviet prisons and forced labor camps. By way of the Middle East Naglerowa reached Italy, where she edited a journal for the Polish service women and published a collection of short stories, LUDZIE SPONIEWIERANI (The Mistreated People, 1945). After the war she settled in England. Her last unfinished work, ZA ZAMKNIĘTYMI DRZWIAMI (Behind the Closed Door) had been conceived as a cycle of novels, of which SPRAWA JÓZEFA MOSTA (The Case of Józef Most, 1953) is a part.

Chleb. Translated as *Bread.*

Résumé. Janek's mother went out in the dawn with his older brother Jędrek to work in the steppe. The boy remained alone in the mud-cottage which later in the day crumbled in the blazing heat of the sun. The light made its way through the cracks, and the movement of the light was Janek's sun-dial.

Janek was ill with malaria. He was hungry. He was not accustomed to hunger yet; he complained, he even cried. The hunger had already begun in the railway car on the long journey from Poland to this distant Kazakstan.

On September 22, 1939, the Red Army entered Lwów. On January 10, 1940, his father left home to join the Polish Army in France. They were deported to Russia April 13, and arrived in Kazakstan on May 10. Now it was June, and his birthday would be the day after tomorrow.

Without opening his eyes Janek reached for the bread and water. He consumed the whole portion of the bread and drank the whole cup of water. Mother would admonish him because he did not divide the bread and leave a little for later. He was still hungry, although it was just after breakfast. In the evening mother would prepare "kasza" or barley-soup.

Janek began to think of how much he would like to eat. If every one of them had a whole loaf of bread every day, perhaps they would not be hungry then.

For the whole next day Janek repelled the dream of bread, as though it were an obnoxious bee. He became delirious. When his mother and brother came back, he recovered for a short while. He was holding a whole loaf of bread. "I am going to give it to you," his mother said, "on the eve of your birthday." He asked for a knife. His voice was so weak that his mother had to kneel before him to hear. The knife fell from his hand. He could only whisper, "Divide the bread for you . . . for Jędrek . . . and for . . ." He had no breath to say the word "me" any more.

Darkness and silence embraced him.

Bread, by Herminya Nagler. Translation anonymous. In THE POLISH SHORT STORIES. Edited by Umadevi. [Bombay] Indo-Polish Library. No. 35 [c1946]. p.151-160.

Dunia. Translated as *Dunia.*

Résumé. Helena, Wanda, Janka, and the narrator were pushed into the prison cell at Pietropavlovsk. Helena cried out and drew back, but the Russian warder silently barred her way. It was late at night and the women already occupying the cell were asleep. At the very door their feet were entangled in a layer of human bodies.

Two feet dropped down from the first tier of the bunks: huge calloused soles beneath grey calves like tree trunks. The voice sounded like a gorilla's roar, "The newcomers can stand by the bucket; they're to go there!"

Early in the morning a yawn that rose to a howl announced that the invisible monster was awakening. A whisper passed through the cell, "Dunia's up!" She was now threatening to "smash [the newcomers'] brain-pans" and "suck the blood from their throats." A hundred and thirty women grew still; even the Tartar devotees ceased moving their lips in prayer.

A Russian prisoner, Masha, told the narrator Dunia's story. She had grazed cattle on the steppe, and had meditated on various things. Then she talked about those things aloud. Before long people began to flock around her. She could not read or write, but her speech had a fascinating charm. People believed in Dunia. Someone informed against her. They killed her small husband before her eyes. Her own sentence was twenty-five years in prison. She was then twenty-two, and had a child. It was possible that her child was still alive.

Once, after a scene with Helena, who, to everybody's surprise dared stop Dunia from what she had thought was singing, the monster moved to the door, and beating with her fists until they bled on the sheet-iron, she gabbled, "Take me to the governor!" She wanted to know what had happened to her child.

When Dunia was thrown back into the cell, her body was swollen and violet-hued. Her pulped lips mumbled broken phrases about her child. "They have killed him . . . in a children's home . . ."

Helena went over to her and with her beautiful hands stroked Dunia's swollen cheeks. Dunia took Helena's hand and raised it to her lips.

From her LUDZIE SPONIEWIERANI (*The Mistreated People*).

Dunia, by Herminia Naglerova. Translated by H. C. Stevens. In THE PEN IN EXILE; a Second Anthology. Edited by Paul Tabori. [London] The International P.E.N. Club Centre for Writers in Exile, 1956. p.204–210.

Nałkowska, Zofia (1885–1954)

Nałkowska established her name as a distinguished novelist during the years between the two world wars. A subtle knowledge of feminine psychology characterizes her novels ROMANS TERESY HENNERT (Teresa Hennert's Love Affair, 1923), *Dom nad łąkami* (A House on the Meadow, 1925), and a play, DOM KOBIET (House of Women, 1930). She belonged to the so-called "Przedmieście" (Suburbia), a literary group organized in the thirties. Her best-known prewar novel, GRANICA (The Border, 1935), gave expression to her stand on social matters. After the war Nałkowska was appointed a member of the Commission investigating Nazi crimes in Poland. The volume MEDALIONY (The Medallions, 1946), is a result of this appointment.

Dno. Translated as *Nadir.*

Résumé. (This is one of the stories which grew out of the author's experiences while she was participating in the work of the committee that reviewed Nazi crimes in Poland. The author presents it as it was told by an elderly woman.)

She was grey-haired, rather good-looking, plump and soft. She looked very tired. All she wanted was friendliness; she wanted people to be kind to her. Her son had not returned from the POW camp. She had no news of her daughter. Nor did she know anything about her husband. She was completely alone. She really did not know what should she tell first.

Yes, the women were tortured in Ravensbrück. They were given injections, they were experimented on, their wounds were opened up. . . . But it did not last long. After three weeks she and her daughter were taken from Ravensbrück to a munitions factory.

Her daughter? She was good, she was pretty and talented. And she belonged to the Organization;[12] so did her son. Before the camp they had been for two months at Pawiak.[13] She could not describe all the atrocities there. The prisoners themselves had to

---

[12] The Underground Organization of the Home Army.
[13] A prison on Pawia Street in Warsaw.

carry the corpses of the tortured-to-death fellow-prisoners out of the storerooms in the morning. Yes, she was flogged terribly, but she did not say anything.

In that munitions camp they worked at the machines twelve hours every day. They would be wakened at three in the morning. Morning and evening they were given black unsweetened coffee; ten decagrammes of bread had to last the whole day. They were served a soup "made of leaves or something" in the factory. For the slightest offense they were ordered to the bunker. During the night those in the bunker ate meat from the corpses.

She still had "something interesting" to say. From the Pawiak to Ravensbrück they were transported in cattle wagons, packed in, a hundred to a car. They travelled standing, one close to the other, for several days. They slept standing; everything had to be done standing, down the legs. They started howling like animals. When the car was unsealed and a German officer looked inside, he became frightened. Several women went mad. They were shot the same day. "Even a German was frightened when he saw us," she finished her story. "No wonder the women couldn't stand it."

From her MEDALIONY (*Medallions*), *1946*.

Nadir. Translated by Jadwiga Zwolska. In CONTEMPORARY POLISH SHORT STORIES, selected by Andrzej Kijowski. Warsaw, Polonia Publishing House, 1960. p.[181]–188.

Dwojra Zielona. Translated as *Dwojra Zielona.*

Dwojra Zielona, by Zofia Nalkowska. Translation anonymous. In *Poland of Today,* II, No. 12, 1947. p.8–9, 16.

From her MEDALIONY (Medallions).

Macierzyństwo. Translated as *Motherhood.*

Motherhood. Translated by Geoffrey Potocki of Montalk. In *Pologne littéraire,* No. 94–95, 1934. p.4.

"*P.P.C.*" Translated as "*P.P.C.*"[14]

---

14 "P.P.C." is a French abbreviation for "pour prendre congé," i.e., "to bid farewell."

Résumé. ("An incident during the early part of the World War [One], when the Russians, retreating before the victorius Austro-German armies, destroyed everything." Told in the first person.)

At the time when the bridges over the Vistula still existed, the narrator drove to the opposite side of the river into the country to her abandoned home. She thought she might still bring to town the rest of the articles she had left behind. Upon arrival, old Martin told her that her house had been robbed. Strewn about on the upper floor were articles of all kinds, dragged from chests of drawers; in the attic scores of books had been dumped and scattered about from their boxes and parcels, and maps and single sheets were everywhere.

Near the house four soldiers were playing cards. She went to them to be assured that no one would come into the house again. One of the soldiers insisted that they had nothing to do with the books; they did not even understand the language. She went to see the officers. They, too, had nothing to do with it. However, in spite of the lateness of the hour, some officers accompanied her to examine the damage. They discovered "a veritable pogrom," and appointed a sentry who went on guard at midnight.

The following day she began packing the books. One soldier showed great interest and volunteered to help packing. He said he loved books, and appeared to be a thoughtful and a sensitive man. He belonged to the detachment of machine gunners.

Early next day Martin informed her that in the night all the soldiers had gone away. The soldier who had helped her pack had tried to see her very early. Failing to do so, he left his visiting card with a bent edge. At the bottom was written, in pencil and in Roman letters, 'p.p.c.'. A strange souvenir after a plunder!

"*P.P.C.*" (A Lady's Narrative), by Mme. Rygier-Nałkowska. Translated by Joseph Solomon. In SELECTED POLISH TALES. Translated by Else C. M. Benecke and Marie Busch. London, New York [etc.] H. Milford, Oxford University Press [1921]. p.339-348.

Translators' note: "This sketch has been translated by Mr. Joseph Solomon, whose knowledge of Slavonic languages makes him a most valuable co-operator." (Preface, p. x.)

Profesor Spanner. Translated as *Professor Spanner.*

Professor Spanner. Translated by Jadwiga Zwolska. In *Poland; Illustrated Magazine,* No. 4 (68) 1960. (Am. ed.) p.13–15.

Narbutt, Ignacy

Łabędzie gniazdo. Translated as *The Swan's Nest.*

The Swan's Nest. Translation anonymous. In *Poland; Illustrated Magazine,* No. 2 (30) 1957. p.26–27.

Niedźwiecki, Zygmunt (1865–1918)

This is the only Polish writer who turned almost entirely to the production of short stories. He wrote only one novel, MALOWANY ŚWIAT (The Painted World), which was never published. He is also an author of a few dramatic works. The number of short stories left by Niedźwiecki is about two hundred and fifty. He is sometimes referred to as the Polish Maupassant. Niedźwiecki was a successful translator too, and rendered into Polish stories of Poe, Zola, Daudet and Maupassant. His collections of short stories appeared in the following volumes: SŁOŃCE (The Sun, 1892), JEDYNE DZIEŁO (The Only Masterpiece, 1893), U OGNISKA (At the Campfire, 1894), LIŚĆ FIGOWY (The Fig Leaf, 1900) and EROTYKI (The Erotica, 1904).

Kura. Translated as *The Chicken.*

Résumé. An old woman, deserted and lonely, makes a chance purchase of a lean live chicken that nobody wanted. The chicken becomes a poetic experience in her life when a strange friendship develops between the two, much to the irritation (motivated by jealousy) of the janitress, who keeps a dozen hens of her own in the spacious courtyard of the house. In view of such a hostile environment the very life of the chicken is in constant danger.

One morning the chicken is found shaking with spasms of fever, its eyes blurred. The vegetable peddler whom the old woman serves and whose meagre apartment she shares, decides to kill the bird before it dies. It now becomes the painful duty of the old woman to roast her friend.

In the evening they sit down to the hearty meal. The chicken's fragrance is overpowering. Alarmed by her appetite, the peddlar warns the woman (and this is the closing sentence of the story), "Don't eat so fast, for Heaven's sake, or you'll choke to death."

The Chicken. Translated by Olga Scherer-Virski. In her THE MODERN POLISH SHORT STORY. 's-Gravenhage, Mouton, 1955. (Slavistic printings and reprintings, 5). p.160–162.

Za mąż. Translated as *The Dowry.*

Résumé. A young woman greeted one of her lovers with the unexpected, "Nothing doing, today. I'm going out." At first he took it for a joke, but he soon found out that she meant it. Astonished, he learned that Fela was going out with her fiancé "to attend to some business." He never knew that she had a fiancé. She was to marry him in a year. Why so late? Because her dowry was not yet ready. How was she to get it? Well, she would continue her present mode of living for another year until she had collected enough money. Then she would start another life and be an "honest woman."

Casually Fela announced that her fiancé would be here in a few minutes. Though the visitor wanted to take his hat and leave, she stopped him. To his surprise, she wanted to introduce him to her fiancé. And anyway, he could not go since he could not find his hat.

The fiancé arrived and proved to be a waiter who had waited on Fela's friend quite often. He was very polite. When the missing hat was finally found on the window-sill behind the shade which the visitor himself had pulled down, the fiancé only remarked that such things happened quite often with hats, not at all angry or upset. Bidding good-bye, the waiter bowed low and said, "Always at your service, Sir."

(The story is told in the first person by the visitor.)

From his collection SŁOŃCE (*The Sun*), *1892.*

The Dowry. Translated by Ilona Ralf Sues. In POLISH SHORT

STORIES, selected by Zbigniew Żabicki. Warsaw, Polonia Publishing House, 1960. p.215–[220].

Niemojewski, Andrzej (1864–1921)

For Niemojewski two ideas reigned supreme, social justice and independence of thought. He wrote poetry, drama, novels, short stories, works of literary criticism and, between 1906 and and 1921 while he was the editor of *Myśl Niepodległa* (Independent Thought), he filled with his own articles a great deal of space in 578 issues of the periodical. His broad humanitarianism made him cross boundaries not only between social classes and speak on behalf of factory workers, but also between religions. His short story, *Boruch* (1907), in which his sympathy went to a young Warsaw Jew "who died for freedom," was translated into Hebrew a year after its first appearance in print. His works include a collection of poetry POLONIA IRREDENTA (1895–96), a play FAMILIA (Family, 1901), a novel LISTY CZŁOWIEKA SZALONEGO (Letters of a Madman, 1899) and a literary study DAWNOŚĆ I MICKIEWICZ (Old Times and Mickiewicz, 1921).

Dziennikarz. Translated as *The Journalist*.

Résumé. For many years Mr. Casimir had edited the street rag, *Dawn*, featuring the Warsaw gossip. From time to time he would dabble in politics by publishing news embarrassing the Russian authorities.[15] On one occasion he exposed scandalous cheating in a bureau of the State Lottery which happened to be sponsored by Maria Andrejewna, wife of no less a personage than the Governor himself, General Hurko. Arrested by the captain in charge of the investigation, Mr. Casimir was set free when his accusation proved to be true. He then turned his attention to the Franco-Prussian war, and in his reports France was always victorious. As he himself put it, Mr. Casimir "stood at his journalistic post." During the Russo-Japanese crisis, all of his laudatory remarks about Japan were faithfully based on Russian sources from pre-war days.

---

15 The action takes place before World War I, when Warsaw was occupied by Russia.

When the "ukase" of toleration reached Warsaw from Moscow, the *Dawn* had become a first-rate, excellently edited, popular newspaper. Mr. Casimir had brought talented journalists from Galicia who filled the pages of his paper with brilliant articles scourging the Russian administration and its bureaucracy. The Russians finally suspended publication of *Dawn,* but Mr. Casimir managed to reach the public with a paper under a different name. When the Russians stopped this one too, he continued using the same tactics of simply changing the paper's name. At last arrested and imprisoned by the Russians, he outwitted them even then by getting out his *Gazette for Hermits* from behind the prison walls. His printing office was placed under arrest. As he heard the Socialists singing the "Red Flag" in the corridor, Mr. Casimir declared that he was at the end of his rope, and that only with the Socialists in power could he return to his post.

The Journalist, by A. Niemojewski. Translated from the Polish by K. Malecka. In SAVED FROM SIBERIA; the True Story of My Treatment at the Hands of the Russian Police, by Katie Malecka. London, Everett and company [1914], p.133–143. (Appendix I.)

Translator's note: "This story was produced in Court as evidence against me."

Norwid, Cyprian Kamil (1821–1883)

This great lyric poet, whose name is now often pronounced in the same breath with the great trio of the Polish romantic poetry, Mickiewicz, Słowacki, Krasiński, was almost unknown to his own generation. After going into exile, Norwid led a life of poverty, struggle and self-denial. He was rediscovered by the writers of the so-called Young Poland. Zenon Przesmycki, known under the pseudonym Miriam, takes credit for bringing the poet into the limelight. Norwid visited the United States. His works include a collection of lyrical poetry, VADEMECUM (1865–66), a treatise on poetry, PROMETHIDION (1851), and a drama KLEOPATRA (Cleopatra).

"*Ad leones.*" Translated as "*Ad leones.*"

Résumé. (This is a satire on café-type artists told by the author with tongue in cheek. Some of the subtle irony with which Norwid treats his characters is untranslatable.)

The principal among his heroes is a red-bearded sculptor, famous at the Café Greco in Rome as the creator of "Ad leones." His main qualification as an artist seems to be the ownership of a fine Kirghisian greyhound bitch. There is an editor of a political and literary gazette, the very existence of which we begin to suspect; a handsome singer who gives lessons to foreigners; a young tourist sent by his parents "to form his opinion on things," followed unsuccessfully by his tutor during the day until their inevitable reunion at the Café Greco in the evening; and finally a gifted painter who is not quite sure whether his own latest painting represents Cleopatra or . . . the Assumption.

The whole artistic group (including the narrator; the story is told in the first person) had been invited to view the sculpture, "Ad leones." The lions proved to have existed only in the imagination of the sculptor; temporarily the only lion in the unfinished group had the form of a lump of clay. There were two figures, one male, promising a beautiful torso, and the other that of a girl. They were to represent Christians thrown to the lions at the time of Domitian.

An American correspondent of a big United States newspaper became interested in the now famous sculpture. But to him the group clearly represented "Capitalization." The woman symbolized thrift, the man—energy (the crosses had been removed just in time by the sculptor), the would-be-lion looked to him very much like a coffer. For a considerable sum of money he ordered the sculpture to be executed in white marble.

Written in 1881.

"*Ad leones.*" Translated from the Polish of C. K. Norwid by N. B. Jopson. In *The Slavonic (and East European) Review*, XI, 1932–33. p.163–172.

"*Ad leones.*" Translated by Ilona Ralf Sues. In POLISH SHORT

STORIES, selected by Zbigniew Żabicki. Warsaw, Polonia Publishing House, 1960. p.15–[29].

Tajemnica Lorda Singlewortha. Translated and abridged as *Lord Singleworth's Secret.*

Résumé. Lord Singleworth became known in many European cities as an eccentric person who undertook, for some mysterious reason, aerial trips in a balloon. These affairs became intriguing and there were many conjectures as to the real purpose of the trips, two principal ones being that the eccentric lord was in pursuit of meteorological scientific data, or that he needed exercise for the sake of his health. Finally a bet was made in Venice and an appointment was sought with Lord Singleworth himself.

The author accompanied by three prominent citizens of Venice went to Lord Singleworth's apartment in the White Lion Hotel in the hope of solving the mystery. Neither of the opposing parties was satisfied with the reply, as the real reason for the trips as given by Lord Singleworth appeared to be no less mysterious than the trips themselves: it was his concept of cleanliness.

To avoid uncleanliness which became synonymous with descent, cleanliness meant for him rising high. "I rise up high," declared Lord Singleworth, "in order to be loyal to my concept of cleanliness and to confirm the truth of my seemingly empty words with a stamp of fulfillment."

Lord Singleworth's Secret. Translated by Olga Scherer-Virski. In her THE MODERN POLISH SHORT STORY. 's-Gravenhage, Mouton, 1955. (Slavistic printings and reprintings, 5) p.54–62.

In this translation two pages which "digress in order to satirize the decadence and impoverishment of the old Venetian aristocracy," plus one other page are omitted, thus making a total of three untranslated pages.

Nowakowski, Tadeusz (1917–   )

Syn zadżumionych. Translated as *Born of the Plague.*

Born of the Plague. Translation anonymous. In *Poland; Illustrated Magazine,* No. 9 (61) 1959. p.13–18, 27–32.

"Excerpts from a short story published in the monthly magazine, *Kultura,* No. 1, 1959, Paris."

Olechowski, Gustaw (1874–   )

The author studied commerce in Antwerp, law in the Hague, and he also graduated from the University in Montreal. Between 1905 and 1906 he was the editor of the Polish patriotic periodical, *Naród a państwo* (The Nation and the State). His works include RZECZY WIDZIANE (The Things Seen, 1911), DZIEJE MĘŻCZYZNY (The Story of a Man, 1912), RYCERZ (The Knight, 1914), and U WRÓT BARBARII (At the Gate of Barbarism, 1921). Olechowski also published a treatise in English, POLAND AND PRUSSIA (Copenhagen, 1915), and is the author of a novel about Józef Piłsudski, WÓDZ; POWIEŚĆ O JÓZEFIE PIŁSUDSKIM (1929).

Potęga złota (?) Translated as *The Might of Gold.*

Résumé. The old woman was breathing her last. Her confession to a young priest was continually interrupted by spasmodic gasps and sobs.

She drove her daughter-in-law into the grave to deprive her of her inheritance . . . She cheated the Church . . . She threw her serving maid, an orphan, into the street on the eve of her giving birth. The maid died in the street together with the unborn child . . . She hated her son and poisoned his only child . . . She rented out a whole floor in her palace to a brothel. She made money on usury . . . She denounced to the authorities a writer who had lived in her attic and could not pay his rent. He was arrested and hanged . . .

The woman was dead. The last will of the deceased stated that her immense wealth was left to the church. An old priest made the funeral oration at the grave. He addressed the crowd: "Mourning friends! Your noblest mother, grandmother, relative and devoted friend was taken from you, etc., etc."

When he finished the warm September sun suddenly hid behind a dark cloud.

The Might of Gold. Translated by Irena Morska. In POLISH AUTHORS OF TODAY AND YESTERDAY . . . Selected by Irena Morska, New York, S. F. Vanni [c1947]. p.57–60.

Orwid-Bulicz, Roman

> The author is a graduate of the University of Cracow in philosophy and of the University of Poznań in law. He began writing in exile after World War Two. EUROPA NIE ODPOWIADA (Europe Does Not Answer, 1950) is, perhaps, the best known of his several novels. His play, ŚWIADEK (The Witness, 1953) is based on the materials collected by the author in his ZBRODNIA KATYŃSKA W ŚWIETLE DOKU-MENTÓW (The Katyń Crime in the Light of Documents).

Kanały (?) Translated as *The Sewers.*

Résumé. Dr. Rozenzweig was told at the Jewish Committee meeting that he would be taken through the sewers.[16] Before he even reached the bottom of the sewer, the doctor started to shiver with cold and strain. The air striking him from below was fetid and damp. His face burned, his eyes smarted. His guide, young Zagajski, urged him to keep close. The doctor hugged tight an important parcel; he was afraid of dropping it into the slime.

They were going through the sticky fluid of human excrement and slime. The doctor was almost blinded by the mephitic vapors. He called to the guide that he could not go on. The young boy gave him his hand and urged him to be brave. Dr. Rozenzweig

---

[16] Sewers were used as underground thoroughfares during the tragedy of the Jewish ghetto in Warsaw in 1943, and during the Warsaw Uprising in 1944.

nerved himself to move. The glutinous mess reached above his knees. To return was now unthinkable.

Zagajski put off the torch; they had to move in the dark. A violent tremor; a building above came tumbling down. Passing through a recess, they were in the stinking stream up to their necks. The liquid lapped over the collar of the doctor's coat and trickled down his body. Zagajski was now taking care of the parcel. A rat slipped past them. Rozenzweig felt dizzy. Every now and again he knelt down to rest on his hands and knees. His beard dipped in the excrement. Tears streamed down his face.

A series of loud explosions shook the ground. Zagajski murmured that the Germans, lying in ambush, were throwing hand-grenades into the sewer. Whole packs of rats, frightened by the explosion, slithered between their legs. Rozenzweig, who had "nothing in common" with any religion, began to whisper, "God of Abraham! God of Isaac! God of Jacob! . . ."

The Sewers, by Roman Orwid-Bulicz. Translated by Stefan Cedric Potocki. In THE PEN IN EXILS; AN ANTHOLOGY. Edited by Paul Tabori. [London] The International P.E.N. Club Centre for Writers in Exile, 1954. p.109–115.

Orzeszko, Eliza, *see* Orzeszkowa, Eliza

Orzeszkowa, Eliza (1841–1910)

An outstanding realist writer, Orzeszkowa née Pawłowska, was at the beginning of her career close to the Polish Positivism. For her, as for Prus, art was a means subordinated to the cause. She fought for equal rights for women, social justice for all, including the ghetto Jews, she bitterly criticized all forms of social backwardness, and was an untiring champion of education. As a Positivist, she stressed the importance of trade and commerce, though her novels abound in poetic and most "romantic" descriptions of nature. Orzeszkowa lived most of her life in Grodno. Some of her novels, e.g. DZIURDZIOWIE (The Dziurdzios, 1885) and

NIZINY (Lowlands, 1883) are excellent social and psychological studies of a Byelo-Russian village. The most prominent among her novels are MEIR EZOFOWICZ (1878), BENE NATI (1891), and NAD NIEMNEM (On the Niemen, 1887). GLORIA VICTIS (1910) is a well-known collection of her short stories.

A . . . B . . . C . . . Translated as *A . . . B . . . C . . .*

Résumé. Every day Joan Lipska had been passing the building of the Court of Justice without paying the slightest attention to it. She looked for a job. She wanted to do something useful.

One evening she happily told her brother, Michael, that a Mrs. Roshnovska had asked her to teach her two grandchildren. Mrs. Roshnovska also promised to recommend her to her friends. In her happiness Joan kept repeating, "This is only the beginning, but later, later . . ."

Soon the kitchen was filled with the children's happy chattering. In the thin-walled room of the attic small voices were heard repeating: a . . . b . . . c . . . Until there came one day when Joan entered the Court of Justice and sat on the bench of the accused. She was charged with "the crime of running a school without permission of the authorities."[17] The sentence was two hundred marks fine or three months in jail.

Michael borrowed the impossible sum from the town usurer to pay the fine. The children returned to the kitchen, but they ran away when they heard Michael's angry voice in the adjoining room. Little Mańka stayed on. The baby choked her silvery voice, and kept reading in a whisper, "a . . . b . . . c . . . a . . . b . . . c . . ."

A . . . B . . . C . . . , by Eliza Orzeszko. Translated by Irena Morska. In POLISH AUTHORS OF TODAY AND YESTERDAY . . . Selected by Irena Morska. New York, S. F. Vanni [c1947]. p.61–77.

Czy pamiętasz? Translated as *Do You Remember?*

Résumé. He was just under fifty, a highly esteemed man who had once regarded himself as fortunate. He had preserved his dark thick hair, his smooth skin and easy polished movements. He had

---

17 This was before World War One, when Poland was divided between Russia, Austria and Prussia.

attained a high position and had everything that he desired. The success was due to him alone. His parents were poor.

For the past two years he was less satisfied and gay; something was lacking. Wrinkles appeared on his formerly smooth brow. Neither his friends nor he himself knew what was the matter.

One night during the Christmas season, he returned home from the theatre disgusted with himself and his friends. He ordered his man servant to brew some tea, flung himself on a couch and sighed. Beside his valet, there was not a living soul in the house; he was unmarried. He stepped up to his writing desk and picked up in his soft white hand an unopened letter. A new light suddenly came into his eyes, and he smiled. The letter was from his sister, Anulka. She lived in obscurity in their little native village. For twenty years they had not seen each other. She seldom wrote to him, and he replied very briefly or not at all. She inherited the little village estate from their parents.

"Do you remember," she was asking in her letter, "the first time our parents took us out to the hunter's lodge in the depths of the forest?" The same pine trees and the tall ferns were still there. "And do you remember our children's room?" In that same room her own children, Stach and Julka, now grew up. But long ago she found in the attic Vladya's (she always addressed him that way) wooden pony which he had gotten as a small boy. And did he remember the old nurse, Kacenka Holubowa? She died a year ago, and before her death she kept speaking of him. He would never see her grave . . .

After a few moments, without finishing the reading, he himself sat writing. He had forgotten it all—he wrote—and yet recalled it all again. With Stach and Julka, with her cares and joys, she was happier than he was. He was asking many questions. He will take a trip to see her soon. Or better yet—in a year or two he will return completely to her and to his own people. A great tear dropped down on the next word.

Do You Remember? Translated by Šarka B. Hrbkova. In GREAT STORIES OF ALL NATIONS; One Hundred Sixty Complete Short Stories from the Literatures of All Periods and Countries. Edited by Maxim Lieber and Blanche Colton Williams . . . New York, Brentano's Publishers, 1927. p.809–812.

Preceded by a note about the author.

Daj kwiatek! Translated as *"Give Me a Flower!"*

Résumé. Old Chaita lived in a small provincial Polish town, Ongród. Her clothes betrayed her trade: she was a ragpicker. All the members of her family were resting at the Hebrew cemetery. But she was not alone: Heiemke, a six-year-old boy, whom her daughter had left behind in the world, was with her. Heiemke was a pretty child; the only rose in the thorny garland of Chaita's life.

Once when Heiemke and other Jewish children gathered on the boulevard were listening to Henoch's story of the exodus of the people of Israel from Egypt, they saw a beautiful lady crossing the boulevard, accompanied by several handsome gentlemen. The lady carried an immense bouquet of beautiful flowers.

Heiemke was enchanted. He ran in front of the lady and, stretching his hands toward the flowers, lifted entreating eyes to her. "Ask for it nicely," she said. The boy did not understand Polish. Say, "Give me a flower!" The boy exclaimed the words loudly and distinctly in the language of the country he lived in, but which was foreign to him. The woman took a large part of her bouquet and gave it to the child. Heiemke covered her hand with ardent kisses.

The boy ran home. Chaita clapped her hands at the sight of the beautiful flowers, and wanted to know how the boy had got them. Heiemke would not part with his enchanting gift even at night. He placed the bouquet under his pillow. When he saw the crumpled stems in the morning, Heiemke wept bitterly and his grandmother was unable to console him.

Chaita suddenly realized her responsibility towards the boy. Reluctant as she was to part with the child, afraid of leaving her grandson alone in the world, Chaita placed Heiemke under the care of the rabbi. Reb Nohim took the boy to his home. Once, when listening to the rabbi's story of the angel of prayer, Heiemke had a vision of the beautiful lady with flowers. He exclaimed in Polish: "Give me a flower!" Reb Nohim was puzzled by the foreign words spoken by the child.

First published 1878.

"Give Me a Flower!" Translated by Szymon St. Deptula. In CANDLES IN THE NIGHT; Jewish Tales by Gentile Authors. Edited by Joseph L. Baron; with a preface by Carl van Doren. Philadelphia, The Jewish Publication Society of America, 1940 (5700). p.209–239.
"... A slightly abridged version."

Panna Antonina. Translated as *Miss Antonina.*

Résumé. "If I had twelve daughters I should educate every one of them to be professors of the university," was her favorite saying. Miss Antonina was a private teacher. She never married (after some deliberation she rejected the proposal which was her last chance). She was an embodiment of the fight for equal rights for women and a vigorous "champion of education." She educated others, and also by reading widely and incessantly, though without any special plan, she never ceased educating herself.

She held herself erect, always walking briskly, her bloodless complexion giving an impression of early fading. There was never anything gay or ornamental about her dress.

After seventeen years of teaching, living in other people's homes, Miss Antonina had an irresistible yearning for a home of her own. She came to the city and rented a room in an attic. Miss Antonina continued to give lessons privately, but in the evening she also taught and even fed some children gratis.

Her room was cold and damp, but she was soon forced to take another one still colder and damper. She developed arthritis. When she fell ill, she lay in her own room for a few months, but later, when the arthritis had reached her lungs, she had to be taken to a hospital. Some kind people kept paying for her private room.

Her only occupation now was searching her soul and reliving her past. Helpless, in physical and spiritual pain, she was awaiting her death.

(The story is told in the first person by the narrator who had been meeting Miss Antonina at the various stages of her life.)
Written in 1881.
First printed 1883.

Miss Antonina. Translated by Janina Rodzińska. In POLISH SHORT STORIES, selected by Zbigniew Żabicki. Warsaw, Polonia Publishing House, 1960. p.107–[148].

Pieśń przerwana. Translated as *The Interrupted Melody.*
The Interrupted Melody. Translated from the Polish of Eliza Orzeszko by M. Ochenkowska. London, Andrew Melrose, 1912. 140 p.
Border-line with a novel.

"Silny Samson"; obrazek miejski. Translated as *Powerful Samson.*

Powerful Samson. Translated by Krystyna Cękalska. In *Poland; Illustrated Magazine,* No. 11 (75) 1960. (Am. ed.) p.25–27.
"Excerpts."
First published 1879 in her Z RÓŻNYCH SFER (From Various Walks of Life).

Parandowski, Jan (1893–)

Roscher. Translated as *Roscher.*

Roscher. Translated by Andrzej Konarek. In *Polish Perspectives; Monthly Review,* [II], No. 12 (20), 1959. p.24–28.
From his GODZINA ŚRÓDZIEMNOMORSKA (The Mediterranean Hour), 1949.
Followed by "An Hour with Jan Parandowski," by Lesław M. Bartelski, p.29–33.
A border-line with an essay.

Perzyński, Włodzimierz (1878–1930)

This playwright, novelist and short story writer, popular at his time, is today remembered for some of his plays. His LEKKOMYŚLNA SIOSTRA (The Light-Minded Sister, 1905) is occasionally still produced on the stage. Another of his popular plays was ASZANTKA (1907). A master of witty dialogue, Perzyński never probes deep into the mysteries of life. His novels include TRYUMFATOR (The Triumpher, 1919) and KLEJNOTY (Jewels, 1930). TO, CO NIE PRZEMIJA (Things That Do Not Pass, 1907), NOWELE (Short Stories, 1909), MIŁOŚĆ, SZTUKA I PIENIĄDZE (Love, Art and Money, 1912), ZNAMIĘ (The Stigma, 1927) and PRALNIA SUMIENIA (The Laundering of Conscience, 1930) are among his collections of short stories.

Protekcja. Translated as *A Question of Influence.*

Résumé. The owner of the store where Mr. Everest Winkiewicz had worked for three years ran away with his customers' money to a foreign country, and Winkiewicz found himself without a job.

He desperately tried to find some work while living on his savings. An ad in the paper produced no results whatsoever. His friends kept repeating to him that the question of finding employment is solely that of influence.

When his situation was rapidly becoming desperate, a school friend accidentally met in a restaurant suddenly raised his hopes. He knew an influential Szyszkowski family in Warsaw who surely would help. Mr. Szyszkowski's weak point was that he loved old Warsaw and abhorred the new buildings.

On Sunday Winkiewicz presented himself to the Szyszkowskis. He was greeted most cordially. He took the first opportunity to steer the conversation to the problem of Warsaw architecture, and giving a false address, expressed his disgust with the new house he was supposedly living in. Mr. Szyszkowski was delighted. Winkiewicz was overjoyed with his success.

All of a sudden a quarrel ensued between the Szyszkowskis over the date of tearing down the old structure on the spot where that new house in question was now standing. Mrs. Szyszkowski indignantly left the room. Rudely and angrily Mr. Szyszkowski bid his guest farewell.

First printed approximately 1910.

A Question of Influence. Translated by Janina Rodzińska. In POLISH SHORT STORIES, selected by Zbigniew Żabicki. Warsaw, Polonia Publishing House, 1960. p. 247–[256].

Sercem za serce. Translated as *Gratitude.*

Gratitude. In his THREE TALES . . . Translated by K. Żuk-Skarszewska. In *Poland* (New York), VII, 1926. p.635–637.

Terminologja. Translated as *Terminology.*

Terminology. In his THREE TALES . . . Translated by K. Żuk-Skarszewska. In *Poland* (New York), VII, 1926. p.606–607.

Uczeń Sherlock Holmsa. Translated as *The Way to Success.*

The Way to Success. In his THREE TALES . . . Translated by K. Żuk-Skarszewska. In *Poland* (New York), VII, 1926. p.607-608, 633-635.

Wybraniec losu. Translated as *A Stroke of Luck.*

Résumé. Seated on a bench in a public park of Warsaw, absorbed in thought, was Pan Mizerski, the sculptor. He was at the end of his rope. He had been disappointed in his ambitions, and he was almost destitute. He was intelligent, good-looking and healthy. But due to his pride, he was unable to court the good graces of influential personages. Hungry, cold and exhausted, he decided to take his life; and he had made up his mind to die from a bullet.

He returned to his studio-apartment and lay on his bed made of the books of poems, inherited from his friend the poet who had died young. The only thought which filled his mind was how to get a revolver. Suddenly a strange thing happened. Mizerski saw the poet sitting near him on a chair. His long-dead friend pointed to the cupboard in the wall. On the shelf inside lay a pair of cuffs and a freshly washed shirt. Believing it was all an hallucination, Mizerski fell into a heavy, dreamless sleep. He was awakened by the police, handcuffed, and taken to prison as a dangerous criminal.

Mizerski was accused of murdering, in an access of erotic frenzy, a woman of seventy, well known for her acts of charity. The shirt supposedly had traces of blood. In the prison Mizerski began to thrive again. His cell was filled with flowers. As a result of all the publicity about his crime, there appeared long articles in the papers about his art.

His lawyer secured his release from prison. He soon was able to buy himself a splendid villa in a spacious garden. In the garden was his studio. One day a mysterious visitor announced to him that it was he who had murdered the old woman, and had put the blood-stained shirt into the cupboard. Mizerski seized his revolver, and shot down the intruder like a dog.

A Stroke of Luck, by Wlodzimierz Perzynski. Translation anonymous. In POLISH SHORT STORIES, by Joseph Weyssenhof, Piotr Choynowski, Kornel Makuszynski [and others] . . . London, Minerva Publishing Company [1943]. p.70–76.

Pietrkiewicz, Jerzy (1916–   )

Like Joseph Conrad, this Polish author has made English his adopted language. His first poems had appeared in a Warsaw weekly *Prosto z mostu,* and his collections of poetry, such as WIERSZE I POEMATY (Verses and Poems) had been published in Poland before the war. His first collection of poetry written in exile, POGRZEB EUROPY (The Funeral of Europe), was published in London in 1946. In 1953 his series of novels in English, which have received wide acclaim, began to appear. The first was THE KNOTTED CORD, followed by a novel about Scots in Poland in the seventeenth century, LOOT AND LOYALTY (1955); then came FUTURE TO LET (1958), ISOLATION (1959), THE QUICK AND THE DEAD (1961) and THAT ANGEL BURNING AT MY LEFT SIDE (1963). The most recent one is his surrealistic and unclassifiable INNER CIRCLE (1966). Since 1950 Jerzy Pietrkiewicz has lectured on Polish literature at the School of Slavonic and East European Studies of the University of London.

His latest titles have appeared under the name Jerzy Peterkiewicz.

Pustelnik. Translated as *A "Sadhu."*

Résumé. (A story of a Polish underground newspaper editor during World War II, told in the first person.)

The editorial offices of a secret weekly paper, "The Brave," were moved six times in six weeks. When the Germans occupied the Eastern part of Poland, the editorial staff bolted across the river Bug. They chose a suitable spot in the woodlands with a railway line running nearby, and the printer was confident of releasing the first issue within a week. There was a problem of a press agency. The narrator asked his colleague in the underground organization about a radio set. He was assured that he would have first-class assistance for the distribution of his paper. His friend thought that "The Brave" might even become a daily. The narrator would have to go to the hermit. Any child knew the way. At the hermit's den the narrator was to ask for "an actor."

The peasant who had accommodated the team and who had no idea who his lodgers were, promised to take the narrator to the hermit's den the following afternoon. On the way the peasant talked about the hermit. He had been there for a long time. The hermit had been dumb before, but he miraculously regained his speech about six months ago. The miracle brought to his den a lot of people anxious to see the saintly man. He talked about birds and trees, knights and saints, and about Saint Andrew Bobola too. The peasant was taking two loaves of bread for him.

The den was on top of a high precipitous ravine. A long-legged unshaven young man was standing under the arch of a pine tree shading the entrance. He evidently was acting as the hermit's private secretary and doorkeeper. A crowd had gathered around and the young man was collecting the bundles brought by the visitors. An old man with a long beard suddenly appeared at the den's entrance. Dressed in a long coat made of homespun linen cloth, he held a long staff in one hand and a book in black leather in the other. The hermit made a short speech in a clear sonorous voice. He urged the people to go home to work and pray. He spoke of fortitude and courage, and proclaimed a great miracle to come soon.

The crowd dispersed. When his guide went home, the narrator was taken to the den by the hermit's assistant. The young man was the "actor," the hermit's beard proved to be a false one, and the hermit himself was a member of the Polish underground army who had replaced the dumb hermit six months after his death.

> From his UMARLI NIE SĄ BEZBRONNI (The Dead Are Not Helpless), 1943.

A "Sadhu," by J. Pietrkiewicz. Translation anonymous. In THE POLISH SHORT STORIES. Edited by Umadevi. [Bombay] Indo-Polish Library, No. 35 [c1946]. p.141–150.

Witaj dostojny gościu! Translated as Welcome Our Distinguished Guest.

Résumé. (A story from the German occupation of Poland.)

A group of dignitaries and specially invited guests waited in a sweltering heat of the Polish countryside near Cracow for the ceremony of welcoming the Governor-General of occupied Poland, Dr. Frank, in celebration of third anniversary of the outbreak of war. It was September 1, 1942. Among those waiting were a Swedish and a Swiss journalist.

A group of Cracovian peasants rode by on horseback. When they were returning from the village the Swiss journalist, who could speak some Polish, soon found out that the "Cracovians" could not speak Polish. They were Germans disguised in Polish national costumes.

Meanwhile a crowd of villagers had gathered on the meadow behind the military band. It was a silent and pensive crowd, almost menacing in its composure. These were Poles. It was exactly noon.

The Governor-General was supposed to meet the dignitaries outside the birch grove at 10 A.M. The ceremony of the salute was to be followed by a triumphal march through the village of Czarna Gruda. A reception at the castle and a tour of exemplary German settlements were to complete the programme. It was to show the country-folk and the "new order" in perfect harmony.

At 9 A.M. Dr. Frank started on his way. His open car was stopped at the cross-roads by a priest in a black robe. The priest ordered the car back, but before he vanished he said in a hypnotic tone of voice to the Governor, "There is blood on your hands." Dr. Frank's hands were dripping with blood. He turned back.

The same priest appeared on the road before the crowd waiting for the Governor. When he passed under the first triumphal arch bearing the German inscription, "Welcome our distinguished guest," it collapsed. The withered boughs of the second one recovered, as he approached, their radiant green hue. The priest sparkled with light like a second sun above the kneeling crowd. An old patriotic song filled the air.

As soon as the priest had disappeared the Germans assaulted the kneeling Poles, knocked them to the ground, pulled them by the hair. A little girl with two red streaks across her face showed the Swiss journalist the picture of the priest who had just appeared. It was Saint Andrew Bobola.[18]

> From his UMARLI NIE SĄ BEZBRONNI (*The Dead Are Not Helpless*).

Welcome Our Distinguished Guest, by J. Pietrkiewicz. Translation anonymous. In THE POLISH SHORT STORIES. Edited by Umadevi. [Bombay] Indo-Polish Library. No. 35 [c1946]. p.130–140.

Promiński, Marian (1908–   )

Tak się bawią wariaci. Translated as *A Crazy Game*.

A Crazy Game. Translation anonymous. In *Poland; Illustrated Magazine*. No. 5 (69) 1960. (Am. ed.) p.25.

From his ATRAMENT I KREW (Ink and Blood).

---

[18] Editor's note: "St. Andrew Bobola is Poland's fighters' patron. He was himself martyred by Russian Cossacks in the 17th century for his religious and patriotic work and was canonized in 1938 in Rome. He was adopted by the Polish Underground Organizations and fighting Poland abroad as their beloved Saint and helper."

Maj na kółkach. Translated as *May on Wheels.*

May on Wheels. Translation anonymous. In *Poland; Illustrated Magazine,* No. 5 (69) 1960. (Am. ed.) p.25.
Preceded by a brief note about the author.
From his ATRAMENT I KREW (Ink and Blood).

Prus, Bolesław, pseud. (1845–1912)

Better known under this pseudonym (his real name was Aleksander Głowacki), Prus belongs among the greatest Polish writers. A mouthpiece for Polish Positivism, the author was the most prominent exponent of the realist school of which the other talented representative was Eliza Orzeszkowa. Prus collaborated with many periodicals, and most of his sketches and short stories appeared in print in magazines first. For Prus the pen was a sword to fight for his ideas; he subordinated art to his cause. His LALKA (1890), an epic tale about life in nineteenth century Poland, has been announced to appear in English (in translation of David J. Welsh) as LALKA (THE DOLL). Another novel, EMANCYPANTKI (Emancipated Women, 1894), still awaits its translation. The author's great historical novel, set in ancient Egypt, FARAON (1897), was published in English as THE PHARAOH AND THE PRIEST (1902).

Dziwna historia. Translated as *A Curious Story.*

A Curious Story. Translated from the Polish of Bolesław Prus by W. J. Rose. In *The Slavonic (and East European) Review,* XXVI, 1947–48. p.534–42.

Kamizelka. Translated as *The Waistcoat.*

Résumé. An underpaid clerk develops tuberculosis. Both he and his wife try to cheer each other and they pretend that everything is going well.

He assures her that he is gaining weight, because his waistcoat feels tighter on him as the days go by. Every night in great secrecy he moves the belt-buckle of his waistcoat a little. He does not realize that in order to comfort him his wife had resorted to the very same trick.

One snowy night in March he dies. She has to give up their one-room apartment and is compelled to sell everything—even the waistcoat, a tragic symbol of their love.

The Waistcoat. Translated from the Polish of Bolesław Prus by N. B. Jopson. In *The Slavonic (and East European) Review,* IX, 1930–31. p.283–291.

The Waistcoat. Translated by Olga Scherer-Virski. In her THE MODERN POLISH SHORT STORY. 's-Gravenhage, Mouton, 1955. (Slavistic printings and reprintings, 5) p.111–118.

The Waistcoat. Translated by Ilona Ralf Sues. In POLISH SHORT STORIES, selected by Zbigniew Żabicki. Warsaw, Polonia Publishing House, 1960. p.89–[103].

Omyłka. Translated as *A Mistake.*

Résumé. The narrator, his mother and his teacher and the family friend, Mr. Dobrzański, were seated at dinner a few days before Easter, when a special delivery letter was handed to the mother. She read it, and her face turned white.

Władysław, her older son, for patriotic reasons had volunteered for the army. He was a student at the University of Warsaw. Mother was his sole supporter. She worked very hard and denied herself even a decent pair of shoes for the sake of her sons' education. For her the news was as if somebody stuck a knife into her heart. Mr. Dobrzański offered to write to Władysław to bring him home at once.

Just at that moment an elderly man was passing by the house. He had bought his son's release from military service, and people called him "the traitor." Mother's lips trembled. Mr. Dobrzański was now ready to write. "Tell him," she whispered, sobbing, "that his mother sends him her blessing, which he had forgotten to take from her."

A Mistake (fragment), by Boleslaw Prus. Translated by Irena Morska. In POLISH AUTHORS OF TODAY AND YESTERDAY . . . Selected by Irena Morska. New York, S. F. Vanni [c1947]. p.81–84.

Placówka. Translated as *The Outpost.*

The Outpost. In SELECTED POLISH TALES. Translated by Else C. M. Benecke and Marie Busch. London, New York [etc.] H. Milford, Oxford University Press [1921]. p.1–226.

A novel rather than a short story.

Powracająca fala. Translated as *The Returning Wave.*

Résumé. Two German school-mates made their home on Polish soil: Pastor Boehme, poor as a church mouse, but liked and respected by the Polish peasants, and Gottlieb Adler, a wealthy factory owner whose dream, now close to realization, was to make a million roubles.

The pastor had a son and a daughter. Józio, about to graduate from a technical college at Riga, was planning to work hard and support his family and his parents in their old age. Adler's son, Ferdinand, a typical member of the golden youth, never completed his education, and instead kept dissipating his father's wealth by drinking and debauchery. The more money Ferdinand spent, the stronger were the "economy" measures in the factory. During one such period, a young, able and ambitious mechanic, Gosławski, feverish and weakened from overworking, suffered an accident at work and died.

One day Pastor Boehme demonstrated to old Adler "the returning wave" by throwing bits of wood and cork on the pond. He was warning Adler that evil begets evil, and that his overindulgence with Ferdinand and the ruthless exploitation of his workmen might bring the wave of evil back to where it had started. The old man laughed these warnings off.

Soon after, Ferdinand, following a night of drinking in the company of his friends, fought a duel with the respected judge Zapora, whom he had provoked. Wounded in the fight, he was brought home and died in his father's arms. Old Adler went mad with grief. Rejecting the words of comfort from Pastor Boehme, he set his factory afire and died in the flames. The wave had returned.

The Returning Wave, by Bolesław Prus. In MORE TALES BY POLISH AUTHORS. Translated by Else C. M. Benecke and Marie

Busch. New York, Longmans, Green and company, 1916. p.186–288.

Sen. Translated as *The Dream.*

   The Dream. Translated from the Polish of Bolesław Prus by Peter Rennie. In *The Slavonic and East European Review,* XXIX, 1950–51. p.6–19.

W górach. Translated as *In the Mountains.*

   In the Mountains. Translation anonymous. In *Poland; Illustrated Magazine,* No. 8 (60) 1959. p.13–15.

Z legend dawnego Egiptu. Translated as *From Legends of Ancient Egypt/From the Legends of Ancient Egypt.*

   Résumé. Old Rameses, the great Pharaoh in whose lifetime the Nile had ebbed a hundred times, fell ill. He called his wisest physician from the temple at Carnac and gave orders for the preparation of potent medicine which would either heal or kill him at once. Then he commanded Prince Horus, his grandson and his successor, to be led into the hall of the Pharaohs to await there the ring which, after the death of Rameses, would invest him with the authority of the Pharaoh.

   While awaiting the ring, Horus suddenly gave a cry of pain. He thought a bee had stung his foot; it proved to be a venomous spider. Impatient Horus ordered several edicts to be written so that they could be executed as soon as he had touched them with the ring.

   One edict would conclude peace with Ethiopia, another stated that no prisoner should have his tongue torn from his mouth upon the field of battle. Further edicts were to lower people's lease-rents and taxes by half; the slaves were to have three days in the week free from labor. Horus's preceptor, the wise and noble Jetron, was to be recalled from banishment. Under another edict the mortal remains of Horus's mother Zefora would be transferred to the catacombs. Finally, his beloved Berenice was to be liberated from her cloistered captivity.

   But when the wisest physician from Carnac gazed upon the prince's foot, Horus understood that he was soon to die. His only hope now was that he would have enough strength to touch the edicts with the ring before his death.

When the high priest's deputy came to announce a miracle—that mighty Rameses had miraculously regained his health and desired to ride forth for lions at sunrise—Horus was dead.

Such is the fate of human hopes before the decrees of the heavens.

From Legends of Ancient Egypt. Translation anonymous. In *Poland; Illustrated Magazine,* No. 8 (60) 1959. p.15–16.

From the Legends of Ancient Egypt, by Boleslaw Prus. In ANTHOLOGY OF MODERN SLAVONIC LITERATURE IN PROSE AND VERSE. Translated by P. Selver; with an introduction and literary notes. London, Kegan Paul, Trench, Trubner and company; New York, E. P. Dutton and company, 1919. p.76–87.

Żywy telegraf. Translated as *The Human Telegraph.*

Résumé. Countess X was shocked to see four boys fighting over a half-torn book in the Orphanage. The Sister in charge explained the cause of the quarrel: the children loved to read and the Orphanage was lacking books.

The Countess mentioned the incident to the Chief Counselor. The Counselor passed it on to Mr. Z. who, in turn, rushed into the editorial rooms of the "Daily News" and implored the editor to print an appeal to the public to donate books for the orphans.

A few days later a shabbily dressed workman knocked on the door of the editorial room. His pale, thin little daughter brought a bundle of old books. They left the gift and disappeared without leaving their names.

The author compares the incident to a system of telegraphy. The main station was the Orphanage, the receiving station—the workman. The others functioned as telegraph poles.

The Human Telegraph, by Boleslav Prus. Translated by Irena B. Hrbkova. In GREAT SHORT STORIES OF THE WORLD; a Collection of Complete Short Stories Chosen from the Literatures of All Periods and Countries by Barrett H. Clark and Maxim Lieber. New York, Robert M. McBride and company, 1926. p.714–715.

"This story is translated—for the first time into English—by Sarka B. Hrbkova, by whose permission it is here printed."

Preceded by a note about the author: p.713.

The Human Telegraph, by Boleslaw Prus. Translated by Irena Morska. In POLISH AUTHORS OF TODAY AND YESTERDAY . . . Selected by Irena Morska. New York, S. F. Vanni [c1947]. p.78–80.

Pruszyński, Ksawery (1907–1950)

Pruszyński's CZERWONA HISZPANIA (Red Spain), published in 1937, was a direct result of his assignment as war correspondent in Spain during the Civil War. The author spent his war years partly with the Polish émigré government in London, and partly as a combat officer. DROGA WIODŁA PRZEZ NARWIK (The Road Through Narvik, 1941) describes his experiences in the Norwegian campaign. Since the war Pruszyński has published the collections: TRZYNAŚCIE OPOWIEŚCI (Thirteen Tales, 1946) and KARABELA Z MESCHEDU (The Sabre of Meshed, 1948). After his return to Poland the author lost his life in a tragic accident.

Człowiek z rokokowego kościoła. Translated as *The Man from the Rococo Church.*

The Man from the Rococo Church. Translated by Ilona Ralf Sues. In *Polish Perspectives; Monthly Review*, III, No. 8–9, 1960. p.52–62.

From his TRZYNAŚCIE OPOWIEŚCI (Thirteen Tales), 1946.

Preceded by an article on the author by Lesław M. Bartelski, "The Two Worlds of Ksawery Pruszyński." p.47–51.

O głowę murzyńskiego króla. Translated as *For the Head of a Negro King.*

Résumé. (The story is told in the first person.)

The narrator was a newcomer to the regiment. When the tanks began moving that morning, he was ordered to ride on a big two-ton lorry. A cavalry sergeant who sat at the wheel was introduced to him as the "live archives" of the regiment. Even at that early hour the "live archives" reeked of liquor.

The regiment was on the way to Aldershot; from there it was to go straight to the port, and embark for France. The road was monotonous and the "live archives" silent. But when the narrator asked him if he knew France, he opened up. France was to him like his own backyard, he said. He could say the same about Italy. Did he know Lamadria di Chiavasso?—the sergeant put the question to the narrator.

It was there that the 10th regiment of Mounted Rifles was set up in 1918. The sergeant was there from the start. He crossed over the front-line to the Italians in an Austrian uniform at night, and later on, together with other Poles, was sent to Lamadria di Chiavasso. In the winter of 1918 the regiment was transferred to a big military camp at Guer in Brittany, France. There were many cafés in the camp which served "poor coffee, lousy wine and worn-down females." The French soldiers nicknamed the camp Putainville, while the Poles called it Kurwidołki.

The Poles went to action against the Germans and they fought well. They met Senegalese riflemen in the front-lines. The Negroes were brave. Asked why they were fighting, they explained that their relic, the dried head of some king from the Congo Negroes, had been stolen by the Germans and put in a Berlin museum. They were determined to get it back. They wondered if the Poles were fighting for a similar reason.

The sergeant was wounded, was confined to a hospital, and never returned to his native Wolica, as that village was not included in free Poland after the war. He later returned to his old regiment.

During World War Two he was again in action against the Germans. Interned by the Hungarians he escaped, was wounded, and he again made for France. In 1940 he went through the same movements and places exactly as he had in 1918. Many situations of 1940 were almost identical with those of 1918; sometimes they seemed to have taken place only a few minutes earlier.

Moving to France the sergeant was musing whether once again it was going to be Guer at Coëtquidan . . .

From his TRZYNAŚCIE OPOWIEŚCI *(Thirteen Tales), 1946.*

For the Head of a Negro King. Translated by Ilona Ralf Sues. In CONTEMPORARY POLISH SHORT STORIES, selected by Andrzej Kijowski. Warsaw, Polonia Publishing House, 1960. p.[191]–208.

Pomiędzy wilki. Translated as *Back to the Wolves.*

Back to the Wolves. Translation anonymous. In *Poland; Illustrated Magazine,* No. 2 (54) 1959. p.13–16, 26–28.

Przerwa-Tetmajer, Kazimierz, *see* Tetmajer, Kazimierz Przerwa

Przybyszewski, Stanisław (1868–1927)

A playwright and a novelist, Przybyszewski is the outstanding representative of modernism and "decadentism" in Polish letters. His first works, written in German, included CHOPIN UND NIETZSCHE (1887). HOMO SAPIENS, his novel trilogy, was published between 1899 and 1901. At that time, as an editor of the weekly, *Życie* (Life, 1898–1901), he exercised a powerful influence upon the literary trend of Młoda Polska (Young Poland).

Best known among his novels are: DZIECI SZATANA (Satan's Children, 1899), SYNOWIE ZIEMI (Sons of the Earth, 1904), and MOCNY CZŁOWIEK (The Strong Man, 1912). His TANIEC MIŁOŚCI I ŚMIERCI (The Dance of Love and Death, 1901) and GODY ŻYCIA (The Feast of Life, 1910) may serve as examples of the type of plays he wrote. "Art for art's sake" was the essence of Przybyszewski's literary credo.

Chopin. Translated as *Chopin.*

Chopin, by Stanislaw Przybyszewski. In ANTHOLOGY OF MODERN SLAVONIC LITERATURE IN PROSE AND VERSE. Translated by P. Selver, with an introduction and literary notes. London, Kegan Paul, Trench, Trubner and company; New York, E. P. Dutton and company, 1917. p.88–111.

Chuć (?) Translated as *Sex*[19]

Résumé. In the beginning there was sex. Out of the voice box of the human being sex tore the first long stretched sounds, directed them to the tempo of the pulsing heart, formed them into rhythm and melody.

Sex gave birth to the world. Sex diffused itself with super-power into the muscles of the human body; it handed man the club, as it came upon him, to destroy his rival in the contest for his mate. It helped him to clear forests, to direct into new beds rivers and lakes, to subdue seas and to conquer mountains. Sex awakened the brain from its slumber, forcing it into incomprehensible suffering and into the labors of never-heard-of work.

Sex gave birth to the deed. And sex forced its way into the heart of man, and filled it out completely. It awakened in man the desire to see everybody as happy as sex itself was in its sacred elevation of happiness. Sex created pity and consolidation, it created father and mother, brother and sister; it united the human sex through bonds of blood and of friendship. But at the same time it became the origin of revengefulness and of inordinate desire for murder and crime.

Sex craved for divinity, and it expanded the chest of man with fervent longing. The Holy Spirit descended upon sex and thus sex created love. Sex was the first one [*sic*] to talk to God. The super-power of sex grew with love and the consciousness of its divinity. And thus sex became the confidant of God and carried Him glad messages of how man had been drawn nearer to Him through Art.

Sex gave birth to Art. And so sex is the Androgyne, "father-mother" of all that is, that was, that will be: the powerful original fountain of might, of eternal strength, of enthusiasm and intoxication, of the most sacred attempt to storm the heavens and of the greatest, most detestable Fall of Man.

Sex, by Stanislav Przybyszyewsky. Translation anonymous. In

---

19 *Chopin* and *Sex* are not truly short stories. Both are borderline cases resembling essays. Taking exception to the rule, the résumé of *Sex* is offered here as an example of Przybyszewski's creative writing on the border of the short story.

JUDAS ISCARIOT AND OTHER STORIES, by W. Doroschewitch, Catulle Mendes, Feodor Sologub and others. Guido Bruno, 1919. p.15–17.

Putrament, Jerzy (1911–   )

Several collections of poetry were published by this author before the war. Putrament spent the war years in the Soviet Union. His war reminiscences were the theme of a collection of short stories, ŚWIĘTA KULA (The Holy Bullet), published in 1946. The author concerns himself critically with prewar Poland in the novels, RZECZYWISTOŚĆ (Reality, 1947) and WRZESIEŃ (September, 1952). Putrament continued his war reminiscences in a volume of stories to which one of them gave the title, viz., WYPADEK W KRASNYM-STAWIE (The Accident at Krasnystaw, 1957).

Wypadek w Krasnymstawie. Translated as *The Accident at Krasnystaw.*

Résumé. (The story is based on the author's World War Two reminiscences, and is told in the first person.)

Four Polish officers, plus the driver, were in the car on the way to Lwów. All four had fled from there three years earlier. Now the Germans had been driven out, and Lwów was taken by the Soviet Army. Colonel Błoński was sent to Lwów on some official business, the other three managed to get a few days' leave and joined him in the newspaper's jeep. Lieutenant Cymmerman, a youngish ensign, Kołoda, and the narrator sat in the back; Błonski, as host, sat next to the driver.

They were all in excellent mood, and their conversation soon took the form of bragging. Their wives were the subject. Błoński's wife, Clara, according to his account, was so beautiful that people in the neighborhood would give directions by means of the house "where that lovely Clara lives." Błoński pulled out a photograph. Clara was dark and she was really beautiful. Cymmerman's wife was sunshine itself, while the narrator praised the absolute fairness of his wife's hair. Even Kołoda said he was married, and he too pulled out a photograph.

Suddenly the car swerved at full speed, and all were thrown out. Only the narrator and the driver came out unscathed; the others suffered minor injuries and had to be detained in the hospital. The narrator was charged with the responsibility to go on with the trip and look up their respective wives; then come back and report.

First the narrator tried to find his own wife. He had to give up the attempt, and decided to look up Clara Błońska. After many trials and tribulations he learned that, because of some admixture of Jewish blood, Clara had been cremated by the Germans. Kołoda's wife had been a nurse in a hospital. She was taken by the Germans and sentenced to death for giving illegal injections for abortion. Cymmerman's "wife" had turned to prostitution. She kept repeating she knew that Cymmerman was dead.

The narrator came back to the hospital. He told the truth to Błoński and Kołoda, and somehow extricated himself from Cymmerman's inquisitive questions. He reaped the wrath and anger of them all.

When he came to Lublin, the narrator found a letter from one of his friends about the sad fate of his own wife. (We never learn what that fate was.)

> From his collection WYPADEK W KRASNYMSTAWIE (*The Accident at Krasnystaw*), *1957*.

The Accident at Krasnystaw. Translated by Edward Rothert. In CONTEMPORARY POLISH SHORT STORIES, selected by Andrzej Kijowski. Warsaw, Polonia Publishing House, 1960. p.[211]–240.

Pytlakowski, Jerzy

24 [*dwadzieścia cztery*] *godziny śmierci.* Translated as *Twenty-Four Hours of Dying.*

Twenty-Four Hours of Dying. Translation anonymous. In *Poland; Illustrated Magazine,* No. 6 (70) 1960. (Am. ed.) p.13–16. Preceded by a brief note about the author.

Rejmont Władysław, *see* Reymont, Władysław Stanisław

Rey, Sydor (1908–)

Born in Eastern Poland, this novelist and poet has lived in the United States since 1939. His literary debut in Poland goes back to 1929. In 1933 Rey joined a literary group, called "Przedmieście" (Suburbia). His prewar novel, KROPIWNIKI, appeared in Poland in 1937. A small volume of poetry in Polish, PIEŚNI MÓWIONE (Spoken Songs) was published in New York in 1945. Rey's recent novel (about the people of Europe, thrown on the American continent by the fate of war and trying to start life anew), KSIĘGA ROZBITKÓW (The Book of Survivors) was published by the "Czytelnik" in Poland in 1959.

Generał. Translated as *The General.*

Résumé. When the general appeared in the village he wore a blue suit, light tan shoes, loud socks, a red tie, and a hat the color of cream. The general was a miner from Wilkes-Barre, Pa., and his name was Matuszek. He arrived there from Poland as a boy of fifteen. Now he came to visit his birthplace, the village of Podhorki.

When Matuszek himself hinted that he had been an officer in America, it was decided that he must have been a general. He scattered dollars all round, but he never got drunk when he wore his uniform.

One Sunday news was brought to the inn that the landlord had seized the mare of the poorest peasant in the village. The general led the crowd against the landlord. As soon as they reached the estate, Pyentak's mare appeared at the gate, released by the frightened landlord. Carried on the shoulders of the men, Matuszek confessed to the grateful villagers that he never was an officer. But now more than ever he was for them a general. When leaving, he was escorted by the crowd of villagers with the village band. "Long live the general," thundered the crowd.

Matuszek saluted as he started on his journey back to his home in Wilkes-Barre.

The General. [Translated by Edward Falkowski.] In POLISH AUTHORS OF TODAY AND YESTERDAY . . . Selected by Irena Morska. New York, S. F. Vanni [c1947]. p.85–90.

Iwańcio. Translated as *Iwancio.*

Résumé. Iwancio was forty years old and an idiot. He was illegitimate. It was not known who his father was, and three nationalities laid claim to him: Ukrainians, Poles and Jews. Accordingly Iwancio would say his prayers in Ukrainian, Polish or Jewish, depending on who asked for them. He slept outdoors during the summer, and in stables during the winter. Iwancio was infinitely gentle.

Soon after the war Nachman made his appearance in Wojniłów. Nachman spoke with difficulty and thought somewhat indolently, but he was a man of the world. Iwancio attached himself to Nachman immediately and idolized him.

One day Iwancio, delighted with a gift of two Turkish cigarettes and a large piece of chocolate, stretched his hand to Nachman, and called, "Nachman, have some!" He looked at Iwancio and spat out contemptuously, "Not from you," and turned around. Iwancio grew pale and threw himself on the floor in a fit of frenzy. But suddenly he composed himself and returned to his own, gentle self.

One never knows what may spring from a man, concludes the author.

Iwancio. Translated by Samuel Sorgenstein. In POLISH AUTHORS OF TODAY AND YESTERDAY . . . Selected by Irena Morska. New York, S. F. Vanni [c1947]. p.91–98.

Szulim. Translated as *The Story of Shulim.*

The Story of Shulim. [Translated by Norbert Guterman.] In *Commentary,* XXIX, 1960. p. 324–332.
From his KSIĘGA ROZBITKÓW (The Book of Survivors), 1959.

Reymont, Ladislas, *see* Reymont, Władysław Stanisław

Reymont, Władysław Stanisław (1867–1925)

Reymont is best known for his epic CHŁOPI (THE PEASANTS, 1902–1909) which brought him the Nobel Prize in 1924. Although it describes a peasant community somewhere in central Poland, its appeal has proved universal. Despite the difficulty presented by its somewhat stylized dialect, the novel has been widely translated. Reymont started his literary career as an author of short stories. His varied experiences furnished him the subjects. As a youth he ran away from home and tried such jobs as factory worker, office clerk, and actor. His realistic description of various manifestations of human brutality may, perhaps, be traced to the hardships that he experienced in his youth. Among other works, Reymont is the author of a novel about life in the Polish industrial town ŁÓDŹ, ZIEMIA OBIECANA (The Promised Land, 1899) and a historical novel, ROK 1794 (The Year 1794, 1913–1919).

Contrasts. Fragment from his CHŁOPI (THE PEASANTS).

Contrasts, by W. Reymont. [Translated by Michael H. Dziewicki.] In THE WINTER MAIDENS AND OTHER SHORT STORIES. Edited by Umadevi. [Bombay] The Indo-Polish Library, 1947. p.89–114.

Dwie wiosny. Translated as *Spring.*

Spring. Translated by K. Żuk-Skarszewska. In *Poland* (New York) VII, 1926. p.261–262, 264, 322.

I wynieśli. Translated as *In Spite of All.*

In Spite of All. In his TWO SHORT TALES . . . Translated by K. Żuk Skarszewska. In *Poland* (New York), IX, 1928. p.683–685.

In the Old Town at Lodz. Fragment from his ZIEMIA OBIECANA (The Promised Land).

In the Old Town at Lodz, by W. S. Reymont. In ANTHOLOGY OF MODERN SLAVONIC LITERATURE IN PROSE AND VERSE. Translated by

P. Selver, with an introduction and literary notes. London, Kegan Paul, Trench, Trubner and company; New York, E. P. Dutton and company, 1919. p.111–116.

Komurasaki. Translated as *Komurasaki.*

Komurasaki; the Sad History of a Broken Heart. Translated by K. Żuk-Skarszewska. In *Poland* (New York), IX, 1928. p.80–84.

Legenda. Translated as *Legend.*

Legend. Translated by Victoria de Kreuter. In *Poland* (New York), IX, 1928. p.152–159.

O zmierzchu. Translated as *Twilight.*

Résumé. The old horse, Sokół, lay dying. He had fallen sick a long time ago, and was kicked about like a useless carcass. Good people said it would be wrong to kill him; they let him die slowly, alone and forgotten. Only Łapa, an old blind Siberian hound, stayed with him longer than the rest.

The old horse was left to his misery. He was afraid of the short, stifling nights of June. He became frantic with terror. He would tear at his halter, and beat with his hoofs against the wall. He wanted to escape and run . . .

One day, as the sun was setting, somber panic seized him. He broke his halter, and fled into the yard. The sun blinded him, a sharp pain gnawed at his entrails. He came close to the manor house, and began to neigh pleadingly, piteously. But no one had a kind word for him; all was deserted and still. He approached the veranda, neighing plaintively, but no one heard him. He stood gazing at the curtained windows, then he walked all around the house.

Suddenly he seemed to forget everything. He shivered. He dragged himself into the meadow, and sank exhausted to the ground. The crows came near him. He saw their terrible round eyes and half-open beaks. He gave one savage neigh and sprang to his feet. The crows flew away, screeching. Sokół felt himself sinking. A cold shiver ran over his body, and he lay still. Łapa ran up to his friend, but Sokół did not recognize him. Thousands of living things began to crawl over his body, and rend his flesh.

Twilight, from the Polish of Władysław Rejmont. Translation anonymous. In *The Pagan; a Magazine for Eudaemonists,* I, No. 4, 1916. p.33–36.

Twilight, by Wladyslaw Reymont. Translation anonymous. In GREAT STORIES OF ALL NATIONS; One Hundred Sixty Complete Short Stories from the Literatures of All Periods and Countries. Edited by Maxim Lieber and Blanche Colton Williams . . . New York, Brentano's Publishers, 1927. p.813–815.

"Reprinted from the *Pagan* magazine, copyright 1916."

Twilight, by Wladyslaw Reymont. Translation anonymous. In STORIES OF MANY NATIONS, selected and arranged by Irwin H. Braun . . . and D. Edward Safarjian . . . Illustrated by Armstrong Sperry. Boston, D. C. Heath and company [c1942]. p.457–461.

Twilight, by Wladyslaw Stanislaw Reymont. Translation anonymous. In GREAT SHORT STORIES FROM THE WORLD'S LITERATURE, edited by Charles Neider. New York, Rinehart & Co. [c1950]. p.364–367.

Preceded by a brief note about the author.

Peasant Wedding. Fragment from his CHŁOPI (THE PEASANTS).

Peasant Wedding, by W. Reymont. [Translated by Michael H. Dziewicki.] In THE WINTER MAIDENS AND OTHER SHORT STORIES. Edited by Umadevi. [Bombay] The Indo-Polish Library, 1947. p.55–88.

Pęknięty dzwon. Translated as *The Sacred Bell.*

The Sacred Bell. In his TWO SHORT TALES . . . Translated by K. Żuk-Skarszewska. In *Poland* (New York), IX, 1928. p.680–683.

The Polish peasants. (I.) Fragment from his CHŁOPI (THE PEASANTS).

The Polish Peasants. (I.) Translated from the Polish of W. S. Reymont by Roman Dyboski. In *The Slavonic Review,* I, 1922–23. p.[428]–436.

The Polish peasants. (II.) Fragment from his CHŁOPI (THE PEASANTS).

The Polish Peasants. (II.) From the Polish of W. S. Reymont. [Translated by Roman Dyboski.] In *The Slavonic Review,* I, 1922–23. p.[598]–603.

A Polish Scene. Fragment from his CHŁOPI (THE PEASANTS).

Résumé. (The place is a solitary inn in Russian Poland, near the Prussian frontier, kept by a Jew named Herszlik, part of whose occupation is to smuggle emigrants for America across the border by night. Besides emigrants and Herszlik are present an old beggar man and his wife 'doxy' and a couple of peasants drinking together.)

It was a rainy, windy and cold night in March. The inn stood in the middle of the forest at cross-roads. Jasiek Winciorek, a youth who had just escaped from prison to which he had been unfairly sentenced, pushed forward cautiously from the wood to the road. He peeped in through the window, hesitated, turned back, crossed himself, and finally entered. He moved to the fire. His wet coat began steaming. A blind beggar was at the fire, drying the soaked strips he wore round his legs. He was talking endlessly in a low voice to the woman beside him. She was cooking soup in a pot which stood on a tripod in the fire. They treated Jasiek to the soup and some whisky, while the beggar was expounding his philosophy of life based on his grossly over-simplified religion.

In the middle of the night Herszlik led out a column of ragged shadows whose destination was Brazil. Jasiek returned to the now dark inn, crouched by the fire, and fell asleep. He was awakened by a sharp tug and a demand to show his passport. Two policemen stood over him. Jasiek struck one of them with his fist between the eyes, darted to the door and ran out. The policeman fired. Jasiek shrieked, fell in the mud, then jumped up again and was lost in the darkness of the forest.

A Polish Scene. Translated by Joseph Solomon. In SELECTED POLISH TALES. Translated by Else C. M. Benecke and Marie Busch. London, New York [etc.] H. Milford, Oxford University Press [1921]. p.269–281.

Remorse. Fragment from his ZIEMIA OBIECANA (The Promised Land).

Remorse, by Ladislas Reymont. Translated by Michael H. Dziewicki. In THE WORLD'S GREAT CATHOLIC LITERATURE, edited by George N. Shuster . . . New York, Macmillan, 1942. p.344–345.

Sąd. Translated as *The Trial.*

Résumé. On a cold March night the miller was finishing his supper when a crowd of peasants began to pour into his room. When he finished eating they firmly demanded to know the identity of the thieves who had robbed him. Pressed by the threatening and angry peasants, the miller finally confessed that the robbers were the two Gajdas and the Starszy (the policeman). They had robbed not only the miller, but also many peasants in the village.

One of the peasants, Jędrzej, led the crowd to punish the guilty. A smaller group was sent to the policeman's house. Jędrzej led the larger group to the house of the Gajdas. The two men were bound with ropes and taken to the church door. The people's trial followed. The priest was out, so they were asked to make a confession to the crowd. Old Gajda yielded and confessed his crimes. Young Gajda was still defiant when the crowd fell upon them, and a few minutes later nothing remained of the two men at the church door but a black, shapeless mass.

Soon the news spread that the policeman escaped unpunished. It was the miller's daughter who had warned him. Jędrzej gave orders to follow him.

Slowly the miller dragged himself homewards. So it was his own daughter. . . . He was trembling as in a fever and he wept.

The Trial, by Władysław Reymont. In MORE TALES BY POLISH AUTHORS. Translated by Else C. M. Benecke and Marie Busch. New York, Longmans, Green and company, 1916. p.86–111.

The Trial, by Wladyslaw Reymont. [Translated by Else C. M. Benecke and Marie Busch.] In POLISH AUTHORS OF TODAY AND YESTERDAY . . . Selected by Irena Morska. New York, S. F. Vanni [c1947]. p.107–127.

Śmierć. Translated as *Death.*

Résumé. The old man was dying. His daughter, Antkowa,[20] was tugging at him and threatening that she would not let him die in her hut. Let him go to Julina to whom the old man had left his property. The sick man begged for a priest, to which the woman

---

[20] Antek's wife.

answered with curses and abuses. Fifteen acres of land, the pigs, three cows, furniture and clothes—all had gone to Julina and Tomek! But the priest came, and the old man received the holy sacrament.

When night fell Antkowa suddenly clutched the dying man under the armpits, and ordered her daughter Magda to open the door. The penetrating cold restored the dying man to consciousness. She dragged him across the yard, pulled him into the pigsty and dropped him there, close to the wall. She opened his shirt, tore off his chaplet, and took it with her. The chaplet contained abundant money for the funeral.

Next morning, when Antek and his wife entered the pigsty, a sight of horror struck them. One half of the dead man's body had frozen to the floor. They brought the corpse into the hut; the deaf-mute washed the body. They gave notice to the priest and to the sołtys[21] of their inability to pay for the funeral. Tomek, under pressure of public opinion, finally agreed to bear the expense. When Tomek's wife came to the house there was a fight between the two women.

After the funeral Tomek invited everybody to his hut. Antek, his wife and two others went to the inn. He soon got drunk. In the raging storm Antkowa brought her husband home and dragged him into bed.

Death, by Władysław St. Reymont. In SELECTED POLISH TALES. Translated by Else C. M. Benecke and Marie Busch. London, New York [etc.] H. Milford, Oxford University Press [1921]. p.282–306.

Death. Translated by Else C. M. Benecke and Marie Busch. In A WORLD OF GREAT STORIES; edited by Hiram Haydn and John Cournos [and] Board of Editors. New York, Crown Publishers [c1947]. p.649–663.

Preceded by a brief note about the author.

"From POLISH TALES BY MODERN AUTHORS, Oxford University Press."

Death, by Ladislas Reymont. Translated by Else C. M. Benecke

---

21 The village mayor.

and Marie Busch. In THE NOBEL PRIZE TREASURY, edited by Marshall McClintock. Garden City, N.Y., Doubleday, 1948. p.264–277.

Death. Translated by Else C. M. Benecke and Marie Busch. In GREAT STORIES BY NOBEL PRIZE WINNERS, edited by Leo Hamalian and Edmund L. Volpe. New York, the Noonday Press [c1959]. p.[129]–149.

Preceded by a brief note about the author.

The Sowers. Fragment from his CHŁOPI (THE PEASANTS).

The Sowers. Translated by S. Żółtowska. In *Poland* (New York), V, 1924. p.209–211, 258, 260–262.

The Sowers. Translated by S. Żółtowska. In *The Slavonic Review*, III, 1924–25. p.37–45.

Suka. Translated as *The Bitch.*

Résumé. A ten-year-old girl, instead of studying her French grammar, goes for a horse-back ride to the wood with Witek, the young boy who tends the foals. The ride is breathtaking, the games in the woods exhilarating. They are fascinated with the beauty of the forest. There is no end to their joy.

Their forbidden excursion is reported to the mother of the girl who gives a merciless whipping to her daughter and furiously beats the boy. The governess speaks her mind and, as a result, is discharged.

Comforted by his mother, Witek looks for his dog, Finka. She was about to have puppies. When he finds her, Finka behaves very strangely—as though she had rabies. The master brings his gun, aims at her head, shoots, but only wounds her. The dog disappears in the rushing water of the river by the mill. The floodgates had been open, and the water was flooding the lowlands.

At night the wet and bleeding Finka returns home and licks the sleeping boy's face and throat until she wakes him. She has brought two puppies from across the river. She did not have rabies. She behaved strangely, because through the rushing water she could not reach her puppies on the other side. Licking the lad and her little ones, the bitch dies. Trying to warm the orphaned puppies, who were trembling with cold, the boy resolves to bring them up.

(The title of the story may be taken as a play on words. It seems to refer not only to Finka, but also to the girl's mother. It is the dog's love and sacrifice for her puppies which is "human," while supposedly bitch-like is the mother's lashing of her misunderstood daughter.)

First printed 1894.

The Bitch. Translated by Ilona Ralf Sues. In POLISH SHORT STORIES, selected by Zbigniew Żabicki. Warsaw, Polonia Publishing House, 1960. p.191–[211].

Tomek Baran. Translated as *Tomek Baran.*

Résumé. Joy in the tavern was riotous, but on Tomek Baran's heart grievous suffering lay like a stone. He confessed to old Jagustynka that he was discharged without pay from his job on the railroad. As he had never brought any presents to the foreman, they denounced him as a thief. His wife was dead and he had four children. He had no land. Jagustynka advised him to go to the village priest to ask for help.

Tomek went to the priest and told him his story. He was afraid that his children might die of starvation. The Reverend Father gave him a few kopeks, a small piece of bread for the children, and offered to celebrate a holy mass on his behalf. He promised that he would put in a word for him "where it would do some good."

Tomek returned to his hut. He boiled water, poured it on the bread, and woke up his children. Greedily they applied themselves to the bread soup. For two days they had had nothing to eat.

The next day in the afternoon he took his oldest daughter, Marysia, out and the two set themselves to the hard task of digging out the fir trees from under the all-covering snow. For this work Tomek received a ruble in cash from the forest clerk. He took the ruble to the priest to pay for the holy mass, but the priest would not accept it. He was so touched that he presented Tomek with a bushel of potatoes. Elevated in spirit, Tomek returned home.

Then came a blizzard. Tomek exhausted all provisions. He begged the railroad foreman to take him back; he was painfully humiliated in the attempt. In despair he tore away from the dogs a sheep that had died of the rot and was buried in the snow. With a disfigured face and a bitten hand after his fight with the dogs, he brought his booty home. The next day his beloved son, Józiek, fell seriously ill and died soon after.

After the burial the village peasants gathered in Tomek's hut bringing various gifts of food, and offered to take care of the children until spring. Old Jagustynka decided to stay in his hut and cook for him. Tomek went to work cutting faggots.

Written in 1897.

Tomek Baran. Translated by George Rapall Noyes. In GREAT SHORT NOVELS OF THE WORLD; a Collection of Complete Tales Chosen from the Literatures of All Periods and Countries, by Barrett H. Clark. Albert and Charles Boni [1932]. v.2, p.928–961.

Preceded by an introduction and a brief note about the author.

W głębinach. Translated as *The Traitor.*

Résumé. Theodatus, the Syrian, a slave lutist in the powerful house of the Claudians, crept cautiously through the gardens of the Caesars, followed by a string of moving shadows. The night was heavenly: moonlit and serene. Theodatus laid his ear to the ground. The Christians were approaching. He instructed the Roman leader of the armed detachment to keep silent and not to strike. They would take the Christians in the catacombs.

Soon three aged men wearing shepherds' cloaks of goatskin, barefoot, with neglected beards and bald heads appeared in the moonlight. "Lamb of God," murmured Theodatus, falling on his knees. He assured them that all the brethren had passed that way in safety while he had been keeping watch. He received a blessing from one of the men, and the three disappeared in the darkness.

Theodatus told the Roman that it was the archpriest who had just passed. He himself had joined the Christians some time ago and had been tortured for the new faith. But now for betraying the Christians and revealing the entry to the catacombs, he was promised by the Emperor freedom, riches, and the dignity of a Roman citizen.

They marched for about an hour. Theodatus approached one of the houses, knocked, and pronounced the words, "The Lamb." When a man from inside was handing him a flaming torch, Theodatus plunged his sword into his throat. Behind the house, under a stone marked with ivy, was the entry to the catacombs. The Roman, with drawn sword, decided to descend with the Syrian. Flames of small oil lamps flickered in deep recesses. The Roman was now livid with terror. After a prolonged march, they saw the man who had blessed Theodatus on the way, dressed in white robes, reading: "Bless them which persecute you . . ." In an agony of fear and despair, Theodatus began to run. But in any direction he turned, he saw a statue of Christ standing before him with outstretched arms, gazing upon him . . .

In vain that night and thereafter, did the Emperor await the return of the Roman and of Theodatus.

The Traitor. Translated by K. Żuk-Skarszewska. In *Poland* (New York), VIII, 1927. p.331–333, 372–374, 376.

The Traitor, by Ladislas Reymont. [Translated by K. Żuk-Skarszewska.] In POLISH SHORT STORIES, by Joseph Weyssenhof, Piotr Choynowski, Kornel Makuszynska [and others] . . . London, Minerva Publishing Company [1943]. p.158–165.

W pruskiej szkole. Translated as *The Lord's Prayer.*

Résumé. It was the end of the last period. In the school yard mothers were waiting for their children.

The teacher rapidly made the sign of the cross and began to drone monotonously. "Vater unser, der Du bist . . ." Not one voice of the children had joined his. He started again, and again there was silence. He called one of the boys. "I won't say the Lord's prayer in German," was his trembling answer. The teacher slapped the boy's face with all his might, grabbed him by the hair, dragged him to the desk, and beating him furiously, he yelled, "You must speak German, you Polish swine." One by one he called the boys and the girls, and the same scene was repeated over and over again.

He omitted one small girl, about eight years old. Through her tears she whispered, "I am a Pole too, and I won't say the Lord's prayer in German." It was as though he had gone mad. He beat her so hard that the whole class joined in her cries. Almost unconscious, she still gasped between the blows, "I won't say the Lord's prayer in German; I won't, I won't, I won't . . ."

First printed in the Kurjer Warszawski, No. 100, 1919.

The Lord's Prayer, by Wladyslaw Reymont. Translated by Irena Morska. In POLISH AUTHORS OF TODAY AND YESTERDAY . . . Selected by Irena Morska. New York, S. F. Vanni [c1947]. p.103–106.

Winter. Fragment from his CHŁOPI (THE PEASANTS).

Winter, by Ladislas Reymont. Translated by Michael H. Dziewicki. In WORLD'S GREATEST CHRISTMAS STORIES, edited by Eric Posselt. Chicago, Ziff-Davis Publishing Company [c1949]. p.311–336.

Winter, by Ladislas Reymont. Translated by Michael H. Dziewicki. In THE WORLD'S GREATEST CHRISTMAS STORIES. Edited by Eric Posselt . . . New York, Prentice-Hall, 1950. p.293–317.

Wołanie. Translated as *The Mother (the Call).*

Résumé. Mother heard the call distinctly. She dragged herself to the window, praying in a quick feverish whisper. She had offered her only son in the Polish struggle for freedom.

From far distances the voice came back to her calling for help. She recognized the voice of her son. She did not hesitate; she left her home and her loved ones and went on an unknown road. "I am coming, my little one, I am coming to you, my son." "The Mother," whispered women, kissing the bloody stains left by her feet. She went into raging battles. "My son is waiting for me," she would say without fear. Her son had a thousand faces, a thousand wounds. Everyone seemed to be her own son, and suffered likewise. She wiped off their bleeding foreheads and kissed their open wounds. They were dying in her arms with smiles of happiness on their frozen lips.

First published in Słowo Polskie, No. 41, Lwów, 1915.

The Mother (the Call), by Wladyslaw Reymont. Translated by Irena Morska. In POLISH AUTHORS OF TODAY AND YESTERDAY . . . Selected by Irena Morska. New York, S. F. Vanni [c1947]. p.99–102.

Rodziewicz, Marja, *see* Rodziewiczówna, Maria

Rodziewiczówna, Maria (1863–1944)

Rodziewiczówna is the author of a long list of novels which enjoyed a passing popularity. The most characteristic of them and the best known is DEWAJTIS (1889), translated by S. C. de Soissons as DEVAYTIS (London, 1901). It symbolizes a Polish country-estate man whose roots in the Lithuanian soil reached as deep and were as strong as those of the old Dewajtis oak.

Noc. Translated as *A Night's Tragedy.*

Résumé. The sun had set. Within the hut four people were resting. An elderly peasant was smoking his pipe; his wife was peeling potatoes; a young peasant accompanied on his violin a young woman singing by the fire. She was young and beautiful, her eyes large and dark. The door of the hut opened. The song ceased suddenly; the young woman shrank back. The newcomer was a young man, strongly built, with a quiet, sad face. He was dressed in the squire's livery. He took off his hunting-bag and gun and placed them in the corner. "Good evening, Maryuka," he said. She returned the greeting indifferently. To the invitations to stay overnight, the young man replied that he would remain an hour, until the moon should rise. Jacob complained that Maryuka would never sing to him; in their home a song had been a rare pleasure. He asked his wife to get ready. The old man begged Jacob not to punish her too severely. The old woman pleaded that he not beat her daughter.

The couple took the small path leading to the river. The new moon cast its light on them. The young man could hear jeering whispers from the village: "Did you see, stupid Jacob has come for his wife again . . ." He never uttered a word.

They got in a little boat. Jacob crossed to the opposite side of the river in the shadow of the low bushes. They were alone on that quiet May night. Maryuka lay in the shadow, feigning sleep. Suddenly the forester spoke up, softly and caressingly. He spoke of his great, tender and passionate love for Maryuka which had been rejected. When she would run away from him, people advised him to beat her, but he never did. He grew up in the woods, among the animals and birds, where he never saw a male kill his mate. He forgot how to smile, and the world appeared grey and dull to him. Now he decided to put an end to it. She preferred Maciej for whom Maryuka was just a plaything; from her he would return to his wife. Now he would give her to Maciej. He overpowered her with one hand; with the other he bound her head with a kerchief. He wavered a second, and then threw her as a prey to the whirlpools.

The man grovelled at the bottom of the boat, sobbing in abandonment to grief.

From her collection, z GŁUSZY (*From the Wilderness*).

A Night's Tragedy, by Marya Rodziewicz. Translation anonymous. In THE MASTERPIECE LIBRARY OF SHORT STORIES . . . Edited by J. A. Hammerton . . . London, The Educational Book Company [1920] Vol.13, p.328–335.

A fragmentary translation.

Pierścień. Translated as *The Ring.*

The Ring, by Marja Rodziewicz. Translated by Jadwiga Morawska. In *Poland* (New York), VII, 1926. p.298–301, 309–311, 333–334.

W noc grudniową. Translated as *A December Night.*

A December Night. Translated by Jadwiga Morawska. In *Poland* (New York), VII, 1926. p.741–743, 763–764.

Różewicz, Tadeusz (1921–   )

The most prominent of the postwar generation of poets in Poland, Różewicz published his first collection of short stories in 1955. OPADŁY LIŚCIE Z DRZEW (The Trees Have Shed Their Leaves) may be taken to represent an expression of sentiments of the present generation of young people in Poland which has grown up in the shadow of World War Two, and which still cannot rid itself of the nightmare of war.

Nowa szkoła filozoficzna. Translated as *The New Philosophical School.*

Résumé. (The story is told in the first person.)

A young student who had neglected his studies because of his active participation in the war went to a professor of philosophy in Warsaw with a request to attend seminar lectures without having to go through all the preparatory courses of study. The professor asked him what philosophical writings he had read. The student was eighteen when the war broke out. He vaguely mentioned Plato, Nietzsche, Bergson, Spencer, Draper, Freud and Schopenhauer.

Then he returned to his lonely room, and asked himself questions about the meaning of life. He lay on his bed and thought of what it really entailed to be a human being. What did it mean to be a member of the human race? What is left of man when he has ceased eating, washing, reading, talking and buying?

He lay on his bed so intensely that he had almost become one with his bed. He had locked himself up and lit the lamp covered with a hood made from an old newspaper. No one now could throw him out of bed or stop him from eating his sausages. If he were to die instantly, he would have no last wish before his death. So far as he was concerned people just lived and died. Everything had been explained ultimately. There was no morality. And even if there were some remnants of the old morality, people lived apart from them.

The pipes in the house had broken down again, and the inhabitants had to smell their own odors. The neighbor's daughter, sad and flat-chested, stood guard at the toilet door, making sure that nobody forgot to flush the toilet. A moment ago the toilet had been used by an old woman who was soon to die. She had neglected flushing the toilet. The subtle gentleman, the guard's father, who had been feeding his anemic life on the poetry of Claudel, Mallarmé, and Nerval, became as angry as a village dog, and kept barking, "Pigs, pigs . . ." Again the corridor was quiet.

The young man thought that he could be alone. But now he was on the brink of madness. He needed a confirmation of his life by others and wanted to be near people. He yearned for a living man. He waited for him. But he did not come. He walked out, locked the door, and slowly ambled down the stairs. He stopped and listened.

Written between November 1955 and December 1956.
First published in Twórczość, *Warsaw, February, 1957.*

The New Philosophical School (a Postwar Story). Translated by Paul Mayewski. In THE BROKEN MIRROR; A COLLECTION OF WRITINGS FROM CONTEMPORARY POLAND, edited by Pawel Mayewski . . . Introduction by Lionel Trilling. New York, Random House [1958]. p.11–29.

Piwo. Translated as *Beer.*

Résumé. (The story is told in the first person.)

Gustav, the narrator, was pushed by Henry into a murky tavern. Inside, Henry became provoked by the looks of a fat, red-necked man, an ugly opportunist, who came to Gustav to light his cigarette.

The two men soon left the tavern. Henry was on his way to the station; he was leaving town by the night express. He invited Gustav to accompany him. They waded through puddles; a cold, autumn rain was streaming down in buckets. Henry was uneasy. He talked disjointedly, jumping from one subject to another and leaving sentences unfinished.

They walked into the station's stuffy waiting room. Henry pulled Gustav into a corner, sat down at a table, and kept silent. After a while he pointed to a scratched out black sign, and explained that this was the place where the Bahnschutzpolitzei post had been during the German occupation. He used to sit exactly on that same spot waiting for his mother to come back from her food hunting trips in the country. She had a bad heart so Henry, her only son, would help her carry the stuff home.

Once he was waiting for his mother over a glass of beer, when he saw the Bahnschutz strike her on the head. She had the look of a frightened child. Henry did not move. Just at that moment, his imagination worked on a heroic story, how he slaps a German officer's face for behaving improperly toward an unfamiliar, elderly woman.

That night Henry returned home late and drunk. He went to bed and dreamed that he had become an invisible man who performed many heroic deeds against the Germans. When he opened his eyes, his mother was bending over him. She stroked his hair, and said, "I was afraid you'd start defending me. I was so terribly afraid . . ." She kissed his hand and pressed her face to his.

Written in 1947.

From OPADŁY LIŚCIE Z DRZEW (*The Trees Have Shed Their Leaves*), *1955.*

Beer. Translated by Jadwiga Zwolska. In CONTEMPORARY POLISH SHORT STORIES, selected by Andrzej Kijowski. Warsaw, Polonia Publishing House, 1960. p.[243]–252.

Beer. Translated by Jadwiga Zwolska; illustrated by Franciszek Barącz. In *Poland; Illustrated Magazine,* No. 1 (65) 1960. p.26–28.

Wzorowe małżeństwo. Translated as *The Exemplary Couple.*

The Exemplary Couple. Translation anonymous. In *Poland; Illustrated Magazine,* No. 5 (21) 1956. p.27.

Rudnicki, Adolf (1912–   )

Having come from a poor Jewish family, in his early writings the author portrayed Jewish life and customs. Since the war Rudnicki has become the most powerful writer in Poland, dealing with the Nazi crimes against Polish Jews. This is the theme of the author's novel, ZŁOTE OKNA (GOLDEN WINDOWS, 1955), and of his numerous short stories. His short story collections include SZEKSPIR (Shakespeare, 1948) and UCIECZKA Z JASNEJ POLANY (An Escape from Jasna Polana, 1949), a part of the cycle which Rudnicki calls "Epoka pieców" (The Era of Crematoria). Both were later reprinted (without the title story, UCIECZKA Z JASNEJ POLANY) with three new stories added in ŻYWE I MARTWE MORZE (1952), and translated—again with some changes—as THE DEAD AND THE LIVING SEA AND OTHER STORIES (Warsaw, 1957).

A selection of his stories appeared in this country under the title ASCENT TO HEAVEN (New York, 1951). A larger collection of fifty stories, 50 OPOWIADAŃ, was published in Warsaw in 1966.

Czysty nurt. Translated as *The Clear Stream/The Crystal Stream.*

Résumé. (A story of love doomed to perish through the fate of war.)

Abel, a gifted and promising young architect, taken prisoner of war, left his beautiful wife, Amelia, in Warsaw. Abel was assigned to the "Judenblock," the building in the Officers' Camp reserved for the Jews. It was only now that he realized how much he loved his wife. Her postcards sustained his life. When of necessity she was changing her name and there was a break in her correspondence (she lived, like other Jews, continually under sentence of death), his suffering was more than he could bear. To his generous offer of freedom for her, she responded with letters full of passionate love.

But soon after this her letters suddenly stopped. There came one note written with three different kinds of pencil. It was obvious that she was forcing herself to write.

In October 1944, officers who had taken part in the Warsaw Uprising arrived at the camp. One of the new arrivals confirmed that there was someone else in Amelia's life. As much as he expected it and had resigned himself to the fact, Abel was almost choked by the news.

The Russian forces overran Camp 3 E in May 1945, and Abel returned to Poland. He made his home in Łódź. One day he went to Warsaw, and when he was looking over the vast expanse of the rubble on the spot of the former ghetto, he met Amelia. She looked beautiful. Abel's love for her was not dead even now. When hope began to lurk in his soul, she told him that it was not only a question of the other man. She had a six-months-old child.

Abel realized that fate had defeated him. He felt her bend over him, and he saw tears in her eyes. Then—she left him.

From his SZEKSPIR *(Shakespeare), 1948.*

The Clear Stream. In his THE DEAD AND THE LIVING SEA AND OTHER STORIES. Translated by Jadwiga Zwolska. Warsaw, Polonia Publishing House, 1957. p.257–[282].

The Crystal Stream. In his ASCENT TO HEAVEN. Translated by H. C. Stevens. Illustrated by Mieczyslaw Piotrowski. New York, Roy Publishers [c1951]. p.77–104.

Ginący Daniel. Translated as *A Dying Man/The Dying Daniel.*

Résumé. (A story of the tragic fate of an innocent man unsuccessfully trying to clear himself of a false accusation.)

Daniel Dzikowski slipped for a few minutes into No. 22 Trzy Korony Street on August 1, 1944, to thank Zybert for having kept him at his home for the past several weeks. After leaving Zybert he no longer found it possible to get through to the Ochota District, as just then the Warsaw Uprising had begun. He returned to Zybert who welcomed him warmly.

As a sub-tenant in the house he had to do all kinds of hard and dangerous chores. One night Daniel was accused by his former friend Rafael of having sold a Jew named Kaliski into the hands of the Gestapo. (Both Rafael and Dzikowski were Jews.) Daniel was taken to the lock-up.

His "crime" was that Kaliski had bought a "place" in his passport supplied by the Honduras Consulate in Berne and, deceived by the Germans, instead of being taken to safety abroad, was cremated in an extermination camp. Daniel had put Kaliski on his passport only when the latter exerted on him the maximum of pressure.

When released from jail, Daniel learned that his savior was not Zybert, but his maid, omnipotent Jadwiga. Though free, Daniel could not remove the stigma of suspicion. Zybert no longer treated him as friend. Daniel made frantic efforts to clear up his case, but all in vain. Fate was against him. Witnesses of his innocence were either dead or through cowardice refrained from doing anything.

Locked up again, this time without any charge but simply because he looked suspicious, Daniel found himself in the company of the German S.S. men. By the tragic freak of fate he was executed together with the mass-murderers of the Jews.

After the Uprising the bodies of Dzikowski and his friend Kazio were found at No. 22 not burnt, but as though cast in lead. Jadwiga's head had rolled along the street.

From his SZEKSPIR (*Shakespeare*), *1948*.

A Dying Man. In his ASCENT TO HEAVEN. Translated by H. C. Stevens. Illustrated by Mieczyslaw Piotrowski. New York, Roy Publishers [c1951]. p.107–166.

The Dying Daniel. In his THE DEAD AND THE LIVING SEA AND OTHER STORIES. Translated by Jadwiga Zwolska. Warsaw, Polonia Publishing House, 1957. p.201–[255].

Józefów. Translated as *Józefów.*

Résumé. (Written in the first person.)

The narrator's friend, Severyn B., invited him to his weather-beaten, wooden cottage in Józefów. He felt that the author-narrator had done no writing for months because he lacked conditions conducive to contemplation. Severyn told the narrator that he would have a neighbor in the "villa," a young tailor who had spent seven of his twenty-six years of life in prison. He had tuberculosis and was in Józefów on "health leave." Theresa, the "prisoners' auntie" was responsible for "planting him" on Severyn.

Józefów is all pines and sand. The pines are checked by board fences behind which stand ugly wooden cottages. With the beginning of summer all Warsaw comes here. Then, Józefów bubbles over with life not only at the suburban railway station, but also behind the board fences. In the summer, Józefów is wide open; in the winter its cottages are locked and isolated from their neighbors. It was here in December that Joel Filut, the young tailor, was dying. The narrator did not know whether his friend, Severyn, was aware that he was sending him to a dying man rather than to a sick one.

When Joel left prison several months earlier he found the Party dispersed. (Before World War Two the Communist Party in Poland which is here referred to was illegal.) Thanks to "Theresa of the prisoners" Joel was examined by a doctor; he had but a month or two to live. He was sent to Józefów—to die. And Joel Filut was dying the way consumptives die: with moments of excitability, high fevers, hemorrhages, injections, ice packs on his chest, and with the inseparable bottle into which he expectorated phlegm. Joel became very fond of the narrator; the two had become friends.

It was the year of 1936. The dying man never thought of himself; all his thoughts were centered on the Civil War in Spain. General Franco was preparing for a finishing blow to Madrid. The national troops were beginning to flank the city. But Joel did not lose hope.

On the eve of Christmas the narrator bade the sick man goodnight. Hours later he was awakened by the heavy steps of Joel. In agony, Joel caught the narrator's wrist convulsively and managed to whisper his last greetings to the fighting proletariat of Spain. No soldier in Madrid had a more beautiful death.

On a sunny, frosty Christmas Day Joel's body, no longer tormented with pain, was entrusted to the stone-hard earth.

Written in Lwów in 1940.

Józefów; in a Warsaw Suburban Resort. In his THE DEAD AND THE LIVING SEA AND OTHER STORIES. Translated by Jadwiga Zwolska. Warsaw, Polonia Publishing House, 1957. p.7–[21].

Koń. Translated as *The Horse.*

Résumé. Jacob Kagan, a small town tailor, was going to his son in Warsaw. More frequently of late after his wife's death, he would feel lonely, and people advised him to marry again. But Jacob Kagan was very attached to his son, Zacharias, who, because of his great height, was affectionately called "the Horse." The father was small like a child, while the son was a giant. Zacharias had the build of an athlete and the hands of a porter, yet he had hair like a girl's, and eyes like a child's. A gentle smile never left his face. He always worked very hard. No, Jacob would not give his son a stepmother.

One day when Zacharias was eighteen he told his father that he did not believe in God. He called himself an enlightened man. Asked whether this was what he had learned in the back room of Gąsiorowski's bakery, he replied that it was the duty of every working man with a feeling for humanity to help change the world. When Jacob warned his son of the danger of interfering with the course of the world, Zacharias replied that it might be too late for the warning. They had locked up his friend, David, that very afternoon.

Jacob Kagan became frightened and decided that Zacharias should go to Warsaw. He had an acquaintance there, Zelmanowicz, a tailor whose son, Reuben, was Zacharias's age. When things quieted down here, Zacharias would return. In Warsaw "the Horse" did not abandon the dangerous ideas about "turning the world upside down," and waded in deeper and deeper. Soon Jacob received a letter from young Reuben Zelmanowicz, informing him of his son's arrest.

Jacob suffered as only a father can suffer. He was afraid to raise his eyes when for the first time he was permitted to see his son through the bars. "The Horse" greeted him in a voice he might have used had he come home a free man. After five years Zacharias was released. Jacob found himself delaying his request that his son come home immediately.

When Jacob received news of the death of his old friend, he set out immediately for Warsaw. On that June night the journey seemed endless. Arriving at Zelmanowicz's apartment on the fourth floor of the house on Nowolipki Street, he was alarmed to discover that his son had not been in for twelve days. His friend's son, Reuben, had been injured and his head was bandaged. Jacob was completely bewildered. Three days had passed since Jacob's arrival —he rushed about the scorching city like a madman as he searched for his son. He felt that Reuben was concealing something. Finally, Reuben admitted that Zacharias had left with Steve, who was much admired as "one of their best." Police spies, he said, shot them, throwing their bodies into the river. A week ago Steve's body was washed ashore and was buried with proper respect. The police had staged a massacre at the cemetery, where Reuben had sustained his head injury. Only today news had been received that the body of Zacharias was lying in W. . . Street. Jacob's face became deathly pale.

Chaim Leser, the head man in cemetery matters, declared that

223

it must have been a suicide. Thereupon, Jacob went to the head of the Jewish community. Ready to fall on his knees to beg for a humane, Jewish burial for his son, he learned that nothing could be done. To avoid crowds and demonstrations, the order was to bury Zacharias's body at night. A motor-hearse was sent to W. . . Street after midnight, but Jacob was not allowed to walk behind the hearse. The car sped through empty Warsaw streets. Two gravediggers dug the grave near the wall and in the light of the candles Jacob saw earth fall on his son's corpse. He remained at the grave in a state of shock and grief. When the dawn lit up the sky, some strong hands lifted him from the grave, and massaged his benumbed limbs with tenderness. The old tailor heard again the voice of life, and wept.

Written in Lwów, January 1941.

The Horse. In his THE DEAD AND THE LIVING SEA AND OTHER STORIES. Translated by Jadwiga Zwolska. Warsaw, Polonia Publishing House, 1957. p.23–[44].

The Horse. [Translated by Jadwiga Zwolska.] In *Poland; Illustrated Magazine,* No. 8 (60) 1959. p.25–28.

Preceded by a brief note about the author, by Wiktor Woroszylski.

Sądny dzień. Translated as *Yom Kippur.*

Yom Kippur. Translated by Reuben Ainsztein. In *Polish Perspectives; Monthly Review,* III, No. 7, 1960. p.27–37.

From his KROWA (The Cow), 1959.

Preceded by an article on the author by Henryk Bereza, "The Measure of Morality." p.24–26.

Wielkanoc. Translated as *Easter.*

Résumé. The author describes in flashes the annihilation by the Germans of the Warsaw ghetto. The title comes from the date of the massacre which began on the first night of the "Jewish Easter." When the Jews commenced the struggle they did not look to victory; all they hoped for was to die like human beings. Against the might of the Nazis, all they had to offer in resistance was one machine gun, a few rickety small arms and egg-like grenades which did not explode.

At the first sign of resistance, the Germans began a classical siege of the ghetto, as though it were a fortress. Methodically the artillery brought fire and destruction, and the soldiers followed only when the last vestige of life departed from the ruins.

When a ghetto house was aflame, the half-insane inhabitants would slip like lizards from floor to floor, ever higher. If a German bullet did not kill them before they reached the top, the husband would pass the child to his wife, all three would give one another a last kiss and then they jumped.

The tragedy of the ghetto lay not only in the brutal massacre of the helpless human beings, but also in the shameless German lies about the "communists and Poles who helped build the [ghetto] fortress," and in the human indifference. The detonation shook the ground, but the world around seemed deaf.

The narrator, himself a Jew hiding in Warsaw, met a young Jewish woman in the street. Risking detection and the fate of the Jews in the ghetto, they talked to each other. Her only wish was that one day someone would immortalize the death of the Jewish martyrs and heroes.

The author-narrator feels that now he has no creative power; his brain is shattered and his heart dried up. But when his weariness is gone he would like to remember the words of that young woman who did not survive.

> *Written in April 1945.*
> *From his* SZEKSPIR *(Shakespeare), 1948.*

Easter. Translated by Jadwiga Zwolska. In CONTEMPORARY POLISH SHORT STORIES, selected by Andrzej Kijowski. Warsaw, Polonia Publishing House, 1960. p.[255]–264.

Easter. In his THE DEAD AND THE LIVING SEA AND OTHER STORIES. Translated by Jadwiga Zwolska. Warsaw, Polonia Publishing House, 1957. p.191–[199].

Wielki Stefan Konecki. Translated as *The Great Stefan Konecki.*

Résumé. In December 1939 the war flung the narrator into the streets of Lwów. He was not yet thirty. At that time Stefan Konecki, the chairman of the Lwów branch of the Polish Writers Association, was the uncrowned king of Lwów writers. The narrator turned to Stefan Konecki for help, and the help was granted.

When other writers joined the official "Organizational Committee" the narrator was the only one who continued calling on Konecki, although the latter's political orientation was dangerously to the right. Later, when the office for two writers only could no longer be justified to the authorities, he moved to Konecki's private apartment and occupied one of his three rooms.

The narrator, however, longed for Warsaw, and was given an opportunity to go there. Konecki, too, received an invitation from his old friend in Warsaw, Dr. Braun. But he declined, remarking that only a madman would return at a time like this "to the denomination of Moses." Konecki's real name was Kon.

In Warsaw the narrator was appointed one of Dr. Braun's assistants in the distribution of Western funds in relieving the Jewish misery. Once he visited Konecki's flat in Lwów, and was greeted by his secretary who informed him that Konecki had been sent to a camp.

One night someone entered the narrator's room in the dark. Groping for an armchair the newcomer sat down. The narrator had a feeling that it was Konecki, but the visitor did not utter a sound. When the light came on the narrator saw a face that looked as if taken out of its own tomb. It was the face of a terrified owl. His body was wrapped in a sack. And he stank. It was the great Stefan Konecki.

Victim of blackmailers, Konecki had been taken to Gestapo. He had gone through the depths of misery of an extermination camp and had escaped miraculously. (These details were supplied later by Dr. Braun.) Now he started singing an old Jewish song. The narrator turned round and saw an Ukrainian militia-man standing at the door.

The Great Stefan Konecki. In his ASCENT TO HEAVEN. Translated by H. C. Stevens. Illustrated by Mieczyslaw Piotrowski. New York, Roy Publishers [c1951]. p.169–204.

Wniebowstąpienie. Translated as *Ascent to Heaven*/*Raisa's Ascent to Heaven.*

Résumé. The day after the German-Russian war started on June 22, 1941, all Lwów was on the move. Raisa, a Jewish student of the Conservatoire, left the house with the intention of meeting Tamarkin, and then of evacuating with him and the other students. On the way, at a certain corner she decided to turn left instead of right. She wanted to say good-bye to Sebastian. This turn changed her life.

Raisa never left Sebastian's home to meet Tamarkin. She stayed on and married Sebastian, a Jewish doctor of psychiatry, although brutal German persecutions of the Jews in Lwów had already started. From then on they struggled to escape what seemed to be their fate.

After Sebastian's father and mother were murdered by the Germans (taken for the soap, as the saying went), the young couple moved to Warsaw. Every day of their life there was fraught with danger. Enemies were everywhere, even among the Jews, but Sebastian found his greatest enemy in himself. He had carried some seeds of insanity while still in Lwów, but now the seeds came to fruition. Sebastian was dangerous not only to himself and to his wife, but also to their hosts, friends, and neighbors. Every Jew outside of the ghetto lived under an assumed Polish name. To be exposed was synonymous with death.

Raisa made heroic efforts to save Sebastian, but finally she succumbed to her friend Bukin's persuasive insistence (Bukin was in love with her) that it was her duty to poison her husband. They went to Bielany. When he lifted the poisoned tea to his lips, Raisa knocked the bottle away. She still loved him. A stray dog drank the spilled tea and, when Sebastian saw him die, insanity spread on his face again.

Help, so eagerly sought for Sebastian by Raisa, came too late. As a result of his own provocation he was taken by the Germans and shot.

When the Russians occupied Warsaw, Raisa's parents returned to the city from the depth of Russia to search for her. Eventually

Saul Wolkow found out that the Warsaw Uprising had caught his daughter in Żoliborz. Only a few shells fell on this part of the city, but one of them hit the house where she was staying. Raisa was buried in the ruins.

> From his UCIECZKA Z JASNEJ POLANY (*An Escape from Jasna Polana*), *1949*.

Ascent to Heaven. In his ASCENT TO HEAVEN. Translated by H. C. Stevens. Illustrated by Mieczyslaw Piotrowski. New York, Roy Publishers [c1951]. p.11–74.

Raisa's Ascent to Heaven. In his THE DEAD AND THE LIVING SEA AND OTHER STORIES. Translated by Jadwiga Zwolska. Warsaw, Polonia Publishing House, 1957. p.283–[339].

Złote okna. Translated as *Golden Windows.*

Golden Windows. In his THE DEAD AND THE LIVING SEA AND OTHER STORIES. Translated by Jadwiga Zwolska. Warsaw, Polonia Publishing House, 1957. p.[45]–[190].

A novel rather than a short story.

Not included in his Polish collection, ŻYWE I MARTWE MORZE (Warszawa, 1952).

Żywe i martwe morze. Translated as *The Dead and the Living Sea.*

Résumé. (A story of the Warsaw Ghetto during World War Two.)

On a chilly November Saturday when Emmanuel was twenty-one, he marched behind the hand cart piled with the worldly possessions of the Krakowski family. Following the Nazi ordinance, they were moving from Królewska Street to the northern district of the city. At his side walked his father, Jasha Krakowski. Jasha, a bookkeeper, had worked very hard all his life in order to maintain his home at a suitable level, and to give his three sons an education. Emmanuel was the second of them.

The Krakowskis were allotted one room in Nowolipki Street. Fifteen hundred people were squeezed into a medium-sized house, thirteen people in one room. During the first stage, the Germans allowed typhoid fever and starvation to destroy as many as six thousand people every month.

Before long, Emmanuel witnessed the first murders while he happened to be in the Britania Hotel in Nowolipki Street. About midnight a large Mercedes drove up, and six SS men alighted. Fifty-two persons were lined up against a vine-covered wall, and mowed down by a machine gun.

Emmanuel lost his family quite early. The first one was his pretty eighteen-year-old sister, Ann. Her school friend persuaded her to leave the ghetto. She was "pointed out" and taken with a group of about one hundred people to the woods near Warsaw, where they were shot by the Germans.

In the summer of 1942 two-thirds of the people behind the walls lost their lives. Shortly after the drive started, policemen came to the Krakowskis' courtyard, and all the residents were summoned. Trusting her certificate, Mrs. Krakowski went down; but she was taken with the others. The oldest son, a doctor, who came just then, joined his mother. Neither ever returned. Two days later the police came again, with two Latvians dressed in black. Wowa, Jasha's youngest son, stumbled against one of the Latvians. A moment later, he lay near the dust-bin in a pool of his own blood. Jasha was shot praying over his son's body. Emmanuel saw all this from the window.

The massacres continued. After the loss of all his family, Emmanuel left the house to live the life of the poor. On September 6, all who were left in the district were ordered to the neighborhood of Miła and Lubecki Streets. Selection was made on the spot, and those selected were loaded into railway cars. Emmanuel found a friendly boy named Mundek, whom he had met before, in the same car. Hardly able to breathe, they pulled the boards up from the floor; someone had an axe. Emmanuel was the first to jump. He fell, but a moment later he dashed into the woods. Later, returning to the railway line, he saw Mundek's yellow jacket— Mundek was dead. Walking along a side path, Emmanuel was seen by a man. His name was Kajetan Sitek; he lived in a poor cottage in a village forty kilometers from Warsaw. Instead of betraying him to the Germans, as Emmanuel had feared, Sitek hid him in the woods until night, then led him to his barn, where he kept him for three weeks, bringing him food.

229

Several years later, in 1945, the inhabitants driven out of Warsaw returned to their devastated city—a city without houses. Emmanuel found work in the office of an architect, where he designed houses. In the spring of 1949 a young woman of about twenty, a journalist representing a youth magazine, came to the architect's office. Emmanuel later learned that she was Kajetan Sitek's daughter. Kate filled the void in Emmanuel's heart, and three months later they were married. When their child was born, love enveloped everything.

One evening while Kate was out, an old, strangely dressed woman, Regina Borkowska, came to see Emmanuel. She wanted his help because her son, a half-Jew, had run away to marry a non-Jewish girl against his mother's wishes. While listening to the woman and replying to her plea, Emmanuel relived the horrors of the ghetto, and advised the woman to forget the past and to build anew. Her son had already married the girl, anyway. Telling his story, Emmanuel also mentioned that he had been married to "one of our women" before, but she had left him. His first wife had died at the massacre in the Britania Hotel in Nowolipki Street.

The Dead and the Living Sea. In his THE DEAD AND THE LIVING SEA AND OTHER STORIES. Translated by Jadwiga Zwolska. Warsaw, Polonia Publishing House, 1957. p.[341]–[420].

Rygier-Nałkowska, Zofja, *see* Nałkowska, Zofia

Samozwaniec, Magdalena

A Remedy for Robbers. [Original title not established.]

A Remedy for Robbers. Translated from the Polish of Magdalena Samozwaniec by W. A. Morison. In *The Slavonic (and East European) Review,* XXIII, 1945–46. p.7–9.

Schulz, Bruno (1892–1942)

Schulz's prose defies traditional realism. Some of his works could have come from the pen of Kafka, whose PROZESS he translated into Polish. His almost abnormal imagination transposes reality into another dimension. Through their lack of plot Schulz's stories may remind us of some modern French anti-novels of the Nathalie Sarraute type. The principal characters of his most typical work, SKLEPY CYNAMONOWE (1934; translated into English as CINNAMON SHOPS AND OTHER STORIES in London, 1963, and as THE STREET OF CROCODILES in the American edition, New York, 1963), are the adolescent narrator Joseph, his parents and the servant girl Adela. Father becomes the victim of hallucinations; he behaves like a bird, hatches the eggs of exotic species, perches on a curtain-rod, and then, turning into a cockroach, disappears with the sweepings. In Schulz's fantastic world human beings diminish in size and fade away, while inanimate objects acquire human traits. The same four central figures appear in the SANATORIUM POD KLEPSYDRĄ (Sanatorium under the Hourglass, 1937) which continues in the mood similar to that of the CINNAMON SHOPS. The author was shot by the Nazis in 1942.

Manekiny. Translated as *The Mannequins.*

The Mannequins. Translation anonymous. In *Poland; Illustrated Magazine,* No. 10 (50) 1958. p.26–27.
From his SKLEPY CYNAMONOWE (CINNAMON SHOPS AND OTHER STORIES).

Mój ojciec wstępuje do strażaków. Translated as *My Father Joins the Fire Brigade.*

Résumé. After a trip in an old landau through the woods in the darkness of night (the coachman had no matches to light the lanterns), Joseph and his mother arrived home. Joseph, the narrator, was dropping off to sleep. The event described happened then, or it might have been on another occasion, after they had closed the shop and were returning home with the shop assistants. On the threshold of the lobby Mother uttered a cry of astonishment. In the middle of the room stood a magnificent, brazen knight-at-arms, arrayed with golden bucklers and an entire outfit of burnished armor. Sprouting out from beneath the heavy helmet, Joseph recognized Father's bristling beard and moustache.

He was speaking against Adela's petty mind. She, born without any imagination, burned with envy at the thought of anything rising above the commonplace; taking her turn and turning to the Mother, Adela bitterly complained that it was all because of raspberry juice. As a captain of the fire-brigade, Father took every bottle of the juice to those good-for-nothing scoundrels who did nothing but loaf. Father spoke again in defense of the "sons of fire" whose nature was beyond Adela's shallow mind. They seemed a gallant lot to Mother, but they appeared as irresponsible parasites to the senior shop-assistant.

In the middle of the argument Father blew a whistle and four young men in glittering helmets rushed into the room. Before Adela could do anything to stop them, they grabbed a large demijohn of raspberry juice and made a hasty escape with it. Father jumped on the window-sill. Sparkling in the glory of his apparel, he saluted and leaped out. Beneath the window eight firemen were stretching out an enormous sheet of canvas. It was such a wonderful sight that even Adela forgot her temper. Father placed himself at the head of the detachment, and they marched in file in the midst of applauding onlookers.

> From his SANATORIUM POD KLEPSYDRĄ (Sanatorium under the Hourglass), 1937.

My Father Joins the Fire Brigade. Translated by W. Stanley Moss and Zofia Tarnowska. In 10 CONTEMPORARY POLISH STORIES. Edited by Edmund Ordon; with an introduction by Olga Scherer-Virski. Detroit, Wayne State University Press, 1958. p.117–133.

Preceded by a note about the author and the translators.

Ptaki. Translated as Birds.

Birds. Translation anonymous. In Poland; Illustrated Magazine, No. 10 (50) 1958. p.25–26.

Preceded by a note about the author.

From his SKLEPY CYNAMONOWE (CINNAMON SHOPS AND OTHER STORIES).

Sienkiewicz, Henryk (1846–1916)

Probably the best-known Polish writer abroad and certainly the most translated, Sienkiewicz began his career as a journalist, literary critic, and a short story writer. He visited the United States in 1876–78, and a major portion of his LISTY Z PODRÓŻY DO AMERYKI (Letters from America), which he wrote for Warsaw papers, translated in part before, was published in 1959 in English as PORTRAIT OF AMERICA. Apart from such short stories as *The Lighthouse Keeper,* he expressed the patriotic feelings of Poles and their yearning for independence after the tragic end of the Polish Uprising in 1863 in his great historical novels. The most prominent among these are KRZYŻACY (KNIGHTS OF THE CROSS, 1900) and a trilogy based on seventeenth century Poland, consisting of OGNIEM I MIECZEM (WITH FIRE AND SWORD, 1884), POTOP (THE DELUGE, 1886) and PAN WOŁODYJOWSKI (PAN MICHAEL, 1887), all in various English translations. Sienkiewicz was awarded the Nobel Prize in 1905 for his novel set in ancient Rome, QUO VADIS (1896).

Bądź błogosławiona. Translated as *Be Blessed/Be Thou Blessed/ The Blessing.*

Résumé.　Once upon a moonlight night wise and great Krishna, being a god, changed a lotus flower into human form. The beautiful maiden stood in front of the Lord asking where she was now to live. "The mountain tops are cold and covered with snow, storms trample the plains, the caves are dark." She would not choose any of them.

At dawn on the edge of the lake appeared the poet Valniki. The only word he could utter was, "I love. . . ." The face of Krishna brightened. He found in the world the place worthy of his creation: it was the heart of the poet.

When the maiden entered her new dwelling-place, her face grew pale. She saw there all she had feared; the snowy mountain tops, the plains with their storms, and the dark Ellora cave. But good and wise Krishna said: "Be thou a warm breath of the spring to melt the snow, plant flowers of happiness in the plains, and be thou a sunny ray in the dark Ellora cave. The poet Valniki added, "And be blessed."

> *Written in 1893.*
> *First published in book form 1894.*

Be Blessed. In his LET US FOLLOW HIM, AND OTHER STORIES . . . Translated by Vatslaf A. Hlasko and Thos. H. Bullick. New York, R. F. Fenno and company [c1897]. p.129–135.

Be Blessed; an Idyll. In his LET US FOLLOW HIM, AND OTHER STORIES . . . [Translated by Sigmund C. Slupski and Iza Young.] Philadelphia, H. Altemus [c1898]. p.89–95.

"Be Blessed!" In TALES FROM SIENKIEWICZ; translated by S. C. Soissons. London, George Allen, 1899. p.223–227.

Be Thou Blessed. In his HANIA . . . Translated from the Polish by Jeremiah Curtin. Boston, Little, Brown and company, 1897. p.[259]–262.

Be Thou Blessed. In his THE JUDGMENT OF PETER AND PAUL ON OLYMPUS: a Poem in Prose . . . Translated from the Polish by Jeremiah Curtin. Boston, Little, Brown, 1900. p.15–[24].

The Blessing; a Hindoo Legend. Translated by Victoria de Kreuter. In *Poland* (New York), XI, 1930. p.18–19.

Bartek Zwycięzca. Translated as *Bartek the Conqueror/Bartek the Victor/The Fate of a Soldier.*

Résumé. His name was Bartek Słowik, and he came from the village of Pognębina in the province of Poznań. His intellectual qualities won him the nickname of "Bartek the Blockhead."

German authorities mobilized all forces for the war against France. Bartek was called to the army. He bade good-bye to his wife, Magda, and was soon in the front lines.

At the battle of Gravelotte Bartek distinguished himself as a hero, and continued the tradition of a fearless fighter in battle after battle. He was even asked to stay on at the siege of Paris, when his regiment had been recalled from the front lines.

Upon his return home as a hero with a head wound, many medals and no money, Bartek was drawn into a fight with Herr Boege, a German schoolmaster, who had hit his son Franek.

The court ruled that Bartek should serve a prison sentence and pay Boege a fine. Together with his wife he borrowed money from another German until the debts ruined them completely. They lost their farm.

Bartek the Conqueror, the victor of Gravelotte and Sedan, now bent like an old man, his wife Magda, and their son Franek, had to go to the town to seek employment, as they could not find work at Pognębina. In the town Bartek still had to serve the rest of his term of imprisonment during the winter.

Written in 1882.

First published in book form 1882.

Bartek the Conqueror; a Tale of the Franco-Prussian War. Translated from the Polish by Iza Young. In his LET US FOLLOW HIM, AND OTHER STORIES . . . Philadelphia, H. Altemus [c1898]. p.99–234.

Bartek the Conqueror. In TALES BY POLISH AUTHORS . . . Translated by Else C. M. Benecke. Oxford, B. H. Blackwell, 1915. p.1–99.

Bartek the Conqueror. In TALES FROM HENRYK SIENKIEWICZ. Edited and introduced by Monica M. Gardner. Translated by Else Benecke. London, J. M. Dent; New York, E. P. Dutton [1946]. (Everyman's library. [no.871]) p.209–261.

Bartek the Conqueror. Translated by Else Benecke. In THE NOBEL PRIZE TREASURY, edited by Marshall McClintock. Garden City, N.Y., Doubleday, 1948. p.526–564.

Bartek the Victor. In his YANKO THE MUSICIAN, AND OTHER STORIES . . . Translated from the Polish by Jeremiah Curtin, with drawings by Edmund H. Garrett. Boston, Little, Brown and company, 1893. p.155–281.

Bartek the Victor. In his SIELANKA; A FOREST PICTURE AND OTHER STORIES. Authorized unabridged translation from the Polish by

Jeremiah Curtin. Boston, Little, Brown and company, 1898. p.[267]–335.

The Fate of a Soldier, by Henryk Sienkiewicz . . . Translated from the original Polish by J. Christian Bay. New York, J. S. Ogilvie Publishing Company, c1898.

144 p. (The Sunnyside series, no. 103, 1898)

Czy ci najmilszy? Translated as *Is He the Dearest One?*

Résumé. Through an open gate a wanderer walked into the yard and greeted the mistress of the cottage. She saw that he was coming back from a long journey, and offered him bread and milk. He was bringing news from her children. The woman asked about Yasko.

One of her sons worked in forests, another herded horses in the steppe, the third climbed mountains and tended sheep on high pastures. They were all well and were sending mother their greetings.

Again she anxiously inquired about Yasko. The wayfarer said he was keeping sad news for the last. The field did not give him its fruit; he was tormented by poverty and hunger. He had even forgotten his mother tongue.

When he finished, the woman gave the traveller a loaf of bread and a silver coin, and implored him to take it to Yasko. He reminded her of her other sons, and asked if Yasko was her dearest one. To this she replied, "My blessing is for them all, but my gifts are to Yasko, for I am a mother, and he is my poorest son."

(The story is allegorical. Mother, as the translator explains in the preface, represents Poland, and Yasko—the province of Silesia. The silver coin symbolizes one million marks collected among Poles in Russian-occupied Poland for the people of Silesia after the famine in that province about 1880.)

Written in 1880.
First published in book form 1901.

Is He the Dearest One? In his LIFE AND DEATH, AND OTHER LEGENDS AND STORIES. Translated from the original Polish by Jeremiah Curtin. Boston, Little, Brown and company, 1904. p.21–25.

Czyja wina? Translated as *Whose Fault? A Dramatic Picture in One Act.*

Whose Fault? A Dramatic Picture in One Act. In his SIELANKA; A FOREST PICTURE, AND OTHER STORIES. Authorized unabridged translation from the Polish by Jeremiah Curtin. Boston, Little, Brown, 1898. p.[139]–156.

Whose Fault? A Dramatic Picture in One Act. In his SO RUNS THE WORLD . . . Translated by S. C. de Soissons. London, New York, F. Tennyson Neely [1898]. p.[89]–123.

Whose Fault? A Dramatic Picture in One Act. In TALES FROM SIENKIEWICZ; translated by S. C. De Soissons. London, George Allen, 1899. p.[229]–255.

The Days of Nero. Fragment from his QUO VADIS.

The Days of Nero. [Translated by Jeremiah Curtin.] In THE UNIVERSAL ANTHOLOGY . . . Edited by Richard Garnett, Leon Vallée [and] Alois Brandl. London, The Clarke Company [1899]. v.6, p.116–143.
Preceded by a note about the author.

The Death of Radzivill. Fragment from his POTOP (THE DELUGE).

The Death of Radzivill. [Translated by Jeremiah Curtin.] In THE UNIVERSAL ANTHOLOGY . . . Edited by Richard Garnett, Leon Vallée [and] Alois Brandl. London, The Clarke Company [1899]. v.14, p.263–274.
Preceded by a note about the author.

The Death of the Traitors. Fragment from his OGNIEM I MIECZEM (WITH FIRE AND SWORD).

The Death of the Traitors. [Translated by Jeremiah Curtin.] In THE UNIVERSAL ANTHOLOGY . . . Edited by Richard Garnett, Leon Vallée [and] Alois Brandl. London, The Clarke Company [1899]. v.14, p.134–146.
Preceded by a note about the author.

The Duel. Excerpt from his HANIA.

The Duel. In TALES FROM SIENKIEWICZ; translated by S. C. De Soissons. London, George Allen, 1899. p.275–[299].

Dwie łąki. Translated as *Life and Death;* a Hindu Legend.

Résumé. The supreme and almighty Brahma had created two plains, the Plain of Life and the Plain of Death. A clear river was flowing between. He had commanded the good Vishnu to rule in the Region of Life, while the wise Siva was lord in the Region of Death.

In the Plain of Life the kindly god has created Love, which he also made Happiness. Brahma commanded Vishnu that henceforth men must weave the thread of life for themselves unassisted. From their good thoughts came joy, from the evil, sorrow. When men complained to Vishnu that life was grievous, he told them that Love should give them happiness. They multiplied and soon there was not enough food for them all.

Thus Labor appeared among people. When men complained to their Lord that from Labor came toil and weariness, Vishnu made Sleep. When men, still weary, asked Vishnu for sleep eternal, he told them of the neighboring region, the Plain of Death. The sun never rose or set there; the whole plain was a lily-colored absolute clearness and stillness. The people entered the water—the region belonging to Siva seemed to them sweeter and better. They began to pass to the other shore in increasing numbers until only one youth and one maiden remained in the Region of Life.

Frightened Vishnu called on Brahma to preserve life. Almighty Brahma made a thick veil out of darkness. He created Fear and Pain and commanded them to hang that black veil at the Passage.

Vishnu's kingdom was saved; it was now as crowded with life as it had been. Despite the calmness and serenity of Siva's realm, people dreaded the Passage.

Written in 1903.
First published in book form 1908.

Life and Death: a Hindu Legend. In his LIFE AND DEATH, AND OTHER LEGENDS AND STORIES. Translated from the original Polish by Jeremiah Curtin. Boston, Little, Brown and company, 1904. p.3–18.

The Escape. Fragment from his OGNIEM I MIECZEM (WITH FIRE AND SWORD).

The Escape. [Translated by Jeremiah Curtin.] In WAR OR PEACE.

Edited by Alfred Brant . . . and Frederick Houk Law . . . New York and London, Harper and brothers, 1938. p.195–215. "Reprinted by permission of Little, Brown & Company."

Escape of Zagloba and Helena. Fragment from his OGNIEM I MIECZEM (WITH FIRE AND SWORD).

Escape of Zagloba and Helena. [Translated by Jeremiah Curtin.] In THE UNIVERSAL ANTHOLOGY . . . Edited by Richard Garnett, Leon Vallée [and] Alois Brandl. London, The Clarke Company [1899]. v.14, p.146–157.

Hania. Translated as *Hania.*

Résumé. Hania, the granddaughter of the old serving-man Nicholas, had been left at his death to the care of the author-narrator when he was only sixteen. The young protector duly fell in love with his protegée, as did his close friend and school mate, Selim.

After an ill-fated elopement of Selim with Hania the two young men fought a duel. The narrator was seriously wounded, and when he recovered he found that Hania had had smallpox, which had left terrible marks on her beauty. Selim gallantly expressed his readiness to marry Hania. She refused in order to become a Sister of Charity.

For some time the author lost sight of her, but after a number of years he saw her unexpectedly again. All traces of the terrible disease had disappeared; she looked in her nun's cap more beautiful than ever before. It was a beauty more angelic than human.

> *Written in 1876.*
> *First published in book form 1880.*

Hania. In his HANIA . . . Translated from the Polish by Jeremiah Curtin. Boston, Little, Brown and company, 1897. p.[21]–167.

Hania. In his HANIA. Translated from the Polish by Casimir W. Dynicwicz (i.e. Dyniewicz). Chicago, Donohue, Henneberry and company [c1898]. p.31–257.

Hania. In his HANIA . . . Translated from the Polish by Casimir Gonski. Philadelphia, Henry Altemus [c1898]. p.27–297.

Hania. In TALES FROM HENRYK SIENKIEWICZ. Edited and introduced by Monica M. Gardner. Translated by H. E. Kennedy and Z. Umińska. London, J. M. Dent; New York, E. P. Dutton [1946]. (Everyman's library. [no.871]) p.14–123.

Jamioł. Translated as *The Angel/Yamyol.*

Résumé. After the funeral of widow Kaliksta, some women remained to finish the hymn in the church of the little town Lupiskory. After church the women went to the inn, and took Marysia, the orphan, with them. One of the women, Kulik, spoke tenderly to the orphan, and reminded the girl and everybody else of the priest's words that a yamyol[22] was above to protect her.

Voytek Margula who was to take Marysia to another village had had a few drinks before the two started out in a sleigh.

On the way Voytek fell asleep, and didn't waken even when the horses overturned the sleigh. Marysia tried to wake him up, but finally gave up and decided to walk. Soon she entered the forest.

Night fell, and the tired and sleepy girl sat under a tree, confident that a yamyol was above her. Falling asleep she heard some quiet and quick steps. When she raised her sleepy eyes she saw in front of her the terrible, gray, three-cornered face of a wolf.

Written in 1880.
First published in book form 1882.

The Angel. Translated by Virgilia Peterson. In *Poland-America,* XII, 1931. p.418–421.

Yamyol (Angel); a Village Sketch. In his LILLIAN MORRIS, AND OTHER STORIES . . . Translated by Jeremiah Curtin, with illustrations by Edmund H. Garrett. Boston, Little, Brown, 1894. p.179–197.

Yamyol; a Village Sketch. In his SIELANKA; A FOREST PICTURE, AND OTHER STORIES . . . Authorized unabridged translation from the Polish by Jeremiah Curtin. Boston, Little, Brown, 1898. p.[463]–473.

---

[22] The Polish word for "angel," as it is pronounced by peasants in some regions of the Polish countryside.

Janko Muzykant. Translated as *Janko the Musician/Little Janko/ Yanko the Musician.*

Résumé. The baby came into the world so frail and weak that it was decided to baptize him at once. He was given the name Yan, but instead of dying, he went on living until he reached the age of ten.

Yanko was always lean; his eyes were gazing into some immense distance. He heard music in the woods, in the fields, and by the river. He heard the violin played in the public house, and he made himself one out of a shingle and horsehair, but it would not play as beautifully as did the other.

One night through the open door he saw the fiddle of his dream in the pantry of the mansion. He was caught when he touched it, and the next day he stood before the tribunal of the village mayor.

"Mamma, will the Lord God give me a real fiddle in heaven?" was his last question, as he lay on his deathbed as a result of the whipping by the village policeman.

On the second day after Yanko's death the master and mistress of the mansion returned to their residence, very much impressed by the artistic qualities of the people in beautiful Italy. "The talents are sought and protected there," added their daughter in French.

> *Written in 1879.*
> *First published in book form 1880.*

Janko the Musician. Translation anonymous. In THE MASTER-PIECE LIBRARY OF SHORT STORIES . . . Edited by J. A. Hammerton . . . London, The Educational Book Company [1920]. Vol. 13, p.321–327.

Janko the Musician. Translated by N. B. Jopson. In *The Slavonic (and East European) Review,* XV, 1936–37. p.29–36.

Janko the Musician. Translated by Peter A. Ostafin. Orchard Lake, Michigan, Sodalis Press, 1938.

Janko the Musician. Translated by N. B. Japson (i.e. Jopson). In STORIES OF MANY NATIONS, selected and arranged by Irwin H.

Braun . . . D. Edward Safarjian . . . Illustrated by Armstrong Sperry. Boston, D. C. Heath and company [c1942]. p.462–471.

Little Janko. Translated by C. O'Conor-Eccles. In *The Ave Maria,* a Catholic Magazine, XXXIV, 1892. p.60–64.

Yanko the Musician. In his YANKO THE MUSICIAN, AND OTHER STORIES . . . Translated from the Polish by Jeremiah Curtin, with drawings by Edmund H. Garrett. Boston, Little, Brown, 1893. p.9–27.

Yanko the Musician. In his SIELANKA; A FOREST PICTURE AND OTHER STORIES . . . Authorized unabridged translation from the Polish by Jeremiah Curtin. Boston, Little, Brown, 1898. p.[255]–264.

Yanko the Musician. [Translated by Jeremiah Curtin.] In POLISH AUTHORS OF TODAY AND YESTERDAY . . . Selected by Irena Morska. New York, S. F. Vanni [c1947]. p.149–158.

The text of the translation of Jeremiah Curtin has been slightly altered by the editor.

Keeper of the Faith. Fragment from his QUO VADIS.

Keeper of the Faith. Translation by Jeremiah Curtin. In THE WORD LIVES ON; a Treasury of Spiritual Fiction. Edited by Frances Brentano; introduction by Halford E. Luccock. Garden City, N.Y., Doubleday, 1951. p.312–314.

Komedia z pomyłek. Translated as *A Comedy of Errors;* a Sketch of American Life.

Résumé. (This sketch of American life in a small town is told "as if it happened" in California, but the question of locality is here not of importance.)

A paraffin well was discovered in a certain place which became known as Struck-Oil, and soon rightfully changed its name to Struck-Oil City. The town grew, and with the growth of the city so grew the animosity between the owners of two competitive grocery stories, Hans Kasche and a young lady, Lora Neuman, both German.

When their fight came to a climax, they decided to seek justice through the town's judge who, misunderstanding the nature of their visit (neither of them spoke English), duly—married them!

When the two mortal foes discovered the bond which was to unite them, they burst into anger, but finally resigned themselves to the fact.

Peace returned to Struck-Oil City.

Written in 1878.
First published in book form 1880.

A Comedy of Errors; a Sketch of American Life. In his YANKO THE MUSICIAN, AND OTHER STORIES . . . Translated from the Polish by Jeremiah Curtin, with drawings by Edmund H. Garrett. Boston, Little, Brown, 1893. p.117–151.

A Comedy of Errors; a Sketch of American Life. In his FOR DAILY BREAD, AND OTHER STORIES. [Translated by Iza Young.] Philadelphia, Henry Altemus [c1898]. p.[173]–209.

A Comedy of Errors. In his SIELANKA; A FOREST PICTURE, AND OTHER STORIES . . . Authorized unabridged translation from the Polish by Jeremiah Curtin. Boston, Little, Brown, 1898. p.[519]–538.

A Comedy of Errors; a Sketch of American Life. In TALES FROM HENRY SIENKIEWICZ. Edited and introduced by Monica M. Gardner. Translated by H. E. Kennedy and Z. Umińska. London, J. M. Dent; New York, E. P. Dutton [1946]. (Everyman's library. [no.871]) p.[124]–138.

Latarnik. Translated as *The Lighthouse Keeper/The Lighthouse Keeper of Aspinwall.*

Résumé. By chance a small package of Polish books containing a copy of Mickiewicz's great epic, PAN TADEUSZ, reaches the lighthouse keeper, an old Pole stranded in a far corner of the world, at Aspinwall near Panama. Skawiński had fought in many lands, including America, and had won several medals for his bravery.

He throws his food to the sea-gulls and reads aloud the opening lines of the poem which take him back to his native land, last seen about forty years ago. Elated and transfixed, he continues to read and forgets for the first time his duty of lighting the lantern of the lighthouse. Thus he loses the long coveted job which was to him a perfect haven of peace after the long life of adversity and adventure.

> *Author's note: "This story is founded on a real occurrence, of which J. Horain wrote in one of his letters from America." Written in 1881.*
> *First published in book form 1882.*

The Lighthouse-Keeper. Translated by Monica M. Gardner. In TALES FROM HENRYK SIENKIEWICZ. Edited and introduced by Monica M. Gardner. London, J. M. Dent; New York, E. P. Dutton [1946] (Everyman's library. [no.871]) p.194–208.

The Lighthouse-Keeper, by H. Sienkiewicz. Translated by Monica Gardner. In THE POLISH SHORT STORIES. Edited by Umadevi. [Bombay] Indo-Polish Library. No. 35 [c1946]. p.104–121.

The Lighthouse Keeper. Translated by Ilona Ralf Sues. In POLISH SHORT STORIES, selected by Zbigniew Żabicki. Warsaw, Polonia Publishing House, 1960. p.33–[54].

The Light-House Keeper of Aspinwall. In his YANKO THE MUSICIAN, AND OTHER STORIES . . . Translated from the Polish by Jeremiah Curtin, with drawings by Edmund H. Garrett. Boston, Little, Brown, 1893. p.31–69.

The Light-House Keeper of Aspinwall. In his SIELANKA; A FOREST PICTURE, AND OTHER STORIES . . . Authorized unabridged translation from the Polish by Jeremiah Curtin. Boston, Little, Brown, 1898. p.[441]–460.

The Light-House Keeper of Aspinwall. Translated by Jeremiah Curtin. In STORIES BY FOREIGN AUTHORS: Polish, Greek, Belgian, Hungarian. New York, Charles Scribner's Sons, 1898. p.11–38.

"From 'Yanko the Musician and other Stories.' Translated by Jeremiah Curtin. Published by Little, Brown & Co. Copyright, 1893."

The Lighthouse-Keeper of Aspinwall. [Translated by Jeremiah Curtin.] In THE MASTERPIECE LIBRARY OF SHORT STORIES . . . Edited by J. A. Hammerton . . . London, The Educational Book Company [1920]. Vol. 13, p.307–320.

The Lighthouse Keeper of Aspinwall. [Translated by Jeremiah Curtin.] In MASTERPIECES OF ADVENTURE . . . Stories of the Sea and Sky. Edited by Nella Braddy. Garden City, N.Y., Doubleday, Page and company, 1922. p.98–121.

"Reprinted by permission of Little, Brown and company."

The Lighthouse Keeper of Aspinwall. Translated by Jeremiah Curtin. In GREAT SHORT STORIES OF THE WORLD; a Collection of Complete Short Stories Chosen from the Literatures of All Periods and Countries by Barrett H. Clark and Maxim Lieber. New York, Robert M. McBride and company, 1926. p.701–713.

Preceded by a brief note about the author.

"The present version is reprinted from the volume YANKO THE MUSICIAN, etc., translated by Jeremiah Curtin. Copyright, 1893, by Little, Brown & Co., by whose permission it is used here."

The Lighthouse Keeper of Aspinwall. Translated by Jeremiah Curtin. In GREAT SEA STORIES OF ALL NATIONS, by Giovanni Boccaccio, David Bone, Joseph Conrad . . . and Many Others from Ancient Greece to Modern Japan; edited and with an introduction by H. M. Tomlinson. Garden City, N.Y., Doubleday, Doran, and company, 1930. p.969–980.

From Jeremiah Curtin's translation of YANKO THE MUSICIAN. Reprinted by permission of Little, Brown and company.

The Light-House Keeper of Aspinwall. [Translated by Jeremiah Curtin.] In POLISH AUTHORS OF TODAY AND YESTERDAY . . . Selected by Irena Morska. New York, S. F. Vanni [c1947]. p.128–148.

The Light-House Keeper of Aspinwall. [Translated by Jeremiah Curtin.] In TREASURY OF WORLD LITERATURE, edited by Dagobert D. Runes. New York, Philosophical Library [c1956]. p.1165–1178.

Preceded by a brief note about the author.

Legenda żeglarska. Translated as *A Legend of the Sea.*

Résumé. There was a ship named "The Purple," so strong and so great that she feared neither winds nor waves. Life on that ship was one ceaseless holiday. On other ships stern discipline ruled, but on "The Purple" each man did what seemed good to him. And "The Purple" sailed; she was proud and splendid. Long years passed, and she was invincible.

Then the crew grew slothful and forgot their own art. They still sailed for a very long period. Finally the ship began to decay.

There came a raging storm. The weak rigging snapped and "The Purple" was sinking. The crew unaccustomed to work did not know how to save her. Enraged, they began to cannonade the wind and to flog that sea which was drowning them. But the waves had more strength than the mariners. The crew kept decreasing every minute.

At last they felt that death was approaching. In that moment of despair they realized that it was useless to cannonade the wind and to flog the waves. "The Purple" was yet afloat and they rushed to mend the vessel. And they worked from morning till night in the sweat of their brows.

(Like *Is He the Dearest One?* the story is allegorical. The ship represents Poland. Through this allegory the author endeavors, as the translator indicates in the preface, to explain the meaning of Polish history.)

> *Written in 1884.*
> *First published in book form 1900.*

A Legend of the Sea. In his LIFE AND DEATH, AND OTHER LEGENDS AND STORIES. Translated from the original Polish by Jeremiah Curtin. Boston, Little, Brown, 1904. p.29–37.

Listy o Zoli. Translated as *Zola.*

Zola ("*Doctor Pascal*"). In his SIELANKA; A FOREST PICTURE, AND OTHER STORIES . . . Authorized unabridged translation from the Polish by Jeremiah Curtin. Boston, Little, Brown, 1898. p.[571]–592.

Zola. In his SO RUNS THE WORLD . . . Translated by S. C. de Soissons. London, New York, F. Tennyson Neely [c1898]. p.[43]–85.

Lux in tenebris lucet. Translated as *An Artist's End/Light in Darkness/Lux in tenebris lucet/True to His Art.*

Résumé. Kamionka fell ill and stopped working on his statue of

"Mercy." The bad November weather annoyed him. Heavy mist hung over the earth; everything was damp. For the sake of economy Kamionka slept in his gloomy studio. The walls were dark, the floor was covered with dirt.

After the death of his wife whom he had loved dearly, he had begun to sculpture figures for her monument. This work was a labor of love. Now, when he was ill, no one called upon him except his servant, who made his tea. He took no nourishment; he did not want to eat, work, or live.

One day his servant told Kamionka that she could no longer come as often as she had done before, and advised him to call in a Sister of Mercy. At dawn he saw a figure sitting by his bedside. It was a Sister of Mercy. In the morning he recognized in the Sister his wife, Sophia. She put her arms around him. "I am ready to die," said the sculptor. "You have died already," replied his wife. He looked in the direction of her finger. In the distance under his feet, he saw his gloomy studio; on his bed lay his own body. But now the brightness surrounded them and lifted them into infinitude.

Written in 1891.
First published in book form 1894.

An Artist's End (Lux in tenebris lucet). In his FOR DAILY BREAD, AND OTHER STORIES. [Translated by Iza Young.] Philadelphia, Henry Altemus [c1898]. p.[151]–172.

Light in Darkness; lux in tenebris lucet. In his LET US FOLLOW HIM, AND OTHER STORIES . . . Translated by Vatslaf A. Hlasko and Thos. H. Bullick. New York, R. F. Fenno and company [c1897]. p.139–159.

Lux in tenebris lucet. In his HANIA . . . Translated from the Polish by Jeremiah Curtin. Boston, Little, Brown, 1897. p.[387]–398.

True to His Art. In TALES FROM SIENKIEWICZ; translated by S. C. De Soissons. London, George Allen, 1899. p.259–272.

Na jasnym brzegu. Translated as *In Monte Carlo/On the Bright Shore/On the Sunny Shore.*

Résumé. Świrski, the painter, was sitting beside Pani Elzen in an open carriage driving from Nice to Monte Carlo. The front seats were occupied by Pani Elzen's twin sons, Romulus and Remus. Pani Elzen placed her hand on the painter's arm; she gazed with dreamy eyes over the mirror of the sea. Świrski felt the touch; had it not been for Romulus and Remus, he might have placed his arm around the young and beautiful widow. But then, he thought with a certain fear, his hesitation would be settled.

That night during the dinner given by Pani Elzen at the Hôtel de Paris in Monte Carlo, the painter met the incurably consumptive Mr. Kresowicz, the tutor of the twins. Kresowicz was a man of another style who hated that society in which he was forced to appear.

Świrski's landlady at Nice, where he had his studio, had found for him a model whom he badly needed for an unfinished painting. The model came next morning. She was young and beautiful, but she refused to undress to the waist as was required for the picture. She begged him to accept her as a model for the head alone. At first the painter was impatient, but when he began talking to her he discovered that she could speak Polish. Her mother was Polish, so was her grandfather; her father was Italian. Her name was Maria Cervi. Świrski arranged for the sittings for the head, visited the family, and left three hundred francs with Pani Cervi as an advance payment. Maria's father was dead, her grandfather was ill, and the family was in great poverty.

The sittings were interrupted by Pani Elzen's telegram that Kresowicz had committed suicide. Świrski went to her immediately. Pani Elzen had released Kresowicz from his duties as tutor the day before the tragedy. Her only concern now about the tutor (who had been in love with her) was what would society say about it. Without realizing it, she openly displayed her selfishness.

This was the turning point. From that time the painter's feelings of attachment to his new model quickly deepened into love, while his admiration for Pani Elzen melted away fast. The last telegram from Pani Elzen, after he had left word with her sons that he was going on a journey, contained only one word: "Scoundrel." Świrski announced to Panna Maria that he would like to take her to Rome, no longer as his model, but as his—wife.

Written in 1897.
First published in book form 1897.

In Monte Carlo. Translated by S. C. de Soissons from the original Polish of Henryk Sienkiewicz . . . London, Greening and company, 1899.

x,13–160 p.

Chapter contents: Introduction, by S. C. de Soissons.—I. An interrupted proposal.—II. Mrs. Elzen at home.—III. The next morning.—IV. The ruling passion.—V. A night of speculation.—VI. A new model.—VII. Mrs. Elzen shows herself.—VIII. A new interest in life.—IX. A tragical farce.—X. Love.

"First English edition pub. September 11th, 1899. Reprinted September 18th, 1899."

In Monte Carlo . . . Popular edition. [Translated and] with an introduction by S. C. De Soissons. London, Greening and company, 1902.

x,13–160 p. (On cover: The Thistledown series)

Reprinted 1903 [with date 1904].

In Monte Carlo; a story by Henryk Sienkiewicz . . . Translated from the Polish, with an introduction by Count S. C. de Soissons. London, Stanley Paul and company; Philadelphia, David McKay Company, n.d.

159 p. front.(port.)

Also published with imprint: London, Stanley Paul and company, The International Library [1927].

On the Bright Shore. In his HANIA . . . Translated from the Polish by Jeremiah Curtin. Boston, Little, Brown, 1897. p.[401]–480.

On the Bright Shore, by Henryk Sienkiewicz . . . Authorized unabridged translation from the Polish by Jeremiah Curtin. Boston, Little, Brown, 1898.

147 p.

"Copyright, 1897, 1898, by Jeremiah Curtin."

On the Bright Shore. To which is added, *That Third Woman.*

By Henryk Sienkiewicz . . . Authorized and unabridged translation from the Polish by Jeremiah Curtin. Boston, Little, Brown, 1898. 82,[3]–68 p. (On cover: The Beacon series)

On the Sunny Shore (by Henry Sienkiewicz). Translated from the Polish by S. C. de Soissons . . . New York, R. F. Fenno [c1897]. 161 p.

Na Olimpie. Translated as *The Judgment of Peter and Paul on Olympus/On Mount Olympus.*

Résumé. One calm night in May, when the full moon was sailing above Olympus (it was an ambrosial night), Peter and Paul sat on the highest grassmound of the slope to pass judgment on the gods of antiquity. The heads of the Apostles were encircled by halos. Below were assembled the gods awaiting their sentence.

First came Zeus. He looked still mighty, but his face was gloomy. His old eagle had a broken wing, his thunderbolt had grown reddish from rust. Peter pronounced his sentence: "Thou art cursed and condemned through all eternity." The god vanished through the earth.

Next came Poseidon, and when he heard his sentence, he turned into vanishing mist.

Then rose Apollo, the silver-bowed, with a hollow lute in his hand. Behind him moved slowly the nine Muses. Radiant Apollo turned to Paul with an appeal to be spared; with his death would die Song. There was a moment of silence. Paul rose, made the sign of the cross above the head of the god, and said: "Let Song live." Apollo sat down with his lute at the feet of the Apostle. The Muses began to sing a song of praise to the holy Mother of God.

The turn was for Pallas Athene. She did not beg for life. She confessed that she had always been only a shadow, an illusion.

Finally came the most beautiful and the most honored goddess. She was sweet and marvelous. Her lips quivered like those of a child. She cried in fear and humility: "I am sinful, I deserve blame, but I am Joy. Have mercy—I am the one happiness of mankind." Paul touched her with a white field-lily, and said: "Joy, be henceforth like this flower, and live thou for mankind."

When dawn came, the earth awoke and smiled, because Song and Joy had not been taken from it.

> *Written in 1900.*
> *First published in book form 1902.*

The Judgement of Peter and Paul on Olympus; a Poem in Prose. Translated by Jeremiah Curtin. In *The Century Illustrated Monthly Magazine,* LIX, 1899. p.316–17.

The Judgment of Peter and Paul on Olympus; a Poem in Prose . . . In his THE JUDGMENT OF PETER AND PAUL ON OLYMPUS . . . Translated from the Polish by Jeremiah Curtin. Boston, Little, Brown, 1900. p.1–[13].

The Judgment of Peter and Paul on Olympus; a Poem in Prose. In his LIFE AND DEATH, AND OTHER LEGENDS AND STORIES. Translated from the original Polish by Jeremiah Curtin. Boston, Little, Brown, 1904. p.55–65.

On Mount Olympus. Translated by J. P. Wachowski. In *Poland–America,* XII, 1931. p.313–315.

Niewola tatarska. Translated as *Tartar Captivity.*

Résumé. (The story is told in the first person.) Although of noble birth, Alexis Zdanobarski, in love with Marysia, the daughter of Pan Tworjanski, was refused her hand because of lack of wealth. The dejected noble decided to improve his fortunes by offering his services to Col. Koszyc, an old friend of his father, at the farthest Polish outpost against the Tartars in Ukraine.

During the first battle, when his wounded horse fell under him, Zdanobarski was taken prisoner by a rich Tartar, Aga Sukyman, who at first treated him well in the hope of receiving a high ransom. Disappointed, even though his own daughter fell in love with the prisoner, the Tartar tried to bend the Polish noble's spirit by cold, hunger, and threats of torture. In the midst of all his misery, the noble proudly rejected the offer to marry Sukyman's daughter.

In the meantime Pan Tworjanski had died, and Marysia accidentally learned of her suitor's plight. The ransom came just as the captive noble fainted while hot coals had been placed under his feet.

From a short postscript we learn that, although miraculously returned to freedom, Zdanobarski did not marry Marysia. For all we know, he never married at all.

Written in 1880.

First published in book form 1882.

Tartar Captivity. In his HANIA . . . Translated from the Polish by Jeremiah Curtin. Boston, Little, Brown and company, 1897. p.[171]–215.

Organista z Ponikły. Translated as *A Country Artist/The Organist of Ponikla.*

Résumé. Klen had long legs, and he walked briskly from Zagrabie to Ponikła. He was dressed scantily, but he had a hautboy[23] in his hand, a couple of glasses of arrack in his stomach, and in his heart—delight.

That morning he had signed a contract with Canon Krajewski as the future organist of Ponikła. Though a first-rate musician, up to the time when the old organist had still been alive he had strolled about like a gypsy; now he was to settle down. He was to have a house, a garden, a hundred and fifty rubles a year, and an occupation in the service of God.

Important as all these things might have been, the source of greatest delight to the newly-appointed organist was, however, the fact that at long last he was to have his Olka, the daughter of the tile-maker in Zagrabie. Up to now the father was unwilling to give Olka to Klen.

After signing the contract, Klen went with all speed to the tile-maker's. Now everything was different. He was invited into the house, treated to arrack, and feasted. So Klen had sat there from midday till evening, to his own great delight and to Olka's. Now he was returning by the road to Ponikła, on squeaking snow and in twilight, with a song in his heart. Darkness came and the

---

[23] An oboe-like musical instrument.

frost grew severe. To reach his house more quickly Pan Klen decided to cut across the field. To kill time he played his hautboy. He repeated the same songs that he had played earlier in the day, when Olka had accompanied him so gladly with her thin voice. They had laughed most at the "Green pitcher," so now Klen played it to himself.

It was hard to walk cross-country. In some places Pan Klen had to wade through the drifted snow to the knee. He grew so tired that he finally decided to sit down. When he sat down he again started to play "My green pitcher." The notes grew weaker until silence fell. He murmured, "Olka! where art thou?" The hautboy dropped from his stiffened hands.

Next morning the dawn shone on the organist's sitting figure with the hautboy near his long legs.

Written in 1893.
First published in book form 1894.

A Country Artist. In TALES FROM SIENKIEWICZ; translated by S. C. De Soissons. London, George Allen, 1899. p.3–15.

The Organist of Ponikla. In his HANIA . . . Translated from the Polish by Jeremiah Curtin. Boston, Little, Brown and company, 1897. p.[375]–383.

Orso. Translated as *A Circus Hercules/Orso.*

Résumé. Hirsch's Circus from Los Angeles has come to Anaheim, a town in Southern California. Many attractions are in store for the town inhabitants and the vineyard hands filling the city after the grape gathering. The greatest of them all is the "unconquerable Orso," the athlete, and the "aerial angel," Jenny. The two are friends.

Jenny often reads to Orso from the "good book," the Bible, and Orso, whose father was white and mother an Indian, tells Jenny of his dreams of going to the desert with her.

Ill-tempered Mr. Hirsch catches them talking instead of working. Orso swallows the indignity of his own whipping, but he cannot endure the punishment inflicted by the "artist of the whip" upon Jenny. He descends upon Mr. Hirsch. Four Negroes run to the help of their master. Orso defeats them all and leaves Mr. Hirsch beaten unconscious on the floor.

Orso and Jenny flee the circus. They escape into the mountains and keep going until they reach the dwelling of an old, lonely squatter. Since then these three have lived together.

Written in 1879.
First published in book form 1880.

A Circus Hercules. In TALES FROM SIENKIEWICZ; translated by S. C. De Soissons. London, George Allen, 1899. p.113–147.

Orso. In his LET US FOLLOW HIM, AND OTHER STORIES . . . Translated by Vatslaf A. Hlasko and Thos. H. Bullick. New York, R. F. Fenno [c1897]. p.163–213.

Orso. Translated by Vatslaf A. Hlasko and Thos. H. Bullick. New York, R. F. Fenno and company, 1898 [c1897].

Unpaged.

Issued with his SIELANKA . . . New York, R. F. Fenno and company, 1898 [c1897].

Orso. In his SIELANKA; A FOREST PICTURE, AND OTHER STORIES . . . Authorized unabridged translation from the Polish by Jeremiah Curtin. Boston, Little, Brown, 1898. p.[111]–136.

Orso, by Henry Sienkiewicz. [Translated by Vatslaf A. Hlasko and Thomas H. Bullick.] Foreword by Carey McWilliams . . . [San Francisco] Published for its members by the Book Club of California, 1939.

viii,33 p. (Book Club of California. Six California tales, no. 3)

"Limited to 650 copies . . . designed and printed by the Ward Ritchie Press, Los Angeles."

Reprinted from the author's LET US FOLLOW HIM, AND OTHER STORIES . . . New York, R. F. Fenno and company [c1897].

Pan Michael at Kamenyets. Fragment from his PAN WOŁODYJOWSKI (PAN MICHAEL).

Pan Michael at Kamenyets. Translated by Jeremiah Curtin. In THE WORLD'S GREAT CATHOLIC LITERATURE, edited by George N. Shuster . . . with an introduction by William Lyon Phelps. New York, Macmillan, 1942. p.366–369.

Pójdźmy za Nim. Translated as *Anthea/Let Us Follow Him.*

Résumé. Caius Septima Cinna, a Roman patrician, married beautiful Anthea, the daughter of wise and scholarly Greek Timon. After a year of marriage Anthea was afflicted with a cruel disease. Her former poetic and inspiring dreams changed to horrible visions which drained her life. A famous Jewish physician advised Cinna to leave Egypt for the change of climate, and go to Jerusalem.

In Jerusalem the Procurator, Pontius Pilate, paid them a visit and, in order to take Anthea's mind off her affliction, he told them the story of a strange Jewish prophet of Nazareth. He invited them to witness the crucifixion on Golgotha.

Anthea had heard of the teachings of the Nazarene and was sympathetic with the prophet. Cinna and Anthea witnessed the crucifixion. Anthea's heart leaped to the Nazarene, and while Jewish crowds shouted and jeered, she whispered, "Thou art truth." No horrible vision afflicted Anthea that day or returned the following noon. Instead she had a vision of the Nazarene, and exclaimed to Cinna, "Whithersoever He calleth us, let us follow Him."

A moment later Pontius Pilate brought the news that the Nazarene reportedly had risen from the dead.

> *Written in 1893.*
> *First published in book form 1894.*

Anthea. In TALES FROM SIENKIEWICZ; translated by S. C. De Soissons. London, George Allen, 1899. p.169–220.

Let us Follow Him, by Henryk Sienkiewicz . . . Translated from the Polish by Jeremiah Curtin. Boston, Little Brown, and company, 1897.

vi,91 p. front.

"Publishers' note": p.v–vi.

"Copyright 1897."

Let Us Follow Him. In his HANIA . . . Translated from the Polish by Jeremiah Curtin. Boston, Little, Brown, 1897. p.[219]–255.

Let Us Follow Him. In his LET US FOLLOW HIM, AND OTHER

STORIES . . . Translated by Vatslaf A. Hlasko and Thos. H. Bullick. New York, R. F. Fenno and company [c1897]. p.9–83.

Let Us Follow Him; a Story of the Time of the Crucifixion. In his LET US FOLLOW HIM, AND OTHER STORIES . . . [Translated by Sigmund C. Slupski and Iza Young.] Philadelphia, H. Altemus [c1898]. p.7–85.

Let Us Follow Him. In TALES FROM HENRYK SIENKIEWICZ. Edited and introduced by Monica M. Gardner. Translated by S. C. de Soissons. London, J. M. Dent; New York, E. P. Dutton [1946]. (Everyman's library. [no. 871]) p.[308]–332.

Przez stepy. Translated as *Across the Plains/Across the Prairies/ Lillian Morris/Where Worlds Meet.*

Résumé. (The story is told in the first person. During his visit in California the author heard it directly from a Pole, Captain R., known as "Big Ralph.")

As a result of his varied experience in the prairies, Captain R. is called upon to be a leader of a big caravan to cross from the East to California. To reduce the danger to a minimum he organizes the party so as to cross the great prairies between the Mississippi and the Rocky Mountains in the spring. For the same reason he decides to lead his men not by the southern route from St. Louis, but through Iowa, Nebraska, and Northern Colorado.

On the way a young, delicate and beautiful girl, Lillian, going West to join her father, melts the heart of Big Ralph, and the two, by the common custom of the times, become husband and wife. Their love is as great as it is tender.

But despite all the precautions the party is struck by one misfortune after another. Adversities multiply until a small group of skeletons dragging their feet westward is left on the scene—with no mules, horses, wagons or any kind of provisions.

The climax comes when Lillian catches an infectious disease and dies in the arms of her husband. In blind despair he tears the bandages on his wounded head, and faints.

A month later he awakes in California at the home of a Polish squatter. He is never able to discover the place of Lillian's grave.

His only hope now is to find his great love in the prairies of Heaven.

Written in 1879.
First published in book form 1880.

Across the Plains. In his SIELANKA; A FOREST PICTURE, AND OTHER STORIES . . . Authorized unabridged translation from the Polish by Jeremiah Curtin. Boston, Little, Brown, 1898. p.[339]–414.

Across the Prairies; Captain R.'s Tale. In TALES FROM HENRYK SIENKIEWICZ. Edited and introduced by Monica M. Gardner. Translated by Eveline Blackett. London, J. M. Dent; New York, E. P. Dutton [1946]. (Everyman's library. [no.871]) p.139–193.

Lillian Morris of Boston. In his LILLIAN MORRIS, AND OTHER STORIES . . . Translated by Jeremiah Curtin, with illustrations by Edmund H. Garrett. Boston, Little, Brown, 1894. p.3–154.

Where Worlds Meet, by Henryk Sienkiewicz . . . Translated by J. Christian Bay; with the introduction by S. C. de Soissons. Chicago, New York, F. Tennyson Neely [c1899].
216 p.

Sachem. Translated as *Sachem.*

Résumé. In the town of Antelope on the river by the same name in Texas, crowds were hurrying to the circus. This was the first time that a circus had visited the town.

Some fifteen years ago on the very spot of the present Antelope there was an Indian village, Chiavatta, the capital of the Black Snakes. The Indians had molested the neighboring German settlements, and one night some four hundred German settlers fell upon sleeping Chiavatta, burned the village to the ground, and massacred all the inhabitants, including women and children. Those few Indians who escaped were hanged later. The only survivor of the Black Snakes, Sachem, was to appear as an acrobat in the circus that very night.

During his breath-taking performance the Indian chief suddenly addressed the audience in German. He told the tragic story of his tribe, and related the cowardly act of the Germans who attacked the women and children at night. He sounded terrible and threatening. What will he do? The guilty audience expected something horrible.

Suddenly the Indian acrobat jumped down to collect money for the last survivor of the tribe. His fiery speech was a pretence: it was a clever trick of the circus director. The Germans relaxed.

After the performance the last of the Black Snakes drank beer and ate dumplings at the "Golden Sun."

Written in 1883.
First published in book form 1889.

Sachem. In his LILLIAN MORRIS, AND OTHER STORIES . . . Translated by Jeremiah Curtin, with illustrations by Edmund H. Garrett. Boston, Little, Brown, 1894. p.157–176.

Sachem. In his SIELANKA; A FOREST PICTURE, AND OTHER STORIES . . . Authorized unabridged translation from the Polish by Jeremiah Curtin. Boston, Little, Brown, 1898. p.[505]–515.

Sielanka. Translated as *Sielanka; a Forest Picture/Sielanka; an Idyll.*

Résumé. In an open glade amid the deep woods stands the house of the forester Stefan. Tomorrow is Ascension Day and Stefan's daughter, Kasia, begs permission to go to the woods to gather herbs for the church. Singing happy songs, she departs.

Soon she meets Yasio, a young turpentine worker from the edge of the woods. Yasio helps Kasia in gathering plants. Stefan's dog, Burek, escapes from the house, and joins the two.

Now Yasio starts a song, and both sing the refrain in unison. The woods, the birds and even the smallest plants, all sing to the glory of God.

Kasia sits down under a mossy stone to weave garlands. Holding the unfinished garland in her hands, she falls asleep. Suddenly the Angelus bell rings from the church on the other side of the lake. Both kneel by the mossy stone as if before an altar, and begin to pray. The angels hover above their heads. Their souls are bright, pure and innocent like the souls of angels.

Written in 1875.
First published in book form 1889.

Sielanka; a Forest Picture. In his SIELANKA . . . AND OTHER STORIES
. . . Authorized unabridged translation from the Polish by Jeremiah
Curtin. Boston, Little, Brown and company, 1898. p.[3]–22.

Sielanka; an Idyll. In his LET US FOLLOW HIM, AND OTHER STORIES
. . . Translated by Vatslaf A. Hlasko and Thos. H. Bullick. New
York, R. F. Fenno and company [c1897]. p.87–125.

Sielanka; an Idyll. Translated by Vatslaf A. Hlasko and Thos.
H. Bullick. New York, R. F. Fenno and company, 1898 [c1897].
Unpaged.

With this is issued his *Orso.*

Stary sługa. Translated as *The Old Servant / The Old Serving-Man.*

Résumé. His name was Nicholas Suchowolski. The author's
father inherited him from his father whom Nicholas had served as
orderly during the Napoleonic wars.

Nicholas performed various duties. He was butler and footman;
in summer he acted as steward; he had the keys of the cellar and
of the storehouse; he wound the clocks. Whatever else he did, he
grumbled all the time. He was the type of serving-man that is now
disappearing from the face of the earth.

Nicholas' silhouette is delightfully drawn. Despite all his grumbling and harmless lying about his courageous and heroic acts of
war, he was, above anything else, faithful, loyal, and absolutely
devoted to the family he served.

Once, badly beaten because he would not hear a word against
his master from anybody, he refused to say anything about the
circumstances of the beating even though he was unjustly scolded
on that account by the author's father himself. After recovery he
returned to his own old ways.

The story closes with a moving description of his death, when
the old servant had almost reached his ninetieth year.

Written in 1875.
First printed in book form 1880.

. . . *The Old Servant.* In his HANIA . . . Translated from the
Polish by Jeremiah Curtin. Boston, Little, Brown and company,
1897. p.[3]–20.

At head of title: Prologue to Hania.

The Old Servant; Prologue [to Hania]. In his HANIA. Translated from the Polish by Casimir W. Dynicwicz (i.e. Dyniewicz). Chicago, Donohue, Henneberry and company [c1898]. p.5–30.

The Old Servant; Prologue [to Hania]. In his HANIA . . . Translated from the Polish by Casimir Gonski. Philadelphia, Henry Altemus [c1898]. p.[3]–25.

The Old Serving-Man. Translated by H. E. Kennedy and Z. Umińska. In TALES FROM HENRYK SIENKIEWICZ. Edited and introduced by Monica M. Gardner. London, J. M. Dent; New York, E. P. Dutton [1946]. (Everyman's library. [no.871]) p.1–13.

Szkice węglem. Translated as *Charcoal Sketches/The New Soldier.*

Résumé. Pan Zołzikiewicz, secretary to the Mayor of the commune of Barania Głowa, had a design on peasant Rzepa's wife. In order to get rid of Rzepa, he decided to put his name, instead of the Mayor's son's, on the conscription list. The Mayor's son was single, while Rzepa was married and had a year-old baby. To insure the success of his plot Zołzikiewicz tricked Rzepa into signing his name on the "contract," whereby for fifty roubles he was supposed to go to service to replace the Mayor's son.

Rzepa took to drinking more heavily than ever, while his wife, Marysia, left no stone unturned in her efforts to get help in a desperate situation. No one in the commune would help her, the priest could not do anything, neither would Pan Skorabiewski at the mansion. Shmul, the Jewish innkeeper, suggested that she should go to Pan Zołzikiewicz herself. He had heard the "Lord Secretary" say that if only Rzepa's wife came for the contract herself, he would tear the document.

Marysia, went, and when she returned, she threw herself at her husband's feet. Weeping, she confessed that Pan Zołzikiewicz deceived her, abused her, and then turned her out. She did it for him, her husband, whom she loved above everything in the world. Rzepa took an axe out of the box. He asked her to make the sign of the cross; her end had come. He calmly told her that soon she would lie in the churchyard. Soon after a dull blow was heard, followed by more blows. A quiver passed through the woman, her body stretched and was motionless. Soon after a huge flame rent the darkness; the buildings of the mansion were blazing.

In the epilogue the author explains that the "contract" signed by Rzepa at the inn had no legal value whatsoever. Zołzikiewicz, who was at the mansion at the time of the fire, safely escaped. He now continues in his office of secretary in Barania Głowa, and at present he has the hope of being chosen judge.

Written in 1877.
First published in book form 1880.

Charcoal Sketches. In his HANIA . . . Translated from the Polish by Jeremiah Curtin. Boston, Little, Brown and company, 1897. p.[291]–372.

The New Soldier; or, Nature and Life, by Henryk Sienkiewicz . . . Translated by J. Christian Bay [with the introduction by S. C. de Soissons]. New York, Hurst and company [c1901].

235 p.

"Copyright, 1899, by F. Tennyson Neely in the United States and Great Britain."

"Copyright, 1901, by Hurst & Company."

Ta trzecia. Translated as *In Bohemia/That Third Woman/The Third Woman.*

Résumé. (The story is told in the first person.) The narrator, a painter, shares his studio, workroom and bedchamber—all in one unpaid-for room—with his friend Światecki, who makes a pretense of being a complete degenerate.

The narrator is supposedly in love with the daughter of a wealthy snob. As soon as it is discovered that the young artist's painting had received a prize (which would bring him both fame and money) quick arrangements are made for the official engagement. This is later broken off by the fiancée because of a suspicion that her husband-to-be is unfaithful to her.

While trying to court a beauty of Warsaw, the young artist discovers his true love for another, the third woman, his old friend and a talented actress. In the end our painter marries the actress, and Światecki, to everybody's usrprise, becomes the husband of the snob's daughter. To make the story complete, the Warsaw beauty also finds her mate.

Written in 1888.
First published in book form 1888.

In Bohemia. In TALES FROM SIENKIEWICZ; translated by S. C. De Soissons. London, George Allen, 1899. p.19–109.

That Third Woman. In his HANIA . . . Translated from the Polish by Jeremiah Curtin. Boston, Little, Brown and company, 1897. p.[483]–548.

That Third Woman. [Authorized and unabridged translation from the Polish by Jeremiah Curtin. Boston, Little, Brown and company, 1898].

[3]–68 p.

Issued with his *On the Bright Shore* . . . Boston, Little, Brown and company, 1898.

The Third Woman, by Henryk Sienkiewicz . . . Translated from the original Polish by Nathan M. Babad . . . New York, J. S. Ogilvie Publishing Company, 1898.

iv,[5]–158 p. (Peerless series. No.107)

Translator's preface: p.[iii]–iv.

The Third Woman. In TALES FROM HENRYK SIENKIEWICZ. Edited and introduced by Monica M. Gardner. Translated by S. C. de Soissons. London, J. M. Dent; New York, E. P. Dutton [1946]. (Everyman's library. [no.871]) p.[262]–307.

U źródła. Translated as *At the Source.*

Résumé. A young and poor doctor of philosophy asked for the hand of Tola with whom he had been long in love. Her parents not only refused, but insulted him claiming that he had abused their confidence. The young man suffered a shock. He fell ill with typhus. What follows was his dream during the illness. (The author purposely makes the reader mistake the dream for reality.)

The next day Tola's father comes to apologize for their mistake. He and his wife are now ready to give him Tola for his wife. The father leads the young man to his house, and the parents leave the young man alone with his beloved. Soon they are engaged.

Plans are made for the wedding. At her fiancé's impatient request Tola begs her mother to allow their wedding to take place sooner than it was planned originally. Reluctantly both parents give their consent to this. Every day their love grows. The wedding takes place soon after Easter. Blissfully happy, the young man brings his bride to his newly redecorated house. The next morning Tola begins to behave strangely.

The young man regained consciousness and learned that in reality Tola's parents had taken her to Venice.

Written in 1892.
First published in book form 1894.

At the Source. In his HANIA . . . Translated from the Polish by Jeremiah Curtin. Boston, Little, Brown and company, 1897. p.[265]–288.

Walka byków. Translated as *The Bull-Fight.*

The Bull-Fight; a Reminiscence of Spain. In his LILLIAN MORRIS, AND OTHER STORIES . . . Translated by Jeremiah Curtin, with illustrations by Edmund H. Garrett. Boston, Little, Brown and company, 1894. p.201–247.

The Bull-Fight; a Reminiscence of Spain. In his SIELANKA; A FOREST PICTURE, AND OTHER STORIES . . . Authorized unabridged translation from the Polish by Jeremiah Curtin. Boston, Little, Brown and company, 1898. p.[477]–501.

Wspomnienia z Maripozy. Translated as *Memories of Mariposa.*

Résumé. On his way to the Big Trees the narrator visited Mariposa. The town had been a booming "golden" city in the past and was now reduced to a population of about one thousand inhabitants. The Polish traveler stopped at the only hotel in town.

When Mr. Biling, the proprietor, learned that the visitor was from Poland, he paid him a visit. He was from Baden, but greeted our visitor as warmly as if he were a Pole himself. In his younger days, Mr. Biling explained, he had served in the army under Mierosławski, and that had left a warm spot in his heart which he extended to all the countrymen of his beloved leader.

Upon leaving the room, Mr. Biling suddenly remembered that a Pole lived in the woods near the city. Next morning he brought a tall gentleman with white hair, white beard, and blue eyes, who introduced himself as Putrament. He had lived near Mariposa for twenty years, and the present visitor was the first Pole he had talked to in all those years. His Polish was fluent but it was as archaic as the language of Piotr Skarga. The old man was deeply moved meeting his countryman.

Toward the end of the conversation Putrament explained the secret of his bizarre language. In order to keep his Polish, he read the Polish Bible daily. This was the only book he owned. He had no relatives in Poland, but his attachment to his country was that of the Lighthouse Keeper of Aspinwall.

> *Written in 1882.*
> *First published in book form 1889.*

Memories of Mariposa. In his LET US FOLLOW HIM, AND OTHER STORIES . . . Translated by Vatslaf A. Hlasko and Thos. H. Bullick. New York, R. F. Fenno and company [c1897]. p.217–241.

Wycieczka do Aten. Translated as *An Excursion to Athens/A Journey to Athens.*

An Excursion to Athens. [Translated from the Polish by Vatslaf A. Hlasko and Thomas H. Bullick. New York, R. F. Fenno and company, c1897].

[5–59] p.

Issued with his *After Bread; a Story of Polish Emigrant Life to America* . . . New York, R. F. Fenno and company [c1897].

A Journey to Athens. In his SIELANKA; A FOREST PICTURE, AND OTHER STORIES . . . Authorized unabridged translation from the Polish by Jeremiah Curtin. Boston, Little, Brown, 1898. p.[541]–567.

Wyrok Zeusa. Translated as *The Decision of Zeus/The Verdict.*

Résumé. One evening Apollo and Hermes met on the Pnyx and made a wager. If a woman of Hermes' choice in Athens resisted

Apollo's charms, Hermes would win lovely Lampetia. If Hermes lost the wager, he would have to steal for Apollo a herd of long-horned oxen.

Hermes' choice fell on beautiful Eriphyle, a baker's wife. Apollo brought his lyre and sang a song, then another, until disgruntled Eriphyle threw at the god a bowl of acid for making yeast. His face covered with the liquid, Apollo withdrew angry and abashed. In anger he refused to give Lampetia to Hermes.

The gods went to Zeus to present their case. The father of gods frowned and gave this verdict. A virtuous woman could, in his judgment, resist Apollo. But Eriphyle did not resist the god out of virtue, but because of her stupidity. Therefore Lampetia should not go to Hermes. The gods heard the verdict and departed.

>*Written in 1891.*
>*First published in book form 1894.*

The Decision of Zeus. In his SIELANKA; A FOREST PICTURE, AND OTHER STORIES . . . Authorized unabridged translation from the Polish by Jeremiah Curtin. Boston, Little, Brown and company, 1898. p.[159]–171.

The Decision of Zeus. In TALES FROM SIENKIEWICZ; translated by S. C. De Soissons. London, George Allen, 1899. p.151–166.

The Verdict. In his SO RUNS THE WORLD . . . Translated by S. C. de Soissons. London, New York, F. Tennyson Neely [c1898]. p.[127]–149.

Z pamiętnika poznańskiego nauczyciela. Translated as *From the Diary of a Tutor in Poznan/Paul.*

Résumé. More than once at two or three o'clock in the morning I saw Michaś bent over a book. Mechanically he repeated Latin and Greek conjugations. I loved Michaś, as I secretly loved his mother, a widow whose only hope now was this little boy of eleven.

Michaś loved and adored his mother. She considered him a boy of more than average abilities, and he did not want to disappoint her. But the harder he tried the poorer were the results. He beamed when he received a good mark. But often enough he got poor marks because he could not "tongue it out" in German.[24] His absolute honesty was misinterpreted by his German teachers as obstinacy. When I tried to explain the true circumstances to them, I was accused of defending the boy's supposed laziness. Michaś was rapidly losing weight; he grew very pale and was weaker every day.

Just before Christmas holidays, for no other reason but his scholastic record, Michaś was expelled from school. Right after the tragic expulsion which also happened to be on the eve of his starting for holidays in Zalesin, where he was to join his mother, I was awakened in the middle of the night. By the light of the lamp I saw Michaś repeating fervently Latin conjugations. The boy developed inflammation of the brain.

I summoned his mother at once, and soon after her arrival the little boy, her only hope in the world, was dead.

> *Written in 1879.*
> *First published in* Gazeta Lwowska *in October, 1879, under the title Z pamiętnika Korepetytora.*
> *First published in book form 1880.*

From the Diary of a Tutor in Poznan. In his YANKO THE MUSICIAN, AND OTHER STORIES . . . Translated from the Polish by Jeremiah Curtin, with drawings by Edmund H. Garrett. Boston, Little, Brown, and company, 1893. p.73–113.

From the Diary of a Tutor in Poznan. In his SIELANKA; A FOREST PICTURE, AND OTHER STORIES . . . Authorized unabridged translation from the Polish by Jeremiah Curtin. Boston, Little, Brown and company, 1898. p.[417]–438.

Paul. Translated from the Polish of H. Sienkiewicz-Litwos by W. R. Thompson. In *The Catholic World*, IV, 1884. p.406–419.

Za chlebem. Translated as *After Bread/For Bread/For Daily Bread /Her Tragic Fate/In the New Promised Land/Peasants in Exile.*

Résumé. Vavron Toporek, a successful farmer at Lipińce near Poznań, was almost ruined as a result of a dispute when his cow

---

24 The story took place at the time when the Poznań region was under Prussian occupation.

was caught in somebody else's clover. In despair, lured by a German agent, he decided to emigrate to America with his eighteen-year-old daughter, Marysia.

Upon arrival they waited on the street in New York for the governor who, according to the assurances of the agent, was supposed to greet them and give them free land. The governor never came, and for several months they suffered poverty and hunger until every penny of their scant resources was spent. Turned out into the street Vavron was on the verge of taking the life of his daughter and his own. Finally they met a well-to-do countryman who fed them, gave them money, and paid their fare to a new settlement in Arkansas.

The settlement turned out to be a failure. It was flooded, and in the flood not only Vavron was drowned, but also Orlik, a young man in love with Marysia, who had tried to rescue her. Left alone, Marysia returned to her benefactor in New York. His house was now occupied by strangers. He was dead and his children had moved elsewhere.

Marysia lost her mind. Hungry and in rags she went every day to the wharf to look for her beloved Yasko whom she had left behind in her native village, and who was to follow her to the end of the world. After two months her body was found washed ashore at the end of the pier. The police could not identify her.

> *Written in 1880.*
> *First published in book form 1880.*

After Bread; a Story of Polish Emigrant Life to America, by the Author of "Quo vadis" (Henryk Sienkiewicz). Translated from the Polish by Vatslaf A. Hlasko and Thomas H. Bullick. New York, R. F. Fenno and company [c1897].

165 p.

With this is issued his *An Excursion to Athens.* [New York, R. F. Fenno and company, c1897].

For Bread. In his SIELANKA; A FOREST PICTURE, AND OTHER STORIES . . . Authorized unabridged translation from the Polish by Jeremiah Curtin. Boston, Little, Brown and company, 1898. p.[25]–107.

For Daily Bread. Translated by C. O'Conor-Eccles. In *The Ave Maria,* a Catholic Magazine, XXXIV, 1892. p.257–62, 288–93, 311–15, 340–43, 368–71, 402–05, 424–28, 452–57, 483–86.

Issued also in book form under title: PEASANTS IN EXILE (FOR DAILY BREAD).

For Daily Bread; a Story from the Life of American Emigrants. In his FOR DAILY BREAD, AND OTHER STORIES. [Translated by Iza Young.] Philadelphia, Henry Altemus [c1898] p.3–150.

Her Tragic Fate . . . Translated by J. Christian Bay [with the introduction by S. C. de Soissons]. Chicago, New York [etc.] F. Tennyson Neely [c1899].

216 p.

Also published with imprint: New York, Hurst and company [c1901].

In the New Promised Land; a Novel by Henryk Sienkiewicz . . . Translated by S. C. de Soissons. London, Jarrold and sons, n.d.

139 p. front.(port.)

Chapter contents: Introduction; Henryk Sienkiewicz, by S. C. de Soissons.– I. Upon the ocean.– II. Landing.– III. In New York.– IV. A countryman's help.– V. In the railway.– VI. Pioneer life.– VII. Black Orlik.– VIII. Alone.

In the New Promised Land, a Novel by Henryk Sienkiewicz . . . Translated [and with the introduction] by S. Count de Soissons. 2nd ed. London, Jarrold and sons [1900].

139 p.

Peasants in Exile (For Daily Bread). Translated from the Polish by C. O'Conor-Eccles. Notre Dame, Indiana, *The Ave Maria* [c1898].

172 p.

"Copyrighted, 1898, by D. E. Hudson, C.S.C."

Żurawie. Translated as *The Cranes.*

Résumé. During his visit in America the author recalls sojourning at Anaheim Landing on the shore of the Pacific Ocean. His sole company were some sailor fishermen, for the most part Norwegians, and a German who prepared food for them and lodged them. He was happy among them.

One evening the author heard cries in the sky. He recognized the voices of cranes. A whole flock of cranes was flying above his head toward the island of Santa Catalina.

He suddenly remembered that he had heard cries like these, when as a boy he journeyed from school for vacation, and he was seized by homesickness. He returned to his cabin. Pictures of Poland passed before his mind. The next morning the ocean and the sky seemed to him absolutely foreign. In succeeding days he began to create a world of his own.

A week later, on a night when the Norwegians went out on the ocean, the author sat down in his little room, and from his pen flowed the following words: "In Barania Głowa, in the chancellery of the village mayor, it was as calm as in time of sowing poppy seed."

And thus, because cranes flew over the shore of the Pacific, he composed his *Charcoal Sketches*.[25]

> *Written in 1896.*
> *First published in book form 1902.*

The Cranes. In his LIFE AND DEATH, AND OTHER LEGENDS AND STORIES. Translated from the original Polish by Jeremiah Curtin. Boston, Little, Brown and company, 1904. p.41–52.

Sieroszewski, Wacław (1858–1945)

A novelist and short story writer, Sieroszewski was one of the noblest figures of his time in Poland. As in the case of Szymański, the author's revolutionary activities led to his deportation to the land of Yakuts in Northern Siberia. His studies of the Asiatic peoples furnished him with subjects for his numerous tales. He described life in Siberia, Mongolia, Korea, and even China and Japan. Best known among

---

[25] The idea of *Charcoal Sketches* was conceived and the story was written in California.

Sieroszewski's works are: NA KRESACH LASÓW (At the Edge of the Forests, 1894), DWANAŚCIE LAT W KRAJU JAKUTÓW (Twelve Years in the Land of Yakuts, 1900), BRZASK (The Dawn, 1900), POWIEŚCI CHIŃSKIE (Chinese Tales, 1903), OL-SONI-KISAN (1906), Z FALI NA FALĘ (From Wave to Wave, 1910), BENIOWSKI (1916), TOPIEL (Abyss, 1921) and DALAJ-LAMA (1927).

Czukcze. Translated as *The Chukchee.*

Résumé. (A story from life of the Polish political exiles in Siberia.)

Józef visited his friend Stefan in the Arctic cold of Siberia bringing the news from the town that the Chukchee were encamping there. The Chukchee, who lived a primitive life in the tundras, traded with the Yankees. Józef had a vague dream of a possible escape from Siberia by making friends with the Chukchee.

Soon the Cossack, Buza, brought a Chukchee party to Stefan's house. Among them was sombre Kituwia. Józef and Stefan revisited the Chukchee camp, but neither of them realized that they were stepping into the very heart of a family feud inherited, perhaps, from another generation.

On one occasion, powerful and rich Otowaka paid Stefan a visit with his sons and daughters. The visit was interrupted by the intrusion of Kituwia. Buza discovered in time that the intruder was armed with a knife. Kituwia had a grudge against one of Otowaka's sons who was married to his sister. He was disarmed and arrested.

Father Pantelay had a design for baptizing powerful Otowaka. Stefan bought dogs and sledges, and the caravan started for the tundra in the terrible cold and blizzard under Buza's leadership. After having reached a tent filled with the murdered and distorted bodies of Otowaka's family, the party started back, losing in the blizzard their furs and provisions. They met Otowaka with only one boy saved from the clan. Now the Chukchee wanted to be baptized and bring the boy up as an avenger of the massacre.

The Chukchee. In MORE TALES BY POLISH AUTHORS. Translated by Else C. M. Benecke and Marie Busch. New York, Longmans, Green and company, 1916. p.146–185.

Jesienią. Translated as *In Autumn.*

Résumé. (While he was exiled to the depths of Russia, the author made a study of Siberian tribes. The Yakut tribe was one of them.)

The rain had kept the inhabitants of the tiny and stuffy Yakut hut, "Talaki," indoors. When Kuimis began quarrelling with her husband and our host, Kyrsa, I shouldered my gun and went out of the cottage in order to avoid being a witness to his possible defeat.

I was attracted by the "demons' forest" which looked gloomy and horrible. When it became dark, I lost my way. Cold and wet, I resolved to wait for daybreak. I loaded my gun, and crouching against a tree, tried to sleep.

Soon I heard sounds like measured strokes of an oar and a small Yakut pirogue emerged from the shadows. The man drew the boat to land. When I approached, he recognized me. He was a poor Yakut who lived about five versts from me.

Together we travelled back in the pirogue. My companion was to spend the night at Chachak's home. I had known Chachak too. I walked towards his yurta first, and got a warm welcome. When my companion came in he mentioned a bear that had been seen in the district.

In the past Chachak was a great bear hunter of fabulous fame. Once, late in the season, he killed a big elk. He decided to build a larder on the spot, and to lay the elk in it for a time, till the road became frozen. Suddenly "He" came. Chachak reached for his knife, and tried in vain to drag it out; it had frozen to the sheath. He seized the bear by the throat with his right hand, and laid his left on its jaws. His boy frightened the Black One away, but in the confusion he had hit Chachak in the chest with his knife. From that time on, besides suffering from the horrible wound, Chachak's mind had been troubled. The old man believed that "He" would still take his revenge.

A few years later I heard that Chachak had disappeared without trace in the wood.

In Autumn. In TALES BY POLISH AUTHORS . . . Translated by Else C. M. Benecke. Oxford, B. H. Blackwell, 1915. p.137–161.

W matni. Translated as *Caught in a Snare.*

Caught in a Snare. Translated by Geoffrey Potocki of Montalk. In *Pologne littéraire*, No.100–101, 1935. p.2–3.

". . . A fragmentary translation."

W ofierze bogom. Translated as *A Sacrifice to the Gods/In Sacrifice to the Gods.*

Résumé. Every year in the spring the nomad Tungus tribes assemble for a week in the broad valley of the Sheroka river. It is the time when the family elders collect the tribute of hides and settle all important matters. The young men use the time for love and merrymaking, dancing and races.

But this year there was no laughter and no singing. A terrible pestilence was raging among the tribes, mercilessly killing men and reindeer. Now they were all waiting for the coming of old, rich and powerful Seltichan with his family. While Tumara was telling the tragic story of his family, Seltichan's caravan arrived.

The following morning, under the sky clear and blue, men assembled at the conference. Old Oltungaba was chosen to prophesy. He sat until a shiver ran through his body, followed by a violent sob. The shivering and sobs passed into convulsions and groans. Beating the drum he uttered the awful words that he who was proud and rich and respected, whose sons were famed for their shooting and the daughters for their beauty, should offer himself to the gods.

The following day, when Seltichan asked his son Miore to call the people, the young man threw himself at his father's feet and begged him not to leave the family. Once more the people assembled in the valley. On the third day Miore charged that while performing the ceremony Oltungaba was lying, bribed by jealous Kniaź. Summoned by Seltichan, Oltungaba did not deny taking gifts from Kniaź, but he asserted that there was no deceit on his part in the performance of the ceremony. Saying this, he put his hand into the flame. Seltichan drew the old man away from the fire, and with a quick movement plunged a knife up to the hilt into his own heart. Seltichan sacrificed himself to the gods.

A Sacrifice to the Gods. Translated by Janina Rodzińska. In
POLISH SHORT STORIES, selected by Zbigniew Żabicki. Warsaw,
Polonia Publishing House, 1960. p.259–[288].

In Sacrifice to the Gods. In TALES BY POLISH AUTHORS . . . Translated by Else C. M. Benecke. Oxford, B. H. Blackwell, 1915. p.163–
198.

Widmo sakurskie. Translated as *The Vision of Sakura.*

The Vision of Sakura. Translated by K. Żuk-Skarszewska. In
Poland (New York), IX, 1928. p.270–275.

Słowacki, Juliusz (1809–1849)

With Mickiewicz and Krasiński, Słowacki belongs to the
Polish trio of the great Romantic poets. Like the others,
he spent most of his short life in exile. In KORDIAN (1834)
the poet based the plot on the coronation of the tsar as
king of Poland and the mission of his Hamletic hero to
kill the tsar in Warsaw. In his tragedy LILLA WENEDA
(1840), by presenting ruthless Lechits against the dreamy
and defenseless Weneds, the poet pointed to the clash in
the Polish national character between the vulgar and the
refined. In KRÓL DUCH (King-Spirit, 1847) Słowacki made an
attempt to grasp the spirit of Polish history. His *Anhelli*
published in Paris in 1838, appeared in English in Dorothea
Prall Radin's translation in 1930 (London, George Allen
and Unwin).

Anhelli. Translated as *Anhelli.*[26]

Résumé. A thousand Polish exiles came to the land of Siberia;
they built a wooden house that they might dwell together in
brotherly love. There was among them great sorrow; they were
longing for their fatherland.

---

[26] This is not a short story. The work is *sui generis,* and can be described as a
poem in prose. An exception has been made for inclusion of *Anhelli* with a
résumé in this work because of the special significance and unique position
this poem in prose holds in Polish letters. (The résumé is based on the
fragmentary translation in THE BLUE FLOWER, ed. by Hermann Kesten.)

When a caravan of Siberian people arrived, their ruler whom they called the Shaman, took pity on the exiles. Forsaking his own people, he came to abide with the exiles, because they were more unfortunate.

The Shaman soon found that their hearts were weak, and that they allowed themselves to be conquered by grief. He feared that misery might transform them into evil and mischievous men. He decided to choose from among them one whom he would love as a son, and to whom he would pass his burden so that in him there might be redemption. He called a youth by the name of Anhelli, and he breathed into him heartfelt love for man and compassion. He said he would go away with this youth to show him many grievous things. The rest were to remain to learn how to endure hunger, wretchedness and sorrow.

One night the Shaman waked Anhelli. After he had put on a white garment, Anhelli followed the old man. They saw a camp of little children. A Russian priest sat on a Tartar horse with two baskets of bread at his saddle. He began to instruct those children according to the new Russian faith. The Shaman pronounced the word of malediction. The priest caught fire and burned to ashes.

Then the Shaman passed with Anhelli over the desert ways of Siberia. Beside the prisons they fell in with men bearing coffins. The dead were still in chains. Anhelli asked the Shaman to waken an old man with a grey beard and white hair. It seemed to him that he had known the man when he was alive. Three times the Shaman waked the man from the dead, but every time Anhelli spoke to him of the past, the old man died again.

Siberian fishermen complained to the Shaman that he had deserted them. They were now full of doubts. They even doubted the very existence of a soul. The Shaman laid Anhelli to sleep, and showed them his spirit in a beautiful form of varying colors with white wings. When Anhelli awoke, he learned from the Shaman that, as soon as it was free, his soul would fly in the direction of his fatherland.

Written in 1838.

Anhelli. Translated by Dorothea Prall Radin. In THE BLUE

FLOWER; edited by Hermann Kesten, illustrated by Z. Czermanski. New York, Roy Publishers [c1946]. p.510–518.
  Fragment.

Anhelli. Translated from the Polish by Dorothea Prall Radin. Edited with an introduction by George Rapall Noyes. London, George Allen and Unwin, Ltd. [1930].
  118 p.
  At head of title: Juljusz Słowacki.

Strug, Andrzej pseud. (1873–1937)

Known under the pseudonym as Andrzej Strug, Tadeusz Gałecki was throughout his life an ardent socialist, concentrating on the revolutionary struggle against Imperial Russia. He was also preoccupied with the futility of war. In his KLUCZ OTCHŁANI (Key to the Abyss, 1929) the author's pacifism reminds us of Remarque. In most of Strug's writings there is a marked influence of Stefan Żeromski. In his best-known novel, ŻÓŁTY KRZYŻ (The Yellow Cross, 1933), the plot is centered on international espionage and the iron rule of Clemenceau during the last year of World War One. Foremost among his volumes of short stories is the collection LUDZIE PODZIEMNI (The Underground People, 1908).

Na stacji. Translated as *At the Station*.

Résumé. It had happened at last. The police got him at the station. As soon as they recognized him they immediately posted men at every exit and on the platform. They telephoned their chief and watched him closely. The chief was to arrive very shortly.

He (probably a prominent socialist leader, when socialism in the Russian-occupied part of Poland was considered a crime) had been watching what was going on all around. This was the end. There was no question about it. He felt relief. He had suitcases with illegal literature, but fortunately he carried nothing to incriminate others.

Everyone had been warning him for a long time that this was going to happen. His friends had advised him to go abroad. They had even given him money for the journey. The party doctors had insisted that he needed a change of air, and advised him to go to . . . Bad Reinerz. He had merely poked fun at them. He had already had several narrow escapes.

Now he was so tired that for a moment he imagined that there was no one around. All this was the hallucination of an exhausted brain. Just get up and go, he thought, and nobody will stop you.

All of a sudden a rumbling thunder rent the air. A teeming crowd of people poured into the hall. That was the train from the frontier. Back was all his strength like a steel spring suddenly released. He plunged into the tumult and got lost in the crowd.

First printed 1905.

At the Station. Translated by Ilona Ralf Sues. In POLISH SHORT STORIES, selected by Zbigniew Żabicki. Warsaw, Polonia Publishing House, 1960. p.311–[319].

Stryjkowski, Julian (1905–   )

Chiwu. Translated as *Chiwu.*

Chiwu. Translated by Krystyna Cękalska; drawings by Mieczysław Piotrowski. In *Poland; Illustrated Magazine,* No. 4 (68) 1960. (Am. ed.) p.25–28.

"Excerpts from a short story."

Preceded by a brief note about the author, by Jacek Bocheński.

Świętochowski, Aleksander (1849–1938)

Writer, playwright, publicist and historian, Świętochowski (known also under the pseudonym as Wł. Okoński) was one of the most important exponents of Polish Positivism which he also voiced in his weekly, *Prawda* (Truth), established 1881. Author of the original treatise on ethics, ŹRÓDŁA MORALNOŚCI (The Sources of Morality, 1912), he also wrote dramas such as OJCIEC MAKARY (Father Makary, 1876), NIEWINNI (The Innocent, 1876), and ASPAZJA (1885).

Świętochowski published several novels, e.g. DRYGAŁOWIE (The Drygals, 1915), and a historical work, HISTORIA CHŁOPÓW POLSKICH W ZARYSIE (An Outline of the History of Polish Peasants, 1928). All his works are permeated with the ideas of Polish Positivism. *Damian Capenko* (1878), *Karl Krug* (1879) and *Klemens Boruta* (1880) are some of the titles of his short stories.

Chawa Rubin. Translated as *Chava Ruby.*

Résumé. Chava Ruby, a young but prematurely withered Jewish woman, struggled on a working capital of three roubles to keep alive herself, her husband Simcha, and four children in a small Polish town, Kazimierz-on-Vistula. Simcha did not do any work. As a Hasid he spent a great deal of time in the temple; apart from that his weak chest had rendered him unfit for any manual work.

Chava, dreaming about prosperity, seized a risky opportunity of buying directly from fishermen, who had just caught the fish, three sturgeons weighing about one hundred and fifty pounds. She did not make the fabulous profit she was hoping for, but the transaction seemed to have turned the tide in Chava's favor. When she was busy selling the rest of the sturgeons, Franek, the Post Office delivery boy, was caught taking money out of two registered letters and dismissed. The postmaster Chrząstkiewicz appointed Chava Ruby as postwoman "to deliver ordinary and registered mail in the town and in the countryside."

Life smiled on Chava. Now she looked much younger, and her children no longer went to sleep hungry. She was on her way to deliver a reigstered letter in Polanówka (which could bring her about a rouble's tip), wearing her new skirt and shoes and a white bonnet, when she was brutally attacked and robbed by the jealous Franek.

Chava died after two days of suffering, and she was too weak to tell anybody that it was Franek who had beaten her, took her letter, and robbed her of ten roubles which she had hidden in a little sack in her bosom.

First printed 1879.

Chava Ruby. Translated by Ilona Ralf Sues. In POLISH SHORT

STORIES, selected by Zbigniew Żabicki. Warsaw, Polonia Publishing House, 1960. p.57–[85].

Szaniawski, Jerzy (1887–)

Melonik profesora Tutki. Translated as *Professor Tutka's Derby.*

Professor Tutka's Derby. Translated by Janina Rodzińska; illustrated by Zbigniew Geppert. In *Poland; Illustrated Magazine,* No. 1 (65) 1960. p.13–[15].
Preceded by a note about the author, by Tadeusz Drewnowski.
From his PROFESOR TUTKA (Professor Tutka).

Wykład profesora Tutki. Translated as *Professor Tutka's Lecture.*

Professor Tutka's Lecture. Translation anonymous. Drawings by Lech Zahorski. In *Poland; Illustrated Magazine,* No. 3 (19) 1956. p.[28]–29.
Preceded by a brief note about the author, by S. K.
From his PROFESOR TUTKA (Professor Tutka).

Szaniawski, Klemens Junosza

Łaciarz. Translated as *The Patcher.*

The Patcher, by Klemens Junosza-Szaniawski. Translated by N. B. Jopson. In *Pologne littéraire,* No. 94–95, 1934. p.[1]–2.

Szczepański, Jan Józef (1919–)

Buty. Translated as *Shoes.*

Shoes. Translated by Janina Rodzińska; drawings by Jan Młodożeniec. In *Poland; Illustrated Magazine,* No. 6 (58) 1959. p.13–16, 25–27.
Preceded by a note about the author, by Wojciech Żukrowski.

Sznaper-Zakrzewska, Stanisława

Młoda lekarka z Prezydenckiej. Translated as *The Young Woman Doctor on Prezydencka Street.*

Résumé. The child was ill. Each day when she came back from the day nursery her cold was worse. Several times her mother thought of letting her stay home, but now she had used the last lump of coal to feed the fire.

(She had finished a play to order and delivered it to the Ministry of Culture. Those being the last days of December, the fiscal books were closed. No more funds were available for the year.)

The mother decided to go to the pediatric branch of the hospital clinic. The weather was freezing. The mother carried her child into the waiting room. The lazy receptionist at the window slipped her nail file into a drawer; she stared at the newcomer reproachfully, and told her to come for her number tomorrow morning at eight. The mother pleaded that she had a card from the district doctor, but the receptionist slammed the window in her face. Only when she threatened to report her to the Director of Staff did she learn that the laryngologist would be there at one.

The mother wheeled the carriage aimlessly through the streets. After an hour she returned to the clinic. Another hour of waiting and she was told that the laryngologist would not come at all. The child's cold was worse; she was more feverish. The mother decided to wait for the afternoon hours beginning at three. Other women waiting with their children would not hear of letting her through. The child's breathing was getting heavier. It was dark when the mother decided to return home and herself apply camomile, oil of camphor, and other home drugs.

The next morning the fever fell. The mother decided to see a doctor anyway, this time privately. She chose the first woman doctor close by, on Prezydencka Street. A young, delicate blonde opened the door. Unfortunately, she said, she could not see the child at home. The mother mentioned something about a "private visit." She smiled indulgently. The mother said she thought the child's condition was bad. The doctor asked them in, examined the child carefully, and gave a prescription, but she declined a payment. The envelope with a modest fee passed back and forth. Finally the woman doctor tucked it into the little girl's coverlet, asking the mother to buy her lemons and orange. Back in the street, the mother comforted her little one, promising to buy her all those things which would give her joy.

First published in Nowa Kultura, *Warsaw, January 8, 1956.*

The Young Woman Doctor on Prezydencka Street, by Stanisława Sznaper-Zakrzewska. [Translated by Elizabeth K. Valkenier.] In BITTER HARVEST; the Intellectual Revolt Behind the Iron Curtain. Edited by Edmund Stillman; introduction by François Bondy. London, Thames and Hudson [1959]. p.138–142.

Szymański, Adam (1852–1916)

Deported to Siberia in 1878 as a result of his patriotic stand against Russia (after the unsuccessful Polish Uprising in 1863), Szymański began writing his SZKICE (Sketches) in exile, of which volume one appeared in print in 1887, volume two in 1890. They show not only the author's deep love for his native land, but are a testimony to his broad humanitarianism embracing all humanity. His Z JAKUCKIEGO OLIMPU (Olympus of the Yakuts, 1910), which extols the virtue of sacrifice among the wild Siberian tribes, precedes similar works on a larger scale by Wacław Sieroszewski.

Dwie modlitwy. Translated as *Two Prayers.*

Résumé.

I.

Long ago for the first time in my life I heard a fine men's choir singing in unison in one of the largest churches of Podlasie. The church was filled to overflowing, and soon everybody joined in the chants which streamed from the choir like burning lava. Loud at first, the voices passed into sobbing until they became scarcely audible .

I stood by my father, and my small body shivered as with fever.

I prayed that those people in the choir might sing less sadly, and that they might feel brighter and happier. I prayed so fervently that I expected God by miracle to stop this unbearable singing instantly. But the organ joined in, the people wept, and a second wave of the imploring chants filled the church. I felt as though the prayers like birds rose high in the church, and there, confined by the vaulting, were circling and clamoring. I flung myself into my father's arms. "Father! Father! Let us go outside to pray," I cried, "there in the sunshine! God Almighty will hear us there, and nothing will hinder our prayers."

II.

In a fit of painful nostalgia I decided to spend Christmas of 18— amongst a group of my countrymen who in desperation had taken over a deserted, fear-inspiring house on the outskirts of X (an unnamed town in Siberia), where some years before people had died of smallpox.

When I reached the house Pan Józef, the shoemaker, was still busy working. Helping him was Pan Jan Horodelski, a former medical student. Other inhabitants of the place were: a stalwart peasant known as Bartek the Shepherd, the locksmith Porankiewicz with a back bent like a bow, and the ex-landowner, Pan Feliks Babiński. That night everybody tried to look his best. Soon Porankiewicz solemnly announced that the dinner was ready in the other room. We entered and saw an unusual sight.

Two candles lighted the table from which wafted the savory odors of the local titbits (the "oładis" and the "pępki"). From the holes in the white table linen peeped hay which had been spread underneath. Present were the bottle of wine and the ceremonial plate of wafer fragments.

As Babiński broke a wafer he became white and speechless with awe on the solemnity of the occasion, and did not recover until Bartek handed him half a glass of vodka.

The faces were wet with tears of sympathy, and everybody began to show penitence by acknowledging his failings and sins. In the final episode the six of us sang all the Polish songs we remembered until our repertoire was exhausted. Bartek was the first to fall on his knees, and then all began to pray. "Turn from us hunger and grievous plague, protect us from bloodshed and war . . ." Suddenly, dressed as he was, Bartek rose and went out of "this den of infection" to pray in the open. He returned singing a joyful Christmas carol and we all joined in. Again we prayed long and fervently, filling our hearts with the fire of truth, confidence, and hope.

Two Prayers. In MORE TALES BY POLISH AUTHORS. Translated by Else C. M. Benecke and Marie Busch. New York, Longmans, Green and company, 1916. p.52–85.

Maciej Mazur. Translated as *Maciej the Mazur*.

Résumé. After leaving Yakutsk I settled in X, a miserable little town further up the Lena river in Siberia. I had promised the shoemaker Stanisław Światełki to write his home letters for him, and although it was a stormy night. I set out from the house. I wrote a letter to Światełki's son and to the priest, asking him to take the young man under his protection. When, reading the letter out loud, I came to the passage in which I requested a Mass for Światełki's dead parents, huge and clumsy Maciej, who lived at the shoemaker's house and did household chores for him, suddenly offered his own three roubles, imploring that the priest should pray for God's mercy for them all.

Soon Maciej, who hardly ever talked to anybody, told us how through his hard and honest work he had saved several hundred roubles toiling as a baker in the gold mines. I prompted him to tell us his life story.

Maciej the Mazur came from the village Mocarze on the Narev river. He was a serf on Pan Olszeski's estate. When Maciej got married, he was set free and given a farm of twenty acres. At the time of the Revolution of 1863, Pan Olszeski did not let him go with the others, but kept him as his private and confidential messenger.

Suddenly Maciej noticed that he had lost his former master's confidence and the village people's respect. He did not know that his own brother Mateus, an outcast of the family, had turned a spy for the Germans, and everyone seemed to be certain that Maciej had a part in the dirty work. When Maciej's wife finally told him about it, he visited his brother's house, went out with him for a walk, and at one point made Walek, whom Mateus took for his own protection, stab him. Maciej confessed the crime and was sentenced for life.

Maciej the Mazur. In MORE TALES BY POLISH AUTHORS. Translated by Else C. M. Benecke and Marie Busch. New York, Longmans, Green, 1916. p.1–51.

Srul z Lubartowa. Translated as *Srul from Lubartów.*

Résumé. It happened in Yakutsk at the beginning of November. On a very cold day we buried one of our men in the colony, Peter Kurp, nicknamed Bałdyga. I came back from the funeral, and unable to write, I allowed my thoughts to be carried away to my native plains on the Vistula. I was interrupted in my thoughts. Dressed in ox and stag's hide, a typical Polish Jew from a small town stood before me.

He was a hawker, and he said that he had spent in Yakutsk three long years. He was a Husyt, a Law abiding Jew. His name was Srul and he lived here with his wife and a daughter. His other three children had died during the journey.

What did he want? He wanted to hear about his country. But he did not want news about politics, about the prices of goods in Poland, and the like. What he did want was to listen to a tale about the plants and flowers which grow in Poland, about the trees and the birds whose names he even no longer remembered. Stroking his red beard he listened, while tears rolled down his cheeks . . .

Written 1885.

Srul—from Lubartów. In TALES BY POLISH AUTHORS . . . Translated by Else C. M. Benecke. Oxford, B. H. Blackwell, 1915. p.119–136.

Srul from Lubartów. Translated by Else C. M. Benecke. In *Poland* (New York), XII, 1931. p.174–176, 227–229.

Srul—from Lubartów. Translated by Else C. M. Benecke. In CANDLES IN THE NIGHT; Jewish Tales by Gentile Authors. Edited by

Joseph L. Baron; with a preface by Carl van Doren. Philadelphia, The Jewish Publication Society of America, 1940 (5700). p.179–191.

Srul from Lubartow. [Translated by Else C. M. Benecke.] In POLISH AUTHORS OF TODAY AND YESTERDAY . . . Selected by Irena Morska. New York, S. F. Vanni [c1947]. p.159–171.

Stolarz Kowalski. Translated as *Kowalski the Carpenter.*

Résumé. It was in Yakutsk, and I made his acquaintance quite accidentally during the Yakut spring. He was of middle stature, greyheaded, and he looked very neglected. He spoke Polish correctly and with a pure accent. He carefully avoided any direct or indirect allusion to his past. He talked principally about his dog. When he got up and tried to walk, I had to turn away my eyes, for his clump feet seemed to cause him the greatest agony. Now Kowalski was ill. Whatever carpentry work he had been dabbling at before, he had to give up. Some weeks passed and he was no better; we were all convinced that this illness was his last.

One morning I was asked to go to see him. Fearing that it was his last hour I took with me the New Testament. Kowalski looked like a dead man, but his voice was clear and loud as never before. He spoke. About forty years ago he was exiled to the steppes of Orenburg. He was young and strong, and after two years he escaped. He was punished for it by being sent to Tomsk, and he escaped again. He was severely punished for this second flight, but he escaped a third time. It was during that escape that his feet were frostbitten and he lost his toes. This time he was sent beyond the Yenessi. He waited six years for another chance to escape, and even with his clump feet, he started off again. His recurring dream now was to die on his mother's grave. He got farther than ever before but, when he was thanking God for His mercy, he was caught and sent to Yakutsk. He had trusted God like a child; now he cursed Him. For him God had become only the God of the wicked.

I began to pray, and then I read passages from the New Testament. Hearing the prayer the dying man tried in vain to lift his hands, but he only murmured, "Lord, by Thy pain forgive me." Kowalski's eyes closed. The life of suffering was ended.

Kowalski the Carpenter; a Siberian Sketch. In SELECTED POLISH TALES. Translated by Else C. M. Benecke and Marie Busch. London, New York [etc.] H. Milford, Oxford University Press [1921]. p.239–260.

Uroczysta wigilja. Translated as *A Pinch of Salt.*

Résumé. In the fourth year of my exile to Siberia, a few days before Christmas, we got the news that an ex-student and fellow-sufferer was to pass through our town on his way back from far-distant Yakut, where he had lived for three years. He was due to arrive on Christmas Eve. The fact that a human being had been able to survive in that remote world bore witness to the strength of the human spirit. The life in the Yakut yurtas was miserable; there was a want of the most necessary European foods, above all, bread.

I was charged with the arrangement of the dinner, assisted by a young student and by the intense interest of the whole colony. My scullion and I were proud of our work. The menu included many elaborate courses; everything was rich and plentiful. A huge fish, weighing twenty pounds, boiled whole, was the crowning success of our art.

At last our guest arrived. He was small and very thin. We sat to our dinner. "Let us be cheerful!" Even the gloomiest faces brightened. A storm of applause greeted the first course. The student filled the guest's plate heaping full. The guest, however, did not eat. The next course followed, and he still did not touch the food. At last he got up and timidly explained. For three years he had tasted no salt. Now he tried to swallow a tiny piece of bread, but—he could not. He entreated the others to eat and be merry, and with tears he sank back into his seat. The spell was broken. All gaiety had vanished and a dead silence brooded over the frightened assembly.

A Pinch of Salt. In SELECTED POLISH TALES. Translated by Else C. M. Benecke and Marie Busch. London, New York [etc.] H. Milford, Oxford University Press [1921]. p.227–238.

Tetmajer, Kazimierz Przerwa (1865–1940)

The author belonged to the group of poets of so-called "Young Poland." His poetry expressed the moods of the "decadentism" of the period: pessimism, disdain for action, longing for nirvana. Seven collections of his poetry were published between 1891 and 1912. Tetmajer received many literary prizes for his poetry; some came for his stories, e.g. *Ksiądz Piotr (Father Peter)*. The most treasured of Tetmajer's poems are those inspired by the Tatra Mountains. His stories, collected in NA SKALNEM PODHALU, published in 1914 and translated into English as TALES OF THE TATRAS have as their inspiration the same source. The author died tragically in Warsaw during the German occupation.

Dziki juhas. Translated as *The Savage Shepherd.*

Résumé. There was a shepherd from Jurgow who was terribly savage; his name was Bronisław Luptowski. His face was as black as charcoal, and he was not only fierce but as strong as a bear. Folk called him "the savage shepherd." The girls ran away from him, but when he caught one by the hand, she was his.

There was, however, one girl whom he could not manage; she was from the Zdziar region and her name was Agnes Hawrancówna. He talked to her as to a saint's picture, and she to him as to a dog. Once when she refused to be his, he grew so furious that he threatened to throw her down the precipice. She stood her ground and he let her go unharmed. Instead he threw down fifty sheep that he was shepherding. At night he was about to throw a huge stone on Agnes's shed where she was sleeping. He would have killed her, but again he did not.

As though afraid of himself he jumped into the forest, and he really went mad. He broke the trees, pulled them up by the roots, tore the bark with his teeth till blood spurted from his lips.

In the morning the huntsmen from Zakopane found him covered with blood, with wounds and holes all over his body. One of them recognized him. Whispering that it was a wench and the forest that had finally got the better of him, the savage shepherd died.

The Savage Shepherd. Translated from the Polish of K. P. Tetmayer by H. E. Kennedy. In *The Slavonic (and East European) Review,* XIV, 1935–36. p.550–556.

The Savage Shepherd. In his TALES OF THE TATRAS . . . Translated by H. E. Kennedy and Zofia Umińska. Foreword by William John Rose. London, Minerva Publishing Company [1941]. p.123–133.

The Savage Shepherd. In his TALES OF THE TATRAS. Translated by H. E. Kennedy and Zofia Umińska. Foreword by Carl Carmer. New York, Roy Publishers [1943]. p.161–173.

Jak się Józek Smaś pojechał wysłuchać. Translated as *How Jozek Smas Went to Confession.*

Résumé. Józek Smaś Solicarz was a mighty hunter but a still mightier robber. He robbed not from need but because he loved to. He was as godless as Antichrist himself. In spite of this everything went well with him.

But as luck had favored him, so it left him. When he was about fifty-five, a storm caught him while he was hunting near Frozen Pond. For three days and three nights he sat in the shelter of a rock. When he reached home, illness crept upon him. Neither bear fat nor marmot fat did him any good. Herbs and charms did not help. Old women urged the robber to go to confession. After deliberation Józek Smaś made up his mind to go to the Lord God in Ludzimir. He took with him two fiddlers and a double-bass player. He had two pistols and two knives in his belt, he held an axe in his fist and a flint-lock was flung over his shoulder. He confessed to the priest that he hanged many high up in the trees, but he never did so on the Polish side of the mountains, only over in Hungary.

After the confession Smaś got well. He gave up his robber's trade. He was not afraid of the devils the little priest prated about, but if Lord God was good to Smaś, so he would be to Lord God. He always was like that.

How Jozek Smas Went to Confession. In his TALES OF THE TATRAS. Translated by H. E. Kennedy and Zofia Uminska. Foreword by William John Rose. London, Minerva Publishing Company [1941]. p.153–163.

How Jozek Smas Went to Confession. In his TALES OF THE TATRAS. Translated by H. E. Kennedy and Zofia Uminska. Foreword by Carl Carmer. New York, Roy Publishers [1943]. p.201–213.

Jak umarł Jakób Zych. Translated as *The Departure of Jacob Zych.*

Résumé. One morning in December Jacob Zych said to his wife Katherine, "Till today I've lived and today I shall die." He was ninety-three or, perhaps, ninety-five years old. He recollected that he had married Kate who was much younger than he, only because he had threatened her parents that he would set fire to their cottage.

When his crony, Francis Gombos, came in, his remembrances went back to the good old times when most people lived to be a hundred. He didn't need a priest, he said, as he did not wish to talk to a farm-hand when he was soon to talk to the Master Himself.

Later Zych's children, grandchildren and great-grandchildren gathered together in his cottage to bid him farewell. He asked everybody to leave except his favorite grandson, Staszek Koys, whom he told of a treasure brought from beyond the Tatra Mountains, and hidden close to Saint John's chapel near Novy Targ.

Towards evening Jacob Zych got very weak and kissed his wife good-bye. He got up by himself and took a last look at the mountains. He made three crosses with his robber's knife in the air, and crossed himself with it three times. Then with the point he made a circle round himself on the floor. Within that circle he lay down, closed his eyes, sighed a few times and died.

The Departure of Jacob Zych. In his TALES OF THE TATRAS . . . Translated by H. E. Kennedy and Zofia Umińska. Foreword by William John Rose. London, Minerva Publishing Company [1941]. p.27–36.

The Departure of Jacob Zych. In his TALES OF THE TATRAS. Translated by H. E. Kennedy and Zofia Uminska. Foreword by Carl Carmer. New York, Roy Publishers [1943]. p.35–46.

Jak wzieni Wojtka Chrońca. Translated as *How Wojtek Chroniets Was Taken*.

Résumé. Wojtek Chroniets had deserted from the Austrian army and was hiding in the upper pastures in the hut of the chief shepherd. Little Jacob was sent on an errand to the inn, where he saw that Kasia Penckowska, Wojtek's sweetheart, was dancing—contrary to her promise—with Bronisław Walencak of Kosny Forge. When Wojtek threw the little boy a twenty-crown piece, little Jacob told him what he had seen.

Wojtek took his hatchet and ran out of the shed. Two faithful Hajaceks followed him. At the inn Wojtek met Florian Francuz, an ugly and rich fellow, who was also in love with Kasia. As he couldn't get her himself, he wanted Wojtek to take her. Florian's poisoned words against Walencak only added fuel to the fire already burning in Wojtek's heart.

Walencak continued to dance with Kasia. An exchange of songs followed between Walencak and Wojtek. Then Wojtek rushed forward, caught Kasia by the pigtail, flung her on the floor, and kicked her in the chest reminding her of her broken vows. Kasia's brother moved in defense of his sister, while two Hajaceks went forward to help Wojtek. Soon the floor was smeared with blood. Walencak's brain spurted out under the blow of Wojtek's hatchet. Wojtek called for the music to play, and asked the innkeeper to bring paper and ink. Wojtek dictated a statement about his killing Kasia and Walencak, and also pleading guilty as a deserter; he promised to wait for the gendarmes to get him. Then he let his chin fall on to his chest—and he slept.

How Wojtek Chroniets Was Taken. In his TALES OF THE TATRAS . . . Translated by H. E. Kennedy and Zofia Umińska. Foreword by William John Rose. London, Minerva Publishing Company [1941]. p.165–177.

How Wojtek Chroniets Was Taken. In his TALES OF THE TATRAS. Translated by H. E. Kennedy and Zofia Uminska. Foreword by Carl Carmer. New York, Roy Publishers [1943]. p.217–232.

Krystka. Translated as *Krystka.*

Résumé. It was on an afternoon late in September, when Krystka was sixteen, that she met her Jaś. While she was herding cows she was singing a song about being lonely, when suddenly she heard a man's voice above her head. Jaś had an eagle's feather in his cap, and Krystka thought with delight that he might be a robber. They kissed and Jaś was gone.

He was away for a long time, but when he came back Jaś became Krystka's lover. After three years of his visits off and on, Jaś left her. Krystka learned that it was Yadviga who had stolen Jaś's heart, and she ran after him to Wołoszyn.

Her heart was filled with sorrow and a desire for vengeance. She found Jasiek in the shed. She fell on her knees before him and implored him to come back to her. He refused with scorn. It was Yadviga's grey eyes that now fascinated him. Hearing this, Krystka said that she would presently bring Yadviga to him. She seized a big brand from the hearth, and ran straight to Yadviga's hut. Crying, "I want your eyes," she thrust the flaming brand into her rival's face. When Jaś arrived on the scene Yadviga's grey eyes were burnt out. "Now you'll be mine," she said to Jaś.

Krystka took his hand and drew him, unresisting, into the dark wood.

Krystka. In his TALES OF THE TATRAS . . . Translated by H. E. Kennedy and Zofia Umińska. Foreword by William John Rose. London, Minerva Publishing Company [1941]. p.135–152.

Krystka. In his TALES OF THE TATRAS. Translated by H. E. Kennedy and Zofia Uminska. Foreword by Carl Carmer. New York, Roy Publishers [1943]. p.177–198.

Ksiądz Piotr. Translated as *Father Peter.*

Résumé. Father Peter discussed everything with his organist, Pan Dzięgielewski, from oats to politics. He teased him about his nobility, turning the name of his coat of arms, Ozory, into Chicory. (His curate passed his days and nights studying theological works.) Father Peter lacked thirteen years to be a hundred; he had spent about fifty as a priest in Kłonice. He would not give away to God even one day of those thirteen years; he was determined to live to a hundred.

It was not always that Father Peter had worn a cassock. In his youth he had been a cavalry officer. When his servant had failed to polish his sword to his satisfaction, he clouted him just as all the Załański family had always done. He had stolen Panna Jadwiga Karśnicka from his friend Hilary Roszczewski, and hoped to die with the epaulettes of a general. Then he decided to make expiation for his sins and for the sins of other Załańskis; he became a priest.

The estate on which Father Peter now lived resembled Noah's Ark. Apart from the usual domestic animals, the priest had a small menagerie where deer, hares and foreign geese lived in perfect harmony. This menagerie as well as the garden were under the care of old men and women, all the cripples and orphans that could be found in the vicinity.

But one autumn evening, when the sun had slipped behind the horizon, Father Peter suddenly remarked to Pan Dzięgielewski that it was his time to go. His eyes gazed over to the peaceful view bathed in the moonlight. He told Pan Dzięgielewski that he should be dressed in the new cassock, and his boots ought to be polished. His military orders were to be put on his breast and the sword hidden in the folds of his cassock so that the curate would not see it. Everything had been taken care of in the will. Nothing was to be sold. There were funds for everything: for the old men and women, for the orphans and the cripples. Two bulls, ten thousand in cash and various other things were left for Pan Dzięgielewski (who now wept).

When little Ignace came to lead Father Peter to bed, he was dead.

Father Peter. Translated by K. Żuk-Skarszewska. In *Poland* (New York), VII, 1926. p.206–209, 232–238.

Father Peter. Translated from the Polish of Kazimierz Przerwa Tetmayer by D. F. Tait. In *The Slavonic (and East European) Review*, XVI, 1937–38. p.291–306.

Preceded by a short note about the author's silver jubilee.

Father Peter, by Casimir Tetmajer. [Translated by K. Żuk-Skarszewska.] In POLISH SHORT STORIES, by Joseph Weyssenhof, Piotr Choynowski, Kornel Makuszynski [and others] . . . London, Minerva Publishing Company [1943]. p.77–91.

Ku niebu. Translated as *Towards Heaven.*

Résumé. Hanka was crossing the Skupni foothills. The wind was blowing hard, and the freezing cold penetrated to her very bones. She moved like a ghost amid the falling snow. Her heart was filled with cruel pain and grief. It was all the fault of Woytek Mrowca of Olcha.

Hanka had fallen madly in love with him until he had his way with her. But when she spoke of marriage to him, he only jeered and called her a beggar. When she told him of the coming baby, his answer was, "How do I know that? You serve in a Jewish house. Maybe it won't even be a Christian."

These words were now ringing in her ears. She made her way down towards the shelters—not by the path, for there was no trace of that, but over the snow. She had been bypassing the shelter where Woytek used to sleep. She went on toward the Green Mountains. Hanka looked up and saw the Queen of Angels. The brilliance began to advance in the direction of the Lily Mountain. Hanka followed it.

"Lady, I'd like to sit down," she whispered. "Sit down, then," replied the soft voice from the brilliance. Hanka sat down. She began to feel sleepy. Frightened, she made an effort to get up, but she no longer had the strength. "Give me your hand!" said the Mother of God. And Hanka gave Her her hand.

Towards Heaven. In his TALES OF THE TATRAS . . .Translated by H. E. Kennedy and Zofia Umińska. Foreword by William John Rose. London, Minerva Publishing Company [1941]. p.179–189.

Towards Heaven. In his TALES OF THE TATRAS. Translated by H. E. Kennedy and Zofia Uminska. Foreword by Carl Carmer. New York, Roy Publishers [1943]. p.235–247.

O Marysi dalekiej. Translated as *Far-away Marysia/Far-off Marisya/ Far-off Marysia.*

Résumé. Jasiek Mosienzny played beautifully on the fiddle, and he knew how to make up songs. He wandered continually from place to place, and girls everywhere wanted him to marry them. But he paid them no attention. And then he became acquainted with Marysia Chocholovska from Kościeliska Valley who cared for cattle near the Ornak Mountain.

She was a strange lass. She had misty blue eyes that seemed to look around her, but she saw nothing in the world. Folk called her "far-off Marysia." Many boys wanted to marry her, but she thanked them for their offers, and refused.

Jasiek Mosienzny fell in love with that far-off Marysia. She listened to his playing, but when he asked her to be his wife, she refused him, too. Jasiek was desperately unhappy; he loved her so much.

Later on, between sobs, she told him that she had loved the boy with the grey eyes who had led Zosia Tsayovna to the altar. He did not want her, so she made a vow to die a maiden. She did like Jasiek very much, but all the same she asked him to leave her alone. She cared now for nothing but death.

Jasiek went, and, while he played his fiddle, he understood Marysia's vow.

Part I of his Jak Jasiek Mosiężny nie mógł znaleźć szczęścia.

Far-away Marysia. Translated from the Polish of K. P. Tetmayer by H. E. Kennedy and Z. Umińska. In *The Slavonic (and East European) Review,* XV, 1936–37. p.532–542.

Far-off Marisya, by K. Tetmayer. [Translated by H. E. Kennedy and Zofia Umińska.] In THE POLISH SHORT STORIES. Edited by Umadevi. [Bombay] Indo-Polish Library. No. 35 [c1946]. p.57–69.

Far-off Marysia. In his TALES OF THE TATRAS . . . Translated by H. E. Kennedy and Zofia Umińska. Foreword by William John Rose. London, Minerva Publishing Company [1941]. p.11–26.

Far-off Marysia. In his TALES OF THE TATRAS. Translated by H. E. Kennedy and Zofia Uminska. Foreword by Carl Carmer. New York, Roy Publishers [1943]. p.13–31.

O wójtowej Marynie. Translated as *Maryna/The Miller's Maryna.*

Résumé. Maryna, the miller's daughter of Rogoźnik village, was tall and straight and held her head high. Her eyebrows were black, her eyes dark blue. When she walked, even through the greatest crowd, everyone made way for her.

One day Kuba Gonsiorek sent Jasiek Mosienzny, called the Musician (the same one who had been rejected by far-off Marysia from Chochlov) to take a sack of spring wheat to the mill. Jasiek took the sack, and when he later returned for the flour, Maryna asked him to leave Gonsiorek and take a job at the mill.

When Jasiek took service with Maryna, he could not eat, he could not sleep, he was so much in love with her. He hardly dared look at her. Maryna, like a king's daughter, appeared to pay no attention to him. Then at a wedding at which Jasiek played the fiddle, Mat, son of a former mayor of Rogoźnik, led Maryna in a dance. Four weeks later the betrothal of Mat to Maryna was announced.

Later, Jasiek found out from crying Maryna (Mat had left his betrothed in no doubt as to who would be the master in their house) that she had engaged him to work because she had a liking for him. But he was soft and did not take advantage of the situation, so now she was marrying Mat.

Jasiek played at their wedding. Then he went toward Hungary, and no one heard of him any more.

Part II of his Jak Jasiek Mosiężny nie mógł znaleźć szczęścia.

Maryna. In his TALES OF THE TATRAS . . . Translated by H. E. Kennedy and Zofia Umińska. Foreword by William John Rose. London, Minerva Publishing Company [1941]. p.37–58.

Maryna. In his TALES OF THE TATRAS. Translated by H. E. Kennedy and Zofia Uminska. Foreword by Carl Carmer. New York, Roy Publishers [1943]. p.49–75.

Maryna, by K. P. Tetmajer. [Translated by H. E. Kennedy and Zofia Umińska.] In THE WINTER MAIDENS, AND OTHER SHORT STORIES. Edited by Umadevi. [Bombay] The Indo-Polish Library, 1947. p.3–21.

The Miller's Maryna. Translated from the Polish of K. P. Tetmayer by H. E. Kennedy. In *The Slavonic (and East European) Review*, X, 1931–32. p.684–701.

Editor's note: "In the translation of this fine story the names have been somewhat transliterated for the convenience of the Western readers."

O Zosi Walcakównej. Translated as *Old Waltsak's*[27] *Daughter.*

Résumé. Johym Walcak's new wife abused Zosia and Jaś, Walcak's children from his first marriage, but after Jaś—then only eight years old—had once hit his stepmother on the arm with a poker, she did not dare beat them. Jaś and Zosia loved each other greatly.

When they grew up, and Jaś was once dancing at the inn, two famous bandits, Isidor Capek of Capkovka and Maciek Nowobilski, walked in. "Flint" Nowobilski asked Jaś to come out; he wanted to talk to him. Soon Jasiek Walcak passed the test and joined the bandits. For two years he went out plundering. Zosia was a pious girl and she suffered terribly.

One June night Zosia had a dream that she saw Jaś's head, cut from his body, rolling down over the rocks. She decided to speak to him. When she begged him to stay at home, Jaś told her the magnificent stories of the great and dangerous life of adventure with the bandits. But Zosia finally triumphed, and made Jaś go to the Miracle-working Mother of God at Ludzimir. Jasiek could not make his confession, for the priest was ill, but the brother and sister knelt before the altar, and repeating after Zosia, Jaś made a secret vow to God never to go plundering any more.

When the bandits called on Jaś the same evening, he forgot all about his vows, and went off with them again. Zosia stayed by her bedside praying the whole night and the whole day, when the figure of Jaś, pale and bloody, suddenly appeared beckoning toward her.

---

27 The spelling "Waltsak" in the title, and "Walcak" in the text has been preserved in this résumé as it appears in the translation. (This applies to both the London and the New York editions.)

"Jaś" and "Jasiek" have been used interchangeably.

Zosia followed the phantom into the woods until she found Jaś's corpse in the clearing among the limestone rocks.

Old Waltsak's Daughter. In his TALES OF THE TATRAS . . . Translated by H. E. Kennedy and Zofia Umińska. Foreword by William John Rose. London, Minerva Publishing Company [1941]. p.99–121.

Old Waltsak's Daughter. In his TALES OF THE TATRAS. Translated by H. E. Kennedy and Zofia Uminska. Foreword by Carl Carmer. New York, Roy Publishers [1943]. p.131–158.

On. Translated as *He*.

Résumé. The immense black bear was born and reared in the dark fir forest beneath the Great Peak. In all, a tribe of fifteen bears lived in the Dark Fir Wood. But "he" had no rival. He had sides like a tree trunk and a head as big as a bush. He was the most terrible bear of them all. It was he who in broad daylight first killed an ox on the meadow which the shepherds had taken for their own.

In the autumn, when most of the shepherds with their herds had gone down to the village, there remained a couple of them with a flock of sheep which were shut up in a pen. One frosty night "He" fell like an avalanche upon the meadow and massacred the crowded sheep. "He" killed more than thirty. Another time he fell upon a fierce bison near Mount Krzyvan. "He" was victorious in the deadly fight. He slept through the winter somewhere in the Hlinska Valley. In the spring "He" began again to kill the oxen and molest the herds and shepherds.

One drizzly night, when on the way to renew his attack, he suddenly felt a terrible pain; the iron teeth of a trap had sunk into his hind leg. In the morning men saw him and attacked him with a hail of stones and arrows. One man at a close encounter pierced his breast with the iron point of a pike. Soon after "His" monstrous skin was drying in the sun.

He. Translated from the Polish of K. P. Tetmayer by H. E. Kennedy. In *The Slavonic (and East European) Review*, XII, 1933–34. p.13–21.

He. In his TALES OF THE TATRAS . . . Translated by H. E. Kennedy and Zofia Umińska. Foreword by William John Rose. London, Minerva Publishing Company [1941]. p.59–71.

He. In his TALES OF THE TATRAS. Translated by H. E. Kennedy and Zofia Umińska. Foreword by Carl Carmer. New York, Roy Publishers [1943]. p.79–94.

Orlice. Translated as *Eaglets*.

Eaglets. Translated from the Polish of K. Tetmayer by H. E. Kennedy and Z. Umińska. In *The Slavonic (and East European) Review*, XVI, 1937–38. p.520–538.

Szkice opowieści o Zwyrtałowi muzyce (o Zwyrtale muzykancie). Translated as *Zwyrtala the Fiddler*.

Résumé. Old Maciek Zwyrtała died and his soul set out to heaven with a fiddle under his arm. Waiting for heaven's gate to open he began to play. Little angels from all over came to listen. He played robber music and the little angels were delighted.

In a flash the news was all over heaven that a highlandman who played the fiddle had come. Eventually it came to the ears of Lord God Himself. Lord God sent for him, and smoking a pipe (Lord God was resting that day as it was Sunday) commanded Zwyrtała to play the robber's dance. No young men from Podhale were to be found in heaven to dance, but Zwyrtała played and played until all the little angels, the grown-up angels, and the archangels, the saved souls, and even Saint Cecilia, all sang robbers' tunes.

Archangel Gabriel was very much distressed. Zwyrtała would make highlandmen in heaven of them all. Saint Peter called Zwyrtała and said he had to go. But where? Saint Peter did not know. Zwyrtała suggested that he come down to earth, to the woods and valleys, to play his fiddle and see to it that old tunes were not forgotten. With Saint Peter's permission Zwyrtała came down the Milky Way, singing as he went, till he reached the peaks of the Tatras.

Zwyrtala the Fiddler. In his TALES OF THE TATRAS . . . Translated by H. E. Kennedy and Zofia Umińska. Foreword by William John Rose. London, Minerva Publishing Company [1941]. p.87–97.

Zwyrtala the Fiddler. In his TALES OF THE TATRAS. Translated by H. E. Kennedy and Zofia Umińska. Foreword by Carl Carmer. New York, Roy Publishers [1943]. p.115–127.

Zwyrtala the Fiddler, by K. P. Tetmajer. Translated by H. E. Kennedy and Zofia Umińska. In THE WINTER MAIDENS, AND OTHER SHORT STORIES. Edited by Umadevi. [Bombay] The Indo-Polish Library, 1947. p.32–41.

Zimowe panny albo o Maćku, który przepadł w górach. Translated as *The Winter Maidens.*

Résumé. Maciek Scyrbularz was a highland shepherd until something went wrong with his heart. For twenty years he had been sitting at home like an old woman, and he was now sixty years old. He had neither wife nor children, so he talked to his old dog, Singer. When the dog died, Maciek had nobody to talk to.

One day in May a lovely scented breeze was coming from the Tatras. Maciek came out of his cottage, and began to walk straight ahead. He entered the forest, and came across a spring. When Maciek drank from it, something bright and glorious filled his head. He left the forest behind and reached the rocks. He drank again from the mountain spring, and then he saw a strange sight.

Andrysh Michna had told him in his youth about the winter maidens. It was dangerous to fix your eyes on them. The maidens were the souls of sixty nuns killed by a plague, all at the same hour. An angel was carrying the souls to heaven, when he decided to leave the whole sack of them under a rock until the next morning. The devil asked the wind to undo the sack, and the souls flew out all over the place. The wind took them, and ran off with them toward the frozen sea.

It was these winter maidens that Maciek now saw before him. They were dancing on the ice. Maciek joined them in the dance. Suddenly the wind blew, and the maidens disappeared. Terrible pain shot through Maciek's heart. He lay down on the ice waiting for death to come.

The Winter Maidens. In his TALES OF THE TATRAS . . . Translated by H. E. Kennedy and Zofia Umińska. Foreword by William John Rose. London, Minerva Publishing Company [1941]. p.73–85.

The Winter Maidens. In his TALES OF THE TATRAS. Translated by H. E. Kennedy and Zofia Uminska. Foreword by Carl Carmer. New York, Roy Publishers [1943]. p.97–112.

The Winter Maidens, by K. P. Tetmajer. [Translated by H. E. Kennedy and Zofia Umińska.] In THE WINTER MAIDENS AND OTHER SHORT STORIES. Edited by Umadevi. [Bombay] The Indo-Polish Library, 1947. p.22–31.

Tetmayer, Casimir, *see* Tetmajer, Kazimierz Przerwa

Weyssenhoff, Józef (1860–1932)

At the beginning of his literary career, Weyssenhoff was under the influence of Sienkiewicz; later he came under the spell of Anatole France. He is best known for his ŻYWOT I MYŚLI ZYGMUNTA PODFILIPSKIEGO (Life and Thought of Zygmunt Podfilipski, 1898) in which he created the character of Mr. Podfilipski, now famous throughout Poland. Podfilipski is a Warsaw snob, a pompous dilettante and a shallow *arbiter elegantiarum,* treated by the author with subtle irony. Weyssenhoff's novel, SOBÓL I PANNA, was translated into English by K. Żuk-Skarszewska and published under the title, THE SABLE AND THE GIRL (1929).

Dwa sumienia. Translated as *The Voice.*

Résumé. Beautiful Elżbieta's unpractical mind was a constant theme of discussion in the family circle. After the death of her parents she found herself under the protection of her relatives. At seventeen she married Mieczysław Humański, a millionaire scion of a family of recently acquired importance.

Pan Humański who had many business interests expected his wife to help him occasionally. But Pani Elżbieta did not feel that religious respect for money that characterizes sensible and well-born people. Right now she left the gentlemen's company after her husband tried in vain to use her influence and beauty in the case of a certain firm (Izidor Rodyn & Co.) which was anxious to have its gas stoves introduced on Russian railways.

At that moment Antoni, the valet, announced unwillingly that some peasant wished to see his mistress. Although still young, the peasant's face was worn and haggard, and he had a wild, hunted look in his eyes. For a long time he could not utter a word besides saying that he came from the forest and that his name was Jan Kłoda. He had waited for the voice within him to speak, and now he came to the gracious lady, for people said that she was a saint. He had seen people felling trees. When the case was brought to court, he had accepted ten roubles for not speaking against them. He was very poor and his wife was sick. He had sworn a false oath. Will she, please, take those ten roubles from him. He never touched them. Pani Elżbieta took the hateful roubles from his hands, kissed the peasant's unkempt locks, and assured him that God would forgive him.

That evening Pani Elżbieta was so stubborn and absent-minded that her husband never even mentioned the subject of gas stoves. There was talk, started by the servants, that their mistress was kissing peasants.

The Voice. Translated by Żuk-Skarszewska. In *Poland* (New York), VIII, 1927. p.272–274, 302–304, 306.

The Voice, by Joseph Weyssenhof. [Translated by K. Żuk-Skarszewska.] In POLISH SHORT STORIES, by Joseph Weyssenhof, Piotr Choynowski, Kornel Makuszynski [and others] . . . London, Minerva Publishing Company [1943]. p.7–15.

The Voice, by Jozeph [Jozef, in the table of contents] Weyssenhof. [Translated by K. Żuk-Skarszewska.] In THE POLISH SHORT STORIES. Edited by Umadevi. [Bombay] Indo-Polish Library. No. 35 [c1946]. p.1–11.

Introducing Varshulka. Fragment from his SOBÓL I PANNA (THE SABLE AND THE GIRL).

Introducing Varshulka; an Episode from the Famous Novel THE SABLE AND THE GIRL. Translated by K. Żuk-Skarszewska. In *Poland* (New York), VII, 1926. p.478–480, 509–512.

Rendezvous. Fragment from his SOBÓL I PANNA (THE SABLE AND THE GIRL).

Rendezvous; Another Episode from THE SABLE AND THE GIRL. Translated by K. Żuk-Skarszewska. In *Poland* (New York), VII, 1926. p.533–534, 536, 567–571.

Wierzyński, Kazimierz (1894–   )

Wierzyński has published other works besides poems, but first and foremost he belongs to poetry. One of the five leading lyric poets between the wars, he is known internationally for his LAUR OLIMPIJSKI (The Olympic Laurel) of the Olympic Games fame. Competing in poetry, as the athletes did in the stadium, he won for it the first prize in 1928. He has been publishing poetry ever since his first collection, WIOSNA I WINO (Spring and Wine) appeared in 1919, followed by WRÓBLE NA DACHU (Sparrows on the Roof) in 1920. All of them, including the last one, SIEDEM PODKÓW (Seven Horse-Shoes, 1954), are contained in his POEZJE ZEBRANE (Collected Poems, London and New York, n.d.). His best known prose work is THE LIFE AND DEATH OF CHOPIN (1949) with a foreword by Artur Rubinstein. Wierzyński's most recent titles include a collection of poems, KUFER NA PLECACH (A Trunk on my Back, Paris, 1964) and a volume of his correspondence, personal reminiscences, etc., entitled CYGAŃSKIM WOZEM (My Gypsy Life, London, 1966). The author now resides in Rome.

Chłopi. Translated as *The Peasants.*

Résumé. "According to the account of Private M."

Besides the regular Polish army, there was still another one during the war with the Germans: the army of the peasants. When a regular army unit had no maps, the peasant became map, compass and guide. When a halt was called in a strange region, the peasant became the quartermaster. When the units lost contact with their bases, the peasant provided them with food. Often the peasant's home became a soldier's hospital. All this was done without compulsion; the peasants' "army for everything" was a volunteer army.

The peasants' special enemy were German fighting planes and bombers, which hunted and killed a great many civilian men, women, and children in the fields.

This is what Private M., later a well-known public figure among the Polish émigrés, told the author.

On the ninth of September M. was between Warsaw and X., near a certain village which he preferred not to name. It was a village of the past. All that remained of it were heaps of ruin. Clouds of smoke were still rising from glowing embers. To the question of when the village was set afire, one of the peasants replied, "Every day." Even the ruins were repeatedly bombed by the Germans.

At that very moment a plane appeared in the sky. Immediately Polish anti-aircraft guns opened fire. The plane did not increase its speed, but kept descending. Its motor was choking. It dived sharply downward. It was now about a kilometer away.

M. and his colleagues started out for the plane, but the peasants were ahead of them. They began running as they stood. The pilot hid himself behind the fuselage and began to shoot. He killed one of the attackers and wounded three, before one of the peasants jabbed at him with a pitchfork. Then the others got to him. When the soldiers reached the plane, the job was finished.

"It was," said M., "as if they wanted to keep the whole event for themselves . . . they had avenged themselves. It was their own business."

The Peasants. In his THE FORGOTTEN BATTLEFIELD. Translated from the Polish by Edmund Ordon. Illustrated by Zdzislaw Czermanski. New York, Roy Publishers [c1944]. p.133–141.

Garść wody. Translated as *A Handful of Water.*

    Résumé. "According to the account of Commander L."

In the summer of 1940, after the fall of France, Lisbon became the asylum for all European refugees simply because the trains went no further. The only country which permitted entry into its boundaries without any special difficulties was Brazil. That was why the author and his family went there.

In Rio during his visits to the port and other spots on the coast, the author had met a participant in the battles on the Hel peninsula, Commander L. The Commander knew every millimeter of the Polish coast. For some time he had commanded one of the Polish submarines. From him the author heard the following account of the heroic coastal battles.

Near Gdańsk there was a small promontory called Westerplatte, leased to Poland by the Free City. Westerplatte had an area of one square kilometer. A force of 175 soldiers and five officers defended itself there for seven days. It was smashed to pieces by sea and ground artillery, but never taken by storm.

When Gdynia was taken by the Germans, the remaining Polish forces gathered in the naval port of Oksywie. The free coast diminished to five square kilometers. Colonel Dąbek defended himself there until he was left with only thirty men in the torrential rain of fire from air, land and sea. When he had only one last bullet in his rifle, he left it for himself.

From Oksywie the Polish resistance was transferred to the Hel peninsula whose length is thirty-five, with a coastline of about seventy kilometers. The widest spot measured only two kilometers. All attacks were successfully repulsed by counterattacks, but, like Oksywie, it came under the crushing fire from all directions, meter by meter. To cut themselves off from the Germans it was decided to use the torpedo heads as mines, and blow up the narrowest portion of the peninsula. Commander L. was commanded to carry out the orders. Five days later ten tons of mines exploded underground. Hel became an island. It was a volcano. Impregnable Hel defended itself until the first of October, and surrendered only when all provisions and ammunition were exhausted.

A Handful of Water. In his THE FORGOTTEN BATTLEFIELD. Translated from the Polish by Edmund Ordon. New York, Roy Publishers [c1944]. p.91–107.

Nie wszystko skończone. Translated as *All Is Not Yet Finished.*

Résumé. "According to the account of Second Lieutenant R."

The worst was that it came after the victories. After the attack on Łódź, after the taking of Łowicz, after defeating the Germans, R. and his unit knew nothing about the fate of other fronts. Suddenly they were ordered to stop operations and withdraw.

On the sixteenth of September Second Lieutenant R. received orders to prepare a crossing over the Bzura River. R.'s task was to find the shallowest spot of the river. Around midnight he had located a ford. Two other crossings were being readied, and sappers were building a bridge nearby. R. was ordered to remain at the crossing until the evening of the next day.

At dawn the entire plain before the river was crowded with wagons, artillery, and cars. About two hundred wagons with wounded men were to cross first. Eighty of those were filled with Germans. About thirty wagons had crossed when something frightful occurred; the throbbing of plane engines was heard. Dive bombers attacked R.'s crossing, two other crossings, the troops and supply columns. The frightened horses tore their harnesses and jumped on one another. Dust rose above the earth like a moving ceiling. The fields were full of bomb craters and multilated corpses. The river was congested with overturned wagons and the dead bodies of men and horses. The attacks continued throughout the day. R. learned later that this had been an attack by the entire German air force on the Polish front.

More fighting with great losses was in store for R. and his men even after they had finally made the crossing. When their ammunition was exhausted, they left their horses, and divided into platoons. They tried to get through as best they could.

All Is Not Yet Finished. In his THE FORGOTTEN BATTLEFIELD. Translated from the Polish by Edmund Ordon. New York, Roy Publishers [c1944]. p.161–168.

Nieznani żołnierze. Translated as *Unknown Soldiers.*

Résumé. "According to the account of Lieutenant P."

On the ninth or tenth of September (1939) Lieutenant P. was

riding on horseback from Lwów to Przemyśl with an important mission. He chanced to meet his former commander at the officers' artillery school, Colonel Z. The road to Lwów was cut off and there was no other way of getting there. Colonel Z. asked the lieutenant to stay with him. He was lacking a commander for an anti-tank battery.

That was how Lieutenant P. came to command a unit which he had never seen. Searching for the battery, Lieutenant P. and his five men, already quite hungry, stopped before a peasant hut. The housewife immediately began to prepare some eggs. They had barely begun eating when German planes appeared above the road. Their horses could be seen from the air. To save the hut P. suggested that he and his men clear out. The woman's answer was: "Let them burn it, let them kill my children, as long as we win. . . ."

It was evening before Lieutenant P. found his battery. The first news he brought his men, whom he now saw for the first time, was that they had to change their position at night. The following day the battery was ordered to carry out a flanking maneuver. At nine in the evening they moved out of the forest. Colored rockets began to explode, illuminating the terrain, and perhaps signalling the battery's presence. Firing began simultaneously. The battery's targets were German gun flashes. To mislead the enemy P. fired alternately at their right and left wings, pretending that they had two batteries.

An explosion threw Lieutenant P. to the ground. After regaining consciousness he arose without pain. The Germans had been thrust back by the attack. Two tanks were destroyed. At every step there was a burning German car.

Only then P. noticed that he was wounded. Unknown soldiers were now his devoted men with whom he had been in battle.

Unknown Soldiers. In his THE FORGOTTEN BATTLEFIELD. Translated from the Polish by Edmund Ordon. New York, Roy Publishers [c1944]. p.153–160.

Patrol. Translated as *Patrol.*

Résumé. A small segment of the Russo-Austrian front line presents a perfect example of an almost idyllic peace. The narrator, an officer in the Austrian army, fights against the Russians. The scenery is so beautiful that, in spite of war, it makes one Lieutenant sing the incredible: "Here I could live and love forever."

At the foot of the ridge between the Russian and the Austrian positions a few ramshackle peasant huts can be seen. The sight of the huts irritates the Austrian artillery officer. When one of the peasants begins quietly to plow his field, the fate of the huts, that is, their destruction by the Austrian artillery, seems to be sealed.

The narrator decides to warn the peasants. He sets out on the mission with a small patrol. Before they reach their destination the Russian artillery opens fire and destroys the very huts which were to be the aim of the Austrians.

The plowing peasant becomes a tragic symbol of peace caught in the midst of an irrational conflict.

> *From his* GRANICE ŚWIATA (*The Frontiers of the World*), *1933.*

Patrol. Translated by Julius Balbin. In 10 CONTEMPORARY POLISH STORIES . . . Edited by Edmund Ordon; with an introduction by Olga Scherer-Virski. Detroit, Wayne State University Press, 1958. p.39–51.

Puhacz. Translated as *The Falcons.*

> *Résumé.* "According to the account of Lieutenant D."

The story relates the superhuman acts of bravery of one squadron of the Polish Air Force in its plight against the crushing invasion of the Nazi Air Force, which covered the sky with swarms of faster, better armed and more maneuverable planes.

Every flight of the Polish pilots was then a challenge to reason and a renewed act of heroism. Daring missions were accomplished and many German fighters and bombers were shot down. Four owls (German planes) were downed by Lieutenant D. himself, one of them in the course of executing his most important and his most difficult mission.

He was ordered to locate the forces of General Sosnkowski, which were fighting somewhere in the triangle Lwów-Przemyśl-Stryj, and deliver to the General a letter containing orders of extreme importance. Under most adverse conditions Lieutenant D. miraculously accomplished the mission.

Lieutenant D.'s squadron had originally been stationed on the airfield near Jabłonna in the vicinity of Warsaw. It kept moving eastward. It was immediately after his mission was accomplished that Lieutenant D. learned that the Bolsheviks were marching against Poland. He and his colleagues took off for Roumania.

The author had found Lieutenant D. in a small hotel in Paris, where he lived with the remaining members of the squadron. Later the author learned that his friend was no longer in Paris. He had returned to the air.

The Falcons. In his THE FORGOTTEN BATTLEFIELD. Translated from the Polish by Edmund Ordon. New York, Roy Publishers [c1944]. p.39–66.

Śpiew w nocy. Translated as *The Song in the Night.*

Résumé. The author visited General Duch in Windsor where the Polish Army in Canada was being formed. They started playing a game of chess, but soon they found themselves talking about reasons why Poles were being called incorrigible romantics by the world. The subject brought up General Duch's story of an incident from the campaign in Poland.

On the twenty-second of September (1939), the Poles were being pressed by the Germans from the west and by the Russians from the east. General Duch's unit was in the center, in the Lublin area, making its way south. The General and his men were not thinking of capitulation. They had captured a town "forgotten by God" called Miasteczko. In the evening they struck the edge of the forest. The forest descended gradually to the south, toward the village Barchaczów. Barchaczów became strategically important. With it they had passage toward Tomaszów Lubelski, Krasnobród, etc.; without it they could be squeezed between two walls.

They took the edge of the forest by storm. The next day, September twenty-third, they began further attacks, but the fire-power of the Germans proved too strong. By that time the Russians were only thirty kilometers away. Unsuccessful attacks came alternately from the Polish and the German side.

About five the firing increased, and the Germans were attacking again. Everyone went into action, including a platoon of 'phone operators, the divisional staff, and the General himself. Barchaczów was taken and the roads cleared.

At night a glow spread over the sky; Barchaczów was burning. Suddenly from the right flank which had borne the hardest trials in those battles, there floated an unexpected echo. The melody was becoming ever clearer. The echo sounding among the trees repeated from all sides:

> Poland is not dead yet
> While we are alive . . .[28]

The song, begun by no one knew whom, was taken up by the others. It moved among the units invisible in the darkness.

The Song in the Night. In his THE FORGOTTEN BATTLEFIELD. Translated from the Polish by Edmund Ordon. New York, Roy Publishers [c1944]. p.169–179.

Tajemnica lasu. Translated as *The Secret of the Forest.*

Résumé. "According to accounts of the soldiers, officers and the Commander of the Eleventh Division of the Polish Army."

This is a story of how the Eleventh Division or, rather, its remnants made up of three thousand bayonets, gained a splendid victory in the region of the Janów forests, stretching northwest of Lwów, occupied by five German divisions.

Two Polish divisions under command of General Sosnkowski were completely surrounded. The battle took place on an impenetrably dark night. The fighting was face to face. Polish soldiers emptied their rifles. The bayonets decided the issue. Rushing madly from attack to attack, the Poles finally shattered all opposition.

At dawn the area in which the battles had been fought presented an unbelievable sight. All the available space, stretching from the village Mużyłowice on, was filled with every kind of motorized equipment. Spick and span tanks, trucks, fuel transports, cars, motorcycles, motorized artillery, ammunition trailers, anti-aircraft batteries, anti-tank guns seemed to have no end. It was the same in village after village. On General Sosnkowski's order all these riches had to be burnt. The fire lasted a whole day.

---

[28] The opening lines of the Polish national anthem.

The Eleventh Division went on to new battles.

The Secret of the Forest. In his THE FORGOTTEN BATTLEFIELD. Translated from the Polish by Edmund Ordon. New York, Roy Publishers [c1944]. p.19–37.

Talizman. Translated as *The Talisman.*

Résumé. "According to the account of Major A."

The author recalled that it had happened in the same month of April. He was now in Brazil under the Tropic of Capricorn; then he had been in France with an army theatrical unit visiting a Polish battalion. They were greeted by Major A., a robust man with a ruddy face and a sweeping mustache. During the first performance the author stood backstage with the Major and heard the buildings shake with applause. The soldier Michalski, who was pulling at the curtain ropes, was the son of an émigré long settled in France; he did not speak Polish.

One evening the Major invited the author to his quarters. While wet pieces of wood hissed loudly on the fire, the author heard this story:

It happened in Józefów estate between Włocławek and Kowal. On the ninth of September Major A. found himself there with the 22nd Regiment in which he served. Men of his battalion were tired beyond endurance. For four days they had been without food or sleep, all the time on the go. Now the battalion was in the rear and was promised a breathing spell. The kitchen arrived, and for the first time in four days they got something to eat. Dried out and dirty, the men lay as they had fallen.

Just then the regimental adjutant brought Major A. the order to organize another defensive attack behind the regiment. When the officers aroused the men and the companies of human ghosts started moving, the adjutant appeared again with the news that the Germans had broken through the right flank. Major A. was ordered to fill the gap.

Almost blindly they kept moving forward. When the soldiers sensed the vicinity of the Germans, the battalion of ghosts became alive again. Suddenly there were shouts from the front of the line, "Germans," and then a storming, "Hurrah!" The battalion passed the German front lines, taking the enemy by surprise. A cruel slaughter followed. It was amazing how fast it happened. Large numbers of Germans were bayoneted. Their equipment was lying in disorder. Light machine guns, trucks, and three armored cars were among the booty. But, even after this victory, the soldiers had to get up and march again. . . .

The Talisman. In his THE FORGOTTEN BATTLEFIELD. Translated from the Polish by Edmund Ordon. New York, Roy Publishers [c1944]. p.109–131.

Tysiąc lat. Translated as *A Thousand Years.*

Résumé. "According to the account of Lieutenant Colonel K."

Lieutenant Colonel K.'s task was to block the route of the advancing Germans near Kielce. His position was on the pass near Zagnańsk beside the large rock quarries. He transported as many men as he could from different formations to his position. His order was to hold it at least two days, until the arrival of the Twelfth Division.

The first point of resistance on the line from Kielce to Radom was established beside the highway on the cliffs near Dąbrowa. It was entrusted to Lieutenant Colonel I. The second line of resistance was formed on the right side of the highway. The narrator chose for himself a spot in the middle.

The Germans succeeded in flanking Lieutenant Colonel I.'s position. It was taken and his force completely annihilated. The Germans were now advancing towards the main position.

In a flash the situation changed. In a sweeping attack under K.'s command the Poles reached the German lines. The Germans wavered: some fell and the rest began to flee. A doctor, a Second Lieutenant in the reserve, who refused to stay behind, was leading his platoon. The Poles set out after the fleeing Germans. They were tasting victory.

Unfortunately the situation was bad in other sectors. The narrator was ordered to retreat to Suchedniów. As he was driving to meet his troops, he noticed a mass of people coming from the opposite direction. He thought it was a procession of refugees. He soon discovered it was a ghastly march of wounded soldiers. Perhaps they were a thousand, perhaps two thousand. Among them was the front-line volunteer, the doctor, with both hands bandaged. "What will be left of Poland?" he cried when he saw K. "What will hold us back?" "A thousand years, a thousand Polish years, that will remain and that will hold us back," the narrator shouted in reply.

A Thousand Years. In his THE FORGOTTEN BATTLEFIELD. Translated from the Polish by Edmund Ordon. New York, Roy Publishers [c1944]. p.67–90.

Zasadzka. Translated as *Ambush.*

Résumé. "According to the account of Second-Lieutenant S."

S. served in the Forty-ninth Infantry regiment. On the highway between Rzeszów and Łańcut lies the town Błażowa. The Lieutenant's regiment, after a forced twenty-four hour march of seventy kilometers from the river Wisłoka, halted in the village of Barycz, south of Błażowa. On the morning of the tenth of September (1939) S. was ordered to reach Błażowa to determine whether any Germans were there.

The whole company volunteered for the reconnaissance. S. chose thirty men. Second-Lieutenant A. joined the group. They took one light machine gun and one armor-piercing rifle.

They reached Błażowa as if on maneuvers. There were no Germans there. But a local reservist reported that about four hundred tanks and armored cars had passed that way at night. S. decided not to return empty-handed. He thought that probably some messengers or commissary groups would come by during the day. He decided to arrange an ambush.

The road leading from Rzeszów was as visible as the palm of one's hand. On one side of the road stood an inn; opposite it was a school. In front of the school there was a row of corn. Taking advantage of the terrain, S. camouflaged his men.

Soon three motorcycles appeared on the road, two Germans on each. Rounding the hill behind the motorcycles were three armored cars. S. did not order fire until the motorcycles were only about fifty meters away. No one escaped. Forward—hurrah! The grenades finished the task. The highest ranking German officer who lay beside the cars was a Lieutenant-Colonel. Among the captured papers there was the "Order for the tenth of September, 7:05 A.M."

Later, the author met the commander of the division in which the young officer served. It was from him, and not directly from S., that he learned that the captured order was priceless. It revealed the German division's operational plan.

Ambush. In his THE FORGOTTEN BATTLEFIELD. Translated from the Polish by Edmund Ordon . . . New York, Roy Publishers [1944]. p.143–152.

Wittlin, Józef, (1896–   )

The Emperor and the Devil. Fragment from his SÓL ZIEMI (Salt of the Earth).

The Emperor and the Devil, by Joseph Wittlin. Translated by Pauline de Chary. In HEART OF EUROPE; an Anthology of Creative Writing in Europe 1920–1940. Edited by Klaus Mann and Hermann Kesten with an introduction by Dorothy Canfield Fisher. New York, L. B. Fischer [c1943]. p.383–392.

The Emperor and the Devil, by Joseph Wittlin. Translated by Pauline de Chary. In A WORLD OF GREAT STORIES; edited by Hiram Haydn and John Cournos [and] Board of Editors. New York, Crown Publishers [c1947]. p.663–671.

Preceded by a brief note about the author.

Wittlin, Tadeusz (1909–   )

Born in Warsaw, the author now lives in Washington, D.C. He graduated with a degree in law from the University of Warsaw. Between 1931 and 1936 Wittlin was the editor of *Cyrulik warszawski* (The Barber of Warsaw), a witty literary-satirical weekly. Taken prisoner of war in 1939, the author escaped and returned to occupied Warsaw. After he had crossed the German-Russian border, Wittlin was arrested by the Russians, and sent to Siberia. Released to join the Polish Forces under British command in the Middle East, the author took part in the Italian campaign. His first volume of poetry, TRASA NA PARNAS (The Trail to Parnassus) was published in 1929. His novel, MARZYCIEL I GOŚCIE (A Dreamer and the Guests, 1932) was awarded a prize in Poland for the best book of fiction by a young writer. He published two volumes of short stories, PIĘTA ACHILLESA (The Achilles Heel, 1939) and RADOSNE DNI (Happy Days, 1946). Wittlin's RELUCTANT TRAVELLER IN RUSSIA (1952) is based on the author's own experiences in Soviet labor camps. The book was translated into French, Spanish, Dutch and Japanese. Wittlin's biographical novel in two volumes, MODIGLIANI, was published in London in 1965. Its English translation, MODIGLIANI, PRINCE OF MONT-PARNASSE (The Bobbs-Merrill Company) preceded in print by a year the Polish original. His documentary work about the Katyń massacre, TIME STOPPED AT 6:30 (1965), was highly acclaimed by reviewers.

Gdy matka ma kochanka. Translated as *The Lover and the Boy.*

Résumé. Every morning at six in one of the carriages of the suburban train from Ufra to Krasnowodzk, a Turkestan port on the Caspian Sea, one could see a slim brunette with long bright hair and black eyes. At thirty, Sonia was still graceful and good looking. The day her husband was called up, which had been two years before, she swore to herself that she would faithfully wait for his return. She had been all alone except for her sturdy, nine-year-old son, Misha.

She stayed thus till she met a Polish soldier to whom she gave her whole heart, so long starved of affection. Misha took a fierce dislike to the guest. Although they believed that the boy was paying no attention to them, Misha was painfully conscious that his father was being wronged.

The soldier came whenever he was off duty, and often he stole out of camp at night. Sonia, enchanted with the magic of love, grew more beautiful, gay, swift, and full of song. One night Sonia confessed to him that she had been called to the militia-post and warned that if she had a lover he must not be a foreigner but a Soviet soldier.

The next day the soldier, who was the narrator's batman, told him the story. The narrator duly warned him that Sonia was in danger of being sent to Siberia. Worried about his mistress, the soldier stopped his calls.

Some weeks later, one dark and cold evening, the narrator and his batman heard the thud of bare feet outside their tent. It was Misha. He was glad he found the soldier. He told him how his mother had cried until her eyes were swollen. She could not sleep, and she was wasting away. Would the soldier, please, come and visit his mother again? But he should not say that Misha had been here. He seized the soldier's hand, kissed it and ran out of the tent.

The Lover and the Boy. [Translated by Noel E. P. Clark.] In THE PEN IN EXILE; an anthology. Edited by Paul Tabori. [London] The International P.E.N. Club Centre for Writers in Exile, 1954. p.149–153.

Wygodzki, Stanisław (1907–   )

Nad rzeką. Translated as *By the River.*

By the River. Translated by Krzysztof Klinger. In *Polish Perspectives; Monthly Review,* III, No. 2, 1960. p.35–44.
First printed in *Nowa Kultura,* No. 19, 1954.
Preceded by a brief note about the author.

Zakrzewska, Stanisława Sznaper, *see* Sznaper-Zakrzewska, Stanisława

Zapolska, Gabriela (1860–1921)

Actress, playwright, author of novels and short stories, Zapolska followed French naturalists in the treatment of not infrequently salacious details and dramatic episodes in ordinary lives. The principal character of her play,

MORALNOŚĆ PANI DULSKIEJ (Mrs. Dulska's Morals, 1907), became proverbial in Poland. Pani Dulska, a hypocritical
bourgeois woman who did not care for principles but for
the decency of appearances, still attracts Polish theatre
producers. (The play was performed in Cleveland, Ohio.)
In the collection of short stories, MENAŻERIA LUDZKA
(Human Menagerie, 1893), her method is to fight for the
good by attacking the bad. One of the author's recurring
subjects is demand for equal rights for women. Her novels
include KAŚKA KARIATYDA (1888) and SEZONOWA MIŁOŚĆ
(Seasonal Love, 1905).

Koteczek. Translated as *Her Kitten.*

Résumé. (This is a story of a young woman betrayed by her
unscrupulous husband whom she lovingly and tenderly calls her
"Kitten.")

Josie had brought him an orphan's dowry of five thousand
roubles of which she never heard again. Her Kitten held a sinecure
position as an assistant bookkeeper with little work and still less
responsibility. Every month he gave Josie a sum so meager that to
make ends meet she had to pawn the rest of her jewelry, so precious
to her. Worried and half starved, she became prematurely old and
unattractive. He was a broad-shouldered specimen of health with a
powerful neck and rosy complexion. He treated her like a slave,
while she loved and adored her Kitten.

After dinner which, he insisted, always had to be as inexpensive
as possible, her Kitten usually had a nap. After a nap he would go
for a "little walk." He would come back well after midnight. Josie
always waited for him.

One evening on her way back from the pawnshop Josie saw her
husband in a carriage with a pretty woman. He saw her too. He
and Lena were on their way to a restaurant. The thought that her
Kitten was betraying her never entered Josie's mind. Even now she
did not understand. Was it really her Kitten? Could it be?

The kitchen clock had already struck two o'clock. She waited.
At that moment he was drinking the drops of wine from the lips
of his mistress. Josie's faded lips murmured, "Lord, let Kitten come
back to me...!"

First printed 1890.

Her Kitten. Translated by Ilona Ralf Sues. In POLISH SHORT STORIES, selected by Zbigniew Żabicki. Warsaw, Polonia Publishing House, 1960. p.223–[243].

Zawieyski, Jerzy (1902–   )

The author's first novel, GDZIE JESTEŚ PRZYJACIELU? (Where Are You, My Friend?) was published in 1932. In postwar years Zawieyski turned to drama which seemed to suit him better in his expression of Catholic ideology. His plays, ROZDROŻE MIŁOŚCI (Crossroads of Love, 1947), OCALENIE JAKÓBA (Jacob's Salvation, 1947) and MIŁOŚĆ ANNY (Anna's Love, 1948) are all based on the author's religious beliefs, and probe into supernatural life. Closer to everyday life is his collection of short stories, POKÓJ GŁĘBI (Peace of the Depths), published in 1956.

Odwiedziny Prezydenta. Translated as *The President Calls/The President's Visit.*

Résumé. Paul was an unwanted child. After his parents' divorce, he had chosen to stay with his father who had no affection for the boy. Paul reminded him of his first wife whom he called "an idiot." The new mamma had directed all her affection to their new baby, while the new grandma had other interests than children. So Paul's imagination had brought him President Venderdyke of Venderland who was kind to him, stroked his hair, and listened sympathetically to all the stories about his worries. Venderland was the land of joy where everyone was good and happy.

Accidentally the secret of President Venderdyke had leaked out. Instigated by the new grandma, the boy's father decided to "knock" Mr. President out of Paul's head. The boy was taken to a doctor. But the doctor was good and kind and understanding like the President himself. He did not want to knock President Venderdyke out at all. He wanted to see Paul's father instead.

Father had no time for the "charlatan" doctor, and seeing that Paul had cried in bed again (the boy always had tears in his eyes during the President's visits), began to debate whether he should send him to his former wife or place him in a Children's Home.

The President Calls. Translated by Adam Czerniawski. In 10 CONTEMPORARY POLISH STORIES . . . Edited by Edmund Ordon; with an introduction by Olga Scherer-Virski. Detroit, Wayne State University Press, 1958. p.213–240.

The President's Visit. Translation anonymous. In *Poland; Illustrated Magazine,* No. 5 (33) 1957. p.26–29.

Prawdziwy koniec wielkiej wojny. Translated as *The Real End of the Great War.*

Résumé. After the war an architect, Julius Zborski, returned to his wife, Rose, from a P.O.W. camp. He was changed beyond recognition. He had lost his speech. As his writing too was unrecognizable, he practically had lost touch with the outside world. Worst of all were his attacks in the form of insane dances, when Julius whirled with increasing speed, his mouth twisted and saliva dribbling from it, until he dropped to the floor. This dance was a part of the Great War persisting in a ghastly manner in Julius' illness. It was a remnant of the amusement which had been forced on Julius by the German Camp Commandant, Winter, who finally in a wild attack of wrath beat his victim on the head and threw him out of the window. Brain injury was a result, and a repetition of the ghastly dance in the form of periodical attacks, one of its manifestations.

When Julius was late to return home after the war, Rose came under the influence of a professor of mathematics at the University of Warsaw, Bolesław Stęgień. Rose was in charge of the Periodicals Room in the University Library. Their relations developed into a mutual love. Stęgień insisted that Rose should divorce Julius and marry him. But Rose's love for her husband, despite his terrible illness, never died completely. Apart from that, she had a feeling of obligation toward the sick man. Thus Rose found herself in a dilemma.

Under Stęgień's pressure she finally decided to send Julius out to the country with his devoted servant Józia, divorce Julius, and marry Stęgień.

The same afternoon that Rose reached that decision, Julius, independently of her, decided to end the deadlock by stepping out of their life. He hoped that before he dies, Rose would give him one afternoon. That very afternoon Rose went to Stęgień.

It was a surprise to everybody that, when Julius hanged himself on the door of his room, Rose, instead of marrying Stęgień, broke off with him. Soon her beautiful blond hair became grey, her youthful complexion lost its freshness. Rose looked quite an old woman.

A year after Julius' suicide Bolesław Stęgień married a young, attractive woman.

From his POKÓJ GŁĘBI *(Peace of the Depths), 1956.*

The Real End of the Great War. Translated by Jadwiga Zwolska. In CONTEMPORARY POLISH SHORT STORIES, selected by Andrzej Kijowski. Warsaw, Polonia Publishing House, 1960. p.[267]–303.

The Real End of the Great War. Translated by Jadwiga Zwolska; drawings by Jerzy Jarnuszkiewicz. In *Poland; Illustrated Magazine,* No. 12 (76) 1960. (Am. ed.) p.26–[28].

"Excerpts."

Żeromski, Stefan (1864–1925)

One of the greatest Polish writers, Żeromski is the author of novels, short stories, and plays. His prose belongs among the finest in the Polish language. Żeromski frequently tackles the problem of social evils. His typical hero is an idealist who stands up against the wall of human indifference or stupidity, and is eventually defeated. His monumental work, POPIOŁY (ASHES, 1904), partially translated into English, traces lives and problems of a few individuals and families against the background of the Napoleonic wars and Poland's fight for independence. His other novels include SYZYFOWE PRACE (The Tasks of Sisiphus, 1898), LUDZIE BEZDOMNI (The Homeless, 1900), and WIERNA RZEKA (THE FAITHFUL RIVER, 1912). Among his plays the best-known are SUŁKOWSKI (1910) and UCIEKŁA MI PRZEPIÓRECZKA W PROSO (My Little Quail Has Run Away, 1924).

"Cokolwiek się zdarzy—niech uderza we mnie . . ." Translated as *Forebodings;* [the second of] Two Sketches.

Résumé. In the darkest corner of the ward a farm laborer of about thirty years of age had been lying for several months. A black tablet, bearing the words "Caries tuberculosa," hung at the head of the bed. His leg had had to be amputated above the knee, the result of a tubercular decay of the bone. He had been married for three years and had a baby son. He was treated at the expense of the parish.

After the amputation the fever threw him into a bottomless abyss. When the wound began to heal, the fever abated. His mind returned from the other world to the familiar one. Formerly he had felt self-pity arising from terror; now it was the wild hatred of the wounded man.

And then he noticed that his healthy foot was growing stiff and the ankle was swelling. The doctor examined it, and when already at the door, he turned back, bent over the patient, and furtively passed his hand kindly over the sick man's head. The peasant's mind became a blank; it was as if someone dealt him a blow in the dark with a club. He closed his eyes and lay still for a long time, until an unknown feeling of calm came over him. The conception that arose in his mind was that of Christ walking on the waves of the raging sea, quelling the storm. "And may the Lord Jesus . . . may He give His peace to all people," he whispered to himself. "This will do as well for me!"

Forebodings; Two Sketches. In SELECTED POLISH TALES. Translated by Else C. M. Benecke and Marie Busch. London, New York [etc.] H. Milford, Oxford University Press [1921]. p.261–268.

Forebodings; Two Sketches. Translated by Else C. M. Benecke. In GREAT SHORT STORIES OF THE WORLD; a Collection of Complete Short Stories Chosen from the Literatures of All Periods and Countries by Barrett H. Clark and Maxim Lieber. New York, Robert M. McBride and company, 1926. p.716–720.

"This version, translated by Else C. M. Benecke, is reprinted from Polish Tales, Oxford University Press, by permission of the publisher."

The Dance. Fragment from his POPIOŁY (ASHES).

The Dance; an Episode from his Great Historical Novel ASHES. Translated by K. Żuk-Skarszewska. In *Poland* (New York), VII, 1926. p.142–144, 176, 178, 180.

Echa leśne. Translated as *Forest Echoes.*

Résumé. (The theme of the story is a tragic conflict of divided loyalties both for the narrator, General Rozłucki, and for the hero of the tale, his nephew, Rymwid.)

The general inquired of Assistant Forester, Mr. Guńkiewicz (in the presence of other men gathered round the campfire on the edge of the forest, a portion of which was being added to the estate of the author's father) if he knew about a certain cross in the forest near the inn on the way leading from Zagnańsk to Wzdół? Mr. Guńkiewicz knew the cross very well. As a matter of fact he had put it up there himself. A man was buried there.

Suddenly the general broke the news that the man was his own nephew. General Rozłucki was a Pole (he was telling his tale in Polish) in the Russian service. His nephew Rymwid, whom after the death of his brother he had brought up himself, served as a captain in his regiment. When the insurrection of 1863 broke out, Rymwid Rozłucki deserted from the Russian ranks and became a leader of one of the groups of Polish insurgents. He was taken prisoner by a unit under his uncle's command. A court martial consisting of five officers convened immediately. Two voted for punishment on the spot, two for sending him under escort to the prison at Kielce. The general had had to tip the scale. His vote was for death on the spot.

Captain Rozłucki was given permission to express his last wish. He had only one, and he addressed it to his uncle: he wanted his six-year-old son, Peter, to be brought up as a Pole. He was executed early in the morning.

When the general finished his story, the village scribe asked if his nephew's last wish had been respected. "None of your business, and don't you ever dare ask me that question again!" snarled the general in reply.

First printed 1905.

Forest Echoes. Translated by Ilona Ralf Sues. In POLISH SHORT STORIES, selected by Zbigniew Żabicki. Warsaw, Polonia Publishing House, 1960. p.291–[308].

For Our Freedom and Yours. Fragment from his POPIOŁY (ASHES).

For Our Freedom and Yours. (*Za Wolność Naszą i Waszą.*) In A POLISH ANTHOLOGY. Selected by T. M. Filip; translated by M. A. Michael. London, Duckworth [c1944]. p.297–305.
Text English and Polish.

In the Mountains. Fragment from his POPIOŁY (ASHES).

In the Mountains. (*W górach.*) In A POLISH ANTHOLOGY. Selected by T. M. Filip; translated by M. A. Michael. London, Duckworth [c1944]. p.71–85.
Text English and Polish.

The Might of Satan. Fragment from his POPIOŁY (ASHES).

The Might of Satan. (*Moc Szatana.*) In A POLISH ANTHOLOGY. Selected by T. M. Filip; translated by M. A. Michael. London, Duckworth [c1944]. p.205–207.
Text English and Polish.

The Passion of Heaven. Fragment from his POPIOŁY (ASHES).

The Passion of Heaven. (*Namiętność niebieska.*) In A POLISH ANTHOLOGY. Selected by T. M. Filip; translated by M. A. Michael. London, Duckworth [c1944]. p.143–155.
Text English and Polish.

Pokusa. Translated as *Temptation.*

Résumé. The youngest son of Countess Krzywosąd-Nasławska had decided to take Holy Orders. He had been educated in Rome under the eye of a distant cousin, a Cardinal. Still too young to hold a spiritual office, he came back to his own country, and stayed at his mother's house.

His ways were ascetic. He was modest, good and gentle. Every morning he went through the fields to pray in a half-ruined little chapel in the pine forest.

One morning he went there as usual. He prayed on his way during the mystery of the rising sun, opened the wooden door, and fell on his face before the picture of Christ. He was gazing on the face of the Eternal.

Suddenly he heard a man's voice singing a coarse peasant song. A woman's voice answered in the distance. A young man stood at the door of the chapel. A girl was coming along the path, carrying a load of weeds on her back. The corners of her petticoat were turned up and tucked into her belt. She stopped and pushed the young man away with her hands, laughing. They walked again singing together, never completely hidden by the corn.

Temptation. Translated by Else C. M. Benecke. In POLISH AU-THORS OF TODAY AND YESTERDAY . . . Selected by Irena Morska. New York, S. F. Vanni [c1947]. p.210–213.

From TALES BY POLISH AUTHORS translated by Else C. M. Benecke. By permission of Basil Blackwell & Mott, Ltd., Oxford.

Temptation. In TALES BY POLISH AUTHORS . . . Translated by Else C. M. Benecke. Oxford, B. H. Blackwell, 1915. p.113–118.

Rozdziobią nas kruki, wrony. Translated as *The Crows/The Crows and the Ravens.*

Résumé. (An episode from the partisan warfare during the 1863/64 Polish Insurrection against the Russians.)

It was cold, windy, and it was raining. Andrzej Barycki—better known by his adopted name, Szymon Winrych—emerged from behind the hill and turned down into the wide plains towards Nasielsk. He was wet and cold. It was now the third day that he was walking beside his wagon. No one now would recognize in him the former president of the gayest Warsaw fraternity. The hungry and tired horses kept stopping from time to time. Covered with a bit of alder bush and some hay and straw, sixty rifles, a dozen sabres and some lesser weapons lay hidden in the wagon.

Suddenly Winrych heard a dull rumbling sound. He recognized a detachment of the Russians. He turned round on the spot, but the fleeing wagon was spotted. Eight mounted Russian soldiers surrounded it in no time. One of them probed the inside of the wagon with his lance. As it struck the rifle-barrels, the soldier slapped Winrych on the shoulder.

"What unit was he taking this to?" "Idiot," said Winrych in reply. Two soldiers drove their lances through his body. A third horseman, aiming at Winrych's head, instantly killed one of the horses. When the Russians drove away, the eyelids of the dying partisan opened once again. A great hope of immortality embraced his soul; with this hope in heart he died.

The living horse, frightened, kicked in all directions until his hind leg was caught between the spokes of a wagon-wheel, splitting the bone. The crows moved in and attacked the dead bodies of the man and the horse.

Crawling on all fours, a peasant from the near-by village approached the scene. Praying aloud, he took as his loot all he could carry: the corpse's clothes, the leather harness; he even removed the skin of the horse that had been shot. Finally he pushed the man and the horse into one grave. Night and death descended upon the earth.

The Crows. Translated by Olga Scherer-Virski. In her THE MODERN POLISH SHORT STORY. 's-Gravenhage, Mouton, 1955. (Slavistic printings and reprintings, 5) p.168–174.

The Crows and the Ravens; a Story of Revolutionary Poland, by Maurice Zych. Translated by Mrs. Galin. Oxford, Shelley Bookshop, 1906.
11 p.
"Forbidden in Russia."

Siłaczka. Translated as *The Stronger Sex.*

Résumé. Dr. Paweł Obarecki had come to a small town in the provinces called Obrzydłówek six years ago. He wanted to radically improve the world, starting with God-forsaken Obrzydłówek.

He immediately got in trouble with the local drugstore owner and the barbers. The doctor decided to mix and give away free his own medicine. The flame of his idealism burned high and bright until it was extinguished.

One cold wintry day he was summoned to a patient about twenty miles away. It was a village teacher who was ill. Dr. Obarecki was shocked to recognize in the teacher the beautiful Panna Stanisława, with whom he was once in love. When she was a Warsaw student, her mind too was aflame with great ideas. Evidently she was trying to live up to them. She had typhus.

The doctor immediately sent to the nearest town for quinine, offering a large sum of money for the trip. The medicine never arrived. Obarecki set out on the trip himself, but when he came rushing back, Panna Stanisława was dead. Afraid that he would go mad with pain, the doctor left without waiting for the funeral.

Gradually, after this horrible shock, he grew calm. He has grown stout. He is now doing exceedingly well.

The Stronger Sex. In MORE TALES BY POLISH AUTHORS. Translated by Else C. M. Benecke and Marie Busch. New York, Longmans, Green and company, 1916. p.112–145.

The Stronger Sex. [Translated by Else C. M. Benecke and Marie Busch.] In POLISH AUTHORS OF TODAY AND YESTERDAY . . . Selected by Irena Morska. New York, S. F. Vanni [c1947]. p.183–209.

A Soldier's Lot. Fragment from his POPIOŁY (ASHES).

A Soldier's Lot. (Żołnierska dola.) Translated by Jadwiga Morawska. In *The Slavonic Review,* IV, 1925–26. p.561–572.

Spring. Fragment from his POPIOŁY (ASHES).

Spring. (Wiosna.) In A POLISH ANTHOLOGY. Selected by T. M. Filip; translated by M. A. Michael. London, Duckworth [c1944]. p.139–143.
Text English and Polish.

"Tabu." Translated as *"Impossible"*/*Taboo.*

Résumé. Pani Ewa Dąbrowska descended from the train and hurried to the station. A dilapidated carriage took her to the hospital. A young doctor allowed her to see her husband. The doctor was to wait outside in the corridor.

The door opened to admit a gaunt young man with hair disheveled and clothes in disorder. The madman did not take notice either of his visitor or the doctor. He shouted in a hoarse voice a nonsense phrase. Pani Ewa took out a box of sweets and presented it to her sick husband. He swallowed the candy, and pacing the room, amidst a torrent of chaotic phrases, pronounced her name, "Ewunia . . ."

Pani Ewa knew that her sick husband suffered from fears. "Have no fear!" Through her love which never ceased, she tried in a vain effort to instill the words in the sick man's soul. All at once he touched her arm. His face wore a sickening, lascivious expression. He made a hideous, imploring gesture. She rushed to the door, but he caught her. The door flew open and the doctor seized the madman.

Pani Ewa ran out of the hospital grounds, and wandered about the countryside before reaching the station.

This time "that man," a draughtsman in an engineering workshop, who seemed to know her story but had never spoken to her, got into the same compartment. He was holding a bouquet of flowers. She thought she had reached the point when she hated all suffering. As she rose from her seat and approached the window, "that man" placed the flowers on her seat. Returning to her place, oppressed by her thoughts, she untied the bouquet and scattered the flowers over the floor. "My husband is ill, very ill . . ." she whispered. When the train stopped, the young man quickly left the compartment.

"*Impossible*," by Stefan Żeromski. [Translated by Żuk-Skarszewska.] In THE POLISH SHORT STORIES. Edited by Umadevi. [Bombay] Indo-Polish Library. No. 35 [c1946]. p.21–32.

Taboo. Translated from the Polish by K. Żuk-Skarszewska. In *Poland* (New York), VIII, 1927. p.208–210, 241–242, 244.

Taboo, by Stefan Zeromski. [Translated by K. Żuk-Skarszewska.] In POLISH SHORT STORIES, by Joseph Weyssenhof, Piotr Choynowski, Kornel Makuszynski [and others] . . . London, Minerva Publishing Company [1943]. p. 43–51.

Trees in Grudno. Fragment from his POPIOŁY (ASHES).

Trees in Grudno; the Funeral of Peter Olbromski. (*Drzewa w Grudnie;* pogrzeb Piotra Olbromskiego.) In A POLISH ANTHOLOGY.

Selected by T. M. Filip; translated by M. A. Michael. London, Duckworth [c1944]. p.207–211.
Text English and Polish.

Zemsta jest moja . . . Translated as *The Birches.*

Résumé. In a humble village cemetery among crosses long since forgotten stands a lofty monument made of iron. The monument was erected by the descendants of the owner of the fields and forests to perpetuate his memory. Two birch trees of strange beauty grow here, one at each side of the monument. The lofty tops of the trees can be seen from far distances. In the winter wind the birches shake as in fury, their branches moaning and swinging back and forth.

This is the secret of the sin which the birches revealed to a very old peasant:

When alive, the owner of this estate lashed his serfs mercilessly with dry birch switches. When he died and was buried, from one arm-pit a long birch rod shot up into the sky; then from the other arm-pit another rod flashed up. And now the birch trees are growing taller and taller, fed on the heart of the cruel landowner who lashed his own people with birch twigs.

> *From his* SEN O SZPADZIE (DREAM OF A SWORD).
> *First published 1906.*

The Birches. Translation anonymous. In POLISH AUTHORS OF TODAY AND YESTERDAY . . . Selected by Irena Morska. New York, S. F. Vanni [c1947]. p.172–174.

Złe przeczucie. Translated as *Forebodings;* [the first of] Two Sketches.

Résumé. The narrator (the story is told in the first person) was waiting at the railway station for the train to come in when two young students entered the waiting room. They were mud-bespattered and exhausted from travelling. One of them, a fair boy with a charming profile, seemed absent-minded and depressed. The other was trying to comfort him. From their conversation the narrator learned that the fair boy's father was dying. He had suffered from a heart ailment for the last three years. There were eight children in the family, and the mother was of delicate health. In another six months the father would have received his pension.

When the train came in, the two students took seats in the same compartment occupied by the narrator. Before the train started off, the student who had been comforting his colleague left the compartment. The grief-stricken boy gazed out of the window seeing nothing.

The narrator watched him. He noticed that the boy's face turned suddenly pale, and the naked truth which he had not quite faced till that minute struck him through the heart like a sword. The observer did not go to the boy nor speak to him. He did not take his hand. He merely watched him with the interest and insatiable curiosity which the human heart ever aroused in him.

Forebodings; Two Sketches. In SELECTED POLISH TALES. Translated by Else C. M. Benecke and Marie Busch. London, New York [etc.] H. Milford, Oxford University Press [1921]. p.261–268.

Forebodings; Two Sketches. Translated by Else C. M. Benecke. In GREAT SHORT STORIES OF THE WORLD; a Collection of Complete Short Stories Chosen from the Literatures of All Periods and Countries by Barrett H. Clark and Maxim Lieber. New York, Robert M. McBride and company, 1926. p.716–720.

"This version, translated by Else C. M. Benecke, is reprinted from Polish Tales, Oxford University Press, by permission of the publisher."

Zmierzch. Translated as *Twilight.*

Résumé. The marshes belonged to the manor house. The new owner dug holes in the swamp, measured, and finally ordered the bailiff to hire laborers to dig peat until the hole was large enough for a pond. There were to be some thirteen ponds in all.

Walek Gibata, without any land of his own, was hired to cart away the peat. His wife loaded the wheelbarrow, and he wheeled the mud to the field along planks thrown across the swamp. Suddenly the steward decided to pay only twenty kopeks instead of thirty for two cubic yards. Walek went to the inn and got drunk. Next day he beat his wife, and dragged her out to work. Now to dig out four cubic yards they had to work without a break from dawn until night.

A mist fell, and Walkowa[29] wanted to see if her baby in the hut was still alive. Walek brutally refused to let her go. In an attempt to finish their work sooner, both of them now loaded and pushed the wheelbarrow. Her chest rattled, she felt faint, and tears of pain fell from her eyes. The wheels of the barrows clattered and whined. The evening star shone low in the sky.

Twilight. In TALES BY POLISH AUTHORS . . . Translated by Else C. M. Benecke. Oxford, B. H. Blackwell, 1915. p.101–111.

Twilight. Translated by Else C. M. Benecke. In POLISH AUTHORS OF TODAY AND YESTERDAY . . . Selected by Irena Morska. New York, S. F. Vanni [c1947]. p.175–182.

The text of the translation of Else C. M. Benecke has been slightly altered by the editor.

Żesławski Władysław

Szczęście. Translated as *Happiness*.

Happiness. Translation anonymous. Drawings by J. Młodożeniec. In *Poland; Illustrated Magazine*, No. 4 (20) 1956. p.25–[26].

Zieliński, Stanisław (1917–   )

The author's experiences as a prisoner-of-war furnished him with themes for his DNO MISKI (The Bottom of a Bowl, 1949). In the collection of stories, PRZED ŚWITEM (Before Dawn, 1950), Zieliński goes further back in time to describe the collapse of Poland in 1939. More stories were collected in a volume, STATEK ZEZOWATYCH (A Boat of Cross-Eyed People, 1959). The author's trilogy dealing with World War Two published by the Czytelnik in Warsaw in the early fifties consists of OSTATNIE OGNIE (The Last Fires), JESZCZE

---

29 The feminine form of Walek, i.e. Walek's wife.

POLSKA (the title is derived from the initial words of the Polish national anthem), and MINIMUM STRATEGICZNE (A Strategic Minimum).

Bemklau. Translated as *Bemklau.*

Bemklau. Translation anonymous. In *Poland; Illustrated Magazine,* No. 10,(62) 1959. p.25–27.
Preceded by a brief note about the author.

Drzwi. Translated as *The Door.*

The Door. Translated by Christopher J. Klinger. In *Polish Perspectives; Monthly Review,* [II], No. 6 (14), 1959. p.35–41.
From his STATEK ZEZOWATYCH (A Boat of Cross-eyed People), 1959.
Followed by "A Note on the Author" by J. G. p.41–44.

Paryż. Translated as *Paris.*

Paris. Translated by Christopher J. Klinger. In *Polish Perspectives; Monthly Review,* [II], No. 6 (14), 1959. p.30–35.
From his STATEK ZEZOWATYCH (A Boat of Cross-eyed People).
At head of title: Two stories by Stanisław Zieliński.
"A Note on the Author," by J. G. p.41–44.

Przed świtem. Translated as *Before Dawn.*

Résumé. The sergeant and Corporal Mosiejczuk were ordered to contact the next detachment and report to the commander of the battalion there. It was still before dawn. Suddenly there appeared a rocket. The sergeant leaped over a ditch and took cover behind a tree trunk. He lost contact with the corporal. The sergeant continued on his own, and when he discovered an outpost of the detachment, he asked to be led to the commander of the battalion.

Corporal Mosiejczuk left the forester's cottage pleased; the lieutenant commanding the battalion had received him well. The corporal reported that on their way he had lost the sergeant in the woods. Maybe he would join them during the day. The report delivered by Mosiejczuk ordered the detachment hidden in the forest to be on the move. The corporal's ankle was swollen. He was hoping he would get a ride.

The platoon leader walked out of the forester's cottage. "We'll take you," he said to Mosiejczuk. He was fat and he smelled of alcohol. "You've attended to that man?" He directed the question to a lance-corporal. Mosiejczuk asked about "that man" mechanically, without thinking, just to be polite. He had been a fifth columnist, dressed like all the rest of them, but he had no documents and no identity disc. He had had the insignia of a commissioned sergeant.

Suddenly Mosiejczuk grabbed the platoon leader's shoulders and shook him like a sack of dung. "What did he look like?" he shouted. He was a fifth columnist—a youngster with reddish hair, not very tall. They had shot him. They had not even reported the incident to the lieutenant.

Quietly, as though speaking to himself, Mosiejczuk told them that the man they had shot was the sergeant whom he had lost in the woods.

From his collection PRZED ŚWITEM *(Before Dawn), 1950.*

Before Dawn. Translated by Jadwiga Zwolska. In CONTEMPORARY POLISH SHORT STORIES, selected by Andrzej Kijowski. Warsaw, Polonia Publishing House, 1960. p.[307]–314.

Raj Ameru; listy z Amerdagandy. Translated as *Notes from Amerdaganda.*

Notes from Amerdaganda, by Stanislaw Zielinski. Translation anonymous. In *East Europe;* a Monthly Review of East European Affairs, VII, No. 9, 1958. p.11–12.

Fragment.[30]

First published in *Nowa Kultura,* Warsaw, April 7, 1957.

Notes from Amerdaganda, by Stanislaw Zielinski. Translation anonymous. In BITTER HARVEST; the Intellectual Revolt Behind the Iron Curtain. Edited by Edmund Stillman; introduction by François Bondy. London, Thames and Hudson [1959]. p.73–77.

---

[30] Omission of the résumé has been intentional. In the opinion of the compiler a summary of this fragment would not do justice to the plot or the flavor of the story.

Fragment.
Reprinted from *East Europe*.

Żukrowski, Wojciech (1916–   )

Żukrowski's first collection of stories, Z KRAJU MILCZENIA
(From the Land of Silence, 1946), placed him in the forefront of the postwar generation of writers in Poland. Dur-
ing that period his approach to all subjects was from the
Catholic point of view; his paramount problem was that of
salvation. Later he reached into the exotic. Laos, for in-
stance, is the subject of his W KRÓLESTWIE MILIONA SŁONI
(In the Kingdom of a Million Elephants, 1961), while the
Orient in general is featured in his OPOWIEŚCI Z DALEKIEGO
WSCHODU (Tales from the Far East, 1965). A collection of his
short stories was published in 1954 under the title W
KAMIENIOŁOMIE I INNE OPOWIADANIA (In the Quarry and
Other Stories). In collaboration with Tadcusz Marian
Malanowski, Żukrowski selected and edited a short story
anthology which includes translations into Polish, OPOWIEŚCI
Z DRESZCZYKIEM (Tales with a Shudder, 1959). One of his
novels, DNI KLĘSKI (The Days of Calamity, 1952), deals with
Poland's tragedy in World War Two.

Lalka. Translated as *The Doll.*

The Doll, by Wojciech Żukrowski. Translation anonymous. In
Poland of Today, III, No. 9, 1948. p.4–5.

First published in *Przekrój*, Warsaw, No. 150, 1948.

Mli Mli. Translated as *The Milk Sop.*

Résumé. After the war Polish Security Officers were questioning
members of the Home Army in Cracow. Somebody touched John's
shoulder. It was "Murawa," the electrician, who wanted to speak
to his former "chief." They agreed to meet on the bank of the
Vistula shortly before five.

Waiting for Murawa to come, John recollected his underground
activities when, taking orders from the Sector Command, he was in
charge of an underground unit. He had become very attached to
the boys.

When Murawa showed up it was evident that he had been drinking. Something "choked him," as he put it. He had to spill it out to the chief. It concerned a young boy, only fifteen, whom Murawa had brought into the organization and had taken under his wing. The boy's whole family had been murdered by the Germans, he himself had escaped miraculously. The boy took the pseudonym, "the Revenger." His hair was very light and he had an almost girlish face. His comrades nicknamed him "Infant" or "Milk Sop."

Once in a group of boys that was stopped by a patrol he got into a panic and started to run. He was caught and taken to the "educational" camp in Plaszów. Murawa happened to be taken to the same camp and saw how the "Milk Sop" suffered as a result of his act of cowardice, and how ashamed he was before Murawa.

At one roll call the camp was two men short. The German commandant ordered ten men to be shot. The boy volunteered to be one of the ten. He died like a man. During the bloody and brutal execution he turned Murawa's way, blinked his eyes, and smiled to show that it was not so terrible.

John took the stand that, compensating for his act of cowardice, the boy's death was an act of showing off. On no account should Murawa blame himself. But the boy should be remembered as the "Revenger" and not as the "Milk Sop."

> *Written around 1946.*
> *From his* W KAMIENIOŁOMIE *(In the Quarry), 1954.*

The Milk Sop. Translated by Jadwiga Zwolska. In CONTEMPORARY POLISH SHORT STORIES, selected by Andrzej Kijowski. Warsaw, Polonia Publishing House, 1960. p.[317]–339.

Zych, Maurycy, *see* Żeromski, Stefan

Some Folk Tales, Legends, Fairy Tales, Fables, and Children's Stories[1]

Anonymous

The Pig's-Head Magician. Adaptation from a Polish folk tale.

The Pig's-Head Magician (retold). In THE MASTER WIZARD AND OTHER POLISH TALES. Translated from the Polish by Josephine B. Bernhard; revised and adapted by E. Frances Le Valley; illustrated by Marya Werten. New York, Alfred A. Knopf, 1934. p.156–[181]. "Used with the kind permission of Daniel & Co., London."

Stary zegar gdański (?) Translated as *The Old Clock of Danzig.*

The Old Clock of Danzig, a Kashubian Legend. Translated by Mary Wałkuska. In THE WAYSIDE WILLOW; Prose and Verse. Translated from the Polish by members of Klub Polski of Columbia University. Edited by Marion Moore Coleman. Student editor: Loretta M. Bielawska. [Trenton, Printed by the White Eagle Publishing Company, 1945]. p.8–9. "Copyright, 1945, by A. P. and M. M. Coleman."

Baliński, Karol (1812– ?)

Blada panna. Translated as *The Pale Maiden.*

The Pale Maiden, by K. Baliński. In SIXTY FOLK-TALES FROM EXCLUSIVELY SLAVONIC SOURCES. Translated, with brief introductions

---

[1] This list is neither comprehensive, nor in any way representative; it offers sample titles rather than a selection.

and notes, by A. H. Wratislaw . . . Boston, Houghton, Mifflin and company; Cambridge, The Riverside Press, 1890. p.125–127.
From his TALES OF THE PEOPLE.

Barącz, Sadok (1814–1892)

Cygan (?) Translated and adapted as *The Gypsy and the Bear.*

The Gypsy and the Bear. In THE GYPSY AND THE BEAR, AND OTHER FAIRY TALES. Translated from the Polish [and adapted] by Lucia Merecka Borski [Lucia Merecka Szczepanowicz] and Kate B. Miller; with a foreword by Eric P. Kelly; illustrated by James Reid. New York, Toronto, Longmans, Green and company [c1933]. p.85–90.
From his BAJKI, FRASZKI, PODANIA, PRZYSŁOWIA I PIEŚNI NA RUSI (FOLK TALES, LEGENDS, ANECDOTES, PROVERBS AND SONGS IN RUTHENIA).

The Jester Who Fooled a King. Adaptation of a Polish folk tale.

Résumé. The jester Matenko for many years had been the favorite clown of King Jan, but when he became old and his joints stiffened and ached, he could not be funny.

The King gave the jester and his wife, Elżunia, a tiny house in the village. Unfortunately he could give them only a little money to live on, for the last court ball was a tremendous expense, and the treasury was almost empty.

It was not long before husband and wife were penniless. Matenko asked his wife to go to the Queen and inform her that he had died. She rubbed her eyes with a raw onion, and went. Taking compassion on the poor woman, the Queen gave her her little embroidered purse containing fifty pieces of gold.

Then the old joker went to the King and told him that his Elżunia had entrusted her soul to God. The King gave him two hundred pieces of gold.

The two cheats were lying quietly on the bare floor of their cottage, covered with a white muslin sheet, when the King and Queen entered to decide their argument as to which of the two had died first. Silently they prayed for the repose of the departed souls. Just before leaving, the King said to the Queen, "I wonder which of the two old folks died first." "Truly, wise king," answered the jester, "my wife died first, but I was dead before."

King Jan tried to be angry, but he laughed. The King understood that he himself was to blame for the trick they played on him, and he gave Matenko another purse of two hundred pieces of gold. However, he made his old jester promise never again to live dishonestly by his wits.

The Jester Who Fooled a King. In THE MASTER WIZARD AND OTHER POLISH TALES. Translated from the Polish by Josephine B. Bernhard; revised and adapted by E. Frances Le Valley; illustrated by Marya Werten. New York, Alfred A. Knopf, 1934. p.139–146.

The Jester Who Fooled a King. Adapted by Frances Frost from the translation by Josephine B. Bernhard and E. Frances Le Valley. In LEGENDS OF THE UNITED NATIONS, by Frances Frost. New York, London, Whittlesey House, McGraw-Hill book company [c1943]. P.49–54.

Bernhard, Josephine Butkowska

Gwiazdkowa kołysanka. Translated and adapted as *Lullaby; Why the Pussy-Cat Washes Himself So Often.*

Lullaby; Why the Pussy-Cat Washes Himself So Often; a folktale adapted from the Polish by Josephine B. Bernhard. Illustrated by Irena Lorentowicz. New York, Roy Publishers, c1944.

[26] p. illus. (part col.) front.

"Ah, —ah, Pussies Two" (song with accompaniment): p.[21].

9 Cry-Baby Dolls. Adaptation of a Polish folk tale.

9 Cry-Baby Dolls; A Folk-Tale. Adapted by Josephine B. Bernhard; illustrated by Irena Lorentowicz. New York, Roy Publishers [c1945].

unpaged, illus., front.

"This adaptation of the Polish folk-tale is based on the version of Janina Porazinska."

Birkenmajer, Józef (1897–1939)

Jak to święty Józef orał. Translated and adapted as *How Saint Joseph Ploughed the Soil.*

How Saint Joseph Ploughed the Soil. In POLISH FOLK TALES. Translated [and adapted] by Lucia Merecka Borski [Lucia Merecka Szczepanowicz]; illustrated by Erica Gorecka-Egan. New York, Sheed and Ward, 1947. p.[9]–15.
From his OPOWIADANIA STAREJ MARGOŚKI (Tales of Old Margośka).

Dygasiński, Adolf (1839–1902)

Wdzięczność i sprawiedliwość. Translated and adapted as *Gratitude and Justice.*

Gratitude and Justice. In POLISH FOLK TALES. Translated [and adapted] by Lucia Merecka Borski [Lucia Merecka Szczepanowicz]; illustrated by Erica Gorecka-Egan. New York, Sheed and Ward, 1947. p.[113]–118.
From LEGENDA I BAŚŃ (Folk Tales and Legends), by J. Staroś.

Gliński, Antoni Józef (1817–1866)

Madej (?) Translated and adapted as *Madej the Brigand.*

Résumé. Madej had killed his father and had fled from Polish justice to the forest, forcing his old mother to go with him. He made a cavern his hiding-place, and slew everyone who entered the forest.

Władek, a rich merchant's son, stopped at the cavern on his way to the Black Nether World to get back the bond for his soul into which his father had been tricked by the Evil Eye. The boy would have been killed had he not promised to return to Madej and tell him all about the Black Nether World.

The youth saw all the terrors of the Nether World which no one may describe, regained his bond, and on the third day he returned to Madej's cavern. He told the brigand what he had seen, and Madej's heart quivered with remorse and despair. Władek took pity on him and told him to live from now on a blameless life. He promised that some day, when he became a bishop, he would return.

Many years passed, and Władek became a well-beloved archbishop of Kraków. He remembered his promise, and went to the forest to visit the brigand. In the forest his courtiers saw a magnificent apple-tree in full bloom. Among its silver leaves and pink flowers there were many apples of shining gold. When they tried to gather the apples, the tree lifted its branches. Under the tree they noticed a kneeling man, white-haired, frail as a shadow. He asked if the archbishop had come.

When the archbishop appeared and Madej (as he it was) recited to him his evil deeds, the golden apples turned into snow-white doves, and one by one flew away to heaven. These were the souls of those whom Madej had slain. The last apple was the soul of the brigand's father. Scarcely had the archbishop finished a prayer for Madej when his body crumbled to dust. Where it fell, a new flower came up. These were "Madej's tears."

Madej the Brigand (adapted). In THE MASTER WIZARD AND OTHER POLISH TALES. Translated from the Polish by Josephine B. Bernhard; revised and adapted by E. Frances Le Valley; illustrated by Marya Werten. New York, Alfred A. Knopf, 1934. p.102–117.

O czarowniku i jego uczniu. Translated and adapted as *The Wizard's Pupil.*

Résumé. A shoemaker's son had been taught witchcraft by a wizard. When after three years of apprenticeship, the boy was brought home by his mother, he found there poverty and hunger.

The drunkard father was eager to test his son's ability to perform tricks of witchcraft, and the boy turned in succession into a falcon, a bull, a cow, a lamb, etc., and each time was sold by the father on the market. Every time upon return the shoemaker found his son safe at home. The boy warned his father that he should never be commanded to become a horse, for then he would fall into the power of the wizard.

The shoemaker, greedy for money, commanded the boy to turn into a horse nevertheless. The wizard immediately started a pursuit of his pupil until the boy, transformed into a ring, fell at the feet

337

of a beautiful Princess. The Princess was so delighted with the ring that she resolved to wear it for the rest of her life. The wizard changed himself into a Turkish merchant, and the king commanded his daughter to return the ring to him. When the Princess threw the ring on the marble floor, it broke into a thousand small pearls, and the merchant turned into a black rooster. His pupil, quickly transformed into a falcon, caught him, crushed him, and dropped him into the sea. Then he appeared before the Princess as the handsomest youth in the world.

Never afterwards did the pupil use witchcraft. He married the Princess, and asked his pious mother to come to the palace to live. He married his sisters to wealthy husbands. He gave a purse of gold to every tavern-keeper in the land, and asked that they fill his father's glass, whenever he so wished, to overflowing with mead or wine.

Not long after the old King died, and the shoemaker's son became ruler of the kingdom. Kindly and wisely he ruled, and happy were his people.

The Wizard's Pupil. In THE MASTER WIZARD, AND OTHER POLISH TALES. Translated from the Polish by Josephine B. Bernard; revised and adapted by E. Frances Le Valley; illustrated by Marya Werten. New York, Alfred A. Knopf, 1934. p.118–138.

O dziadku i babce, o kogutku i kurce, o lisie i wilku. Translated and adapted as *About an Old Man and an Old Woman, a Cock and a Hen, a Fox and a Wolf.*

About an Old Man and an Old Woman, a Cock and a Hen, a Fox and a Wolf. In THE GYPSY AND THE BEAR AND OTHER FAIRY TALES. Translated from the Polish [and adapted] by Lucia Merecka Borski [Lucia Merecka Szczepanowicz] and Kate B. Miller; with a foreword by Eric P. Kelly; illustrated by James Reid. New York, Toronto, Longmans, Green and company [c1933]. p.55–70.

O Królewiczu Niespodzianku. Translated as *Prince Unexpected.*

Prince Unexpected. In SIXTY FOLK-TALES FROM EXCLUSIVELY SLAVONIC SOURCES. Translated, with brief introductions and notes,

by A. H. Wratislaw . . . Boston, Houghton, Mifflin and company; Cambridge, The Riverside Press, 1890. p.108–121.
From his BAJARZ POLSKI (Polish Story-Teller).

O wilku i jego przygodach. Translated and adapted as *The Adventures of a Wolf.*

The Adventures of a Wolf. In THE GYPSY AND THE BEAR AND OTHER FAIRY TALES. Translated from the Polish [and adapted] by Lucia Merecka Borski [Lucia Merecka Szczepanowicz] and Kate B. Miller; with a foreward by Eric P. Kelly; illustrated by James Reid. New York, Toronto, Longmans, Green and company [c1933]. p.33–45.
From his BAJARZ POLSKI (Polish Story-Teller).

Gliński, Kazimierz (1850–1920)

Król Bartek. Translated and adapted as *King Bartek.*

King Bartek. In THE JOLLY TAILOR, AND OTHER FAIRY TALES. Translated from the Polish [and adapted] by Lucia Merecka Borski [Lucia Merecka Szczepanowicz] and Kate B. Miller; illustrated by Kazimir Klepacki. New York [etc.] Longmans, Green and company [c1928]. p.63–73.
From his BAJKI (Fairy Tales).

Łowy. Translated and adapted as *The Hunting.*

The Hunting. In THE JOLLY TAILOR, AND OTHER FAIRY TALES. Translated from the Polish [and adapted] by Lucia Merecka Borski [Lucia Merecka Szczepanowicz] and Kate B. Miller; illustrated by Kazimir Klepacki. New York [etc.] Longmans, Green and company [c1928]. p.29–40.
From his BAJKI (Fairy Tales).

Majka. Translated and adapted as *Majka.*

Majka. In THE JOLLY TAILOR, AND OTHER FAIRY TALES. Translated from the Polish [and adapted] by Lucia Merecka Borski [Lucia Merecka Szczepanowicz] and Kate B. Miller; illustrated by Kazimir

339

Klepacki. New York [etc.] Longmans, Green and company [c1928]. p.74–83.
From his *Bajki* (Fairy Tales).

Żaba. Translated and adapted as *The Frog*.

The Frog. In THE JOLLY TAILOR AND OTHER FAIRY TALES. Translated from the Polish [and adapted] by Lucia Merecka Borski [Lucia Merecka Szczepanowicz] and Kate B. Miller; illustrated by Kazimir Klepacki. New York [etc.] Longmans, Green and company [c1928]. p.140–156.
From his BAJKI (Fairy Tales).

Goszczyński, Seweryn (1801–1876)

The Legend of Smreczyński Staw. Fragment adapted from his ODA (Ode), 1842.

The Legend of Smreczynski Staw. Translated and adapted by M. M. Coleman. In THE POLISH LAND, ZIEMIA POLSKA; an Anthology in Prose and Verse, compiled by Klub Polski of Columbia University. Edited by Marion Moore Coleman. [Trenton, Printed by the White Eagle Publishing Company, 1943]. p.69–71.

Kasprowicz, Jan (1860–1926)

Bieda z Nędzą. Translated and adapted as *Poverty and Misery*.

Poverty and Misery. In POLISH FOLK TALES. Translated [and adapted] by Lucia Merecka Borski [Lucia Merecka Szczepanowicz]; illustrated by Erica Gorecka-Egan. New York, Sheed and Ward, 1947. p.[97]–102.
From his BAJKI, KLECHDY I BAŚNIE (Folk Tales, Fables and Legends).

Koszałki-opałki. Translated and adapted as *Koshalki-opalki*.

Koshalki-Opalki, or How a Simpleton Became King. In THE JOLLY TAILOR, AND OTHER FAIRY TALES. Translated from the Polish [and adapted] by Lucia Merecka Borski [Lucia Merecka Szczepanowicz] and Kate B. Miller; illustrated by Kazimir Klepacki. New York [etc.] Longmans, Green and company [c1928]. p.41–48.

From his BAJKI, KLECHDY I BAŚNIE (Folk Tales, Fables and Legends).

Ucieczka. Translated and adapted as *The Flight.*

The Flight. In THE JOLLY TAILOR, AND OTHER FAIRY TALES. Translated from the Polish [and adapted] by Lucia Merecka Borski [Lucia Merecka Szczepanowicz] and Kate B. Miller; illustrated by Kazimir Klepacki. New York [etc.] Longmans, Green and company [c1928]. p.134–139.
From his BAJKI, KLECHDY I BAŚNIE (Folk Tales, Fables and Legends).

Kędzierski, Czesław (1881–1947)

The Good Orphan Sunblossom and the Enchanted Treasure. Adaptation of a Polish folk tale.

Résumé. A long time ago a miser lived in a castle in the valley of the river Noteć. He had squeezed a fortune from human lives by greed and injustice.

After his death he guarded his treasure for a century until during the Swedish invasion Sunblossom, a poor and beautiful orphan with a stainless heart, sought refuge in the castle. She released the weary soul of the miser from bondage, promising as he asked her to give one chest of gold and silver to widows and orphans, and one to the monastery. One she was to keep for herself.

When the Swedish army had withdrawn from Polish soil, Sunblossom gladly divided the treasure according to the repentant miser's wish. She was happy to share her riches with those whose lives were darkened by want and misery. Thus her own joy was always full and running over.

The Good Orphan Sunblossom and the Enchanted Treasure. In THE MASTER WIZARD AND OTHER POLISH TALES. Translated from the Polish by Josephine B. Bernhard; revised and adapted by E. Frances Le Valley; illustrated by Marya Werten. New York, Alfred A. Knopf, 1934. p.38–46.

Jaś skrzypek (?) Translated and adapted as *Jaś the Fiddler.*

Résumé. Jaś, a poor young shepherd, was also a fiddler. Queen Bona, the long-dead wife of King Sigismund the Old,[2] had appeared in person to Jaś on the ruins of her castle. She had given him permission to help himself to four hundred pieces of gold so that he would be able to marry the miller's daughter, Małgosia. The Queen had warned him not to take anything more than he needed.

Jaś had visited the castle several times before. In gratitude for his playing for her, Jaś had a standing invitation from Queen Bona to come and ask her for favors; every time he came his request had been granted. He had always taken only as much as he had needed.

On leaving the castle he happened to see a brand-new pair of boots. He really did not need them but he put them on, completely forgetting the Queen's warning. In his excitement and anxiety to get away before the clock had struck midnight, he left the bag of gold behind.

After that last visit, Jaś was never heard of again.

Jaś the Fiddler (adapted). In THE MASTER WIZARD AND OTHER POLISH TALES. Translated from the Polish by Josephine B. Bernhard; revised and adapted by E. Frances Le Valley; illustrated by Marya Werten. New York, Alfred A. Knopf, 1934. p.47–[59].

Mistrz Twardowski i jego pajączek (?) Translated and adapted as *The Master Wizard, Pan Twardowski, and His Spider.*

Résumé. (Twardowski,[3] whose main interest was alchemy, lived in Kraków during the reigns of two Polish kings, Sigismund the Old and Sigismund August. His fame as the greatest wizard in all Poland has endured in Polish folklore to this day. Many of his tricks, including rejuvenation, are described in detail.)

Pan Twardowski's power came from the devil to whom he had

---

[2] Zygmunt Stary.

[3] The legend of Pan Twardowski bears a certain similarity to that connected with Faustus.

sold his soul. He had signed the contract with his own blood, and then succeeded in delaying his obligation until he reached the point of defying the devil himself.

Finally the devil outwitted Twardowski and took possession of his soul. Taken up into the stormy air from his beloved Kraków, the wizard remembered the words of the hymn he had composed as a boy. As soon as he began to sing it, the devil dropped Twardowski and vanished. The falling wizard was caught on the horn of the moon, where he is now, and where he will hang until the Day of Judgment.

Once a year, his faithful servant transformed into a spider, clinging to Twardowski's foot, drops himself slowly to earth by a long gleaming thread. He visits the familiar places, then climbs back and whispers what he has seen in the wizard's ear.

(Although there are many versions of the legend, almost invariably the rooster plays some part in them.)

The Master Wizard, Pan Twardowski, and His Spider (adapted). In THE MASTER WIZARD AND OTHER POLISH TALES. Translated from the Polish by Josephine B. Bernhard; revised and adapted by E. Frances Le Valley; illustrated by Marya Werten. New York, Alfred A. Knopf, 1934. p.3–37.

Wilk i kowal (?) Translated and adapted as *The Wolf and the Blacksmith/Saint Stanislaw and the Wolf.*

Résumé. (A fable about a wolf who had obtained permission from Saint Stanisław to taste human flesh on condition that the person to be devoured be a blacksmith. The saint had warned the wolf that human flesh is bitter and tough.)

The blacksmith played a trick on the wolf, and instead of letting himself be devoured, gave the greedy animal a sound beating. Whistling, he went his way, while the wolf was hardly able to drag himself to the woods.

Saint Stanisław heard the wailing of the injured animal, and set forth to help him. "Ow! Great Saint, human flesh is very bitter," cried the wolf. "Oh, never mention it to me again."

The Wolf and the Blacksmith. In THE MASTER WIZARD AND OTHER POLISH TALES. Translated from the Polish by Josephine B. Bernhard; revised and adapted by E. Frances Le Valley; illustrated by Marya Werten. New York, Alfred A. Knopf, 1934. p.60–66.

Saint Stanislaw and the Wolf. Adapted by Frances Frost from the translation by Josephine B. Bernhard and E. Frances Le Valley. In LEGENDS OF THE UNITED NATIONS, by Frances Frost. New York, London, Whittlesey House, McGraw-Hill book company [c1943]. p.44–49.

Konopnicka, Maria (1842–1910)

Jak to ze lnem było. Translated and adapted as *The Golden Seeds.*

The Golden Seeds; a Legend of Old Poland. Adapted into English by Margaret Sperry; illustrated by the Polish artist Bogdan Zieleniec. Copenhagen, The Golden Mill Press [c1958].
23 p. illus.
"Copyright 1958 by 'Nasza Księgarnia,' Warsaw. Printed in Poland."

Kraszewski, Józef Ignacy (1812–1887)

Był sobie dziad i baba (a poem). Translated and adapted as *There Was an Old Man and an Old Woman.*

There Was an Old Man and an Old Woman. In POLISH FOLK TALES. Translated [and adapted] by Lucia Merecka Borski [Lucia Merecka Szczepanowicz]; illustrated by Erica Gorecka-Egan. New York, Sheed and Ward, 1947. p.[67]–69.

The Foundling. Fragment from his *Iermola.*

The Foundling, by Kraszewski. Translation anonymous. In STORIES FROM FOREIGN NOVELISTS, with Short Notices of Their Lives and Writings, by Helen and Alice Zimmern. New and revised edition with a portrait of Ivan Turgenieff. London, Chatto and Windus, 1884. p.209–219.
"The story from which we quote is one of his most popular folktales, Jermola the Potter."

Kupallo. Frangment adapted from his STARA BAŚŃ (An Old Legend), 1876.

Kupallo, by Józef I. Kraszewski. Translated and adapted by M. M. Coleman. In THE POLISH LAND, ZIEMIA POLSKA; an Anthology in Prose and Verse, compiled by Klub Polski of Columbia University. Edited by Marion Moore Coleman. [Trenton, Printed by the White Eagle Publishing Company, 1943]. p.113–114.

Makuszyński, Kornel (1884–1953)

Bajka o królewnie Marysi, o czarnym łabędziu i o lodowej górze. Translated and adapted as *The Story of Princess Marysia, the Black Swan, and an Iceberg.*

The Story of Princess Marysia, the Black Swan, and an Iceberg. In THE JOLLY TAILOR, AND OTHER FAIRY TALES. Translated from the Polish [and adapted] by Lucia Merecka Borski [Lucia Merecka Szczepanowicz] and Kate B. Miller; illustrated by Kazimir Klepacki. New York [etc.] Longmans, Green and company [c1928]. p.84–116. From his BARDZO DZIWNE BAJKI (Very Strange Fairy Tales).

O tem, jak krawiec pan Niteczka został królem. Translated and adapted as *The Jolly Tailor Who Became King.*

The Jolly Tailor Who Became King. In THE JOLLY TAILOR, AND OTHER FAIRY TALES. Translated from the Polish [and adapted] by Lucia Merecka Borski [Lucia Merecka Szczepanowicz] and Kate B. Miller; illustrated by Kazimir Klepacki. New York [etc.] Longmans, Green and company [c1928]. p.15–28. From his BARDZO DZIWNE BAJKI (Very Strange Fairy Tales).

The Jolly Tailor Who Became King. Translated [and adapted] by Lucia Merecka Borski [and Kate B. Miller]. In ANTHOLOGY OF CHILDREN'S LITERATURE; compiled by Edna Johnson, Carrie E. Scott and Evelyn R. Sickels. Boston, Houghton Mifflin [c1935–48]. p.173–176.

The Jolly Tailor Who Became King. Translated [and adapted] by Lucia Merecka Borski and Kate B. Miller. In ANTHOLOGY OF CHILDREN'S LITERATURE [by] Edna Johnson, Evelyn R. Sickels [and]

Frances Clarke Sayers. 3rd ed. Illustrated by Fritz Eichenberg. Boston, Houghton Mifflin [1959]. p.276–279.

Szewc Kopytko i kaczor Kwak. Translated and adapted as *Cobbler Kopytko and Drake Kwak.*

Cobbler Kopytko and Drake Kwak. In THE JOLLY TAILOR, AND OTHER FAIRY TALES. Translated from the Polish [and adapted] by Lucia Merecka Borski [Lucia Merecka Szczepanowicz] and Kate B. Miller; illustrated by Kazimir Klepacki. New York [etc.] Longmans, Green and company [c1928]. p.117–133.

From his BARDZO DZIWNE BAJKI (Very Strange Fairy Tales).

Markowska, M.

Jak Zawalidroga w niebie został. Translated and adapted as *How Standintheway Remained in Heaven.*

How Standintheway Remained in Heaven. In POLISH FOLK TALES. Translated [and adapted] by Lucia Merecka Borski [Lucia Merecka Szczepanowicz]; illustrated by Erica Gorecka-Egan. New York, Sheed and Ward, 1947. p.[31]–42.

From her ZA SIÓDMĄ GÓRĄ, ZA SIÓDMĄ RZEKĄ (Beyond the Seventh Mountain, Beyond the Seventh River).

O Jóźwie, co na przedpieklu służył. Translated and adapted as *Joe Who Served in Lower Limbo.*

Joe Who Served in Lower Limbo. In POLISH FOLK TALES. Translated [and adapted] by Lucia Merecka Borski [Lucia Merecka Szczepanowicz]; illustrated by Erica Gorecka-Egan. New York, Sheed and Ward, 1947. p.[71]–86.

From her ZA SIÓDMĄ GÓRĄ, ZA SIÓDMĄ RZEKĄ (Beyond the Seventh Mountain, Beyond the Seventh River).

O kozie rogatej. Translated and adapted as *A Horned Goat.*

A Horned Goat. In THE JOLLY TAILOR, AND OTHER FAIRY TALES. Translated from the Polish [and adapted] by Lucia Merecka Borski [Lucia Merecka Szczepanowicz] and Kate B. Miller; illustrated by Kazimir Klepacki. New York [etc.] Longmans, Green and company [c1928]. p.49–62.

From her ZA SIÓDMĄ GÓRĄ, ZA SIÓDMĄ RZEKĄ (Beyond the Seventh Mountain, Beyond the Seventh River).

O psie, co był szewcem. Translated and adapted as *The Cobbler Dog.*

The Cobbler Dog. In THE GYPSY AND THE BEAR AND OTHER FAIRY TALES. Translated from the Polish [and adapted] by Lucia Merecka Borski [Lucia Merecka Szczepanowicz] and Kate B. Miller; with a foreword by Eric P. Kelly; illustrated by James Reid. New York, Toronto, Longmans, Green and company [c1933]. p.23-31.

From her ZA SIÓDMĄ GÓRĄ, ZA SIÓDMĄ RZEKĄ (Beyond the Seventh Mountain, Beyond the Seventh River).

O skowronku, wilku i lisie. Translated and adapted as *The Lark, the Wolf, and the Fox.*

The Lark, the Wolf, and the Fox. In THE GYPSY AND THE BEAR AND OTHER FAIRY TALES. Translated from the Polish [and adapted] by Lucia Merecka Borski [Lucia Merecka Szczepanowicz] and Kate B. Miller; with a foreword by Eric P. Kelly; illustrated by James Reid. New York, Toronto, Longmans, Green and company [c1933]. p.1-13.

From her ZA SIÓDMĄ GÓRĄ, ZA SIÓDMĄ RZEKĄ (Beyond the Seventh Mountain, Beyond the Seventh River).

Perzyński, Włodzimierz (1878-1930)

O szczupaku, który umiał tańczyć. Translated and adapted as *The Dancing Pike.*

Résumé. A poor fiddler had caught a pike that could dance. He bought a bear from a gypsy to serve as partner to the pike, and collected such a great amount of money for his strange performances that he forgot all about his poor wife and hungry children. He married the Yawning Princess whom he had successfully entertained.

At the wedding the bridegroom picked up his fiddle and began to play, when both the pike and the bear who had been killed and prepared for the wedding feast jumped up from their platters and began to dance. When the frightened guests ran away, the pike compelled the fiddler to leave the Princess and return to his family.

Accompanied by the pike and the bear the fiddler went home. He became rich, and his wife and children never lacked anything.

The Dancing Pike (adapted). In THE MASTER WIZARD AND OTHER POLISH TALES. Translated from the Polish by Josephine B. Bernhard; revised and adapted by E. Frances Le Valley; illustrated by Marya Werten. New York, Alfred A. Knopf, 1934. p.67–84.

Pan Rozpędek. Translated and adapted as *Mr. Whirlwind, Shoemaker*.

Résumé. (A tale for children about a shoemaker whose name, Whirlwind, came from the fact that whatever he did, he did with increasing speed.)

When Mr. Whirlwind walked, no matter how slowly he had started, he soon left all the cabs and trolley cars behind. When he worked on a shoe, he nailed faster and faster and harder and harder until the shoe was completely ruined.

By playing tricks on the rich and stingy widow, Mrs. Lovepenny, he induced her to promise to marry him. The shoemaker was truly in love with Mrs. Lovepenny. The widow thought that by marrying Mr. Whirlwind, who appeared to her to be a miraculously industrious craftsman, she would add a great deal of money to her wealth.

Hand in hand they went for a walk. Mrs. Lovepenny wore her best dress and a hat with a white feather. Little by little Mr. Whirlwind increased his pace until he walked so fast that he dragged the screaming woman over the flagstones.

Mrs. Lovepenny fainted and had to be revived. Needless to say, she no longer thought of marrying Mr. Whirlwind.

Mr. Whirlwind, Shoemaker. In THE MASTER WIZARD AND OTHER POLISH TALES. Translated from the Polish by Josephine B. Bernhard; revised and adapted by E. Frances Le Valley; illustrated by Marya Werten. New York, Alfred A. Knopf, 1934. p.85–[101].

Mr. Whirlwind, Shoemaker. Adapted by Frances Frost from the translation by Josephine B. Bernhard and E. Frances Le Valley.

In LEGENDS OF THE UNITED NATIONS, by Frances Frost. New York, London, Whittlesey House, McGraw-Hill book company [c1943]. p.34–44.

Piotrowski, Antoni

O starym psie, ośle, kocie i kogucie. Translated and adapted as *A Dog, a Donkey, a Cat, and a Cock.*

A Dog, a Donkey, a Cat, and a Cock. In THE GYPSY AND THE BEAR AND OTHER FAIRY TALES. Translated from the Polish [and adapted] by Lucia Merecka Borski [Lucia Merecka Szczepanowicz] and Kate B. Miller; with a foreword by Eric P. Kelly; illustrated by James Reid. New York, Toronto, Longmans, Green and company [c1933]. p.47–54.

O takim, co rozumiał jak dzwirzęta gwarzom. Translated and adapted as *How a Sensible Peasant Cured His Wife's Curiosity.*

How a Sensible Peasant Cured His Wife's Curiosity. In THE GYPSY AND THE BEAR AND OTHER FAIRY TALES. Translated from the Polish [and adapted] by Lucia Merecka Borski [Lucia Merecka Szczepanowicz] and Kate B. Miller; with a foreword by Eric P. Kelly; illustrated by James Reid. New York, Toronto, Longmans, Green and company [c1933]. p.121–128.

Szczęśliwy żebrak (?) Translated and adapted as *The Lucky Beggar.*

Résumé. (A lazy Princess was forced by her father, the King, to marry a beggar.) The Princess was so lazy that she only wanted to lie on her plump bed all day, eating sausages and frosted cakes. When the King saw that she had sent all her suitors away, he proclaimed that all beggars throughout his kingdom should assemble at his castle.

When the beggars had gathered in the great hall, the King commanded his daughter to choose one of them for her husband. The Princess cunningly chose a tiny, skinny, puny creature, hoping that he would soon die anyway.

After the wedding the Puny One commanded the Princess to bring him all kinds of fancy dishes from morning until night.

The beggar became fat as a goose, while the Princess seldom ate and slept on a box. The beggar ate and ate until he burst.

When the Princess told the King that she had become a widow, he replied that he had only made believe to marry her to the beggar to teach her a good lesson.

Now the Princess became the busiest girl in the kingdom. She was slender and the most beautiful. Soon she married the most charming and the handsomest of all Princes. The wedding took place with magnificence and splendor amidst the great rejoicing of the people.

The tale ends with the familiar rhyme:

> And I was there among the guests,
> And there I drank both wine and mead;
> And what I saw and heard, I wrote,
> That all of you might read.
> (I ja tam byłem,
> I miód i wino piłem, etc.)

Porazińska, Janina

Moja Wólka. Translated as *My Village.*

My Village, by Janina Porazinska. Illustrated by Stanislaw Bobinski; translated from the Polish by Lucia Merecka Borski [Lucia Merecka Szczepanowicz].

46 p. illus., front.

Rabska, Zuzanna

Dzwony kościelne na Helu (?) Translated and adapted as *The Church Bells of Hel.*

The Church Bells of Hel. Translated and adapted by M. M. Coleman. In THE POLISH LAND, ZIEMIA POLSKA; an Anthology in Prose and Verse, compiled by Klub Polski of Columbia University. Edited by Marion Moore Coleman. [Trenton, Printed by the White Eagle Publishing Company, 1943]. p.12–13.

From her BAŚNIE KASZUBSKIE (?) (Kashubian Legends).

O flondrze bałtyckiej. Translated and adapted as *Why the Flounder Has a Crooked Mouth.*

Why the Flounder Has a Crooked Mouth. In THE GYPSY AND THE BEAR AND OTHER FAIRY TALES. Translated from the Polish [and adapted] by Lucia Merecka Borski [Lucia Merecka Szczepanowicz] and Kate B. Miller; with a foreword by Eric P. Kelly; illustrated by James Reid. New York, Toronto, Longmans, Green and company [c1933]. p.75–78.
From her BAŚNIE KASZUBSKIE (Kashubian Legends.)

O herbie miasta Pucka. Translated and adapted as *The Coat of Arms of Putsk.*

The Coat of Arms of Putsk. In THE GYPSY AND THE BEAR AND OTHER FAIRY TALES. Translated from the Polish [and adapted] by Lucia Merecka Borski [Lucia Merecka Szczepanowicz] and Kate B. Miller; with a foreword by Eric P. Kelly; illustrated by James Reid. New York, Toronto, Longmans, Green and company [c1933]. p.79–83.
From her BAŚNIE KASZUBSKIE (Kashubian Legends.)

Ostatnia syrena Helu (?) Translated and adapted as *The Last Siren of Hel.*

The Last Siren of Hel; a Kashubian Legend. Translated by Mary Walkuska and adapted by Marion Moore Coleman. In THE WAYSIDE WILLOW; Prose and Verse. Translated from the Polish by members of Klub Polski of Columbia University. Edited by Marion Moore Coleman. Student editor: Loretta M. Bielawska. [Trenton, Printed by the White Eagle Publishing Company, 1945]. p.23–27.
From her BAŚNIE KASZUBSKIE (Kashubian Legends.)

Reymont, Władysław Stanisław (1867–1925)

Burek, the Dog That Followed the Lord Jesus. Fragment from his CHŁOPI (The Peasants).

Burek, the Dog That Followed the Lord Jesus. In his BUREK, THE DOG THAT FOLLOWED THE LORD JESUS, AND OTHER STORIES. [Translated by Michael H. Dziewicki.] Cover design and illustration by

M. Walentynowicz. Birkenhead [England] Polish Publications Committee [1944]. p.5–16.

Burek, the Dog That Followed the Lord Jesus. In his POLISH FOLK-LORE STORIES. [Translated by Michael H. Dziewicki.] Illustrated by M. Walentynowicz. Birkenhead [England] Polish Publications Committee [1944]. p.3–8.

Christmas Eve. Fragment from his CHŁOPI (THE PEASANTS).

Christmas Eve. In his BUREK, THE DOG THAT FOLLOWED THE LORD JESUS, AND OTHER STORIES. [Translated by Michael H. Dziewicki.] Cover design and illustrations by M. Walentynowicz. Birkenhead [England] Polish Publications Committee [1944]. p.17–31.

Christmas Eve. In his POLISH FOLK-LORE STORIES. [Translated by Michael H. Dziewicki.] Illustrated by M. Walentynowicz. Birkenhead [England] Polish Publications Committee [1944]. p.8–15.

Christmas Eve, by W. Reymont. [Translated by Michael H. Dziewicki.] In THE POLISH SHORT STORIES. Edited by Umadevi. [Bombay] Indo-Polish Library. No. 35 [c1946]. p.33–51.

The Hawk. Fragment from his CHŁOPI (THE PEASANTS).

The Hawk. In his BUREK, THE DOG THAT FOLLOWED THE LORD JESUS, AND OTHER STORIES. [Translated by Michael H. Dziewicki.] Cover design and illustrations by M. Walentynowicz. Birkenhead [England] Polish Publications Committee [1944]. p.42–[56].

The hawk. In his POLISH FOLK-LORE STORIES. [Translated by Michael H. Dziewicki.] Illustrated by M. Walentynowicz. Birkenhead [England] Polish Publications Committee [1944]. p.19–25.

The Robbers. Fragment from his CHŁOPI (THE PEASANTS).

The Robbers. In his BUREK, THE DOG THAT FOLLOWED THE LORD JESUS, AND OTHER STORIES. [Translated by Michael H. Dziewicki.] Cover design and illustrations by M. Walentynowicz. Birkenhead [England] Polish Publications Committee [1944]. p.38–41.

The Robbers. In his POLISH FOLK-LORE STORIES. [Translated by Michael H. Dziewicki.] Illustrated by M. Walentynowicz. Birkenhead [England] Polish Publications Committee [1944]. p.17–19.

The Slothful Horse. Fragment from his CHŁOPI (THE PEASANTS).

The Slothful Horse. In his BUREK, THE DOG THAT FOLLOWED THE LORD JESUS, AND OTHER STORIES. [Translated by Michael H. Dziewicki.] Cover design and illustrations by M. Walentynowicz. Birkenhead [England] Polish Publications Committee [1944]. p.32–37.

The Slothful Horse. In his POLISH FOLK-LORE STORIES. [Translated by Michael H. Dziewicki.] Illustrated by M. Walentynowicz. Birkenhead [England] Polish Publications Committee [1944]. p.15–17.

Rodziewiczówna, Maria (1863–1944)

The Serpent and the Fir Tree. Fragment adapted from her DEWAJTIS (1889).

The Serpent and the Fir Tree, by Marja Rodziewiczówna. Translated and adapted by Regina Okleyewicz. In THE POLISH LAND, ZIEMIA POLSKA; an Anthology in Prose and Verse, compiled by Klub Polski of Columbia University. Edited by Marion Moore Coleman. [Trenton, Printed by the White Eagle Publishing Company, 1943]. p.108–110.

Rościszewski, M.

Dlaczego kozy mają ucięte ogony. Translated and adapted as *Why Goats Have Short Tails.*

Why Goats Have Short Tails. In THE GYPSY AND THE BEAR AND OTHER FAIRY TALES. Translated from the Polish [and adapted] by Lucia Merecka Borski [Lucia Merecka Szczepanowicz] and Kate B. Miller; with a foreword by Eric P. Kelly; illustrated by James Reid. New York, Toronto, Longmans, Green and company [c1933]. p.71–73.

From LEGENDA I BAŚŃ (Folk Tales and Legends), [compiled] by J. Staroś.

O ojcowskim królu. Translated as *The King and the Peasant/A Tale of the Fatherly King.*

The King and the Peasant. [Adapted from the translation by

Lucia Merecka Borski [Szczepanowicz].] In RIDE WITH THE SUN; an Anthology of Folk Tales and Stories from the United Nations. Edited by Harold Courlander for the United Nations Women's Guild. New York, Whittlesey House, McGraw-Hill Book Company [c1955]. p.142–144.

A Tale of the Fatherly King. In POLISH FOLK TALES. Translated [and adapted] by Lucia Merecka Borski [Szczepanowicz]; illustrated by Erica Gorecka-Egan. New York, Sheed and Ward, 1947. p.[103]–106.

From LEGENDA I BAŚŃ (Folk Tales and Legends), [compiled] by J. Staroś.

"The King referred to in this story is most probably King Kazimir the Great, who merited the title 'The King of the Peasants' for his considerate treatment of them." [Footnote.]

Staroś, J.

O szewczykowej duszyczce. Translated and adapted as *The Cobbler's Soul.*

The Cobbler's Soul. In POLISH FOLK TALES. Translated [and adapted] by Lucia Merecka Borski [Lucia Merecka Szczepanowicz]; illustrated by Erica Gorecka-Egan. New York, Sheed and Ward, 1947. p.[17]–21.

From his LEGENDA I BAŚŃ (Folk Tales and Legends).

Szczepkowski, Jan (1878(?)–   )

Chleb djabelski. Translated and adapted as *The Devil's Bread.*

The Devil's Bread. In POLISH FOLK TALES. Translated [and adapted] by Lucia Merecka Borski [Lucia Merecka Szczepanowicz]; illustrated by Erica Gorecka-Egan. New York, Sheed and Ward, 1947. p.[43]–50.

From his WYSŁUCHANI.

Szelburg-Ostrowska, Ewa (?)

Śnieg. Translated and adapted as *Snow.*

Snow. In POLISH FOLK TALES. Translated [and adapted] by Lucia

Merecka Borski [Lucia Merecka Szczepanowicz]; illustrated by Erica Gorecka-Egan. New York, Sheed and Ward, 1947. p.[61]–65. From her LEGENDY ŻOŁNIERSKIE (Soldiers' Legends).

Szelburg-Zarembina, Ewa (1899–   )

Bajka o gęsim jaju, raku nieboraku, kogucie piejaku, kaczce kwaczce, kocie mruczku i o psie kruczku. Translated and adapted as *The Egg That Went for a Walk.*

The Egg That Went for a Walk. In her WHO CAN TELL. Adapted into English by Margaret Sperry. Warsaw, Nasza Księgarnia [c1959]. p.5–[10].

Goście w glinianym dzbanku. Translated and adapted as *What Happened in the Broken Pitcher.*

What Happened in the Broken Pitcher. In her WHO CAN TELL. Adapted into English by Margaret Sperry. Warsaw, Nasza Księgarnia [c1959]. p.31–[36].

Jak sroczka gości przyjmowała. Translated and adapted as *The Good Housewife?*

The Good Housewife? In her WHO CAN TELL. Adapted into English by Margaret Sperry. Warsaw, Nasza Księgarnia [c1959]. p.37–[38].

Jak żabki Jasia zabawiały. Translated and adapted as *The Little Boy Who Cried Too Much.*

The Little Boy Who Cried Too Much. In her WHO CAN TELL. Adapted into English by Margaret Sperry. Warsaw, Nasza Księgarnia [c1959]. p.25–[30].

Koza, która prawdy nie mówiła. Translated and adapted as *Nothing But a Goat.*

Nothing But a Goat. In her WHO CAN TELL. Adapted into English by Margaret Sperry. Warsaw, Nasza Księgarnia [c1959]. p.48–[51].

O kurce złotopiórce i kogutku szałaputku. Translated and adapted as *The Greedy Rooster.*

The Greedy Rooster. In her WHO CAN TELL. Adapted into English by Margaret Sperry. Warsaw, Nasza Księgarnia [c1959]. p.40–[47].

O tym jak zajączek szaraczek psa burka wywiódł w pole. Translated and adapted as *No Hare Anywhere.*

No Hare Anywhere. In her WHO CAN TELL. Adapted into English by Margaret Sperry. Warsaw, Nasza Księgarnia [c1959]. p.16–[24].

Zabawa myszek. Translated and adapted as *The Mice Give a Ball.*

The Mice Give a Ball. In her WHO CAN TELL. Adapted into English by Margaret Sperry. Warsaw, Nasza Księgarnia [c1959]. p.11–[15].

Szymanowska, Władysława Weychert-, *see* Weychert-Szymanowska,, Władysława

Weychert-Szymanowska, Władysława

Jak sobie mądry chłop poradził ze złodziejami. Translated and adapted as *How a Clever Cottager Outwitted Seven Thieves.*

How a Clever Cottager Outwitted Seven Thieves. In THE GYPSY AND THE BEAR AND OTHER FAIRY TALES. Translated from the Polish [and adapted] by Lucia Merecka Borski [Lucia Merecka Szczepanowicz] and Kate B. Miller; with a foreword by Eric P. Kelly; illustrated by James Reid. New York, Toronto, Longmans, Green and company [c1933]. p.111–120.

From ŚWIAT CZARÓW (The Magic World), by Władysława Weychert-Szymanowska and Wanda Bruner.

O Panu Jezusie i zbójnikach. Translated and adapted as *The Lord Jesus and the Three Robbers.*

The Lord Jesus and the Three Robbers. In POLISH FOLK TALES. Translated [and adapted] by Lucia Merecka Borski [Lucia Merecka Szczepanowicz]; illustrated by Erica Gorecka-Egan. New York, Sheed and Ward, 1947. p.[23]–30.

From ŚWIAT CZARÓW (The Magic World), by Władysława Weychert-Szymanowska and Wanda Bruner.

Pokuta konia zabijaki. Translated and adapted as *The Penance of a Horse Who Was a Bully.*

The Penance of a Horse Who Was a Bully. In POLISH FOLK TALES. Translated [and adapted] by Lucia Merecka Borski [Lucia Merecka Szczepanowicz]; illustrated by Erica Gorecka-Egan. New York, Sheed and Ward, 1947. p.[119]–123.

From ŚWIAT CZARÓW (The Magic World), by Władysława Weychert-Szymanowska and Wanda Bruner.

Powstanie Tatr. Translated and adapted as *Where the Tatra Mountains Came From.*

Where the Tatra Mountains Came From. In POLISH FOLK TALES. Translated [and adapted] by Lucia Merecka Borski [Lucia Merecka Szczepanowicz]; illustrated by Erica Gorecka-Egan. New York, Sheed and Ward, 1947. p.[91]–95.

From ŚWIAT CZARÓW (The Magic World), by Władysława Weychert-Szymanowska and Wanda Bruner.

Prawda i Krzywda. Translated and adapted as *Truth and Falsehood.*

Truth and Falsehood. In POLISH FOLK TALES. Translated [and adapted] by Lucia Merecka Borski [Lucia Merecka Szczepanowicz]; illustrated by Erica Gorecka-Egan. New York, Sheed and Ward, 1947. p.[51]–59.

From ŚWIAT CZARÓW (The Magic World), by Władysława Weychert-Szymanowska and Wanda Bruner.

Sabałowa bajka. Translated and adapted as *A Mountaineer's Tale.*

A Mountaineer's Tale. In POLISH FOLK TALES. Translated [and adapted] by Lucia Merecka Borski [Lucia Merecka Szczepanowicz]; illustrated by Erica Gorecka-Egan. New York, Sheed and Ward, 1947. p.[87]–90.

From ŚWIAT CZARÓW (The Magic World), by Władysława Weychert-Szymanowska and Wanda Bruner.

Szczęście. Translated and adapted as *Fortune.*

Fortune. In POLISH FOLK TALES. Translated [and adapted] by Lucia Merecka Borski [Lucia Merecka Szczepanowicz]; illustrated by Erica Gorecka-Egan. New York, Sheed and Ward, 1947. p.[107]–112.

From ŚWIAT CZARÓW (The Magic World), by Władysława Weychert-Szymanowska and Wanda Bruner.

Wóycicki, Kazimierz Władysław (1807–1879)

Djabli taniec. Translated as *The Demon's Dance.*

The Demon's Dance. In SLAVONIC FAIRY TALES. Collected and translated from the Russian, Polish, Servian, and Bohemian by John T. Naaké . . . London, Henry S. King and company, 1874. p.[17]–18.

From his KLECHDY, STAROŻYTNE PODANIA I POWIEŚCI LUDOWE (Folk Tales and Ancient Legends), 1851.

Duch pogrzebanego. Translated as *The Spirit of a Buried Man.*

The Spirit of a Buried Man. In SIXTY FOLK-TALES FROM EXCLUSIVELY SLAVONIC SOURCES. Translated, with brief introductions and notes, by A. H. Wratislaw . . . Boston, Houghton, Mifflin and company; Cambridge, The Riverside Press, 1890. p.121–125.

From his KLECHDY, STAROŻYTNE PODANIA I POWIEŚCI LUDOWE (Folk Tales and Ancient Legends), 1851.

Dżuma. Translated as *The Plague.*

The Plague. In SLAVONIC FAIRY TALES. Collected and translated from the Russian, Polish, Servian, and Bohemian by John T. Naaké . . . London, Henry S. King and company, 1874. p.[95]–96.

From his KLECHDY, STAROŻYTNE PODANIA I POWIEŚCI LUDOWE (Folk Tales and Ancient Legends), 1851.

Homen. Translated as *The Plague-Omen/The Plague-Swarm.*

The Plague-Omen. In SLAVONIC FAIRY TALES. Collected and translated from the Russian, Polish, Servian, and Bohemian, by John T. Naaké . . . London, Henry S. King and company, 1874. p.[19]–21.

From his KLECHDY, STAROŻYTNE PODANIA I POWIEŚCI LUDOWE (Folk Tales and Ancient Legends), 1851.

The Plague-Swarm. In SIXTY FOLK-TALES FROM EXCLUSIVELY SLAVONIC SOURCES. Translated with brief introductions and notes, by A. H. Wratislaw . . . Boston, Houghton, Mifflin and company; Cambridge, The Riverside Press, 1890. p.127–128.

Jonek. Translated as *Jonek*.

Jonek. In SLAVONIC FAIRY TALES. Collected and translated from the Russian, Polish, Servian, and Bohemian, by John T. Naaké . . . London, Henry S. King and company, 1874. p.[178]–186.

From his KLECHDY, STAROŻYTNE PODANIA I POWIEŚCI LUDOWE (Folk Tales and Ancient Legends).

Madej. Translated as *Madey*.

Madey. In SLAVONIC FAIRY TALES. Collected and translated from the Russian, Polish, Servian, and Bohemian, by John T. Naaké . . . London, Henry S. King and company, 1874. p.[220]–225.

From his KLECHDY, STAROŻYTNE PODANIA I POWIEŚCI LUDOWE (Folk Tales and Ancient Legends).

Oczy uroczne. Translated as *The Evil Eye*.

The Evil Eye. In SLAVONIC FAIRY TALES. Collected and translated from the Russian, Polish, Servian, and Bohemian, by John T. Naaké . . . London, Henry S. King and company, 1874. p.[73]–83.

From his KLECHDY, STAROŻYTNE PODANIA I POWIEŚCI LUDOWE (Folk Tales and Ancient Legends).

Porwany wichrem. Translated as *Carried Away by the Wind*.

Carried Away by the Wind. In SLAVONIC FAIRY TALES. Collected and translated from the Russian, Polish, Servian, and Bohemian by John T. Naaké . . . London, Henry S. King and company, 1874. p.[1]–5.

From his KLECHDY, STAROŻYTNE PODANIA I POWIEŚCI LUDOWE (Folk Tales and Ancient Legends).

Powietrze. Translated as *The Plague and the Peasant*.

The Plague and the Peasant. In SLAVONIC FAIRY TALES. Collected and translated from the Russian, Polish, Servian, and Bohemian by John T. Naaké . . . London, Henry S. King and company, 1874. p.[110]–112.

From his KLECHDY, STAROŻYTNE PODANIA I POWIEŚCI LUDOWE (Folk Tales and Ancient Legends).

Twardowski. Translated as *Twardowski.*

Twardowski. In SLAVONIC FAIRY TALES. Collected and translated from the Russian, Polish, Servian, and Bohemian by John T. Naaké . . . London, Henry S. King and company, 1874. p.[208]–213.

From his KLECHDY, STAROŻYTNE PODANIA I POWIEŚCI LUDOWE (Folk Tales and Ancient Legends).

Wilkołaki. Translated as *Men-Wolves.*

Men-Wolves. In SLAVONIC FAIRY TALES. Collected and translated from the Russian, Polish, Servian, and Bohemian by John T. Naaké . . . London, Henry S. King and company, 1874. p.[135]–140.

From his KLECHDY, STAROŻYTNE PODANIA I POWIEŚCI LUDOWE (Folk Tales and Ancient Legends).

Zajęcze serce. Translated as *The Hare's Heart.*

The Hare's Heart. In SLAVONIC FAIRY TALES. Collected and translated from the Russian, Polish, Servian, and Bohemian by John T. Naaké . . . London, Henry S. King and company, 1874. p.[36]–40.

From his KLECHDY, STAROŻYTNE PODANIA I POWIEŚCI LUDOWE (Folk Tales and Ancient Legends).

Zarembina, Ewa Szelburg-, *see* Szelburg-Zarembina, Ewa

APPENDIX I

List of Anthologies, Collections, and Other Related Titles

Anstruther, Fay Sibyl Marie (Rechnitzer) Carmichael **

OLD POLISH LEGENDS, retold by F. C. Anstruther. Wood-engravings by J. Sekalski; foreword by Z. Nowakowski. Glasgow, The Polish Library, 1945.
66 p. illus.

Contents: Foreword, by Zygmunt Nowakowski.—*The Legend of Lech and Gniezno.—The Story of Popiel.—The Legend of Krakus.—The Legend of Wanda.—The Legend of the Piasts.—The Legend of Mieszko.—The Legend of St. Adalbert.—How the Emperor Otto Visited Gniezno.—The Legend of Boleslaw and His Knights.—The Story of the "Resurrected Brothers."—The Trumpeter of Krakow.*

Baker, Denys Val, ed.

INTERNATIONAL SHORT STORIES (first series). Edited by Denys Val Baker. London, W. H. Allen and company, 1944.

72 p. (New series [*sic!*] No. 1)
Contains: *Banasiowa,* by Marja Konopnicka.

Baron, Joseph Louis, 1894–   ed.

CANDLES IN THE NIGHT; Jewish Tales by Gentile Authors. Edited by Joseph L. Baron; with a preface by Carl Van Doren. Philadelphia, The Jewish Publication Society of America, 1940 (5700).
xxiii,391 p.

Partial contents: *Srul—from Lubartów,* by Adam Szymanski.—*"Give Me a Flower!"* by Eliza Orzeszko.

Each story is preceded by a brief note about the author, translation, etc.

Also published with imprint: New York, Farrar and Rinehart, 1940.

Benecke, Else Cecilia Mendelssohn, 1873–1917, tr.

MORE TALES BY POLISH AUTHORS. Translated by Else C. M. Benecke and Marie Busch. Oxford, B. H. Blackwell, 1916.
viii,288 p.

Contents: *Maciej the Mazur,* by Adam Szymański.—*Two Prayers,* by Adam Szymański.—*The Trial,* by W. St. Reymont.—*The Stronger Sex,* by Stefan Żeromski.—*The Chukchee,* by W. Sieroszewski.—*The Returning Wave,* by Bolesław Prus.

Also published with imprint: New York, Longmans, Green and company, 1916.

Benecke, Else Cecilia Mendelssohn, 1873–1917, tr.

SELECTED POLISH TALES. Translated by Else C. M. Benecke and Marie Busch. London, New York [etc.] H. Milford, Oxford University Press [1921].
x,348 p.

Contents: Preface, by Marie Busch.—*The Outpost,* by Bolesław Prus.—*A Pinch of Salt,* by Adam Szymański.—*Kowalski the Carpenter,* by Adam Szymański.—*Forebodings,* by Stefan Żeromski—*A Polish Scene,* by Władysław St. Reymont.—*Death,* by Władysław St. Reymont.—*The Sentence,* by J. Kaden-Bandrowski.—*"P.P.C.,"* by Mme. Rygier-Nałkowska.

Half-title page: The World's Classics, CCXXX. Selected Polish tales. First published in "The World's Classics," 1921. Reprinted 1928, 1942, 1944.

Benecke, Else Cecilia Mendelssohn, 1873–1917, tr.

TALES BY POLISH AUTHORS: Henryk Sienkiewicz, Stefan Żeromski, Adam Szymański, Wacław Sieroszewski. Translated by Else C. M. Benecke.

Oxford, B. H. Blackwell, 1915.

198 p.

Contents: *Bartek the Conqueror*, by Henryk Sienkiewicz.—*Twilight*, by Stefan Żeromski.—*Temptation*, by Stefan Żeromski.—*Srul—from Lubartów*, by Adam Szymański.—*In Autumn*, by Wacław Sieroszewski. —*In Sacrifice to the Gods*, by Wacław Sieroszewski.

Bernhard, Josephine Butkowska, tr. (S)

THE MASTER WIZARD, AND OTHER POLISH TALES. Translated from the Polish by Josephine B. Bernhard; revised and adapted by E. Frances Le Valley; illustrated by Marya Werten. New York, Alfred A. Knopf, 1934.

ix,180 p. illus.

Contents: Introduction, by Josephine B. Bernhard.—*The Master Wizard, Pan Twardowski, and His Spider* (adapted), by Czeslaw Kedzierski.—*The Good Orphan Sunblossom and the Enchanted Treasure*, by Czeslaw Kedzierski.—*Jas the Fiddler* (adapted), by Czeslaw Kedzierski.—*The Wolf and the Blacksmith*, by Czeslaw Kedzierski.— *The Dancing Pike* (adapted), by Wlodzimierz Perzynski.— *Mr. Whirlwind, Shoemaker*, by Wlodzimierz Perzynski.—*Madej the Brigand* (adapted), by A. J. Glinski.—*The Wizard's Pupil*, by A. J. Glinski.—*The Jester who Fooled a King*, by Baracz.—*The Lucky Beggar*, by A. Piotrowski.—*The Pig's-Head Magician* (retold), anonymous.[1]

Borski, Lucia Merecka, tr. (S)

THE GYPSY AND THE BEAR AND OTHER FAIRY TALES. Translated from the Polish [and adapted] by Lucia Merecka Borski [Lucia Merecka Szczepanowicz] and Kate B. Miller; with a foreword by Eric P. Kelly; illustrated by James Reid. New York, Toronto, Longmans, Green and company [c1933].

xxii,129 p. front., illus., plates.

Contents: *The Lark, the Wolf, and the Fox.*—*How the Animals Lost Their Freedom.*—*The Cobbler Dog.*—*The Adventures of a Wolf.*— *A Dog, a Donkey, a Cat, and a Cock.*—*About an Old Man and an Old Woman, a Cock and a Hen, a Fox and a Wolf.*—*Why Goats Have Short Tails.*—*Why the Flounder Has a Crooked Mouth.*—*The Coat of Arms of Putsk.*—*The Gypsy and the Bear.*—*Ill-Luck.*—*How a Clever Cottager Outwitted Seven Thieves.*—*How a Sensible Peasant Cured his Wife's Curiosity.*[2]

---

1 With the exception of the final one, all these tales have been summarized.
2 No Polish titles have been found, and no analytical entries have been made for the tales, *How the Animals Lost Their Freedom*, and *Ill-Luck*.

"Glossary": p.129.

A bibliographic note, by Lucia Merecka Szczepanowicz: p.[viii].

First edition 1933. Reprinted 1935, 1940, 1943, 1949.

Borski, Lucia Merecka, tr. (S)

THE JOLLY TAILOR, AND OTHER FAIRY TALES. Translated from the Polish [and adapted] by Lucia Merecka Borski [Lucia Merecka Szczepanowicz] and Kate B. Miller; illustrated by Kazimir Klepacki. New York [etc.] Longmans, Green and company [c1928].
158 p. col.front., illus.

Contents: Foreword, by Mary Gould Davis.—*The Jolly Tailor Who Became King.*—*The Hunting.*—*Koshalki-opalki, or How a Simpleton Became King.*—*A Horned Goat.*—*King Bartek.*—*Majka.*—*The Story of Princess Marysia, the Black Swan, and an Iceberg.*—*Cobbler Kopytko and Drake Kwak.*—*The Flight.*—*The Frog.*

"Glossary": p.157.
A bibliographic note, by Lucia Merecka Szczepanowicz: p.6.

First edition 1928. Reprinted 1929, 1938, 1940, 1943, 1946, 1951. Reissued 1957.

Borski, Lucia Merecka, tr. (S)

POLISH FOLK TALES. Translated [and adapted] by Lucia Merecka Borski [Lucia Merecka Szczepanowicz]; illustrated by Erica Gorecka-Egan. New York, Sheed and Ward, 1947.
123 p. front., illus.

Contents: *How Saint Joseph Ploughed the Soil.*—*The Cobbler's Soul.* —*The Lord Jesus and the Three Robbers.*—*How Standintheway Remained in Heaven.*—*The Devil's Bread.*—*Truth and Falsehood.* —*Snow.*—*There Was an Old Man and an Old Woman.*—*Joe Who Served in Lower Limbo.*—*A Mountaineer's Tale.*—*Where the Tatra Mountains Came From.*—*Poverty and Misery.*—*A Tale of the Fatherly King.*—*Fortune.*—*Gratitude and Justice.*—*The Penance of a Horse Who Was a Bully.*

A bibliographic note: p.[8].

"The tales have been not only translated, but also retold and adapted to suit the American reader and the American story teller."

Braddy, Nella, *see* Henney, Nella (Braddy)

Brant, Alfred, ed. *

WAR OR PEACE. Edited by Alfred Brant . . . and Frederick Houk Law . . . New York and London, Harper and brothers, 1938.
xxii,272 p. front., plates.

Contains: *The Escape,* by Henryk Sienkiewicz.

Stories, preceded by brief bio-bibliographic notes, and followed by questions "for class discussion" and on "application to life."

"First edition."

Braun, Irwin H., ed.

STORIES OF MANY NATIONS, selected and arranged by Irwin H. Braun . . . and D. Edward Safarjian . . . Illustrated by Armstrong Sperry. Boston, D. C. Heath and company [c1942].

xvii,588 p. illus.

Partial contents: *Twilight,* by Wladyslaw Reymont.—*Janko the Musician,* by Henryk Sienkiewicz.

Map on lining paper.

Arranged by countries. Poland: p.[453]–471.

"The literature of Poland": p.455–456.

Each story preceded by a brief note about the author, and followed by "Study helps."

Brentano, Frances, ed. *

THE WORD LIVES ON: A TREASURY OF SPIRITUAL FICTION. Edited by Frances Brentano; introduction by Halford E. Luccock. Garden City, N.Y., Doubleday and company, 1951.

xx,355 p.

Contains: *Keeper of the Faith,* by Henryk Sienkiewicz.

Bryde, Elsie, tr. **

THE POLISH FAIRY BOOK. Translated and adapted from the Polish by Elsie Byrde; with illustrations in colour by Livia Kadar. London, T. Fisher Unwin [1925].

231 p. front., col. plates.

Contents: Foreword, by Elsie Byrde.—*About Prince Surprise.—The Wise Simpleton.—Krencipal and Krencipalka* (a Nursery Tale).—*Bogdynek.—The Prince and the Foundling.—The Magic Fife.—The Golden Lynx.—About Jan the Prince.—The Wanderer Who Had Forgotten Who He Was.—About the Hedgehog Who Became a Prince.—The Sheepskin Coat.—Lie-a-Stove.—The Enchanted Doughnuts.—Saturday Mountain.—The Old Man's Son.—The Flight.—The Glass Mountain.—The Three Sisters.—About the Black Crow.—The Giant Twins.—The Dragon Prince.—Goldenhair and Goldenhand.—The Frog Princess.*

Chodźko, Aleksander Borejko, 1804 (?)–1891 **

FAIRY TALES OF THE SLAV PEASANTS AND HERDSMEN. From the French of Alex. Chodsko translated and illustrated by Emily J. Harding. London, George Allen, 1896.

xiii,353 p. illus. front.

Contents: *The Abode of the Gods: 1. The Two Brothers; 2. Time and the Kings of the Elements; 3. The Twelve Months.—The Sun; or, the Three Golden Hairs of the Old Man Vsévède.—Kovlad: 1. The Sovereign of the Mineral Kingdom; 2. The Lost Child.—The Maid with Hair of Gold.—The Journey to the Sun and the Moon.— The Dwarf with the Long Beard.—The Flying Carpet, the Invisible Cap, the Gold-giving Ring, and the Smiting Club.—The Broad Man, the Tall Man, and the Man with Eyes of Flame.—The History of Prince Slugobyl; or, the Invisible Knight.—The Spirit of the Steppes. —The Prince with the Golden Hand.—Imperishable.—Ohnivak.— Tears of Pearls.—The Sluggard.—Kinkach Martinko.—The Story of the Plentiful Table-Cloth, the Avenging Wand, the Sash That Becomes a Lake, and the Terrible Helmet.*

Christy, Arthur E., 1899–1946, ed.

WORLD LITERATURE; an Anthology of Human Experience, edited by Arthur E. Christy [and] Henry W. Wells. New York, American Book Company [c1947].

xxiii,1118 p.

Partial contents: *The Just Hare,* by Adolf Dygasiński.—*Banasiowa,* by Maria Konopnicka.

Clark, Barrett Harper, 1890– ed.

GREAT SHORT NOVELS OF THE WORLD; a Collection of Complete Tales Chosen from the Literatures of All Periods and Countries, by Barrett H. Clark. Albert and Charles Boni [1932].

2v. (Bonibooks)

Contains: A note for critics, by Barrett H. Clark (v.1).—*Tomek Baran,* by Wladyslaw Stanislaw Reymont (v.2).

"Reading list: a brief selective bibliography of the works in English consulted in the preparation of this volume": v.2, p.1301.

Arranged by countries. Each country preceded by a brief introduction. Poland: p.927–961.

First published 1927. First issued in Bonibooks series, 1932.

Clark, Barrett Harper, 1890– ed.

GREAT SHORT STORIES OF THE WORLD: a Collection of Complete Short Stories Chosen from the Literature of All Periods and Countries by Barrett H. Clark and Maxim Lieber. New York, Robert M. McBride and company, 1926.

xv,1072 p.

Partial contents: *The Lighthouse Keeper of Aspinwall,* by Henryk Sienkiewicz.—*The Human Telegraph,* by Boleslav Prus.—*Forebodings,* by Stefan Żeromski.

"First published, December, 1925. Second printing, February, 1926. Third printing, August, 1926."

Also published with imprints:

London, William Heinemann, 1926.

Cleveland, World Publishing Company, n.d.

Cleveland, New York, World Publishing Company, 1947.

"First printed in Bonibooks Series, September, 1931. Second printing, January, 1932. Third printing, July, 1932. Fourth printing, December, 1932. Fifth printing, August, 1933."

"Copyright, 1925, by Robert M. McBride & Co."

Coleman, Marion Moore, 1900– ed. (S)

THE POLISH LAND, ZIEMIA POLSKA; an Anthology in Prose and Verse, compiled by Klub Polski of Columbia University. Edited by Marion Moore Coleman. [Trenton, Printed by the White Eagle Publishing Company, 1943].

xiii,127 p.

Partial contents: *The Church Bells of Hel,* by Zuzanna Rabska.—*The Legend of Smreczyński Staw,* by Seweryn Goszczyński.—*The Serpent and the Fir Tree,* by Maria Rodziewiczówna.—*Kupallo,* by Józef I. Kraszewski.

"List of translators": p.121.

"Copyright, 1943, by A. P. and M. M. Coleman."

Coleman, Marion Moore, 1900– ed. (S)

THE WAYSIDE WILLOW: Prose and Verse. Translated from the Polish by members of Klub Polski of Columbia University. Edited by Marion Moore Coleman. Student editor: Loretta M. Bielawska. [Trenton, Printed by the White Eagle Publishing Company, 1945].

50 p. front.

Partial contents: *The Fern Flower of Happiness,* adapted from Adolf Dygasiński's FEAST OF LIFE.—*The Old Clock of Danzig,* a Kashubian Legend.—*The Last Siren of Hel,* a Kashubian Legend.[3]

"Copyright, 1945, by A. P. and M. M. Coleman."

Courlander, Harold, ed. (S)

RIDE WITH THE SUN; an Anthology of Folk Tales and Stories from the United Nations. Edited by Harold Courlander for the United Nations

---

[3] *The Fern Flower of Happiness* has been included in the main body of the analytical bibliography.

Women's Guild; illustrated by Roger Duvoisin. New York, Whittlesey House, McGraw-Hill Book Company [c1959].
296 p. Illus.
Notes on the stories: p. 283–296.
Contains: *The King and the Peasant* [by M. Rosciszewski].

Dąbrowska, Maria, 1889–1965

A VILLAGE WEDDING AND OTHER STORIES. Translation anonymous. Warsaw, Polonia Publishing House, 1957.
215 p.
Contents: *A Pilgrimage to Warsaw.—The Winter Coat.—The Child.— A Morning at the Zoo.—Night Encounter.—Madame Sophie.—A Change Came O'er the Scenes of My Dream.—The Third Autumn.— A Village Wedding.*

Dynowska, Wanda, ed.

POLISH SHORT STORIES. Edited by Umadevi. [Translated by various hands. Bombay] Indo-Polish Library. No.35 [c1946].
xii,160 p.
Contents: Introduction, by the editor. Part I. *The Voice*, by Jozef Weyssenhof.—*Banasyova*, by Maria Konopnicka.—*"Impossible*," by Stafan [i.e. Stefan] Zeromski.—*Christmas Eve*, by Wladyslaw Raymont [i.e. Reymont].—*The Visitor*, by Feliks Gwizdz.—*Far-off Marisya*, by Kazimir Tetmajer. Part II. *"There Where the Last Gaunt Gallows Stands and Beckons*," by Eugeniusz Malaczewski.—*The Lighthouse Keeper*, by Henryk Sienkiewicz. Part III. *Yanek the Distributor*, by Majewski.—*"Welcome Our Distinguished Guest*," by Jerzy Pietrkiewicz.—*A Saddhu* [spelling varies], by Jerzy Pietrkiewicz.—*Bread*, by Herminia Naglerowa.
"Sole distributors for India"; Padma Publications Ltd., Bombay.

Dynowska, Wanda, ed. (partly)*

THE WINTER MAIDENS AND OTHER SHORT STORIES. [Translated by various hands.] Edited by Umadevi. [Bombay] The Indo-Polish Library, 1947.
182 p.
Contents: Foreword, by Prof. V. B.—*Maryna*, by K. P. Tetmajer.— *The Winter Maidens*, by K. P. Tetmajer.—*Zwyrtala the Fiddler*, by K. P. Tetmajer.—*Temptation*, by Piotr Choynowski.—*Peasant Wedding*, by W. Reymont.—*Contrasts*, by W. Reymont.—*How to Escape*, by J. M. Herbert.—*Sergeant Prot, Night Fighter*, by J. M. Herbert.— *Torture*, by J. Karski.

Eaton, Richard, ed.

THE BEST CONTINENTAL SHORT STORIES OF 1923–1924, AND THE YEAR-

BOOK OF THE CONTINENTAL SHORT STORY. Boston, Small, Maynard, and company [c1924].

452 p.

Contains: *The Forgotten Ghost*, by Kornel Makuszynski.

List of Polish magazines publishing short stories: p.417.

Brief bio-bibliographic notes on seven Polish authors: p.422–423.

List of selected Polish short stories published from July 1923 to July 1924: p.442.

Eaton, Richard, ed.

THE BEST CONTINENTAL SHORT STORIES OF 1924–1925, AND THE YEARBOOK OF THE CONTINENTAL SHORT STORY. Boston, Small, Maynard, and company [c1925].

x,557 p.

Contains: *Jerzy*, by Waclaw Grubinski.

List of Polish magazines publishing short stories: p.524.

Brief bio-bibliographic notes about four Polish authors: p.529.

List of Polish short stories published in 1924–1925: p.551–555.

Eaton, Richard, ed.

THE BEST CONTINENTAL SHORT STORIES OF 1926, AND THE YEARBOOK OF THE CONTINENTAL SHORT STORY. New York, Dodd, Mead, and company, 1927.

x,336 p.

Contains: *Daimonion Bib*, by Waclaw Grubinski.

List of Polish magazines publishing short stories: p.312.

Brief bio-bibliographic notes on selected Polish authors: p.318.

List of Polish short stories published in 1926: p.333–334.

Fiedler, Arkady, 1894– **

THE MADAGASCAR I LOVE. [Translation anonymous.] London, Orbis [1946].

187 p. illus., maps, plates, ports.

Contents: Part I. *The Enticing Isle*. 1. *A Disturbing Smile.*—2. *The Enticing Isle.*—3. *Waves from the East.*—4. *Red Antanana-Rivo.*—5. *Tropical Fear.*—6. *Fadi.*—7. *The Royal Castle of Rova.*—8. *The Tragic Friend of Queen Ranavalo.*—9. *Beautiful Raffia.*—10. *Vari, the Loving Lemur.*—11. *Bare Feet Dance Against Coffee.*—12. *"Our Vasaha Lost His Hat."*—13. *A Night of Dancing.*—14. *Jadanikumba.*—15. *Mipetraka.*—16. *A Girl is Chased.*—17. *The Divine Cruel Voay.*—18. *Bokombolo Was Grey.* Part II. *The Merry Drongo Bird.* 19. *Mimosas.*—20. *An Ordeal.*—21. *Praying Insects.*—22. *My Chameleon.*—

23. *Death in Purple.*—24. *Mount Beniowski.*—25. *The Forest Is My Friend.*—26. *Spiders and Mantises.*—27. *A Breath of Civilization.*—28. *The Merry Drongo Bird.*—29. *Their Flower of Love.*—30. *The Male's Tasty Flesh.*—31. *Odd Humours of the Past.*—32. *Magic of Nature.*—33. *Hungry Blood.*—34. *The Serpent Ankoma.*—35. *Woe Betide the Victor.*—36. *Mountain Aglow.*—37. *What the Dickens!*—38. *Velomody Is Willing.*—39. *River Antanambalana.*—40 *Mother Love.*—41. *The Woman's Right.*—42. *The Hut of Reeds.*—43. *A Moth Is Born.*—44. *Legends Are Stronger Than Life.*

"First published in English, 1946."

Original title: ŻARLIWA WYSPA BENIOWSKIEGO.

Fiedler, Arkady, 1894– *

THE RIVER OF SINGING FISH. [Translated by H. C. Stevens.] With aquatints by Zdzislaw Ruszkowski. London, Hodder and Stoughton [1948].

191 p. front., plates, maps.

Partial contents[4]: *Romantic Passengers.—Little Chicinho and the Great Big Amazon.—The Personal "Great Adventure."—An India-Rubber Tragedy.—The Ants and Parrots of Iquitos.—A Hot-Bed of Racial Rivalry.—Embarrassing Visitors.—Much Ado About—Leticia.—Fifty Yards of Civilization.—Dreaming on the Ucayali.—Spiders.—Europe versus Snake.—A Chapter on Cruelty.—Flowers Which Moved Britons.—Good Old Friends.—A Black Stream of Death.—Where Nature Runs Wild.—Contempt for Whites and Monkeys.—Living Sunbeams.—Water, Water Everywhere.—More Rain.—Butterflies.—Slavery on the Ucayali.—Heat!—Green Parrots and Crimson Macaws.*

"First printed 1948."

Map on lining paper.

Original title: RYBY ŚPIEWAJĄ W UKAJALI.

Fiedler, Arkady, 1894– **

SQUADRON 303; the Story of the Polish Fighter Squadron with the R.A.F. [Translation anonymous.] London, Peter Davies [1942].

116 p. front., plates, ports.

Chapter contents: 1. *"I Am Delighted."*—2. *The Battle of Britain, 1940.*—3. *Comradeship.*—4. *The Fighter Pilot.*—5. *All Bullets Spent.*—6. *Ups and Downs.*—7. *Big Game: Dorniers.*—8. *Suffering.*—9. *Jan Donald Smiles Three Times.*—10. *The Cloud.*—11. *The Best Score.*—12. *The Enemy's Danse Macabre.*—13. *A Gallant Czech, Sergeant*

---

[4] The titles which have no counterparts in the Polish text have been omitted in the analytical bibliography and in Appendix IVa.

Frantisek.—14. *The Grey Roots of Brilliant Flowers.*—15. *Sans peur et sans reproche.*—16. *The Myth of the Messerschmitt 110.*—17. *Stratagems.*—18. *Human Destiny Hangs in the Balance.*—19. *The Balance Tips.*—20. *"We Are Beginning to Understand the Poles."*

First printed by Peter Davies Ltd. 1942. Second edition by Peter Davies Ltd. 1942. Third edition 1944.

Also published with imprint: Letchworth [Herts.] Letchworth Printers [1944].

Original title: DYWIZJON 303.

Fiedler, Arkady, 1894– **

SQUADRON 303; the Story of the Polish Fighter Squadron with the R.A.F. [Translation anonymous.] New York, Roy Publishers, 1943. 182 p. front., plates, ports.

"Copyright, 1943, by Roy, Publishers, A. N. New York. First printing, February 1943. Second printing, June 1943.

Fiedler, Arkady, 1894– *

THANK YOU, CAPTAIN, THANK YOU! Translated by Celina Wieniewska. London, MaxLove Publishing Company [1945]. 145 p. illus.

"First edition in Gt. Britain 1945."

Contents: I. *Thank You, Captain, Thank You!*—II. *La France est morte.*—III. *Roch, the Practical Joker.*—IV. *S.S. Bielsk, a Ship with Character.*—V. *Greaser Loza Is Hungry.*—VI. *A Gallant Captain and a Dauntless Ship.*—VII. *Their Battle.*

Original title: DZIĘKUJĘ CI, KAPITANIE.

Filip, T. M., ed. *

A POLISH ANTHOLOGY. Selected by T. M. Filip; translated by M. A. Michael. London, Duckworth [c1944]. 405 p.

Partial contents: Introduction, by M. A. M[ichael].—*In the Mountains; Spring; The Passion of Heaven; The Might of Satan; Trees in Grudno; For Our Freedom and Yours,* by Stefan Żeromski.

Text English and Polish; added title page in Polish: Moja ojczyzna-polszczyzna; wybór poezji polskiej.

First published 1944. Reprinted 1944, 1947.

Frost, Frances Mary, 1905–1959, ed. (S)

LEGENDS OF THE UNITED NATIONS . . . New York, London, Whittlesey House, McGraw-Hill book company [c1943]. xi,323 p.

Partial contents: *Mr. Whirlwind, Shoemaker* [by Włodzimierz Perzyński].—*Saint Stanislaw and the Wolf* [by Czesław Kędzierski].—*The Jester Who Fooled a King* [by Sadok Barącz].

Garnett, Richard, ed. *

THE UNIVERSAL ANTHOLOGY; a Collection of the Best Literature, Ancient, Mediaeval and Modern, with biographical and explanatory Notes. Edited by Richard Garnett, Leon Vallée [and] Alois Brandl. London, The Clarke Company [1899–1902].
33v. fronts. (partly col.) plates (partly illuminated) ports., facsims.
Partial contents: v.6, *The Days of Nero,* by Henryk Sienkiewicz.—v.14, *The Death of the Traitors; Escape of Zagloba and Helena; The Death of Radzivill,* by Henryk Sienkiewicz.
Edition limited to 1,000 complete sets.
At head of title: Édition de grand luxe.
Also published in Édition nationale, Royal edition, and Westminster edition.

Gawalewicz, Marian, 1852–1910 **

THE QUEEN OF HEAVEN, by Maryan Gawalewicz. Translated from the Polish by Lucia Borski Szczpanowicz [i.e. Szczepanowicz] and Kate B. Miller. New York, Lincoln Mac Veagh, The Dial Press; Toronto, Longmans, Green and company [c1929].
xiv,234 p. front.
Contents: Introduction, by Maryan Gawalewicz.—Part I. *On Earth.*—Part II. *In Heaven.*—Part III. *From Heaven.*
Thirty-four legends about the Blessed Virgin.
Original title: KRÓLOWA NIEBIOS; LEGENDY O MATCE BOSKIEJ.

Giertych, Jędrzej, 1903–

BALTIC TALES. Translated from the Polish. [Translation anonymous.] Preface by Patrick R. Reid . . . Illustrated by S. G. Briault. London, Jędrzej Giertych [1955].
244 p. illus., map.
Contents: Preface, by P. R. Reid.—*A Rat from the Far East.*—*The Rosary.*—*The Sea Nourishes, the Sea Destroys.*—*Hannah.*
"Postscript": p.243.
Map of Northern Cassubia: p.180.
"The engravings by Daniel Chodowiecki (1726–1801) on pages 52, 222 and 223 were originally printed in 'Von Berlin nach Danzig. Eine Künstlerfahrt im Jahre 1773 von Daniel Chodowiecki. 108 Facsimiledrucke. Berlin bei Amsler und Ruthard.' "
"First edition—November 1955."

Gliński, Antoni Józef, 1817–1866 **

THE GLASS MOUNTAIN, AND OTHER STORIES. Translated and adapted from Gliński's fairy-tales by Eileen Arthurton and Norbert Reh. London, F. P. Agency [ca.1946].
71 p. illus., front.

Contents: *The Glass Mountain.—The Sheepskin Coat.—The Adventures of the Two Giants.—The Sword of Yanosik.—The Story of the Three Brothers.—Pavel the Miser.—The Heiress of the Golden Island.—The Knight With the Rabbit's Heart.—King Bartek.—The Frog Queen.—Princess Spring-Maiden.*

Gliński, Antoni Józef, 1817–1866 **

POLISH FAIRY TALES. Translated from A. J. Glinski by Maude Ashurst Biggs; illustrated by Cecile Walton. London, John Lane, The Bodley Head; New York, John Lane Company, 1920.
xiii,96 p. plates, color.front.

Contents: *Tales from Poland,* by Maude Ashurst Biggs.—*The Frog Princess.—Princess Miranda and Prince Hero.—The Eagles.—The Whirlwind.—The Good Ferryman and the Water Nymphs.—The Princess and the Brazen Mountain.—The Bear in the Forest Hut.*

Appendix: p.94–96.

Hamalian, Leo, ed.

GREAT STORIES BY NOBEL PRIZE WINNERS, edited by Leo Hamalian and Edmond L. Volpe. New York, The Noonday Press [c1959].
xv,367 p.

Contains: *Death,* by Wladyslaw Reymont.

Hammerton, Sir John Alexander, 1871–1949, ed.

THE MASTERPIECE LIBRARY OF SHORT STORIES. Selected by an international board of eminent critics. Edited by J. A. Hammerton. With 200 fine art plates. London, The Educational Book Company, limited [1920].
20v. front., plates, ports.

Partial contents of vol. 13, ,"Russian, etc.": *The Lighthouse-keeper of Aspinwall,* by Henryk Sienkiewicz.—*Janko the Musician,* by Henryk Sienkiewicz.—*A Night's Tragedy,* by Marya Rodziewicz.

At head of title: The thousand best complete tales of all times and all countries.

Introductory remarks to the Polish section included in "East European & others" by J. A. H[ammerton]: Vol. 13, p.305–306.

Haydn, Hiram Collins, 1907– ed. (partly) *

A WORLD OF GREAT STORIES; edited by Hiram Haydn and John Cournos [and] Board of Editors. New York, Crown Publishers [c1947]. x,950 p.

Partial contents: Foreword, by Hiram Haydn.—General introduction (including introduction to the American and British section) by John Cournos.—Introduction to the Russian and East European section, by Joseph Remenyi.—*Death*, by Wladyslaw Stanislaw Reymont.— *The Emperor and the Devil*, by Joseph Wittlin.

Each story preceded by a brief note about the author.

Board of Editors: Pierre Brodin, Younghill Kang, Harry Kurz and Joseph Remenyi.

Henney, Nella (Braddy), ed.

MASTERPIECES OF ADVENTURE. Stories of the Sea and Sky. Edited by Nella Braddy. Garden City, N.Y., Doubleday, Page and company, 1922[c1921]. 165 p.

Contains: *The Lighthouse Keeper of Aspinwall*, by Henryk Sienkiewicz.

Herbert, Flight-Lieutenant, *see* Meissner, Janusz

Johnson, Edna, comp. (S)

ANTHOLOGY OF CHILDREN'S LITERATURE; compiled by Edna Johnson, Carrie E. Scott and Evelyn R. Sickels. Boston, Houghton Mifflin [c1935–48]. 1114 p.

Contains: *The Jolly Tailor Who Became King* [by Kornel Makuszyński].

Also published with illustrations by N. C. Wyeth.

Johnson, Edna, comp. (S)

ANTHOLOGY OF CHILDREN'S LITERATURE [by] Edna Johnson, Evelyn R. Sickels [and] Frances Clarke Sayers. 3rd ed. Illustrated by Fritz Eichenberg. Boston, Houghton Mifflin [1959]. 1239 p.

Contains: *The Jolly Tailor Who Became King* [by Kornel Makuszyński].

Includes bibliographies.

JUDAS ISCARIOT AND OTHER STORIES, by W. Doroschewitch, Catulle Mendes, Feodor Sologub [and others]. [New York] Guido Bruno, 1919. 31 p.

Contains: *Sex*, by Stanislav Przybyszewsky.

Karski, Jan, pseud. *
 STORY OF A SECRET STATE. Boston, Houghton Mifflin Company, 1944.
 391 p.
 Contains: *Torture.*
 Also published with imprint: London, Hodder & Stoughton ltd.
 [1945].

Kesten, Hermann, 1900– ed.
 THE BLUE FLOWER. Illustrated by Z. Czermanski. New York, Roy
 Publishers [c1946].
 xv,674 p. illus.
 Partial contents: Introduction, We Live in Romantic Times, by
 Hermann Kesten.—*Zevila,* by Adam Mickiewicz.—*Cholera,* by
 Zygmunt Krasinsky.—*Anhelli,* by Juljusz Slowacki.
 At head of title: Best stories of the romanticists.
 "Authors' Biographies": Mickiewicz, p.672; Krasinski, p.670; Slowacki,
 p. 674.
 Arranged by countries. Poland: p.[487]–518.
 Also published with imprint: Toronto, George J. McLeod [c1946].

Kijowski, Andrzej, 1928– comp.
 CONTEMPORARY POLISH SHORT STORIES, selected by Andrzej Kijowski.
 [Translated by various hands. Polish editor: Jerzy Chociłowski.]
 Warsaw, Polonia Publishing House, 1960.
 339 p. ports.
 Contents: Preface.—*The Sons,* by Jerzy Andrzejewski.—*Ladies and
 Gentlemen, to the Gas Chamber,* by Tadeusz Borowski.—*The Defence
 of the "Granada,"* by Kazimierz Brandys.—*Vexations of Power,* by
 Bohdan Czeszko.—*A Change Came o'er the Scenes of My Dream,* by
 Maria Dąbrowska.—*Victory,* by Kornel Filipowicz.—*The Badger,* by
 Jarosław Iwaszkiewicz.—*Nadir,* by Zofia Nałkowska.—*For the Head
 of a Negro King,* by Ksawery Pruszyński.—*The Accident at Krasny-
 staw,* by Jerzy Putrament.—*Beer,* by Tadeusz Różewicz.—*Easter,* by
 Adolf Rudnicki.—*The Real End of The Great War,* by Jerzy Zawiey-
 ski.—*Before Dawn,* by Stanisław Zieliński.—*The Milk Sop,* by
 Wojciech Żukrowski.
 Each story is preceded by a note about the author.

Kossak-Szczucka, Zofia, 1890–1968 **
 THE TROUBLES OF A GNOME, by Zofja Kossak-Szczucka. Translated from
 the Polish by Monica M. Gardner; with eight full-page illustrations in
 colour by Charles Folkard. London, A. and C. Black, 1928.
 102 p. plates, col.front.

375

Chapter contents: I. *The Old House.*—II. *The Home of the Hob-goblins.*—III. *The White Thief.*—IV. *Where Is the Magic Earring?*—V. *The Stolen Talisman.*—VI. *What Became of the Owl.*—VII. *Plans and Plots.*—VIII. *Plash-Splash to the Rescue.*—IX. *The Battle in the Black Wood.*

Original title: KŁOPOTY KACPERKA, GÓRECKIEGO SKRZATA.

Kuncewiczowa, Maria, 1897– ***

MODERN POLISH PROSE, Birkenhead [England] Polish Publications Committee [1945].
16 p.

(Listed in Zabielska, Janina, comp. BIBLIOGRAPHY OF BOOKS IN POLISH OR RELATING TO POLAND . . . v.1)

Lieber, Maxim, ed.

GREAT STORIES OF ALL NATIONS; One Hundred Sixty Complete Short Stories from the Literatures of All Periods and Countries. Edited by Maxim Lieber and Blanche Colton Williams . . . New York, Brentano's, 1927.[5]
xii,1121 p.

Partial contents: *The Legend,* by Zygmunt Krasinski.—*Do You Remember?* by Eliza Orzeszkowa.—*Twilight,* by Wladyslaw Reymont.

Arranged by countries. Each country preceded by an introduction. Poland: p.800–815.

Each story preceded by a brief note.

Also published with imprint: London, George G. Harrap and company [c1927].

Lieber, Maxim, ed.

GREAT STORIES OF ALL NATIONS; One Hundred Sixty Complete Short Stories from the Literatures of All Periods and Countries. Edited by Maxim Lieber and Blanche Colton Williams . . . New York, Tudor Publishing Company, 1942.
xii,1132 p.

Partial contents: *The Legend,* by Zygmunt Krasinski.—*Do You Remember?* by Eliza Orzeszkowa.—*Twilight,* by Wladyslaw Reymont.
Indices: p.1125–1132.

"Copyright, 1927, by Brentano's Inc."

McClintock, Marshall, 1906– ed.

THE NOBEL PRIZE TREASURY. Garden City, N.Y., Doubleday, 1948.
xvi,612 p.

---

[5] Edition analyzed.

Partial contents: *Death,* by Ladislas Reymont.—*Bartek the Conqueror,* by Henryk Sienkiewicz.

"Biographical and bibliographical notes": Reymont, p.609; Sienkiewicz, p.610.

McCrea, Lilian, ed. **

POLISH FOLK TALES AND LEGENDS. Retold by Lilian McCrea; illustrations by Danuta Laskowska. London, Sir Isaac Pitman and Sons [1959].
vii,88 p. illus. front.

Contents: *The White Eagle of Poland.—Kropelka.—Foolish Bartek. —The Miller's Three Daughters.—Krakus and the Dragon.—Marek of the Loving Heart.—Lazy Marynka.—The Tower of Mice.—Prince and Peasant.—Mieszko the Blind Prince.—The Diamond Necklace. —Maryshka the Little Orphan.—Bishop Adalbert and the Poor Woman.—The Three Gifts.—The Count's Gardener.—A Beloved Queen.—Pan Twardowski.*

"A note on the stories," by Lilian McCrea: p.vii.

Malecka, Katie

SAVED FROM SIBERIA; the True Story of My Treatment at the Hands of the Russian Police, by Katie Malecka. London, Everett and company [1914].
xv,168 p.

Contains: *The journalist,* by A. Niemojewski. (Appendix I.)

Mann, Klaus, 1906—1949, ed. *

HEART OF EUROPE; AN ANTHOLOGY OF CREATIVE WRITING IN EUROPE 1920–1940. Edited by Klaus Mann and Hermann Kesten with an introduction by Dorothy Canfield Fisher. New York, L. B. Fischer [c1943].
xxxvi,970 p.

Contains: The Emperor and the Devil, by Joseph Wittlin.

Introduction [to the Polish section of the volume, titled "Poland"] by Manfred Kridl: p.378–382.

Mayewski, Paweł, ed.

THE BROKEN MIRROR: a Collection of Writings from Contemporary Poland, edited by Pawel Mayewski under the auspices of the East European Institute. [Translated by various hands.] Introduction by Lionel Trilling. New York, Random House [1958].
209 p.

Partial contents: *The New Philosophical School* (a Postwar Story), by Tadeusz Rozewicz.—*The Defense of Granada,* by Kazimierz Brandys.

"About the authors": Rozewicz, p.206; Brandys, p.206–207.

Meissner, Janusz, 1901– *

"G FOR GENEVIEVE," by Flight-Lieutenant Herbert. [Translation anonymous.] Edinburgh, Polish Book Depot, 1944.
185 p. illus.

Chapter contents: Foreword, by the author.—I. *On the Ceiling.*—II. *Evacuation.*—III. *Forget-Me-Nots.*—IV. *The Retreat.*—V. *Pryszczyk Escapes.*—VI. *The Camp in Dobrudja.*—VII. *"The Father's Mountain."*—VIII. *Targu-Jiu.*—IX. *Pryszczyk Escapes Again.*—X. *On the Way to France.*—XI. *La douce France.*—XII. *The Island of Last Hope.*—XIII. *"Genevieve's" Sting.*—XIV. *Sergeant Prot, Night Fighter.*—XV. *Thirteenth Operation: Osnabruck.*—XVI. *A Different Species.*—XVII. *Buyak Fails.*—XVIII. *Sacred Bombs.*—XIX. *A Stain on the Sea.*—XX. *"G for Genevieve"; "L for . . . ."*

Meissner, Janusz, 1901– *

"L FOR LUCY," by Flight-Lieutenant Herbert. [Translation anonymous. illustrated by A. Horowicz.] Edinburgh, Składnica Księgarska, 1945.
140 p. plates.

Chapter contents: Introduction, by the author.—I. *"Lucy" Returns to Base.*—II. *Turin.*—III. *A Few Miles from the Shore.*—IV. *Missing.*—V. *Conclusive Proof.*—VI. *Just Prejudice.*—VII. *Pryszczyk's Adventures.*—VIII. *"A for Aunt Annie."*—IX. *Flying Control.*—Conclusion.

Sequel to *"G for Genevieve."*

"First published 1945."

Morska, Irena, 1895–ca. 1958, ed.

POLISH AUTHORS OF TODAY AND YESTERDAY: Bartkiewicz, Falkowski, Gojawiczynska, Morska, Muszal, Olechowski, Orzeszko, Prus, Rey, Reymont, Sienkiewicz, Szymanski [and] Zeromski. Selected by Irena Morska. New York, S. F. Vanni [c1947].
xvii,213 p.

Contents: *"The Pan Was Bored,"* by Zygmunt Bartkiewicz.—*Our Fathers and We,* by Ed Falkowski.—*Just Another Day,* by Pola Gojawiczynska.—*The Chains* (a reminiscence), by Irena Morska.—*The Pit,* by Kazimiera Muszal.—*The Might of Gold,* by Gustaw Olechowski.—*A . . . B . . . C. . . .* by Eliza Orzeszko.—*The Human Telegraph,* by Boleslaw Prus.—*A Mistake,* by Boleslaw Prus.—*The General,* by Sydor Rey.—*Iwancio,* by Sydor Rey.—*The Mother (the*

Call), by Wladyslaw Reymont.—*The Lord's Prayer*, by Wladyslaw Reymont.—*The Trial*, by Wladyslaw Reymont.—*Yanko the Musician*, by Henryk Sienkiewicz.—*Srul from Lubartow*, by Adam Szymanski. —*The Birches*, by Stefan Zeromski.—*The Stronger Sex*, by Stefan Zeromski.—*Temptation*, by Stefan Zeromski.

Naaké, John T., tr. (S)

SLAVONIC FAIRY TALES. Collected and translated from the Russian, Polish, Servian, and Bohemian by John T. Naaké, of the British Museum; with four illustrations. London, Henry S. King and company, 1874.
viii,272 p. illus. front.

Partial contents: Preface, by J. T. N[aaké].—*Carried Away by the Wind.—The Demon's Dance.—The Plague-Omen.—The Hare's Heart.—The Evil Eye.—The Plague.—The Plague and the Peasant.— Men-Wolves.—Jonek.—Twardowski.—Madey.*

"The translator makes no claim to the honour of having collected these stories. He has selected his materials from the Polish of K. W. Wojcicki." (Preface)

Neider, Charles, 1915– ed.

GREAT SHORT STORIES FROM THE WORLD'S LITERATURE, edited by Charles Neider. New York, Rinehart & Co. [c1950].
viii,502 p.

Contains: *Twilight*, by Wladyslaw Stanislaw Reymont.

Ordon, Edmund, 1918– ed.

10 CONTEMPORARY POLISH STORIES. Translated by various hands and edited by Edmund Ordon; with an introduction by Olga Scherer-Virski. Detroit, Wayne State University Press, 1958.
xxix,252 p.

Contents: *Father Philip*, by Maria Dąbrowska.—*Patrol*, by Kazimierz Wierzyński.—*A Cynical Tale*, by Michał Choromański.—*My Father Joins the Fire Brigade*, by Bruno Schulz.—*Boarding House*, by Piotr Choynowski.—*A Turban*, by Maria Kuncewiczowa.—*Premeditated Crime*, by Witold Gombrowicz.—*The Adventures of an Imp*, by Józef Mackiewicz.—*The President Calls*, by Jerzy Zawieyski.—*The Most Sacred Words of Our Life*, by Marek Hłasko.

Each story is preceded by a note about the author and the translator.

Ossendowski, Ferdynand Antoni, 1876–1944 **

MEMOIRS OF A LITTLE MONKEY: a Diary of the Chimpanzee Ket, by Ferdinand A. Ossendowski . . . Translated from the original Polish

by Francis Bauer Czarnomski. London, Sampson Low, Marston and company [1930].
216 p. illus.
Contents: Part I. *Family and Home.*—Part II. *The Little Monkey in Captivity.*—Part III. *The Return of the Little Monkey.*
Original title: ŻYCIE I PRZYGODY MAŁPKI.

Perzyński, Włodzimierz, 1878–1930 *
Three tales: Terminology, The way to success, Gratitude. Translated by K. Żuk-Skarszewska. In *Poland* (New York), VII, 1926. p.606–608, 633–637.

POLISH SHORT STORIES, by Joseph Weyssenhof, Piotr Choynowski, Kornel Makuszynski [and others] . . . London, Minerva Publishing Company [1943].
165 p.

Contents: *The Voice,* by Joseph Weyssenhof.—*Temptation,* by Piotr Choynowski.—*Calf Time,* by Kornel Makuszynski.—*Taboo,* by Stefan Zeromski.—*The Visitor,* by Feliks Gwizdz.—*The Thimble,* by Waclaw Grubinski.—*Banasiowa,* by Marja Konopnicka.—*A Stroke of Luck,* by Wlodzimierz Perzynski.—*Father Peter,* by Casimir Tetmajer.—*"There Where the Last Gaunt Gallows Stands and Beckons,"* by Eugeniusz Malaczewski.—*Samson and Delilah,* by Ferdynand Goetel.—*The Traitor,* by Ladislas Reymont.
"First published December 1943."

Posselt, Eric, ed. *
WORLD'S GREATEST CHRISTMAS STORIES, edited by Eric Posselt. Chicago, Ziff-Davis Publishing Company [c1949].
xvi,451 p.
Contains: *Winter,* by Ladislas Reymont.

Posselt, Eric, ed. *
THE WORLD'S GREATEST CHRISTMAS STORIES. Edited by Eric Posselt; illustrated by Fritz Kredel. New York, Prentice-Hall, 1950.
xvi,426 p. illus. front.
Contains: *Winter,* by Ladislas Reymont.

[Reymont, Władysław Stanisław] 1876–1925 *
BUREK, THE DOG THAT FOLLOWED THE LORD JESUS, AND OTHER STORIES. [Translated by Michael H. Dziewicki.] Cover design and illustrations by M. Walentynowicz. Birkenhead [England] Polish Publications Committee [1944].
65 p. illus.

Contents: Introduction.—*Burek, the Dog That Followed the Lord Jesus.—Christmas Eve.—The Slothful Horse.—The Robbers.—The Hawk.*

Fragments from his CHŁOPI (The Peasants).

[Reymont, Władysław Stanisław] 1867–1925 *

POLISH FOLK-LORE STORIES. [Translated by Michael H. Dziewicki.] Illustrated by M. Walentynowicz. Birkenhead [England] Polish Publications Committee [1944].
25 p. illus.

Contents: Introductory note.— *Burek, the Dog That Followed the Lord Jesus.—Christmas Eve.—The Slothful Horse.—The Robbers.— The Hawk.*

Fragments from his CHŁOPI (The Peasants).

[Reymont, Władysław Stanisław] 1867–1925 *
Two short tales: The sacred bell. In spite of all. Translated by K. Żuk-Skarszewska. In *Poland* (New York), IX, 1928.
p.680–685.
At head of title: Reymont's rallying-cry during the war.

Rudnicki, Adolf, 1912–

ASCENT TO HEAVEN. Translated by H. C. Stevens. Illustrated by Mieczyslaw Piotrowski. New York, Roy Publishers [c1951].
204 p. illus.

Contents: *Ascent to Heaven.—The Crystal Stream.—A Dying Man. —The Great Stefan Konecki.*

Also published with imprints: London, Dennis Dobson [c1951] and Toronto, George J. McLeod [c1951].

Rudnicki, Adolf, 1912–

THE DEAD AND THE LIVING SEA AND OTHER STORIES, by Adolf Rudnicki. Translated by Jadwiga Zwolska. Warsaw, Polonia Publishing House, 1957.
419 p.

Contents: *Józefów.—The Horse.—Golden Windows.—Easter.—The Dying Daniel.—The Clear Stream.—Raisa's Ascent to Heaven.—The Dead and the Living Sea.*[6]

---

[6] There is little resemblance between this volume and one bearing the same title in Polish. The Polish collection, ŻYWE I MARTWE MORZE, consists of seventeen stories. It does not include *Złote okna* (*Golden Windows*) which has been inserted in the English translation. Thus as many as ten stories have not found their way to the English version.

Runes, Dagobert David, ed.

TREASURY OF WORLD LITERATURE, edited by Dagobert D. Runes. New York, Philosophical Library [c1956].

xxi,1450 p.

Partial contents: *A Legend*, by Zygmunt Krasinski.—*Zevila*, by Adam Mickiewicz.—*The Lighthouse Keeper of Aspinwall*, by Henryk Sienkiewicz.

Sadowska, Krystyna Kopczyńska **

THIRTEEN POLISH LEGENDS. Drawn and told by Krystyna Kopczynska Sadowska. London, The New Europe Publishing Company, 1944.

32 p. illus.

Contents: Introduction, by Jan Sliwinski.—I. *The Legend of the Three Brothers and the White Eagle.*—II. *The Legend of the Wicked King Popiel Whom the Mice Devoured.*—III. *The Legend of Piast the Wheelwright and the Wandering Angels.*—IV. *The Legend of Krak Who Killed the Fearsome Dragon.*—V. *The Legend of Wanda Who, Loving Her Country, Sacrificed Her Own Life.*—VI. *The Legend of Two Brothers Who Loved Liberty More Than Their Lives.*—VII. *The Story of the Witches on the Bald Mountain.*—VIII. *The Legend of Saint Adalbert and the Widow's Farthing.*—IX. *The Story of Madey, the Cruel Outlaw, and his Conversion.*—X. *The Legend of Saint Kinga, of the Ring and the Salt Mines of Wieliczka.*—XI. *The Legend of the Heynal at St. Mary's and the Young Trumpeter.* —XII. *The Story of Pan Twardowski who Lives in the Moon.*—XIII. *The Legend of the Sleeping Knights Who Bring Peace to the World.*

Scherer-Virski, Olga

THE MODERN POLISH SHORT STORY, by Olga Scherer-Virski. 's-Gravenhage, Mouton and Company, 1955.

266 p. (Slavistic printings and reprintings, 5, edited by Cornelis H. van Schooneveld, Leiden University)

Partial contents include the author's translations: *Lord Singleworth's Secret*, by Norwid.—*The Waistcoat*, by Prus.—*The Chicken*, by Niedźwiecki.—*The Crows*, by Żeromski.

Revised version of the author's thesis, Columbia University (1952).

Bibliography: p.[249]–254.

Selver, Paul, 1888– comp and tr. (partly)*

ANTHOLOGY OF MODERN SLAVONIC LITERATURE IN PROSE AND VERSE. Translated by P. Selver; with an introduction and literary notes. London, Kegan Paul, Trench, Trubner and company; New York, E. P. Dutton and company, 1919.

xx,348 p.

Partial contents: *The Ploughman,* by W. Gomulicki.—*From the Legends of Ancient Egypt,* by Boleslaw Prus.—*Chopin,* by Stanislaw Przybyszewski.—*In the Old Town at Lodz,* by W. S. Reymont.

Literary notes: p.323–346.

Bibliography: p.347–348.

Shuster, George Nauman, 1894– ed. *

THE WORLD'S GREAT CATHOLIC LITERATURE, edited by George N. Shuster . . . with an introduction by William Lyon Phelps. New York, Macmillan, 1942.

xxii,441 p.

Partial contents: *Remorse,* by Ladislas Reymont.—*Pan Michael at Kamenyets,* by Henryk Sienkiewicz.

"Biographical notes": Reymont, p.432; Sienkiewicz, p.434.

"First printing."

Sienkiewicz, Henryk, 1846–1916

FOR DAILY BREAD, AND OTHER STORIES, by Henryk Sienkiewicz. [Translated by Iza Young.] Philadelphia, Henry Altemus [c1898].

209 p. front.(port.)

Contents: *For Daily Bread.—An Artist's End.—A Comedy of Errors.*

Half-title: For daily bread; a story from the life of American emigrants.

Sienkiewicz, Henryk, 1846–1916

HANIA, by Henryk Sienkiewicz. Translated from the Polish by Jeremiah Curtin. Boston, Little, Brown, and company 1898 [c.1897].

551 p. front.(port.)

Contents: *Prologue to Hania: The Old Servant.—Hania.—Tartar Captivity.—Let Us Follow Him.—Be Thou Blessed.—At the Source.— Charcoal Sketches—The Organist of Ponikla.—Lux in tenebris lucet.—On the Bright Shore.—That Third Woman.*

Sienkiewicz, Henryk, 1846–1916

HANIA, by Henryk Sienkiewicz . . . Translated from the Polish by Casimir W. Dynicwicz (i.e. Dyniewicz). Chicago, Donohue, Henneberry and company [c.1898].

257 p.

Contents: *Prologue: The Old Servant.—Hania.*

Sienkiewicz, Henryk, 1846–1916

HANIA, by Henryk Sienkiewicz . . . Translated from the Polish by Casimir Gonski. Philadelphia, Henry Altemus [c1898].

297 p. front.(port.)

Contents: *Prologue: The Old Servant.—Hania.*

Sienkiewicz, Henryk, 1846–1916

THE JUDGMENT OF PETER AND PAUL ON OLYMPUS; a Poem in Prose . . . Translated from the Polish by Jeremiah Curtin; [illustrated by Stachiewicz]. Boston, Little, Brown, and company, 1900.

231 p. illus., front.

Contents: *The Judgment of Peter and Paul on Olympus.—Be Thou Blessed.*

"Copyright, 1897, 1899, 1900."

Ornamental borders.

Sienkiewicz, Henryk, 1846–1916

LET US FOLLOW HIM, AND OTHER STORIES; by the author of Quo vadis. Translated from the Polish by Vatslaf A. Hlasko and Thos. H. Bullick. New York, R. F. Fenno and company [c1897].

ix,241 p. front.

Contents: Introduction, by Charles Johnston.—*Let Us Follow Him.—Sielanka.—Be Blessed.—Light in Darkness.—Orso.—Memories of Mariposa.*

Sienkiewicz, Henryk, 1846–1916

LET US FOLLOW HIM, AND OTHER STORIES, by Henryk Sienkiewicz . . . [Translated by Sigmund C. Slupski and Iza Young.] Philadelphia, H. Altemus [c1898].

234 p. front.

Contents: *Let Us Follow Him.—Be Blessed.—Bartek the Conqueror.*

Sienkiewicz, Henryk, 1846–1916

LIFE AND DEATH, AND OTHER LEGENDS AND STORIES BY HENRYK SIENKIE-WICZ . . . Translated from the original Polish by Jeremiah Curtin. Boston, Little, Brown and company, 1904.

vii,65 p. front., plates.

Contents: Preface.—*Life and Death: a Hindu Legend.—Is He the Dearest One?—A Legend of the Sea.—The Cranes.—The Judgment of Peter and Paul on Olympus.*

"Copyright, 1897, 1899, 1900, 1904, by Jeremiah Curtin."

Sienkiewicz, Henryk, 1846–1916 (partly)*

LILLIAN MORRIS, AND OTHER STORIES . . . Translated by Jeremiah Curtin, with illustrations by Edmund H Garrett. Boston, Little, Brown and company, 1894.

247 p. illus.

Contents: *Lillian Morris.—Sachem.—Yamyol.—The Bull-Fight.*

Sienkiewicz, Henryk, 1846–1916 **

PORTRAIT OF AMERICA; Letters of Henry Sienkiewicz. Edited and translated by Charles Morley. New York, Columbia University Press, 1959. xix,300 p. front.(port.)

Contents: Introduction [by Charles Morley].—I. Sojourn in New York. —II. Aboard the Transcontinental: New York to Omaha.—III. Aboard the Transcontinental: Omaha to San Francisco.—IV. American Democracy.—V. American Women.—VI. Idyll in the Santa Ana Mountains.—VII My Mountain Idyll Continued.—VIII. Life among the Squatters.—IX. Bear Hunt.—X. Thoughts from San Francisco.— XI. Virginia City.—XII. The Chinese in California.—XIII. Polish Communities in America.

Letters are arranged in six groups and each group is preceded by a "Prologue."

Frontispiece: "Henry Sienkiewicz, at the time of his visit to America; wood engraving by John de Pol."

Index: p.[293]–300.

Sienkiewicz, Henryk, 1846–1916 (partly)*

SIELANKA; A FOREST PICTURE, AND OTHER STORIES, by Henryk Sienkiewicz. Authorized unabridged translation from the Polish by Jeremiah Curtin. Boston, Little, Brown, and company, 1898. vi,592 p. front.

Contents: *Sielanka.—For Bread.—Orso.—Whose Fault?—Decision of Zeus.—On a Single Card.—Yanko the Musician.—Bartek the Victor.— Across the Plains.—From the Diary of a Tutor in Poznan.—The Light-House Keeper of Aspinwall.—Yamyol.—The Bull-Fight.— Sachem.—A Comedy of Errors.—A Journey to Athens.—Zola ("Doctor Pascal").*[7]

Copyright, 1893, 1894, 1898; reprinted 1899.

Published also with imprint: London, J. M. Dent and company, 1898.

Sienkiewicz, Henryk, 1846–1916 (partly)*

SO RUNS THE WORLD, by Henryk Sienkiewicz . . . Translated by S. C. de Soissons. London, New York, F. Tennyson Neely [c1898]. 290 p.

Contents: Henryk Sienkiewicz, by S. C. de Soissons.—*Zola.—Whose Fault?—The Verdict.—Win or Lose.*[8]

---

[7] A play, ON A SINGLE CARD, has been omitted in the analytical bibliography.
[8] WIN OR LOSE; a Drama in Five Acts, has been omitted in the analytical bibliography.

Sienkiewicz, Henryk, 1846–1916

TALES FROM HENRYK SIENKIEWICZ. Edited and introduced by Monica M. Gardner. [Translated by various hands.] London, J. M. Dent and sons; New York, E. P. Dutton and company [1946].
xvi,332,4 p. (Half-title: Everyman's library, ed. by Ernest Rhys. Fiction. [no.87])
Contents: Introduction.—*The Old Serving-Man.*—*Hania.*—*A Comedy of Errors.*—*Across the Prairies.*—*The Lighthouse-Keeper.*—*Bartek the Conqueror.*—*The Third Woman.*—*Let Us Follow Him.*

"English translations of Sienkiewicz's works": p.xii–xiii.

"For information on Sienkiewicz": p.xiii.

First published in this edition 1931. Reprinted 1946.

Sienkiewicz, Henryk, 1846–1916 (partly)*

TALES FROM SIENKIEWICZ. Translated by S. C. de Soissons. London, George Allen, 1899.[9]
vii,298 p.

Contents: Introduction, by S. C. de S[oissons].—*A Country Artist.*—*In Bohemia.*—*A Circus Hercules.*—*The Decision of Zeus.*—*Anthea.*—*"Be Blessed!"*—*Whose Fault?*—*True to His Art.*—*The Duel.*

Also published with imprint: New York, James Pott and company; London, George Allen [1899].

Sienkiewicz, Henryk, 1846–1916 (partly)*

TALES FROM SIENKIEWICZ. Translated by S. C. de Soissons. Colonial edition; for sale only in the British Colonies and India. London, George Allen, 1901.
vi,281 p.

Sienkiewicz, Henryk, 1846–1916

YANKO THE MUSICIAN, AND OTHER STORIES; by Henryk Sienkiewicz. Translated from the Polish by Jeremiah Curtin, with drawings by Edmund H. Garrett. Boston, Little, Brown, and company, 1893.
281 p. illus.

Contents: *Yanko the Musician.*—*The Light-House Keeper of Aspinwall.*—*From the Diary of a Tutor in Poznan.*—*Comedy of Errors; a Sketch of American Life.*—*Bartek the Victor.*

Reprinted 1895.

Stillman, Edmund, ed. (partly)*

BITTER HARVEST; the Intellectual Revolt Behind the Iron Curtain.

---

[9] Edition analyzed.

Edited by Edmond Stillman; introduction by François Bondy. London, Thames and Hudson [1959].

xxxiii,313 p.

Partial contents: *We Take Off for Heaven,* by Marek Hlasko.—*Long Journey,* by Stanislaw Dygat.—*Notes from Amerdaganda,* by Stanislaw Zielinski.—*"A Point, Mister?"* or, *Everything Has Changed,* by Marek Hlasko.—*The Young Woman Doctor on Prezydencka Street,* by Stanislawa Sznaper-Zakrzewska.

Also published with imprint: New York, Frederick A. Praeger [1959].

STORIES BY FOREIGN AUTHORS: Polish, Greek, Belgian, Hungarian.

New York, Charles Scribner's Sons, 1898.

193 p. front.port.

Contains: *The Light-House Keeper of Aspinwall,* by Henryk Sienkie-wicz.

Reprinted 1902.

"The portrait of Henryk Sienkiewicz prefixed to this volume is used by permission of Messrs. Little, Brown & Co., the authorized American publishers of Sienkiewicz's works."

Strickland, Sir Walter William, 1851– tr. **

NORTH-WEST SLAV LEGENDS AND FAIRY STORIES; a Sequel to Segnius irritant. Tr. from Karel Jaromir Erben's "A hundred genuine popular Slavonic fairy stories in the original dialects." London, Robert Forder, 1897.

[iv],111 p.

Partial contents: *Iskrzycki.—The Whirlwind.—The Shepherd's Pipe.—The Devil's Dance.—The Wan Woman.*

Strickland, Sir Walter William, 1851– tr. **

PANSLAVONIC FOLK-LORE, in four books, by W. W. Strickland. Translated from Karel Jaromir Erben's "A hundred genuine popular Slavonic fairy stories in the original dialects," and compared with notes, comments, tables, illustrative diagrams, introductions and supplementary essays. New York, B. Westermann Company, 1930.

xii,469 p. fold.tables.

Contains: *Iskrzycki,* and some other tales of Polish origin.

Printed in Germany.

Strowska, Suzanne **

TEN POLISH FOLK TALES, by Suzanne Strowska. Translated from the French by M. O'Reilly; with illustrations by Dorothy A. H. Mills. London, Burns Oates and Washbourne, 1929.

150 p. illus.

Contents: *The Tale of the Young Peasant Girl Who Became a Great Lady.—The Story of Bartek, Who Became a Celebrated Doctor Known to the Whole World.—Koiata.—The Tale of a Cock and a Hen Who Set Out for Rome. The Cock Wanted To Be Pope and the Hen Popess.—The Prince, the Stepmother, and the Magician.—The Three Enchanted Princesses.—The Tale of the Orphan and the Four Pots.—The Tale of the Twenty-Four Robbers.—The Bewitched Eyes.—The Wolf and the Farmer's Boy.*

Szczepanowicz, Lucia Merecka, *see* Borski, Lucia Merecka

Szelburg-Zarembina, Ewa, 1899– (S)

WHO CAN TELL. Adapted into English by Margaret Sperry; illustrated by Jerzy Srokowski. Warsaw, Nasza Księgarnia [c1959]. 50 p. illus.

Contents: *The Egg That Went for a Walk.—The Mice Give a Ball.—No Hare Anywhere.—The Little Boy Who Cried Too Much.—What Happened in the Broken Pitcher.—The Good Housewife?—The Greedy Rooster.—Nothing but a Goat.*

"From a book of Polish tales entitled, Wesołe historie."

Szmaglewska, Seweryna ***

SMOKE OVER BIRKENAU. Translated from the Polish by Jadwiga Rynas. New York, H. Holt [1947]. x,386 p.

Original title: DYMY NAD BIRKENAU.

(Listed in Zabielska, Janina, comp. BIBLIOGRAPHY OF BOOKS IN POLISH OR RELATING TO POLAND . . . v.1)

Tabor, Paul, *see* Tabori, Paul

Tábori, Pál, *see* Tabori, Paul

Tabori, Paul, 1908– ed.

THE PEN IN EXILE; an Anthology [of exiled writers]. Edited by Paul Tabori. [Translated by various hands. London] The International P.E.N. Club Centre for Writers in Exile, 1954. 227 p.

Partial contents: *Vengeance,* by Ferdynand Goetel.—"*I see Him,*" by Zofia Kossak.—*The Death of Aza,* by Mieczyslav Lisiewicz.—*Murder on the Waka,* by Josef Mackiewicz.—*The Sewers,* by Roman Orwid-Bulicz.—*The Lover and the Boy,* by Tadeusz Wittlin.

"Biographies": p.221–227.

Tabori, Paul, 1908– ed.

THE PEN IN EXILE; a Second Anthology. Edited by Paul Tabori.
[Translated by various hands. London] The International P.E.N.
Club Centre for Writers in Exile, 1956.

252 p.

Cover title: The pen in exile II.

Partial contents: *The Smile of Destiny*, by Stanislav Balinski.—*Their
Everyday Bread*, by Adolf Fierla.—*The Skies Opened*, by Helena
Heinsdorf.—*Mutton-Fat*, by J. Kowalewski.—*Life of a Drunkard*, by
H.(i.e. M.) J. Lisiewicz.—*Solitude*, by Teodozya Lisiewicz.—*The Red
Flag*, by Josef Mackiewicz.—*Dunia*, by Herminia Naglerova.—*An
Old (i.e. odd) Story*, by Stefan Legezynski.

"Biographies": p.[243]–252.

Tetmajer, Kazimierz Przerwa, 1865–1940.

TALES OF THE TATRAS, by Kazimierz Tetmajer. Translated by H. E.
Kennedy and Zofia Umińska. Foreword by William John Rose. Drawings by Janina Konarska. London, Minerva Publishing Company
[1941].

189 p. illus.

Contents: *Far-off Marysia.*—*The Departure of Jacob Zych.*—*Maryna.*—
He.—*The Winter Maidens.*—*Zwyrtala the Fiddler.*—*Old Waltsak's
Daughter.*—*The Savage Shepherd.*—*Krystka.*—*How Jozek Smas Went
to Confession.*—*How Wojtek Chroniets Was Taken.*—*Towards
Heaven.*

Tetmajer, Kazimierz Przerwa, 1865–1940

TALES OF THE TATRAS, by Kazimierz P. Tetmajer. [Translated by H. E.
Kennedy and Zofia Uminska.] Foreword by Carl Carmer. [Drawings
by Janina Konarska. Initials by T. Zarnover.] New York, Roy Publishers [1943].

247 p. illus.

[Tibbits, Charles John] **

FOLK-LORE AND LEGENDS; Russian and Polish. London, W. W. Gibbings,
1890.

viii,183 p.

Partial contents: *The Wind Rider.*—*The Three Gifts.*—*The Plague.*—
The Wonderful Cloth.—*The Evil Eye.*—*The Stolen Heart.*—*Prince
Slugobyl.*—*Princess Marvel.*—*The Ghost.*

Introductory note: "In this volume I present selections made from
the Russian chap-book literature, and from the works of various
Russian and Polish collectors of Folklore—Afanasief, Erben, Wojcicki,
Glinski, etc.": p.[v].

Tomlinson, H. M., 1873– ed.

GREAT SEA STORIES OF ALL NATIONS, by Giovanni Boccaccio, David Bone, Joseph Conrad . . . and Many Others from Ancient Greece to Modern Japan; edited and with an introduction by H. M. Tomlinson. Garden City, N.Y., Doubleday, Doran, and company, 1930. xxiv,1108 p.

Contains: *The Lighthouse Keeper of Aspinwall,* by Henryk Sienkiewicz.

Also published with imprint: Garden City, N.Y., Garden City Publishing Company [1937].

Umadevi, pseud., *see* Dynowska, Wanda

Virski, Olga Scherer-, *see* Scherer-Virski, Olga

Wierzyński, Kazimierz, 1894–

THE FORGOTTEN BATTLEFIELD. Translated from the Polish by Edmund Ordon. Illustrated by Zdzislaw Czermanski. New York, Roy Publishers [c1944]. 179 p. illus.

Contents: Introduction.—*The Secret of the Forest.—The Falcons.— A Thousand Years.—A Handful of Water.—The Talisman.—The Peasants.—Ambush.—Unknown Soldiers.—All Is Not Yet Finished.— The Song in the Night.*

Wratislaw, Albert Henry, 1822–1892 (S)

SIXTY FOLK-TALES FROM EXCLUSIVELY SLAVONIC SOURCES. Translated, with brief introductions and notes, by A. H. Wratislaw . . . Boston, Houghton, Mifflin and company; Cambridge, The Riverside Press, 1890. xii,315 p.

Partial Contents: *Prince Unexpected* [by A. J. Gliński].—*The Spirit of a Buried Man* [by K. W. Wóycicki].—*The Pale Maiden* [by K. Baliński].—*The Plague-Swarm* [by K. W. Wóycicki]. Arranged by nationalities. Polish Stories: p.[107]–128.

Żabicki, Zbigniew, comp.

POLISH SHORT STORIES, selected by Zbigniew Żabicki. [Translated by Ilona Ralf Sues and Janina Rodzińska. Polish editor: Jadwiga Lewicka.] Warsaw, Polonia Publishing House, 1960. 323 p. ports.

Contents: Foreword.—*"Ad leones,"* by Cyprian Kamil Norwid.—*The Lighthouse Keeper,* by Henryk Sienkiewicz.—*Chava Ruby,* by Aleksander Świętochowski.—*The Waistcoat,* by Bolesław Prus.—*Miss An-*

tonina, by Eliza Orzeszkowa.—*Community Welfare Service,* by Maria Konopnicka.—*For a Coffin,* by Adolf Dygasiński.—*The Bitch,* by Władysław Stanisław Reymont.—*The Dowry,* by Zygmunt Niedźwiecki, —*Her Kitten,* by Gabriela Zapolska.—*A Question of Influence,* by Włodzimierz Perzyński.— *A Sacrifice to the Gods,* by Wacław Sieroszewski.—*Forest Echoes,* by Stefan Żeromski.—*At the Station,* by Andrzej Strug.

Bibliography of translations: p.320–[324].

Each story is preceded by a note about the author.

Zajdler, Zoë, tr. **

POLISH FAIRY TALES. Re-told in English by Zoë Zajdler, with illustrations by Hazel Cook. London, Frederick Muller [c1959].
vii,190 p. illus.

Contents: *The Snake King's Crown.—As the World Pays.—Crookshanks.—The Palace of Rainbow Fountains.—The Drowners.—Kind Brother, Cruel Sister.—The Cock and the Wind.—The Jar of Ducats.—The Pitch Princess.—The Peasant and the King.—The Envious Stepmother.—The Wolf's Breakfast.—Matthew's Bed.—The Horned Goat.—Simon.—The Magical Crock.—The Treasurers.*

A note on "Polish fairy tales," by Zoë Zajdler: p.[i].

Zarembina, Ewa Szelburg-, *see* Szelburg-Zarembina, Ewa

Zimmern, Helen, ed. (S)

STORIES FROM FOREIGN NOVELISTS, with short notices of their lives and writings, by Helen and Alice Zimmern. New and revised edition with a portrait of Ivan Turgenieff. London, Chatto and Windus, 1884.
314 p. front.port.

Contains: *The Foundling,* by Kraszewski.

The story is preceded by a brief note about the author.

Żywulska, Krystyna ***

I CAME BACK. Translated from the Polish by Krystyna Cenkalska. New York, Roy, 1951.
246 p.

Also published with imprints: London, D. Dobson [1951] and Toronto, G. J. McLeod, 1951.

Original title: PRZEŻYŁAM OŚWIĘCIM.

(Listed in Zabielska, Janina, comp. BIBLIOGRAPHY OF BOOKS IN POLISH OR RELATING TO POLAND . . . v.1)

Periodicals Referred To in the Text

Argosy. [London, The Amalgamated Press]

Ave Maria, a Catholic Magazine. Notre Dame, Indiana.
v.1–79 (May 1865–December 1914).
New series beginning with v.1, January 1915–

The Catholic World; a Monthly Magazine of General Literature and Science. New York, N.Y.
April 1865–
Index: v.1–63 (1865–1896).

The Century Illustrated Magazine.

The Century, a Popular Quarterly. New York, N.Y.
v.1–120 (November 1870–May 1930).
v.1–22 (1870–October 1881) as *Scribner's Monthly.*
v.23–110 (November 1881–October 1925) as *The Century Illustrated Magazine.*
v.111–118 (November 1925–August 1929) as *The Century Monthly Magazine.*
United with *Forum* to form *Forum and Century.*
English edition discontinued 1913.

Commentary. A monthly published by the American Jewish Committee. New York, N.Y.
November 1945–

East Europe; a Monthly Review of East European Affairs.
Published by the Free Europe Press (January 1952–October 1953 by the Research and Publications Service) of the Free Europe Committee

(called in January 1952–March 1954, National Committee for a Free Europe). New York, N.Y.

v.1, January 1952–

Title varies.

v.1–5 (January 1952–December 1956) as *News from Behind the Iron Curtain.*

Supersedes an earlier publication with the title *News from Behind the Iron Curtain,* published also by the National Committee for a Free Europe, 1950–1951.

"The National Committee for a Free Europe was founded in 1949 by a group of private American citizens who joined together for direct action aimed at the eventual liberation of the Iron Curtain countries."

New Writing and Daylight, ed. by John Lehmann.

1–7, summer. London, The Hogarth Press.

[1942–1946]

Formed by the union of *Daylight* and *Folios of New Writing.*

Superseded by *Orpheus.*

The Pagan; a Magazine for Eudaemonists. Published monthly by the Pagan Publishing Company, New York, N.Y.

1916–1922.

v.1–16, no.9 (May 1916–January 1922).

No issues March, July–August, 1920.

The Penguin New Writing. No.1–40. Harmondsworth, Middlesex, New York, Penguin Books.

[1940–1950]

Editor: No.1– J. Lehmann.

Includes selections from *New Writing* (later *Folios of New Writing*) and *New Writing and Daylight.*

Ceased publication.

Poland; a Publication and a Service. A monthly magazine for those seeking facts, figures and information regarding any phase of Polish life, business, current conditions.

Copyright, American Polish Chamber of Commerce and Industry, Inc., New York, N.Y.

May 1920–December 1933.

v.1–3, No.1 as the Chamber's *Journal.*

v.3, No. 2–v.12, No.5 (1923–March 1931) as *Poland.*

v.12, No.6–v.14, No.3 (April 1931–March 1933) as *Poland-America.*

No issues June 1931, December 1932, November 1933.

Poland; Illustrated Magazine. Warsaw, Polonia, Foreign Languages Publishing House.

Quarterly, September 1954; monthly, 1955–
Published in Polish, English, French, German, Spanish, and Swedish.
American edition, March 1959–

Poland of Today; Monthly Bulletin of Information. Published by the
Library of the Polish Embassy, New York 21, N.Y.
March 1946–
"It is the purpose of the Bulletin to acquaint the American public
with conditions in Poland today."

Polish Perspectives; Monthly Review. No. 1–
Warsaw, May, 1958–

The Polish Review. v.1–9. August 30, 1941–1949.
New York, N.Y., Polish Information Center, 1941.
Weekly (irregular).
Supersedes *News Bulletin on Eastern European Affairs.*
Caption title.

Pologne Littéraire; revue mensuelle. Warsaw.
1926–1937.
v.1–12 (Nos.1–124) October 1926–1937.

Portfolio. No.1–8; 1959–spring 1964.
[New York, Art News Division, Newsweek, inc., distributed by Macmillan Co.]
8 nos. illus. (part col.)
2 nos. a year, 1959–1961; quarterly, 1962–1964.
Replaced *Art News Annual* between v.28, 1959 and v.29, 1964.
    Title varies: no.2–6, *Portfolio and Art News Annual.*
Edited by A. Frankfurter.
Volumes for 1959–1963 published by Art Foundation Press, New York.

The Slavonic and East European Review; a Survey of the Slavonic
Peoples, Their History, Economics, Philology and Literature. (University of London. School of Slavonic and East European Studies)
London.
June 1922–
v.1–6 (Nos.1–17, 1922–1927) as *Slavonic Review.*
v.6–9 (Nos.18–26) as *Slavonic (and East European) Review.*
v.19 (1939/40–1941) as *Slavonic Yearbook,* being v.19 of *Slavonic and
East European Review.*
v.20–22 (1941–1944) as *Slavonic Yearbook,* being v.20–22 of *Slavonic
and East European Review* (called also American Series I–III). Published for a Committee of American Scholars, in Menasha, Wisconsin.
v.23 (January 1945) publication resumed in England.

Index: v.1–10 (1922–1932).

Subtitle varies. Publisher for the School of Slavonic Studies varies.

"The Slavonic Review will be devoted to the history, institutions, political and economic conditions, and also to the literature, arts, learning and philology of all the Slavonic nations, and in a lesser degree of their neighbours and associates in the former Russian Empire and in the former Dual Monarchy. It will be the joint product of British and American Slavonic scholars, and of representative Slavs in every field of intellectual effort." No.1, June 1922.

List of Translators and Their Translations

Ainsztein, Reuben
Yom Kippur, by Rudnicki

Andrews, Hilda
The Last Battle, by M. Brandys

Babad, Nathan M.
The Third Woman, by Sienkiewicz

Balbin, Julius
Patrol, by Wierzyński

Bay, Jens Christian
The Fate of a Soldier, by Sienkiewicz
Her Tragic Fate, by Sienkiewicz
The New Soldier, by Sienkiewicz
Where Worlds Meet, by Sienkiewicz

Benecke, Else Cecilia Mendelssohn
Bartek the Conqueror, by Sienkiewicz
In Autumn, by Sieroszewski
In Sacrifice to the Gods, by Sieroszewski
Srul—from Lubartow, by Szymański
Temptation, by Żeromski
Twilight, by Żeromski
see also Benecke, Else Cecilia Mendelssohn and Busch, Marie

Benecke, Else Cecilia Mendelssohn and Busch, Marie
The Chukchee, by Sieroszewski
Death, by Reymont
Forebodings; Two Sketches, by Żeromski

Kowalski the Carpenter, by Szymański
Maciej the Mazur, by Szymański
The Outpost, by Prus
A Pinch of Salt, by Szymański
The Returning Wave, by Prus
The Sentence, by Bandrowski
The Stronger Sex, by Żeromski
The Trial, by Reymont
Two Prayers, by Szymański

Bernhard, Josephine Butkowska
The Dancing Pike, by Perzyński
The Good Orphan Sunblossom and the Enchanted Treasure, by Kędzierski
Jas the Fiddler, by Kędzierski
The Jester Who Fooled a King, by Barącz
The Lucky Beggar, by Piotrowski
Lullaby: Why the Pussy-Cat Washes Himself So Often (adapted)
Madej the Brigand, by A. J. Gliński
The Master Wizard, Pan Twardowski and his Spider, by Kędzierski
Mr. Whirlwind, Shoemaker, by Perzyński
9 Cry-Baby Dolls, adapted from Porazińska
The Pig's-Head Magician (retold), anonymous
The Wizard's Pupil, by A. J. Gliński
The Wolf and the Blacksmith, by Kędzierski

Blackett, Eveline
Across the Prairies, by Sienkiewicz

Borski, Lucia Merecka
About an Old Man and an Old Woman, a Cock and a Hen, a Fox and a Wolf, by A. J. Gliński
The Adventures of a Wolf, by A. J. Gliński
The Coat of Arms of Putsk, by Rabska
The Cobbler Dog, by Markowska
Cobbler Kopytko and Drake Kwak, by Makuszyński
The Cobbler's Soul, by Staroś
The Devil's Bread, by Szczepkowski
A Dog, a Donkey, a Cat, and a Cock, by Piotrowski
The Flight, by Kasprowicz
Fortune, by Weychert-Szymanowska
The Frog, by Kasprowicz
Gratitude and Justice, by Dygasiński

Coleman, Marion Moore
    The Church Bells of Hel, by Rabska
    Kupallo, by Kraszewski
    The Legend of Smreczynski Staw, by Goszczyński
Curtin, Jeremiah
    (All the stories listed below are by Sienkiewicz.)
    Across the Plains. Published also as Lillian Morris
    At the Source
    Bartek the Victor
    Be Thou Blessed
    The Bull-Fight
    Charcoal Sketches
    A Comedy of Errors
    The Cranes
    The Days of Nero
    The Death of Radzivill
    The Death of the Traitors
    The Decision of Zeus
    The Escape
    Escape of Zagloba and Helena
    For Bread
    From the Diary of a Tutor in Poznan
    Hania
    Is He the Dearest One?
    A Journey to Athens
    The Judgment of Peter and Paul on Olympus. Published also as *The Judgement of Peter and Paul on Olympus*
    Keeper of the Faith
    A Legend of the Sea
    Let Us Follow Him
    Life and Death
    The Light-House Keeper of Aspinwall
    Lux in tenebris lucet
    The Old Servant
    On the Bright Shore
    The Organist of Ponikla
    Orso
    Pan Michael at Kamenyets
    Sachem

Gardner, Monica Mary
Faith, by Morcinek
The Lighthouse-Keeper, by Sienkiewicz
Silence, by Morcinek

Gay-Tifft, Lola
Cholera, by Krasiński
Zevila, by Mickiewicz

Glinczanka, Agnieszka
The Cuckoo, by Czeszko

Gniatczyński, Wojciech and Czerniawski, Adam
The Most Sacred Words of Our Life, by Hłasko

Gonski, Casimir
Hania, by Sienkiewicz
The Old Servant, by Sienkiewicz

Guterman, Norbert
The Defense of Granada, by Brandys
The Eighth Day of the Week, by Hłasko
The Graveyard, by Hłasko
I Want To Be a Horse, by Mrożek
Next Stop—Paradise, by Hłasko
The Story of Shulim, by Rey

Hłasko, Vatslaf A. and Bullick, Thomas H.
After Bread, by Sienkiewicz
Be Blessed, by Sienkiewicz
An Excursion to Athens, by Sienkiewicz
Let Us Follow Him, by Sienkiewicz
Light in Darkness, by Sienkiewicz
Memories of Mariposa, by Sienkiewicz
Orso, by Sienkiewicz
Sielanka; an Idyll, by Sienkiewicz

Hrbkova, Sarka B.
Do You Remember? by Orzeszkowa
The Human Telegraph, by Prus
A Legend, by Krasiński

Iranek-Osmecki, Jerzy
Mutton-Fat (adapted), by Kowalewski

Jezierski, Bronislas de Leval
Adventures of an Imp, by Mackiewicz
The Red Flag, by Mackiewicz

Jopson, N. B.
"Ad leones," by Norwid
Banasiowa, by Konopnicka
Janko the Musician, by Sienkiewicz
Letter Writing of Long Ago, by Kraszewski
The Patcher, by K. J. Szaniawski
The Waistcoat, by Prus

Kennedy, Harriette Eleanor and Umińska, Zofia
A Comedy of Errors, by Sienkiewicz
The Departure of Jacob Zych, by Tetmajer
Eaglets, by Tetmajer

Far-off Marysia. Published also as *Far-away Marysia,* and as *Far-off Marisya,* by Tetmajer
Hania, by Sienkiewicz
He, by Tetmajer
How Jozek Smas Went to Confession, by Tetmajer
How Wojtek Chroniets Was Taken, by Tetmajer
Krystka, by Tetmajer
The Miller's Maryna. Published also as *Maryna,* by Tetmajer
The Old Serving Man, by Sienkiewicz
Old Waltsak's Daughter, by Tetmajer
The Savage Shepherd, by Tetmajer
Towards Heaven, by Tetmajer
The Winter Maidens, by Tetmajer
Zwyrtala the Fiddler, by Tetmajer

Klinger, Christopher J., *see* Klinger, Krzysztof

Klinger, Krzysztof
By the River, by Wygodzki
The Door, by Zieliński
The End of the War, by Borowski
Journey into a Sea-Shell, by Kotowska
The Lion, by Mrożek
My Boyhood Hero, by Andrzejewski
Paris, by Zieliński
Sunflower, by Czeszko

Konarek, Andrzej
Roscher, by Parandowski

Kowalski, Thad
A Cynical Tale, by Choromański

Kreuter, Victoria de
The Blessing, by Sienkiewicz
Legend, by Reymont
Leval Jezierski, Bronislas de, *see* Jezierski, Bronislas de Leval
Lewicki, Karol
Their Everyday Bread, by Fierla
Łowinski, Jerzy
Schillinger's Death, by Borowski
Maciuszko, George [Jerzy] J.
A Turban, by Kuncewiczowa
Maitland-Chuwen, Ann
The Death of Aza, by M. J. Lisiewicz
Malecka, Katie
The Journalist, by Niemojewski
Mayewski, Paul
The New Philosophical School, by Różewicz
Michael, Maurice A.
For Our Freedom and Yours, by Żeromski
In the Mountains, by Żeromski
The Might of Satan, by Żeromski
The Passion of Heaven, by Żeromski
Spring, by Żeromski
Trees in Grudno, by Żeromski
Montalk, Geoffrey Potocki of, *see* Potocki of Montalk, Geoffrey
Morawska, Jadwiga
A December Night, by Rodziewiczówna
The Ring, by Rodziewiczówna
A Soldier's Lot, by Żeromski
Morison, W. A.
A Remedy for Robbers, by Samozwaniec
Morris, Neil, *see* Wojewoda, Cecylia and Morris, Neil
Morska, Irena
A . . . B . . . C . . ., by Orzeszkowa
The Human Telegraph, by Prus
Just Another Day, by Gojawiczyńska
The Lord's Prayer, by Reymont
The Might of Gold, by Olechowski
A Mistake (fragment), by Prus

A Thousand Years, by Wierzyński
Unknown Soldiers, by Wierzyński

Paczyńska, Maria
The Cross of Valor, by Hen

Peterson, Virgilia
The Angel, by Sienkiewicz

Potocki, Stefan Cedric
The Sewers, by Orwid-Bulicz

Potocki of Montalk, Geoffrey
Caught in a Snare (fragment), by Sieroszewski
Motherhood, by Nałkowska

Radin, Dorothea Prall
Anhelli (fragment), by Słowacki

Rennie, Peter
The Dream, by Prus

Rodzińska, Janina
Miss Antonina, by Orzeszkowa
Professor Tutka's Derby, by J. Szaniawski
A Question of Influence, by Perzyński
A Sacrifice to the Gods, by Sieroszewski
Shoes, by Szczepański

Rose, William John
A Curious Story, by Prus

Rothert, Edward
The Accident at Krasnystaw, by Putrament
Exams on Targowa, by Borowski
Jadwinia (A Day in April), by Iwaszkiewicz
The Sons, by Andrzejewski

Sapieha, Lew
The Red Flag, by Mackiewicz

Scherer-Virski, Olga
The Chicken, by Niedźwiecki
The Crows, by Żeromski
Lord Singleworth's Secret, by Norwid
Premeditated Crime, by Gombrowicz
The Waistcoat, by Prus

Selver, Paul
Chopin, by Przybyszewski

From the Legends of Ancient Egypt, by Prus
In the Old Town at Lodz, by Reymont
The Ploughman, by Gomulicki

Slupski, Sigmund C. and Young, Iza
    Bartek the Conqueror, by Sienkiewicz
    Be Blessed, by Sienkiewicz
    Let Us Follow Him, by Sienkiewicz

Soissons, Guy Jean Raoul Eugene Charles Emmanuel de Savoie-Carignan, comte de
    (All the titles listed below are by Sienkiewicz.)
    "Be Blessed!"
    A Circus Hercules
    A Country Artist
    The Decision of Zeus. Published also as *The Verdict*
    The Duel (excerpt)
    In the New Promised Land
    Let Us Follow Him. Published also as *Anthea*
    On the Sunny Shore. Published also as *In Monte Carlo*
    The Third Woman. Published also as *In Bohemia*
    True to His Art
    Whose Fault?
    Zola

Solomon, Joseph
    "P.P.C." by Nałkowska
    A Polish Scene, by Reymont

Sorgenstein, Samuel
    Iwancio, by Rey

Sperry, Margaret
    The Egg That Went for a Walk, by Szelburg-Zarembina
    The Golden Seeds, by Konopnicka
    The Good Housewife? by Szelburg-Zarembina
    The Greedy Rooster, by Szelburg-Zarembina
    The Little Boy Who Cried Too Much, by Szelburg-Zarembina
    The Mice Give a Ball, by Szelburg-Zarembina
    No Hare Anywhere, by Szelburg-Zarembina
    Nothing but a Goat, by Szelburg-Zarembina
    What Happened in the Broken Pitcher, by Szelburg-Zarembina

Stevens, Henry Charles
    Ascent to Heaven, by Rudnicki

Valkenier, Elizabeth K.

The Young Woman Doctor on Prezydencka Street, by Sznaper-Zakrzewska

Varèse, Louise

(All the stories listed below are by Mrożek.)
Birthday Party
The Children
Fact
The Lion
A Man Saved by a Miracle
Peer Gynt
The Trial
Written in the Darkness

Virski, Olga Scherer-, *see* Scherer-Virski, Olga

Wachowski, J. P.

On Mount Olympus, by Sienkiewicz

Walkuska, Mary

The Last Siren of Hel, by Rabska
The Old Clock of Danzig, anonymous

Wassell, Florence

The Fern Flower of Happiness, by Dygasiński

Wieniawska, Celina

(All the stories listed below are by Fiedler.)
A Gallant Captain and a Dauntless Ship
Greaser Loza is Hungry
La France est morte
Roch, the Practical Joker
S.S. Bielsk, a Ship with Character
Thank You, Captain, Thank you!
Their Battle

Wojewoda, Cecylia and Morris, Neil

The Parable of the Miraculous Salvation, by Mrożek

Wratislaw, Albert Henry

The Pale Maiden, by Baliński
The Plague-Swarm, by Wóycicki
Prince Unexpected, by A. J. Gliński
The Spirit of a Buried Man, by Wóycicki

Young, Iza

An Artist's End, by Sienkiewicz

A Comedy of Errors, by Sienkiewicz

For Daily Bread, by Sienkiewicz

see also Slupski, Sigmund C. and Young, Iza

Żółtowska, S.

The Sowers, by Reymont

Żuk-Skarszewska, Kate

Another *"Paradise" Lost and Regained,* by Makuszyński

Back to Civilization, by Goetel

Banasiowa, by Konopnicka. Published also as *Banasyova*

The Beloved "Nothing," by Grubiński

Calf Time, by Makuszyński

The Childish Arguments of a Sunbeam, by Makuszyński

The Cream-Colored Roses, by Grubiński

The Dance, by Żeromski

Father Peter, by Tetmajer

The Furlough, by Gwiżdż

The Graduate of Smorgonie, by Ejsmond

Gratitude, by Perzyński

"Impossible," by Żeromski. Published also as *Taboo*

In Spite of All, by Reymont

Introducing Varshulka, by Weyssenhoff

Janek's Ordeal, by Choynowski

Komurasaki, by Reymont

Love and Death, by Ejsmond

A Mysterious Visit, by Korzeniowski

Rendezvous, by Weyssenhoff

The Return, by Kossowski

The Sacred Bell, by Reymont

The Sad History of Heydasz the Devil, by Bunikiewicz

Samson and Delilah, by Goetel

The Scream of a Peacock, by Grubiński

Sparrows, by Gwiżdż

Spring, by Reymont

The Story of an Oak, by Ejsmond

The Strongest, by Ejsmond

Temptation, by Choynowski

Terminology, by Perzyński

The Terrible Puppet, by Grubiński

"There, Where the Last Gaunt Gallows Stands and Beckons," by Małaczewski

APPENDIX IVa

English Titles with the Polish Originals

ENGLISH TITLE	ORIGINAL TITLE	AUTHOR
A . . . B . . . C . . .	*A . . . B . . . C . . .*	Orzeszkowa, E.
"A for Aunt Annie" *	*A—jak ciocia Andzia*	Meissner, J.
About an Old Man and an Old Woman, a Cock and a Hen, a Fox and a Wolf (S)	*O dziadku i babce, o kogutku i kurce, o lisie i wilku*	Gliński, A. J.
The Accident at Krasnystaw	*Wypadek w Krasnymstawie*	Putrament, J.
Across the Plains	*Przez stepy*	Sienkiewicz, H.
Across the Prairies	*Przez stepy*	Sienkiewicz, H.
"Ad leones"	*"Ad leones"*	Norwid, C. K.
The Adventures of a Wolf (S)	*O wilku i jego przygodach*	Gliński, A. J.
The Adventures of an Imp	*Przygody małego diabełka*	Mackiewicz, J.
After Bread	*Za chlebem*	Sienkiewicz, H.

411

ENGLISH TITLE	ORIGINAL TITLE	AUTHOR
All Is Not Yet Finished	Nie wszystko skończone	Wierzyński, K.
Ambush	Zasadzka	Wierzyński, K.
The Angel	Jamioł	Sienkiewicz, H.
Anhelli (fragment) (r) *	Anhelli	Słowacki, J.
Another "Paradise" Lost and Regained (P)	Pan z kozią bródką	Makuszyński, K.
Anthea	Pójdźmy za Nim	Sienkiewicz, H.
The Ants and Parrots of Iquitos *	Papugi nad Iquitos	Fiedler, A.
An Artist's End	Lux in tenebris lucet	Sienkiewicz, H.
Ascent to Heaven	Wniebowstąpienie	Rudnicki, A.
At the Source	U źródła	Sienkiewicz, H.
At the Station	Na stacji	Strug, A.
Back to Civilization (P)	Kos na Pamirze	Goetel, F.
Back to the Wolves (P)	Pomiędzy wilki	Pruszyński, K.
The Badger	Borsuk	Iwaszkiewicz, J.
Banasiowa	Banasiowa	Konopnicka, M.
Banasyowa	Banasiowa	Konopnicka, M.
Bartek the Conqueror	Bartek Zwycięzca	Sienkiewicz, H.
Bartek the Victor	Bartek Zwycięzca	Sienkiewicz, H.
Be Blessed	Bądź błogosławiona	Sienkiewicz, H.
Be Thou Blessed	Bądź błogosławiona	Sienkiewicz, H.
Beer	Piwo	Różewicz, T
Before Dawn	Przed świtem	Zieliński, St.
The Beloved "Nothing" (P)	Kochane nic	Grubiński, W.
Bemklau (P)	Bemklau	Zieliński, St.
The Birches	Zemsta jest moja . . .	Żeromski, S
Birds (P)	Ptaki	Schulz, B.
Birthday Party (P)	Imieniny	Mrożek, S
The Bitch	Suka	Reymont, W. St.
A Black Stream of Death *	Czarna struga śmierci	Fiedler, A.
The Blessing	Bądź błogosławiona	Sienkiewicz, H.
Boarding House	Na stancji	Choynowski, P.
Born of the Plague (fragment) (P)	Syn zadżumionych	Nowakowski, T

ENGLISH TITLE	ORIGINAL TITLE	AUTHOR
Bread	Chleb	Naglerowa, H.
The Bull-Fight *	Walka byków	Sienkiewicz, H.
Burek, the Dog That Followed the Lord Jesus (S)	From his CHŁOPI	Reymont, W. St.
Butterflies *	Motyle	Fiedler, A.
Buyak Fails *	Bujak "nawala"	Meissner, J.
By the River (P)	Nad rzeką	Wygodzki, St.
Calf Time	Cielęcy żywot	Makuszyński, K.
The Camp in Dobrudja *	Obóz w Dobrudży	Meissner, J.
Carried Away by the Wind (S)	Porwany wichrem	Wóycicki, K. W.
Caught in a Snare (fragment) (P)	W matni	Sieroszewski, W.
The Chains	Kajdany (?)	Morska, I.
"A Change Came o'er the Scenes of my Dream"	Tu zaszła zmiana	Dąbrowska, M.
A Chapter on Cruelty *	Okrucieństwo	Fiedler, A.
Charcoal Sketches	Szkice węglem	Sienkiewicz, H.
Chava Ruby	Chawa Rubin	Swiętochowski, A.
The Chicken	Kura	Niedźwiecki, Z.
The Child	Dziecko	Dąbrowska, M.
The Childish Arguments of a Sunbeam (P)	Dziecinne argumenty słonecznego promienia	Makuszyński, K.
The Children (P)	Dzieci	Mrożek, S.
Chiwu (P)	Chiwu	Stryjkowski, J.
Cholera	Cholera	Krasiński, Z.
Chopin *	Chopin	Przybyszewski, St.
Christmas Eve (S)	From his CHŁOPI	Reymont, W. St.
The Chukchee	Czukcze	Sieroszewski, W.
The Church Bells of Hel (S)	Dzwony kościelne na Helu (?)	Rabska, Z.
A Circus Hercules	Orso	Sienkiewicz, H.
The Clear Stream	Czysty nurt	Rudnicki, A.

ENGLISH TITLE	ORIGINAL TITLE	AUTHOR
The Coat of Arms of Putsk (S)	O herbie miasta Pucka	Rabska, Z.
The Cobbler Dog (S)	O psie, co był szewcem	Markowska, M.
Cobbler Kopytko and Drake Kwak (S)	Szewc Kopytko i kaczor Kwak	Makuszyński, K.
The Cobbler's Soul (S)	O szewczykowej duszyczce	Staroś, J.
A Comedy of Errors	Komedia z pomyłek	Sienkiewicz, H.
Community Welfare Service	Miłosierdzie gminy	Konopnicka, M.
Conclusive Proof *	Dowód niezbity	Meissner, J.
Contempt for Whites and Monkeys *	Indjanie, pogardzający białymi ludźmi i małpami	Fiedler, A.
Contrasts *	From his CHŁOPI	Reymont, W. St.
Corporal Kid and I (P)	Kapral Koziołek i ja	Konwicki, T.
A Country Artist	Organista z Ponikły	Sienkiewicz, H.
The Cranes	Żurawie	Sienkiewicz, H.
A Crazy Game (P)	Tak się bawią wariaci	Promiński, M.
The Cream-Colored Roses (P)	Kremowe róże	Grubiński, W.
The Cross of Valor (P)	Krzyż walecznych	Hen, J.
The Crows	Rozdziobią nas kruki, wrony	Żeromski, S.
The Crows and the Ravens	Rozdziobią nas kruki, wrony	Żeromski, S.
The Crystal Stream	Czysty nurt	Rudnicki, A.
The Cuckoo (P)	Kukułka	Czeszko, B.
A Curious Story (P)	Dziwna historia	Prus, B.
A Cynical Tale	Opowieść cyniczna	Choromański, M.
Daimonion Bib	Dajmonion-Bib	Grubiński, W.
The Dance *	From his POPIOŁY	Żeromski, S.
The Dancing Pike (rS)	O szczupaku, który umiał tańczyć	Perzyński, W.
The Days of Nero *	From his QUO VADIS	Sienkiewicz, H.
The Dead and the Living Sea	Żywe i martwe morze	Rudnicki, A.

ENGLISH VERSION	ORIGINAL TITLE	AUTHOR
Death	Śmierć	Reymont, W. St.
The Death of Aza	Śmierć Azy	Lisiewicz, M. J.
The Death of Radzivill *	From his POTOP	Sienkiewicz, H.
The Death of the Traitors *	From his OGNIEM I MIECZEM	Sienkiewicz, H.
A December Night (P)	W noc grudniową	Rodziewiczówna, M.
The Decision of Zeus	Wyrok Zeusa	Sienkiewicz, H.
The Defence of the "Granada"	Obrona Grenady	Brandys, K.
The Defense of Granada	Obrona Grenady	Brandys, K.
The Demon's Dance (S)	Djabli taniec	Wóycicki, K. W.
The Departure of Jacob Zych	Jak umarł Jakób Zych	Tetmajer, K. Przerwa
The Devil's Bread (S)	Chleb djabelski	Szczepkowski, J.
A Different Species *	Inny gatunek	Meissner, J.
Do You Remember?	Czy pamiętasz?	Orzeszkowa, E.
A Dog, a Donkey, a Cat, and a Cock (S)	O starym psie, ośle, kocie i kogucie	Piotrowski, A.
The Doll (P)	Lalka	Żukrowski, W.
The Door (P)	Drzwi	Zieliński, St.
The Dowry	Za mąż	Niedźwiecki, Z.
The Dream (P)	Sen	Prus, B.
Dreaming on the Ucayali *	Sny na Ukajali	Fiedler, A.
The Duel *	Excerpt from his Hania	Sienkiewicz, H.
Dunia	Dunia	Naglerowa, H.
Dwojra Zielona	Dwojra Zielona	Nałkowska, Z.
The Dying Daniel	Ginący Daniel	Rudnicki, A.
A Dying Man	Ginący Daniel	Rudnicki, A.
Eaglets (P)	Orlice	Tetmajer, K. Przerwa
Easter	Wielkanoc	Rudnicki, A.
The Egg That Went for a Walk (S)	Bajka o gęsim jaju, raku nieboraku, kogucie piejaku, kaczce kwaczce, kocie mruczku i o psie kruczku	Szelburg-Zarembina, E.

ENGLISH VERSION	ORIGINAL TITLE	AUTHOR
The Eighth Day of the Week	Ósmy dzień tygodnia	Hłasko, M.
The Elephant (P)	Słoń	Mrożek, S.
Embarrassing Visitors *	Odwiedzają mnie czole	Fiedler, A.
The Emperor and the Devil *	From his SÓL ZIEMI	Wittlin, J.
The End of the War (P)	Koniec wojny	Borowski, T.
The Escape *	From his OGNIEM I MIECZEM	Sienkiewicz, H.
Escape of Zagloba and Helena *	From his OGNIEM I MIECZEM	Sienkiewicz, H.
Europe versus Snake *	Polujemy na Binuji	Fiedler, A.
Evacuation *	Ewakuacja	Meissner, J.
The Evil Eye (S)	Oczy uroczne	Wóycicki, K. W.
Exams on Targowa (P)	Matura na Targowej	Borowski, T.
An Exursion to Athens *	Wycieczka do Aten	Sienkiewicz, H.
The Exemplary Couple (P)	Wzorowe małżeństwo	Różewicz, T.
Fact (P)	Fakt	Mrożek, S.
Faith (P)	Wiara	Morcinek, G.
The Falcons	Puhacz	Wierzyński, K.
Far-away Marysia	O Marysi dalekiej (Part I of Jak Jasiek Mosiężny nie mógł znaleźć szczęścia)	Tetmajer, K. Przerwa
Far-off Marysia	O Marysi dalekiej (Part I of Jak Jasiek Mosiężny nie mógł znaleźć szczęścia)	Tetmajer, K. Przerwa
Far-off-Marisya	O Marysi dalekiej (Part I of Jak Jasiek Mosiężny nie mógł znaleźć szczęścia)	Tetmajer, K. Przerwa
The Fate of a Soldier	Bartek Zwycięzca	Sienkiewicz, H.
Father Peter	Ksiądz Piotr	Tetmajer, K. Przerwa
Father Philip	Ksiądz Filip	Dąbrowska, M.
The Father's Mountain *	Góra Ojca	Meissner, J.

ENGLISH TITLE	ORIGINAL TITLE	AUTHOR
The Fern Flower of Happiness *	From his GODY ŻYCIA	Dygasiński, A.
A Few Miles from the Shore *	O kilka mil od brzegu	Meissner, J.
Fifty Yards of Civilization *	Pięćdziesiąt kroków cywilizacji	Fiedler, A.
A First Step into the Clouds (P)	Pierwszy krok w chmurach	Hłasko, M.
The Flight (S)	Ucieczka	Kasprowicz, J.
Flowers Which Moved Britons *	Kwiaty, które poruszyły Anglików	Fiedler, A.
Flying Control *	Flying control	Meissner, J.
For a Coffin	Na trumienkę	Dygasiński, A.
For Bread	Za chlebem	Sienkiewicz, H.
For Daily Bread	Za chlebem	Sienkiewicz, H.
For Our Freedom and Yours *	From his POPIOŁY (Za Wolność Naszą i Waszą)	Żeromski, S.
For the Head of a Negro King	O głowę murzyńskiego króla	Pruszyński, K.
Forebodings; Two Sketches	I. Złe przeczucie II. "Cokolwiek się zdarzy—niech uderza we mnie . . ."	Żeromski, S.
Forest Echoes	Echa leśne	Żeromski, S.
Forget-Me-Nots *	Niezapominajki	Meissner, J.
Forgotten Ghost *	Duch zapomniany	Makuszyński, K.
Fortune (S)	Szczęście	Weychert-Szymanowska, W.
The Fortunes of Count N. (P)	Losy hrabiego N.	Mrożek, S.
The Foundling (S)	From his IERMOLA	Kraszewski, J. I.
The Frog (S)	Żaba	Gliński, K.
From Legends of Ancient Egypt	Z legend dawnego Egiptu	Prus, B.
From the Diary of a Tutor in Poznan	Z pamiętnika poznańskiego nauczyciela	Sienkiewicz, H.
From the Legends of Ancient Egypt	Z legend dawnego Egiptu	Prus, B.

417

ENGLISH TITLE	ORIGINAL TITLE	AUTHOR
The Furlough (P)	Urlop	Gwiżdż, F.
"G for Genevieve"; "L for . . ." *	"G"—jak Genowefa; "L"—jak . . ."	Meissner, J.
A Gallant Captain and a Dauntless Ship *	Wspaniały kapitan i niezłomny statek	Fiedler, A.
The General	Generał	Rey, S.
"Genevieve's" Sting *	Żądło Genowefy	Meissner, J.
"Give Me a Flower!"	Daj kwiatek!	Orzeszkowa, E.
The Golden Seeds (S)	Jak to ze lnem było	Konopnicka, M.
Golden Windows *	Złote okna	Rudnicki, A.
The Good Housewife? (S)	Jak sroczka gości przyjmowała	Szelburg-Zarembina, E.
Good Old Friends *	Starzy, dobrzy przyjaciele	Fiedler, A.
The Good Orphan Sunblossom and the Enchanted Treasure (rS)	Adaptation of a Polish folk tale	Kędzierski, C.
The Graduate of Smorgonie (P)	Akademik smorgoński	Ejsmond, J.
Gratitude (P)	Sercem za serce	Perzyński, W.
Gratitude and Justice (S)	Wdzięczność i sprawiedliwość	Dygasiński, A.
The Graveyard *	Cmentarze	Hłasko, M.
Greaser Loza Is Hungry *	Smarownik Łoza chce jeść	Fiedler, A.
The Great Stefan Konecki	Wielki Stefan Konecki	Rudnicki, A.
The Greedy Rooster (S)	O kurce złotopiórce i kogutku szałaputku	Szelburg-Zarembina, E.
Green Parrots and Crimson Macaws *	Papugi zielone i arary szkarłatne	Fiedler, A.
The Gypsy and the Bear (rS)	Cygan (?)	Barącz, S.
A Handful of Water	Garść wody	Wierzyński, K.
Hania	Hania	Sienkiewicz, H.
Hannah	Hania z międzymorza	Giertych, J.
Happiness (P)	Szczęście	Żesławski, W.
The Hare's Heart (S)	Zajęcze serce	Wóycicki, K. W.

ENGLISH TITLE	ORIGINAL TITLE	AUTHOR
The Hawk (S)	From his CHŁOPI	Reymont, W. St.
He	*On*	Tetmajer, K. Przerwa
Heat! *	*Gorąco!!*	Fiedler, A.
Her Kitten	*Koteczek*	Zapolska, G.
Her Tragic Fate	*Za chlebem*	Sienkiewicz, H.
A Horned Goat (S)	*O kozie rogatej*	Markowska, M.
The Horse	*Koń*	Rudnicki, A.
A Hot-Bed of Racial Rivalry *	*Gorące miasto*	Fiedler, A.
How a Clever Cottager Outwitted Seven Thieves (S)	*Jak sobie mądry chłop poradził ze złodzie-jami*	Weychert-Szymanowska, W.
How a Sensible Peasant Cured his Wife's Curiosity (S)	*O takim, co rozumiał jak dzwirzęta gwarzom*	Piotrowski, A.
How Jozek Smas Went to Confession	*Jak się Józek Smaś pojechał wysłuchać*	Tetmajer, K. Przerwa
How Saint Joseph Ploughed the Soil (S)	*Jak to święty Józef orał*	Birkenmajer, J.
How Standintheway Remained in Heaven (S)	*Jak Zawalidroga w niebie został*	Markowska, M.
How To Escape? *	*Pryszczyk wieje po raz drugi*	Meissner, J.
How Wojtek Chroniets Was Taken	*Jak to święty Józef orał Chrońca*	Tetmajer, K. Przerwa
The Human Telegraph	*Żywy telegraf*	Prus, B.
The Hunting (S)	*Łowy*	Gliński, K.
"I See Him"	*Widzę Go*	Kossak-Szczucka, Z.
I Want To Be a Horse (P)	*Chcę być koniem*	Mrożek, S.
Icarus (P)	*Ikar*	Iwaszkiewicz, J.
"Impossible"	*"Tabu"*	Żeromski, S.
In Autumn	*Jesienią*	Sieroszewski, W.
In Bohemia	*Ta trzecia*	Sienkiewicz, H.
In Monte Carlo	*Na jasnym brzegu*	Sienkiewicz, H.
In Sacrifice to the Gods	*W ofierze bogom*	Sieroszewski, W.
In Spite of All (P)	*I wynieśli*	Reymont, W. St.
In the Mountains (P)	*W górach*	Prus, B.

ENGLISH TITLE	ORIGINAL TITLE	AUTHOR
In the Mountains *	From his POPIOŁY (W górach)	Żeromski, S.
In the New Promised Land	Za chlebem	Sienkiewicz, H.
In the Old Town at Lodz *	From his Ziemia obiecana	Reymont, W. St.
An India-Rubber Tragedy *	Tragedia kauczukowa	Fiedler, A.
The Interrupted Melody *	Pieśń przerwana	Orzeszkowa, E.
Introducing Varshulka (P)	From his Soból i panna	Weyssenhoff, J.
Is He the Dearest One?	Czy ci najmilszy?	Sienkiewicz, H.
The Island of Last Hope *	Wyspa Ostatniej Nadziei	Meissner, J.
Iwancio	Iwańcio	Rey, S.
Jack the Distributor	Kolporter	Majewski, W.
Jadwinia (A Day in April) (P)	Jadwinia (Dzień kwietniowy)	Iwaszkiewicz, J.
Janek's Ordeal (P)	Straszny dzień Janka	Choynowski, P.
Janko the Musician	Janko Muzykant	Sienkiewicz, H.
Jas the Fiddler (rS)	Jaś skrzypek (?)	Kędzierski, C.
Jerzy	Jerzy	Grubiński, W.
The Jester Who Fooled a King (rS)	Adaptation of a Polish folk tale	Barącz, S.
Joe Who Served in Lower Limbo (S)	O Jóźwie, co na przedpieklu służył	Markowska, M.
The Jolly Tailor Who Became King (S)	O tem, jak krawiec pan Niteczka został królem	Makuszyński, K.
Jonek *	Jonek	Wóycicki, K. W.
The Journalist	Dziennikarz	Niemojewski, A.
Journey into a Sea-Shell (P)	Podróż do wnętrza muszli	Kotowska, M.
A Journey to Athens *	Wycieczka do Aten	Sienkiewicz, H.
Józefów	Józefów	Rudnicki, A.
The Judgment of Peter and Paul on Olympus	Na Olimpie	Sienkiewicz, H.
Just Another Day	Powszedni dzień	Gojawiczyńska, P.

ENGLISH TITLE	ORIGINAL TITLE	AUTHOR
The Just Hare	*Sprawiedliwy zając*	Dygasiński, A.
Just Prejudice *	*Zestrzelili nas nad Francją*	Meissner, J.
Keeper of the Faith *	From his QUO VADIS	Sienkiewicz, H.
The King and the Peasant *(S)	*O ojcowskim królu*	Rościszewski, M.
King Bartek (S)	*Król Bartek*	Gliński, K.
Komurasaki (P)	*Komurasaki*	Reymont, W. St.
Koshalki-opalki, or How a Simpleton Became King (S)	*Koszałki-opałki*	Kasprowicz, J.
Kowalski the Carpenter	*Stolarz Kowalski*	Szymański, A.
Krystka	*Krystka*	Tetmajer, K. Przerwa
Kupallo (S)	Adapted from his STARA BAŚŃ	Kraszewski, J. I.
La douce France *	*La douce France*	Meissner, J.
"La France est morte" *	*"La France est morte!" —krzyknął Murzyn i dostał kopniaka*	Fiedler, A.
Ladies and Gentlemen, to the Gas Chamber	*Proszę państwa do gazu*	Borowski, T.
The Lark, the Wolf, and the Fox (S)	*O skowronku, wilku i lisie*	Markowska, M.
The Last Battle (P)	*Ostatnia bitwa*	Brandys, M.
The Last Siren of Hel (S)	*Ostatnia syrena Helu* (?)	Rabska, Z.
A Legend	*Legenda*	Krasiński, Z.
Legend (P)	*Legenda*	Reymont, W. St.
The Legend of Smreczynski Staw (S)	Adapted from his ODA	Goszczyński, S.
A Legend of the Sea	*Legenda żeglarska*	Sienkiewicz, H.
Let Us Follow Him	*Pójdźmy za Nim*	Sienkiewicz, H.
Letter Writing of Long Ago (P)	*Jak się dawniej listy pisało*	Kraszewski, J. I.
The Liaison Man (P)	*Łącznik*	Buczkowski, M. R.
Life and Death; a Hindu Legend	*Dwie łąki*	Sienkiewicz, H.
Life of a Drunkard	*Żywot pijaka*	Lisiewicz, M. J.

ENGLISH TITLE	ORIGINAL TITLE	AUTHOR
Light in Darkness; lux in tenebris lucet	*Lux in tenebris lucet*	Sienkiewicz, H.
The Lighthouse Keeper	*Latarnik*	Sienkiewicz, H.
The Light-House Keeper of Aspinwall	*Latarnik*	Sienkiewicz, H.
Lillian Morris	*Przez stepy*	Sienkiewicz, H.
The Linden Tree (P)	*Lipa*	Gojawiczyńska, P.
The Lion (P)	*Lew*	Mrożek, S.
The Little Boy Who Cried Too Much (S)	*Jak żabki Jasia zabawiały*	Szelburg-Zarembina, E.
Little Chicinho and the Great Big Amazon *	*Mały Czikinjo i wielka Amazonka*	Fiedler, A.
Little Janko	*Janko Muzykant*	Sienkiewicz, H.
Living Sunbeams *	*Kolibry*	Fiedler, A.
Long Journey	*Dalekie podroże*	Dygat, St.
The Lord Jesus and the Three Robbers (S)	*O Panu Jezusie i zbójnikach*	Weychert-Szymanowska, W.
Lord Singleworth's Secret (abridged)	*Tajemnica Lorda Singlewortha*	Norwid, C. K.
The Lord's Prayer	*W pruskiej szkole*	Reymont, W. St.
Love and Death (P)	*Miłość i śmierć*	Ejsmond, J.
The Lover and the Boy	*Gdy matka ma kochanka*	Wittlin, T.
The Lucky Beggar (rS)	*Szczęśliwy zebrak* (?)	Piotrowski, A.
"Lucy" Returns to Base *	*"Lucy" wraca do bazy*	Meissner, J.
Lullaby; Why the Pussy-Cat Washes Himself So Often (S)	*Gwiazdkowa kołysanka*	Bernhard, J. B.
Lux in tenebris lucet	*Lux in tenebris lucet*	Sienkiewicz, H.
Maciej the Mazur	*Maciej Mazur*	Szymański, A.
Madame Sophie	*Pani Zosia*	Dąbrowska, M.
Madej the Brigand (rS)	*Madej* (?)	Gliński, A. J.
Madey (S)	*Madej*	Wóycicki, K. W.
Majka (S)	*Majka*	Gliński, K.
The Man from the Rococo Church (P)	*Człowiek z rokokowego kościoła*	Pruszyński, K.
A Man Saved by a Miracle (P)	*Przypowieść o cudownym ocaleniu*	Mrożek, S.

ENGLISH TITLE	ORIGINAL TITLE	AUTHOR
The Mannequins (P)	*Manekiny*	Schulz, B.
Maryna	*O wójtowej Marynie* (Part II of *Jak Jasiek Mosiężny nie mógł znaleźć szczęścia*)	Tetmajer, K. Przerwa
The Master Wizard, Pan Twardowski, and His Spider (rS)	*Mistrz Twardowski i jego pajączek* (?)	Kędzierski, C.
May on Wheels (P)	*Maj na kółkach*	Promiński, M.
Memories of Mariposa	*Wspomnienie z Mariposy*	Sienkiewicz, H.
Men-Wolves (S)	*Wilkołaki*	Wóycicki, K. W.
The Mice Give a Ball (S)	*Zabawa myszek*	Szelburg-Zarembina, E.
The Might of Gold	*Potęga złota* (?)	Olechowski, G.
The Might of Satan *	From his POPIOŁY (*Moc Szatana*)	Żeromski, S.
The Migration of the Birds (P)	*Tak odlatują ptaki*	Baliński, St.
The Milk Sop	*Mli Mli*	Żukrowski, W.
The Miller's Maryna	*O wójtowej Marynie* (Part II of *Jak Jasiek Mosiężny nie mógł znaleźć szczęścia*)	Tetmajer, K. Przerwa
Miss Antonina	*Panna Antonina*	Orzeszkowa, E.
Missing *	*Missing*	Meissner, J.
A Mistake (fragment)	*Omyłka*	Prus, B.
Mr. Whirlwind, Shoemaker (rS)	*Pan Rozpędek*	Perzyński, W.
More Rain *	*Znów padają deszcze*	Fiedler, A.
A Morning at the Zoo	*Poranek w ogrodzie zoologicznym*	Dąbrowska, M.
The Most Sacred Words of Our Life	*Najświętsze słowa naszego życia*	Hłasko, M.
The Mother (the Call)	*Wołanie*	Reymont, W. St.
Motherhood (P)	*Macierzyństwo*	Nałkowska, Z.
A Mountaineer's Tale (S)	*Sabałowa bajka*	Weychert-Szymanowska, W.

ENGLISH TITLE	ORIGINAL TITLE	AUTHOR
Much Ado about-Leticia *	Wiele hałasu o . . . Letycję	Fiedler, A.
Murder on the Waka	Morderstwo w dolinie rzeki Waki	Mackiewicz, J.
Mutton-Fat (adapted)	Twardy chleb, and Tragarz John	Kowalewski, J.
My Boyhood Hero (P)	Mój chłopięcy ideał	Andrzejewski, J.
My Father Joins the Fire Brigade	Mój ojciec wstępuje do strażaków	Schulz, B.
My Village (S)	Moja Wólka	Porazińska, J.
A Mysterious Visit (P)	From his TADEUSZ BEZI-MIENNY	Korzeniowski, J.
The Mystic Rose (P)	Mistyczna róża (?)	Łuskina, E.
Nadir	Dno	Nałkowska, Z.
The New Philosophical School	Nowa szkoła filozoficzna	Różewicz, T.
The New Soldier	Szkice węglem	Sienkiewicz, H.
Next Stop—Paradise *	Następny do raju	Hłasko, M.
Night Encounter	Nocne spotkanie	Dąbrowska, M.
A Night's Tragedy	Noc	Rodziewiczówna, M.
9 Cry-Baby Dolls (S)	Adaptation of a Polish folk tale	Bernhard, J. B.
No Hare Anywhere (S)	O tym jak zajączek szaraczek psa burka wywiódł w pole	Szelburg-Zarembina, E.
Notes from Amerda-ganda (fragment) *	Raj Ameru; listy z Amer-dagandy	Zieliński, St.
Nothing but a Goat (S)	Koza która prawdy nie mówiła	Szelburg-Zarembina, E.
An Odd Story *	Written originally in English	Legeżyński, S.
The Old Clock of Dan-zig (S)	Stary zegar gdański (?)	Anonymous
The Old Professor (P)	Stary profesor	Dygat, St.
The Old Servant	Stary sługa	Sienkiewicz, H.
The Old Serving-Man	Stary sługa	Sienkiewicz, H.
Old Waltsak's Daughter	O Zosi Walcakównej	Tetmajer, K. Przerwa

ENGLISH TITLE	ORIGINAL TITLE	AUTHOR
On a Beautiful Summer Morning (P)	*W piękny letni poranek*	Dąbrowska, M.
On Mount Olympus	*Na Olimpie*	Sienkiewicz, H.
On the Bright Shore	*Na jasnym brzegu*	Sienkiewicz, H.
On the Ceiling *	*Na pułapie*	Meissner, J.
On the Road (P)	*Na drodze*	Konopnicka, M.
On the Sunny Shore	*Na jasnym brzegu*	Sienkiewicz, H.
On the Way to France *	*W drodze do Francji*	Meissner, J.
The Organist of Ponikla	*Organista z Ponikły*	Sienkiewicz, H.
Orso	*Orso*	Sienkiewicz, H.
Our Fathers and We (r)*	Written originally in English	Falkowski, E.
The Outpost *	*Placówka*	Prus, B.
"P.P.C."	*"P.P.C."*	Nałkowska, Z.
The Pale Maiden *	*Blada panna*	Baliński, K.
Pan Michael at Kamenyets *	From his PAN WOŁODYJOWSKI	Sienkiewicz, H.
"The Pan was Bored"	*"Nudził się Pan"*	Bartkiewicz, Z.
The Parable of the Miraculous Salvation (P)	*Przypowieść o cudownym ocaleniu*	Mrożek, S.
Paris (P)	*Paryż*	Zieliński, St.
The Passion of Heaven *	From his POPIOŁY (*Namiętność niebieska*)	Żeromski, S.
The Patcher (P)	*Łaciarz*	Szaniawski, K. J.
Patrol	*Patrol*	Wierzyński, K.
Paul	*Z pamiętnika poznańskiego nauczyciela*	Sienkiewicz, H.
Peasant Wedding *	From his CHŁOPI	Reymont, W. St.
The Peasants	*Chłopi*	Wierzyński, K.
Peasants in Exile	*Za chlebem*	Sienkiewicz, H.
Peer Gynt (P)	*Peer Gynt*	Mrożek, S.
The Penance of a Horse Who Was a Bully (S)	*Pokuta konia zabijaki*	Weychert-Szymanowska, W.
The Personal "Great Adventure" (adapted) *	*Puszcza nad Amazonką*	Fiedler, A.

ENGLISH TITLE	ORIGINAL TITLE	AUTHOR
The Philosopher Pante-leon (P)	Filozof Panteleon	Dygat, St.
The Pig's-Head Magi-cian (S)	Adaptation of a Polish folk tale	Anonymous
A Pilgrimage to Warsaw	Pielgrzymka do War-szawy	Dąbrowska, M.
A Pinch of Salt	Uroczysta wigilja	Szymański, A.
The Pit	Klimontów	Muszałówna, K.
The Plague (S)	Dżuma	Wóycicki, K. W.
The Plague and the Peasant (S)	Powietrze	Wóycicki, K. W.
The Plague-Omen (S)	Homen	Wóycicki, K. W.
The Plague-Swarm (S)	Homen	Wóycicki, K. W.
The Ploughman	Oracz	Gomulicki, W.
"A Point, Mister?" or, Everything Has Changed	Kancik czyli wszystko się zmieniło	Hłasko, M.
The Polish Peasants (P)	From his CHŁOPI	Reymont, W. St.
A Polish Scene (r) *	From his CHŁOPI	Reymont, W. St.
Poverty and Misery (S)	Bieda z Nędzą	Kasprowicz, J.
Powerful Samson (frag-ments) (P)	"Silny Samson"	Orzeszkowa, E.
Premeditated Crime	Zbrodnia z premedy-tacją	Gombrowicz, W.
The President Calls	Odwiedziny Prezydenta	Zawieyski, J.
The President's Visit	Odwiedziny Prezydenta	Zawieyski, J.
Prince Unexpected (S)	O Królewiczu Niespo-dzianku	Gliński, A. J.
Professor Spanner (P)	Profesor Spanner	Nałkowska, Z.
Professor Tutka's Derby (P)	Melonik profesora Tutki	Szaniawski, J.
Professor Tutka's Lec-ture (P)	Wykład profesora Tutki	Szaniawski, J.
Pryszczyk Escapes *	Pryszczyk wieje	Meissner, J.
Pryszczyk Escapes Again *	Pryszczyk wieje po raz drugi	Meissner, J.
Pryszczyk's Adventures *	"Świńska sprawa"	Meissner, J.

ENGLISH TITLE	ORIGINAL TITLE	AUTHOR
A Question of Influence	Protekcja	Perzyński, W.
Quiet Collaborator (P)	Cichy współpracownik	Mrożek, S.
Raisa's Ascent to Heaven	Wniebowstąpienie	Rudnicki, A.
A Rat from the Far East	Szczur z Dalekiego Wschodu	Giertych, J.
A Rather Narrow Point of View (P)	Bardzo ciasny punkt widzenia	Dygat, St.
The Real End of the Great War	Prawdziwy koniec wielkiej wojny	Zawieyski, J.
The Red Flag *	From his DROGA DO NIKĄD	Mackiewicz, J.
A Remedy for Robbers (P)	–	Samozwaniec, M.
Remorse *	From his ZIEMIA OBIECANA	Reymont, W. St.
Rendezvous (P)	From his SOBÓL I PANNA	Weyssenhoff. J.
The Retreat *	Odwrót	Meissner, J.
The Return (P)	Powroty	Kossowski, J.
The Returning Wave	Powracająca fala	Prus, B.
The Revenant	O żołnierzu błędowcu	Gwiżdż, F.
The Ride	Przejażdżka	Mrożek, S.
The Ring (P)	Pierścień	Rodziewiczówna, M.
The Robbers (S)	From his CHŁOPI	Reymont, W. St.
Roch, the Practical Joker *	Roch płata figle	Fiedler, A.
Roll Call (P)	Apel	Andrzejewski, J.
Romantic Passengers *	Romantyczni pasażerowie	Fiedler, A.
The Rosary	Różaniec	Giertych, J.
Roscher (P)	Roscher	Parandowski, J.
S.S. Bielsk, a Ship with Character *	S.S. Bielsk, statek z charakterem	Fiedler, A.
Sachem	Sachem	Sienkiewicz, H.
The Sacred Bell (P)	Pęknięty dzwon	Reymont, W. St.
Sacred Bombs *	Święte bomby	Meissner, J.
A Sacrifice to the Gods	W ofierze bogom	Sieroszewski, W.

ENGLISH TITLE	ORIGINAL TITLE	AUTHOR
The Sad History of Heydasz the Devil (P)	Żałosny żywot djabła Hejdasza	Bunikiewicz, W.
A "Sadhu"	Pustelnik	Pietrkiewicz, J.
Saint Stanislaw and the Wolf	Wilk i kowal (?)	Kędzierski, C.
Samson and Delilah	Samson i Dalila	Goetel, F.
The Savage Shepherd	Dziki juhas	Tetmajer, K. Przerwa
Schillinger's Death (P)	Śmierć Schillingera	Borowski, T.
The Scream of a Peacock (P)	–	Grubiński, W.
The Sea Nourishes, the Sea Destroys	Morze żywi, morze zabija	Giertych, J.
The Secret of the Forest	Tajemnica lasu	Wierzyński, K.
The Sentence	Wyrok	Bandrowski, J. Kaden
Sergeant Prot, Night Fighter *	Sierżant Prot, nocny myśliwiec	Meissner, J.
The Serpent and the Fir Tree (S)	Adapted from her DEWAJTIS	Rodziewiczówna, M.
The Sewers	Kanały (?)	Orwid-Bulicz, R.
Sex	Chuć (?)	Przybyszewski, St.
Shoes (P)	Buty	Szczepański, J. J.
Sielanka; a Forest Picture	Sielanka	Sienkiewicz, H.
Sielanka; an Idyll	Sielanka	Sienkiewicz, H.
"Sierota" the Dog (P)	Pies sierota (?)	Ligocki, M.
Silence (P)	Cisza	Morcinek, G.
The Skies Opened (r)*	Written originally in English	Heinsdorf, H.
Slavery on the Ucayali *	Niewolnictwo nad Ukajali	Fiedler, A.
The Slothful Horse (S)	From his CHŁOPI	Reymont, W. St.
The Smile of Destiny	Uśmiech losu	Baliński, St.
Snow (S)	Śnieg	Szelburg-Ostrowska, E. (?)
A Soldier's Lot (P)	From his POPIOŁY (Żołnierska dola)	Żeromski, S.
Solitude (r)*	From her SIOSTRA IKARA	Lisiewicz, T.
The Song in the Night	Śpiew w nocy	Wierzyński, K.

ENGLISH TITLE	ORIGINAL TITLE	AUTHOR
The Sons	Synowie	Andrzejewski, J.
The Sowers (P)	From his CHŁOPI	Reymont, W. St.
Sparrows (P)	Wróble	Gwiżdż, F.
Spiders *	Pająki	Fiedler, A.
The Spirit of a Buried Man (S)	Duch pogrzebanego	Wóycicki, K. W.
Spring (P)	Dwie wiosny	Reymont, W. St.
Spring *	From his POPIOŁY (Wiosna)	Żeromski, S.
Srul from Lubartow	Srul z Lubartowa	Szymański, A.
A Stain on the Sea *	Plama na morzu!	Meissner, J.
Still Life (P)	Martwa natura	Konopnicka, M.
Stones for the Rampart *	Kamienie na szaniec	Kamiński, A.
The Story of an Oak (P)	Dzieje dębu	Ejsmond, J.
The Story of Princess Marysia, the Black Swan, and an Iceberg (S)	Bajka o królewnie Marysi, o czarnym łabędziu i o lodowej górze	Makuszyński, K.
The Story of Shulim (P)	Szulim	Rey, S.
A Stroke of Luck	Wybraniec losu	Perzyński, W.
The Stronger Sex	Siłaczka	Żeromski, S.
The Strongest (P)	Dwie moce	Ejsmond, J.
The Sunflower (P)	Słonecznik	Czeszko, B.
The Swan's Nest (P)	Łabędzie gniazdo	Narbutt, I.
Taboo	"Tabu"	Żeromski, S.
A Tale of the Fatherly King (S)	O ojcowskim królu	Rościszewski, M.
The Talisman	Talizman	Wierzyński, K.
Targu-Jiu *	Targu-jiu	Meissner, J.
Tartar Captivity	Niewola tatarska	Sienkiewicz, H.
Temptation	Pokusa	Choynowski, P.
Temptation	Pokusa	Żeromski, S.
Terminology (P)	Terminologja	Perzyński, W.
The Terrible Puppet (P)	Straszny pajac Stasia	Grubiński, W.

ENGLISH TITLE	ORIGINAL TITLE	AUTHOR
Thank You, Captain, Thank You! *	*"Thank you, capt'n, thank you!"*	Fiedler, A.
That Third Woman	*Ta trzecia*	Sienkiewicz, H.
Their Battle *	*Ich bitwa*	Fiedler, A.
Their Everyday Bread	*Chleb na dłoni*	Fierla, A.
There Was an Old Man and an Old Woman (adapted) (S)	*Był sobie dziad i baba* (*a poem*)	Kraszewski, J. I.
"There, Where the Last Gaunt Gallows Stands and Beckons"	*"Tam gdzie ostatnia świeci szubienica"*	Małaczewski, E.
The Thimble	*Naparstek*	Grubiński, W.
The Third Autumn	*Trzecia jesień*	Dąbrowska, M.
The Third Woman	*Ta trzecia*	Sienkiewicz, H.
Thirteenth Operation: Osnabruck *	*Trzynasta wyprawa: Osnabrück*	Meissner, J.
A Thousand Years	*Tysiąc lat*	Wierzyński, K.
Tomek Baran	*Tomek Baran*	Reymont, W. St.
Torture *	From his STORY OF A SECRET STATE	Karski, J.
Towards Heaven	*Ku niebu*	Tetmajer, K. Przerwa
The Traitor	*W głębinach*	Reymont, W. St.
Trees in Grudno *	From his POPIOŁY (*Drzewa w Grudnie*)	Żeromski, S.
The Trial (P)	*Proces*	Mrożek, S.
The Trial	*Sąd*	Reymont, W. St.
True to His Art	*Lux in tenebris lucet*	Sienkiewicz, H.
Truth and Falsehood (S)	*Prawda i Krzywda*	Weychert-Szymanowska, W.
A Turban	*Turban i dzika*	Kuncewiczowa, M.
Turin *	*Turyn*	Meissner, J.
Twardowski (S)	*Twardowski*	Wóycicki, K. W.
Twenty-Four Hours of Dying (P)	*24 [dwadzieścia cztery] godziny śmierci*	Pytlakowski, J.
Twilight	*O zmierzchu*	Reymont, W. St.
Twilight	*Zmierzch*	Żeromski, S.
Two Prayers	*Dwie modlitwy*	Szymański, A.

ENGLISH TITLE	ORIGINAL TITLE	AUTHOR
Unknown Soldiers	*Nieznani żołnierze*	Wierzyński, K.
Vengeance	*Zemsta* (?)	Goetel, F.
The Verdict	*Wyrok Zeusa*	Sienkiewicz, H.
Vexations of Power	*Kłopoty władzy*	Czeszko, B.
Victory	*Zwycięstwo*	Filipowicz, K.
A Village Wedding	*Na wsi wesele*	Dąbrowska, M.
The Vision of Sakura (P)	*Widmo sakurskie*	Sieroszewski, W.
The Visitor	*O żołnierzu błędowcu*	Gwiżdż, F.
The Voice	*Dwa sumienia*	Weyssenhoff, J.
The Voyevoda's Christmas Eve (P)	*Wigilja Wojewody*	Choynowski, P.
The Waistcoat	*Kamizelka*	Prus, B.
Water, Water Everywhere *	*Woda, woda, woda . . .*	Fiedler, A.
The Way to Success (P)	*Uczeń Sherlock Holmsa*	Perzyński, W.
We Take Off for Heaven	*Pierwszy krok w chmurach*	Hłasko, M.
A Wedding in Atomville (P)	*Wesele w Atomicach*	Mrożek, S.
Welcome Our Distinguished Guest	*Witaj dostojny gościu!*	Pietrkiewicz, J.
What Happened in the Broken Pitcher (S)	*Goście w glinianym dzbanku*	Szelburg-Zarembina, E.
Where Nature Runs Wild *	*Szalejąca przyroda*	Fiedler, A.
Where the Tatra Mountains Came From (S)	*Powstanie Tatr*	Weychert-Szymanowska, W.
Where Worlds Meet	*Przez stepy*	Sienkiewicz, H.
Whose Fault? A Dramatic Picture in One Act *	*Czyja wina?*	Sienkiewicz, H.
Why Goats Have Short Tails (S)	*Dlaczego kozy mają ucięte ogony*	Rościszewski, M.
Why the Flounder Has a Crooked Mouth (S)	*O flondrze bałtyckiej*	Rabska, Z.
Winter *	From his CHŁOPI	Reymont, W. St.
The Winter Coat	*Jesionka*	Dąbrowska, M.

THE POLISH SHORT STORY IN ENGLISH

ENGLISH TITLE	ORIGINAL TITLE	AUTHOR
The Winter Maidens	*Zimowe panny albo o Maćku, który przepadł w górach*	Tetmajer, K. Przerwa
Within a Red Circle (P)	*Matka*	Ejsmond, J.
The Wizard's Pupil (rS)	*O czarowniku i jego uczniu*	Gliński, A. J.
The Wolf and the Blacksmith (rS)	*Wilk i kowal* (?)	Kędzierski, C.
Written in the Darkness (P)	*Z ciemności*	Mrożek, S.
Yamyol	*Jamioł*	Sienkiewicz, H.
Yanek the Distributor	*Kolporter*	Majewski, W.
Yanko the Musician	*Janko Muzykant*	Sienkiewicz, H.
Yom Kippur (P)	*Sądny dzień*	Rudnicki, A.
The Young Woman Doctor on Prezydencka Street	*Młoda lekarka z Prezydenckiej*	Zakrzewska, St. S.
Zevila	*Żywila*	Mickiewicz, A.
Zola *	*Listy o Zoli*	Sienkiewicz, H.
Zwyrtala the Fiddler	*Szkic opowieści o Zwyrtałowi muzyce (o Zwyrtale muzykancie)*	Tetmajer, K. Przerwa

Polish Titles with English Versions

For Explanation of Symbols see Appendix IVa

ORIGINAL TITLE	ENGLISH VERSION	AUTHOR
A . . . B . . . C . . .	*A . . . B . . . C . . .*	Orzeszkowa, E.
A—jak ciocia Andzia	*"A for Aunt Annie"* *	Meissner, J.
"Ad leones"	*"Ad leones"*	Norwid, C. K.
Akademik smorgoński	The Graduate of Smorgonie (P)	Ejsmond, J.
Anheli	*Anhelli* (fragment) (r)*	Słowacki, J.
Apel	Roll Call (P)	Andrzejewski, J.
Bądź błogosławiona	1) Be Blessed 2) Be Thou Blessed 3) The Blessing	Sienkiewicz, H.
Bajka o gęsim jaju, raku nieboraku, kogucie piejaku, kaczce kwaczce, kocie mruczku i o psie kruczku	The Egg That Went for a Walk (S)	Szelburg-Zarembina, E.
Bajka o królewnie Marysi, o czarnym łabędziu i o lodowej górze	The Story of Princess Marysia, the Black Swan, and an Iceberg (S)	Makuszyński, K.
Banasiowa	1) *Banasiowa* 2) *Banasyova*	Konopnicka, M.
Bardzo ciasny punkt widzenia	A Rather Narrow Point of View (P)	Dygat, St.

433

ORIGINAL TITLE	ENGLISH VERSION	AUTHOR
Bartek Zwycięzca	1) *Bartek the Conqueror* 2) *Bartek the Victor* 3) *The Fate of a Soldier*	Sienkiewicz, H.
Bemklau	*Bemklau* (P)	Zieliński, St.
Bieda z Nędzą	*Poverty and Misery* (S)	Kasprowicz, J.
Blada panna	*The Pale Maiden* (S)	Baliński, K.
Borsuk	*The Badger*	Iwaszkiewicz, J.
Bujak "nawala"	*Buyak Fails* *	Meissner, J.
Buty	*Shoes* (P)	Szczepański, J. J.
Był sobie dziad i baba (a poem)	*There Was an Old Man and an Old Woman* (adapted) (S)	Kraszewski, J. I.
Chawa Rubin	*Chava Ruby*	Świętochowski, A.
Chcę być koniem	*I Want To Be a Horse* (P)	Mrożek, S.
Chiwu	*Chiwu* (P)	Stryjkowski, J.
Chleb	*Bread*	Naglerowa, H.
Chleb djabelski	*The Devil's Bread*	Szczepkowski, J.
Chleb na dłoni	*Their Everyday Bread*	Fierla, A.
Chłopi	*The Peasants*	Wierzyński, K.
Cholera	*Cholera*	Krasiński, Z.
Chopin	*Chopin* *	Przybyszewski, St.
Chuć (?)	*Sex*	Przybyszewski, St.
Cichy współpracownik	*Quiet Collaborator* (P)	Mrożek, S.
Cielęcy żywot	*Calf Time*	Makuszyński, K.
Cisza	*Silence* (P)	Morcinek, G.
Cmentarze	*The Graveyard* *	Hłasko, M.
"Cokolwiek się zdarzy— niech uderza we mnie . . ."	*Forebodings; [the second of] Two Sketches*	Żeromski, S.
Cygan (?)	*The Gypsy and the Bear* (rS)	Barącz, S.
Czarna struga śmierci	*A Black Stream of Death* *	Fiedler, A.
Człowiek z rokokowego kościoła	*The Man from the Rococo Church* (P)	Pruszyński, K.
Czukcze	*The Chukchee*	Sieroszewski, W.

ORIGINAL TITLE	ENGLISH VERSION	AUTHOR
Czy ci najmilszy?	*Is He the Dearest One?*	Sienkiewicz, H.
Czy pamiętasz?	*Do You Remember?*	Orzeszkowa, E.
Czyja wina?	*Whose Fault?* A Dramatic Picture in One Act *	Sienkiewicz, H.
Czysty nurt	1) *The Clear Stream* 2) *The Crystal Stream*	Rudnicki, A.
Daj kwiatek!	*"Give Me a Flower!"*	Orzeszkowa, E.
Dajmonion-Bib	*Daimonion Bib*	Grubiński, W.
Dalekie podróże	*Long Journey*	Dygat, St.
Djabli taniec	*The Demon's Dance* (S)	Wóycicki, K. W.
Dlaczego kozy mają ucięte ogony	*Why Goats Have Short Tails* (S)	Rościszewski, M.
Dno	*Nadir*	Nałkowska, Z.
Dowód niezbity	*Conclusive Proof* *	Meissner, J.
Drzewa w Grudnie	*Trees in Grudno* *	Żeromski, S.
Drzwi	*The Door* (P)	Zieliński, St.
Duch pogrzebanego	*The Spirit of a Buried Man* (S)	Wóycicki, K. W.
Duch zapomniany	*The Forgotten Ghost*	Makuszyński, K.
Dunia	*Dunia*	Naglerowa, H.
Dwa sumienia	*The Voice*	Weyssenhoff, J.
24 [dwadzieścia cztery] godziny śmierci	*Twenty-Four Hours of Dying* (P)	Pytlakowski, J.
Dwie łąki	*Life and Death; a Hindu Legend*	Sienkiewicz, H.
Dwie moce	*The Strongest* (P)	Ejsmond, J.
Dwie modlitwy	*Two Prayers*	Szymański, A.
Dwie wiosny	*Spring* (P)	Reymont, W. St.
Dwojra Zielona	*Dwojra Zielona* (P)	Nałkowska, Z.
Dzieci	*The Children* (P)	Mrożek, S.
Dziecinne argumenty słonecznego promienia	*The Childish Arguments of a Sunbeam* (P)	Makuszyński, K.
Dziecko	*The Child*	Dąbrowska, M.
Dzieje dębu	*The Story of an Oak* (P)	Ejsmond, J.
Dziennikarz	*The Journalist*	Niemojewski, A.

ORIGINAL TITLE	ENGLISH VERSION	AUTHOR
Dziki juhas	*The Savage Shepherd*	Tetmajer, K. Przerwa
Dziwna historia	*A Curious Story* (P)	Prus, B.
Dżuma	*The Plague* (S)	Wóycicki, K. W.
Dzwony kościelne na Helu (?)	*The Church Bells of Hel* (S)	Rabska, Z.
Echa leśne	*Forest Echoes*	Żeromski, S.
Ewakuacja	*Evacuation* *	Meissner, J.
Fakt	*Fact* (P)	Mrożek, S.
Filozof Panteleon	*The Philosopher Panteleon* (P)	Dygat, St.
Flying control	*Flying Control* *	Meissner, J.
"G"—jak Genowefa; "L"—jak . . .	*"G for Genevieve"; "L for . . ."* *	Meissner, J.
Garść wody	*A Handful of Water*	Wierzyński, K.
Gdy matka ma kochanka	*The Lover and the Boy*	Wittlin, T.
Generał	*The General*	Rey, S.
Ginący Daniel	1) *A Dying Man* 2) *The Dying Daniel*	Rudnicki, A.
Góra Ojca	*The Father's Mountain* *	Meissner, J.
Gorące miasto	*A Hot-Bed of Racial Rivalry* *	Fiedler, A.
Gorąco!!	*Heat!* *	Fiedler, A.
Goście w glinianym dzbanku	*What Happened in the Broken Pitcher* (S)	Szelburg-Zarembina, E.
Gwiazdkowa kołysanka	*Lullaby; Why the Pussy-Cat Washes Himself So Often* (S)	Bernhard, J. B.
Hania	*Hania*	Sienkiewicz, H.
Hania z międzymorza	*Hannah*	Giertych, J.
Homen	1) *The Plague-Omen* (S) 2) *The Plague-Swarm* (S)	Wóycicki, K. W.
I wynieśli	*In Spite of All* (P)	Reymont, W. St.
Ich bitwa	*Their Battle* *	Fiedler, A.
Ikar	*Icarus* (P)	Iwaszkiewicz, J.

ORIGINAL TITLE	ENGLISH VERSION	AUTHOR
Imieniny	*Birthday Party* (P)	Mrożek, S.
Indjanie, pogardzający białymi ludźmi i małpami	*Contempt for Whites and Monkeys* *	Fiedler, A.
Inny gatunek	*A Different Species* *	Meissner, J.
Iwańcio	*Iwancio*	Rey, S.
Jadwinia (Dzień kwietniowy)	*Jadwinia (A Day in April)* (P)	Iwaszkiewicz, J.
Jak Jasiek Mosiężny nie mógł znaleźć szczęścia, see *O Marysi dalekiej* and *O wójtowej Marynie*		
Jak się dawniej listy pisało	*Letter Writing of Long Ago* (P)	Kraszewski, J. I.
Jak się Józek Smaś pojechał wysłuchać	*How Josek Smas Went to Confession*	Tetmajer, K. Przerwa
Jak sobie mądry chłop poradził ze złodziejami	*How a Clever Cottager Outwitted Seven Thieves*	Weychert-Szymanowska, W.
Jak sroczka gości przyjmowała	*The Good Housewife?* (S)	Szelburg-Zarembina, E.
Jak to święty Józef orał	*How Saint Joseph Ploughed the Soil* (S)	Birkenmajer, J.
Jak to ze lnem było	*The Golden Seeds* (S)	Konopnicka, M.
Jak umarł Jakób Zych	*The Departure of Jacob Zych*	Tetmajer, K. Przerwa
Jak wzieni Wojtka Chrońca	*How Wojtek Chroniets Was Taken*	Tetmajer, K. Przerwa
Jak żabki Jasia zabawiały	*The Little Boy Who Cried Too Much* (S)	Szelburg-Zarembina, E.
Jak Zawalidroga w niebie został	*How Standintheway Remained in Heaven* (S)	Markowska, M.
Jamioł	1) *The Angel* 2) *Yamyol*	Sienkiewicz, H.
Janko Muzykant	1) *Janko the Musician* 2) *Little Janko* 3) *Yanko the Musician*	Sienkiewicz, H.

ORIGINAL TITLE	ENGLISH VERSION	AUTHOR
Jaś skrzypek (?)	Jas the Fiddler (rs)	Kędzierski, C.
Jerzy	Jerzy	Grubiński, W.
Jesienią	In Autumn	Sieroszewski, W.
Jesionka	The Winter Coat	Dąbrowska, M.
Jonek	Jonek (S)	Wóycicki, K. W.
Józefów	Józefów	Rudnicki, A.
Kajdany (?)	The Chains	Morska, I.
Kamienie na szaniec	Stones for the Rampart	Kamiński, A.
	*	
Kamizelka	The Waistcoat	Prus, B.
Kanały (?)	The Sewers	Orwid-Bulicz, R.
Kancik czyli wszystko się zmieniło	"A Point, Mister?" or, Everything Has Changed	Hłasko, M.
Kapral Koziołek i ja	Corporal Kid and I (P)	Konwicki, T.
Klimontów	The Pit	Muszałówna, K.
Kłopoty władzy	Vexations of Power	Czeszko, B.
Kochane nic	The Beloved "Nothing"	Grubiński, W.
Kolibry	Living Sunbeams *	Fiedler, A.
Kolporter	1) Jack the Distributor 2) Yanek the Distributor	Majewski, W.
Komedia z pomyłek	A Comedy of Errors: a Sketch of American Life	Sienkiewicz, H.
Komurasaki	Komurasaki (P)	Reymont, W. St.
Koń	The Horse	Rudnicki, A.
Koniec wojny	The End of the War (P)	Borowski, T.
Kos na Pamirze	Back to Civilization (P)	Goetel, F.
Koszałki-opałki	Koshalki-opalki, or How a Simpleton Became King (S)	Kasprowicz, J.
Koteczek	Her Kitten	Zapolska, G.
Koza, która prawdy nie mówiła	Nothing but a Goat (S)	Szelburg-Zarembina, E.
Kremowe róże	The Cream-Colored Roses (P)	Grubiński, W.
Król Bartek	King Bartek (S)	Gliński, K.

ORIGINAL TITLE	ENGLISH VERSION	AUTHOR
Krystka	*Krystka*	Tetmajer, K. Przerwa
Krzyż walecznych	*The Cross of Valor* (P)	Hen, J.
Ksiądz Filip	*Father Philip*	Dąbrowska, M.
Ksiądz Piotr	*Father Peter*	Tetmajer, K. Przerwa
Ku niebu	*Towards Heaven*	Tetmajer, K. Przerwa
Kukułka	*The Cuckoo* (P)	Czeszko, B.
Kura	*The Chicken*	Niedźwiecki, Z.
Kwiaty, które poruszyły Anglików	*Flowers Which Moved Britons* *	Fiedler, A.
La douce France	*La douce France* *	Meissner, J.
"La France est morte!" —krzyknął Murzyn i dostał kopniaka	*"La France est morte"* *	Fiedler, A.
Łabędzie gniazdo	*The Swan's Nest* (P)	Narbutt, I.
Łaciarz	*The Patcher* (P)	Szaniawski, K. J.
Łącznik	*The Liaison Man* (P)	Buczkowski, M. R.
Lalka	*The Doll* (P)	Żukrowski, W.
Latarnik	1) *The Lighthouse Keeper* 2) *The Light-House Keeper of Aspinwall*	Sienkiewicz, H.
Legenda	*A Legend*	Krasiński, Z.
Legenda	*Legend* (P)	Reymont, W. St.
Legenda żeglarska	*A Legend of the Sea*	Sienkiewicz, H.
Lew	*The Lion* (P)	Mrożek, S.
Lipa	*The Linden Tree* (P)	Gojawiczyńska, P.
Listy o Zoli	*Zola* *	Sienkiewicz, H.
Losy hrabiego N.	*The Fortunes of Count N.* (P)	Mrożek, S.
Łowy	*The Hunting* (S)	Gliński, K.
"Lucy" wraca do bazy	*"Lucy" Returns to Base* *	Meissner, J.
Lux in tenebris lucet	1) *An Artist's End* 2) *Light in Darkness* 3) *Lux in tenebris lucet* 4) *True to His Art*	Sienkiewicz, H.
Maciej Mazur	*Maciej the Mazur*	Szymański, A.

ORIGINAL TITLE	ENGLISH VERSION	AUTHOR
Macierzyństwo	*Motherhood* (P)	Nałkowska, Z.
Madej	*Madey* *	Wóycicki, K. W.
Madej (?)	*Madej the Brigand* (rS)	Gliński, A. J.
Maj na kółkach	*May on Wheels* (P)	Promiński, M.
Majka	*Majka* (S)	Gliński, K.
Mały Czikinjo i wielka Amazonka	*Little Chicinho and the Great Big Amazon* *	Fiedler, A.
Manekiny	*The Mannequins* (P)	Schulz, B.
Martwa natura	*Still Life* (P)	Konopnicka, M.
Matka	*Within a Red Circle* (P)	Ejsmond, J.
Matura na Targowej	*Exams on Targowa* (P)	Borowski, T.
Melonik professora Tutki	*Professor Tutka's Derby* (P)	Szaniawski, J.
Miłość i śmierć	*Love and Death* (P)	Ejsmond, J.
Miłosierdzie gminy	*Community Welfare Service*	Konopnicka, M.
Missing	*Missing* *	Meissner, J.
Mistrz Twardowski i jego pajączek (?)	*The master Wizard, Pan Twardowski, and His Spider* (rS)	Kędzierski, C.
Mistyczna róża (?)	*The Mystic Rose* (P)	Łuskina, E.
Mli Mli	*The Milk Sop*	Żukrowski, W.
Młoda lekarka z Prezydenckiej	*The Young Woman Doctor on Prezydencka Street*	Zakrzewska, St. Sznaper
Moc Szatana	*The Might of Satan* *	Żeromski, S.
Mój chłopięcy ideał	*My Boyhood Hero* (P)	Andrzejewski, J.
Mój ojciec wstępuje do strażaków	*My Father Joins the Fire Brigade*	Schulz, B.
Moja Wólka	*My Village* (S)	Porazińska, J.
Morderstwo w dolinie rzeki Waki	*Murder on the Waka*	Mackiewicz, J.
Morze żywi, morze zabija	*The Sea Nourishes, the Sea Destroys*	Giertych, J.
Motyle	*Butterflies* *	Fiedler, A.
Na drodze	*On the Road* (P)	Konopnicka, M.

ORIGINAL TITLE	ENGLISH VERSION	AUTHOR
Na jasnym brzegu	1) *In Monte Carlo* 2) *On the Bright Shore* 3) *On the Sunny Shore*	Sienkiewicz, H.
Na Olimpie	1) *The Judgment of Peter and Paul on Olympus* 2) *On Mount Olympus*	Sienkiewicz, H.
Na pułapie	*On the Ceiling* *	Meissner, J.
Na stacji	*At the Station*	Strug, A.
Na stancji	*Boarding House*	Choynowski, P.
Na trumienkę	*For a Coffin*	Dygasiński, A.
Na wsi wesele	*A Village Wedding*	Dąbrowska, M.
Nad rzeką	*By the River* (P)	Wygodzki, St.
Najświętsze słowa naszego życia	*The Most Sacred Words of Our Life*	Hłasko, M.
Namiętność niebieska	*The Passion of Heaven* *	Żeromski, S.
Naparstek	*The Thimble*	Grubiński, W.
Następny do raju	*Next Stop—Paradise* *	Hłasko, M.
Nie wszystko skończone	*All Is Not Yet Finished*	Wierzyński, K.
Niewola tatarska	*Tartar Captivity*	Sienkiewicz, H.
Niewolnictwo nad Ukajali	*Slavery on the Ucayali* *	Fiedler, A.
Niezapominajki	*Forget-Me-Nots* *	Meissner, J.
Nieznani żołnierze	*Unknown Soldiers*	Wierzyński, K.
Noc	*A Night's Tragedy*	Rodziewiczówna, M.
Nocne spotkanie	*Night Encounter*	Dąbrowska, M.
Nowa szkoła filozoficzna	*The New Philosophical School*	Różewicz, T.
"Nudził się Pan"	*"The Pan Was Bored"*	Bartkiewicz, Z.
O czarowniku i jego uczniu	*The Wizard's Pupil* (rS)	Gliński, A. J.
O dziadku i babce, o kogutku i kurce, o lisie i wilku	*About an Old Man and an Old Woman, a Cock and a Hen, a Fox and a Wolf* (S)	Gliński, A. J.
O flondrze bałtyckiej	*Why the Flounder Has a Crooked Mouth* (S)	Rabska, Z.

ORIGINAL TITLE	ENGLISH VERSION	AUTHOR
O głowę murzyńskiego króla	For the Head of a Negro King	Pruszyński, K.
O herbie miasta Pucka	The Coat of Arms of Putsk (S)	Rabska, Z.
O Jóźwie, co na przedpieklu służył	Joe Who Served in Lower Limbo (S)	Markowska, M.
O kilka mil od brzegu	A Few Miles from the Shore *	Meissner, J.
O kozie rogatej	A Horned Goat (S)	Markowska, M.
O Królewiczu Niespodzianku	Prince Unexpected (S)	Gliński, A. J.
O kurce złotopiórce i kogutku szałaputku	The Greedy Rooster (S)	Szelburg-Zarembina, E.
O Marysi dalekiej (Part I of *Jak Jasiek Mosiężny nie mógł znaleźć szczęścia*)	1) Far-away Marysia 2) Far-off Marysia 3) Far-off-Marisya	Tetmajer, K. Przerwa
O ojcowskim królu	1) The King and the Peasant *(S) 2) A Tale of the Fatherly King *(S)	Rościszewski, M.
O Panu Jezusie i zbójnikach	The Lord Jesus and the Three Robbers (S)	Weychert-Szymanowska, W.
O psie, co był szewcem	The Cobbler Dog (S)	Markowska, M.
O skowronku, wilku i lisie	The Lark, the Wolf, and the Fox (S)	Markowska, M.
O starym psie, ośle, kocie i kogucie	A Dog, a Donkey, a Cat, and a Cock (S)	Piotrowski, A.
O szczupaku, który umiał tańczyć	The Dancing Pike (rS)	Perzyński, W.
O szewczykowej duszyczce	The Cobbler's Soul (S)	Staroś, J.
O takim, co rozumiał jak dzwirzęta gwarzom	How a Sensible Peasant Cured His Wife's Curiosity (S)	Piotrowski, A.
O tem, jak krawiec pan Niteczka został królem	The Jolly Tailor Who Became King (S)	Makuszyński, K.
O tym jak zajączek szaraczek psa burka wywiódł w pole	No Hare Anywhere (S)	Szelburg-Zarembina, E.

442

ORIGINAL TITLE	ENGLISH VERSION	AUTHOR
O wilku i jego przygodach	The Adventures of a Wolf (S)	Gliński, A. J.
O wójtowej Marynie (Part II of Jak Jasiek Mosiężny nie mógł znaleźć szczęścia)	1) Maryna 2) The Miller's Maryna	Tetmajer, K. Przerwa
O zmierzchu	Twilight	Reymont, W. St.
O żołnierzu błędowcu	1) The Revenant 2) The Visitor	Gwiżdż, F.
O Zosi Walcakównej	Old Waltsak's Daughter	Tetmajer, K. Przerwa
Obóz w Dobrudży	The Camp in Dobrudja *	Meissner, J.
Obrona Grenady	1) The Defence of the "Granada" 2) The Defense of Granada	Brandys, K.
Oczy uroczne	The Evil Eye (S)	Wóycicki, K. W.
Odwiedzają mnie czole	Embarrassing Visitors *	Fiedler, A.
Odwiedziny Prezydenta	1) The President Calls 2) The President's Visit	Zawieyski, J.
Odwrót	The Retreat *	Meissner, J.
Okrucieństwo	A Chapter on Cruelty *	Fiedler, A.
Omyłka	A Mistake (fragment)	Prus, B.
On	He	Tetmajer, K. Przerwa
Opowieść cyniczna	A Cynical Tale	Choromański, M.
Oracz	The Ploughman	Comulicki, W.
Organista z Ponikły	1) A Country Artist 2) The Organist of Ponikla	Sienkiewicz, H.
Orlice	Eaglets (P)	Tetmajer, K. Przerwa
Orso	1) A Circus Hercules 2) Orso	Sienkiewicz, H.
Ósmy dzień tygodnia	The Eighth Day of the Week *	Hłasko, M.
Ostatnia bitwa	The Last Battle (P)	Brandys, M.
Ostatnia syrena Helu (?)	The Last Siren of Hel (S)	Rabska, Z.
"P.P.C."	"P.P.C."	Nałkowska, Z.

ORIGINAL TITLE	ENGLISH VERSION	AUTHOR
Pająki	*Spiders* *	Fiedler, A.
Pan Rozpędek	*Mr. Whirlwind, Shoemaker* (rS)	Perzyński, W.
Pan z Kozią bródką	*Another "Paradise" Lost and Regained* (P)	Makuszyński, K.
Pani Zosia	*Madame Sophie*	Dąbrowska, M.
Panna Antonina	*Miss Antonina*	Orzeszkowa, E.
Papugi nad Iquitos	*The Ants and Parrots of Iquitos* *	Fiedler, A.
Papugi zielone i arary szkarłatne	*Green Parrots and Crimson Macaws* *	Fiedler, A.
Paryż	*Paris* (P)	Zieliński, St.
Patrol	*Patrol*	Wierzyński, K.
Peer Gynt	*Peer Gynt* (P)	Mrożek, S.
Pęknięty dzwon	*The Sacred Bell* (P)	Reymont, W. S.
Pięćdziesiąt kroków cywilizacji	*Fifty Yards of Civilization* *	Fiedler, A.
Pielgrzymka do Warszawy	*A Pilgrimage to Warsaw*	Dąbrowska, M.
Pierścień	*The Ring* (P)	Rodziewiczówna, M.
Pierwszy krok w chmurach	1) *A First Step into the Clouds* 2) *We Take Off for Heaven*	Hłasko, M.
Pies sierota (?)	*"Sierota" the Dog* (P)	Ligocki, M.
Pieśń przerwana	*The Interrupted Melody* *	Orzeszkowa, E.
Piwo	*Beer*	Różewicz, T.
Placówka	*The Outpost* *	Prus, B.
Plama na morzu	*A Stain on the Sea* *	Meissner, J.
Podróż do wnętrza muszli	*Journey into a Sea-Shell* (P)	Kotowska, M.
Pójdźmy za Nim	1) *Anthea* 2) *Let Us Follow Him*	Sienkiewicz, H.
Pokusa	*Temptation*	Choynowski, P.
Pokusa	*Temptation*	Żeromski, S.
Pokuta konia zabijaki	*The Penance of a Horse Who Was a Bully* (S)	Weychert-Szymanowska, W.

444

ORIGINAL TITLE	ENGLISH VERSION	AUTHOR
Polujemy na Binuji	*Europe versus Snake* *	Fiedler, A.
Pomiędzy wilki	*Back to the Wolves* (P)	Pruszyński, K.
Poranek w ogrodzie zoologicznym	*A Morning at the Zoo*	Dąbrowska, M.
Porwany wichrem	*Carried Away by the Wind* (S)	Wóycicki, K. W.
Potęga złota (?)	*The Might of Gold*	Olechowski, G.
Powietrze	*The Plague and the Peasant* (S)	Wóycicki, K. W.
Powracająca fala	*The Returning Wave*	Prus, B.
Powroty	*The Return* (P)	Kossowski, J.
Powstanie Tatr	*Where the Tatra Mountains Came From* (S)	Weychert-Szymanowska, W.
Powszedni dzień	*Just Another Day*	Gojawiczyńska, P.
Prawda i Krzywda	*Truth and Falsehood* (S)	Weychert-Szymanowska, W.
Prawdziwy koniec wielkiej wojny	*The Real End of the Great War*	Zawieyski, J.
Proces	*The Trial* (P)	Mrożek, S.
Profesor Spanner	*Professor Spanner* (P)	Nałkowska, Z.
Proszę państwa do gazu	*Ladies and Gentlemen, to the Gas Chamber*	Borowski, T.
Protekcja	*A Question of Influence*	Perzyński, W.
Pryszczyk wieje	*Pryszczyk Escapes* *	Meissner, J.
Pryszczyk wieje po raz drugi	1) *How To Escape?* * 2) *Pryszczyk Escapes Again* *	Meissner, J.
Przed świtem	*Before Dawn*	Zieliński, St.
Przejażdżka	*The Ride* (P)	Mrożek, S.
Przez stepy	1) *Across the Plains* 2) *Across the Prairies* 3) *Lillian Morris* 4) *Where Worlds Meet*	Sienkiewicz, H.
Przygody małego diabełka	*The Adventures of an Imp*	Mackiewicz, J.
Przypowieść o cudownym ocaleniu	1) *The Man Saved by a Miracle* (P) 2) *The Parable of the*	Mrożek, S.

445

ORIGINAL TITLE	ENGLISH VERSION	AUTHOR
	Miraculous Salvation (P)	
Ptaki	*Birds* (P)	Schulz, B.
Puhacz	*The Falcons*	Wierzyński, K.
Pustelnik	*A "Sadhu"*	Pietrkiewicz, J.
Puszcza nad Amazonką	*The Personal "Great Adventure"* (adapted)	Fiedler, A.
Raj Ameru; listy z Amerdagandy	*Notes from Amerdaganda* (fragment) *	Zieliński, St.
Roch płata figle	*Roch, the Practical Joker* *	Fiedler, A.
Romantyczni pasażerowie	*Romantic Passengers* *	Fiedler, A.
Roscher	*Roscher* (P)	Parandowski, J.
Rozdziobią nas kruki, wrony	1) *The Crows* 2) *The Crows and the Ravens*	Żeromski, S.
Różaniec	*The Rosary*	Giertych, J.
S.S. Bielsk, statek z charakterem	*S.S. Bielsk, a Ship with Character* *	Fiedler, A.
Sabałowa bajka	*A Mountaineer's Tale* (S)	Weychert-Szymanowska, W.
Sachem	*Sachem*	Sienkiewicz, H.
Samson i Dalila	*Samson and Delilah*	Goetel, F.
Sąd	*The Trial*	Reymont, W. St.
Sądny dzień	*Yom Kippur* (P)	Rudnicki, A.
Sen	*The Dream* (P)	Prus, B.
Sercem za serce	*Gratitude* (P)	Perzyński, W.
Sielanka	1) *Sielanka; a Forest Picture* 2) *Sielanka; an Idyll*	Sienkiewicz, H.
Sierżant Prot, nocny myśliwiec	*Sergeant Prot, Night Fighter* *	Meissner, J.
Siłaczka	*The Stronger Sex*	Żeromski, S.
"Silny Samson"	*Powerful Samson* (fragments) (P)	Orzeszkowa, E.
Słoń	*The Elephant* (P)	Mrożek, S.
Słonecznik	*The Sunflower* (P)	Czeszko, B.

ORIGINAL TITLE	ENGLISH VERSION	AUTHOR
Smarownik Łoza chce jeść	*Greaser Loza Is Hungry**	Fiedler, A.
Śmierć	*Death*	Reymont, W. St.
Śmierć Azy	*The Death of Aza*	Lisiewicz, M. J.
Śmierć Schillingera	*Schillinger's Death* (P)	Borowski, T.
Śnieg	*Snow* (S)	Szelburg-Ostrowska, E. (?)
Sny na Ukajali	*Dreaming on the Ucayali* *	Fiedler, A.
Śpiew w nocy	*The Song in the Night*	Wierzyński, K.
Sprawiedliwy zając	*The Just Hare*	Dygasiński, A.
Srul z Lubartowa	*Srul from Lubartow*	Szymański, A.
Stary profesor	*The Old Professor* (P)	Dygat, St.
Stary sługa	1) *The Old Servant* 2) *The Old Serving-Man*	Sienkiewicz, H.
Stary zegar gdański (?)	*The Old Clock of Danzig* (S)	Anonymous
Starzy, dobrzy przyjaciele	*Good Old Friends* *	Fiedler, A.
Stolarz Kowalski	*Kowalski the Carpenter*	Szymański, A.
Straszny dzień Janka	*Janek's Ordeal* (P)	Choynowski, P.
Straszny pajac Stasia	*The Terrible Puppet*	Grubiński, W.
Suka	*The Bitch*	Reymont, W. St.
Święte bomby	*Sacred Bombs* *	Meissner, J.
"Świńska sprawa"	*Pryszczyk's Adventures* *	Meissner, J.
Syn zadżumionych	*Born of the Plague* (fragment) (P)	Nowakowski, T.
Synowie	*The Sons*	Andrzejewski, J.
Szalejąca przyroda	*Where Nature Runs Wild* *	Fiedler, A.
Szczęście	*Fortune* (S)	Weychert-Szymanowska, W.
Szczęście	*Happiness* (P)	Żesławski, W.
Szczęśliwy żebrak (?)	*The Lucky Beggar* (rS)	Piotrowski, A.
Szczur z Dalekiego Wschodu	*A Rat from the Far East*	Giertych, J.
Szewc Kopytko i kaczor Kwak	*Cobbler Kopytko and Drake Kwak* (S)	Makuszyński, K.

447

ORIGINAL TITLE	ENGLISH VERSION	AUTHOR
Szkic opowieści o Zwyrtałowi muzyce (o Zwyrtale muzykancie)	*Zwyrtala the Fiddler*	Tetmajer, K. Przerwa
Szkice węglem	1) *Charcoal Sketches* 2) *The New Soldier*	Sienkiewicz, H.
Szulim	*The Story of Shulim* (P)	Rey, S.
Ta trzecia	1) *In Bohemia* 2) *That Third Woman* 3) *The Third woman*	Sienkiewicz, H.
"Tabu"	1) *"Impossible"* 2) *Taboo*	Żeromski, S.
Tajemnica lasu	*The Secret of the Forest*	Wierzyński, K.
Tajemnica Lorda Singlewortha	*Lord Singleworth's Secret* (abridged)	Norwid, C. K.
Tak odlatują ptaki	*The Migration of the Birds* (P)	Baliński, St.
Tak się bawią wariaci	*A Crazy Game* (P)	Promiński, M.
Talizman	*The Talisman*	Wierzyński, K.
"Tam gdzie ostatnia świeci szubienica"	*"There, Where the Last Gaunt Gallows Stands and Beckons"*	Małaczewski, E.
Targu-jiu	*Targu-Jiu* *	Meissner, J.
Terminologja	*Terminology* (P)	Perzyński, W.
"Thank you, capt'n, thank you!"	*Thank You, Captain, Thank You!* *	Fiedler, A.
Tomek Baran	*Tomek Baran*	Reymont, W. St.
Tragarz John	*Mutton-Fat* (adapted)	Kowalewski, J.
Tragedja kauczukowa	*An India-Rubber Tragedy* *	Fiedler, A.
Trzecia jesień	*The Third Autumn*	Dąbrowska, M.
Trzynasta wyprawa: Osnabrück	*Thirteenth Operation: Osnabruck* *	Mcissner, J.
Tu zaszła zmiana	*"A change Came o'er the Scenes of My Dream"*	Dąbrowska, M.
Turban i dzika	*A Turban*	Kuncewiczowa, M.
Turyn	*Turin* *	Meissner, J.
Twardowski	*Twardowski* (S)	Wóycicki, K. W.
Twardy chleb	*Mutton-Fat* (adapted)	Kowalewski, J.

ORIGINAL TITLE	ENGLISH VERSION	AUTHOR
Tysiąc lat	*A Thousand Years*	Wierzyński, K.
U źródła	*At the Source*	Sienkiewicz, H.
Ucieczka	*The Flight* (S)	Kasprowicz, J.
Uczeń Sherlock Holmsa	*The Way to Success* (P)	Perzyński, W.
Urlop	*The Furlough* (P)	Gwiżdż, F.
Uroczysta wigilja	*A Pinch of Salt*	Szymański, A.
Uśmiech losu	*The Smile of Destiny*	Baliński, St.
W drodze do Francji	*On the Way to France* *	Meissner, J.
W głębinach	*The Traitor*	Reymont, W. St.
W górach	*In the Mountains* (P)	Prus, B.
W górach	*In the Mountains* *	Żeromski, S.
W matni	*Caught in a Snare* (fragment) (P)	Sieroszewski, W.
W noc grudniową	*A December Night* (P)	Rodziewiczówna, M.
W ofierze bogom	1) *A Sacrifice to the Gods* 2) *In Sacrifice to the Gods*	Sieroszewski, W.
W piękny letni poranek	*On a Beautiful Summer Morning* (P)	Dąbrowska, M.
W pruskiej szkole	*The Lord's Prayer*	Reymont, W. St.
Walka byków	*The Bull-Fight* *	Sienkiewicz, H.
Wdzięczność i sprawiedliwość	*Gratitude and Justice* (S)	Dygasiński, A.
Wesele w Atomicach	*A Wedding in Atomville* (P)	Mrożek, S.
Wiara	*Faith* (P)	Morcinek, G.
Widmo sakurskie	*The Vision of Sakura* (P)	Sieroszewski, W.
Widzę Go	*"I See Him"*	Kossak-Szczucka, Z.
Wiele hałasu o . . . Letycję	*Much Ado about— Leticia* *	Fiedler, A.
Wielkanoc	*Easter*	Rudnicki, A.
Wielki Stefan Konecki	*The Great Stefan Konecki*	Rudnicki, A.
Wigilja Wojewody	*The Voyevoda's Christmas Eve* (P)	Choynowski, P.

449

ORIGINAL TITLE	ENGLISH VERSION	AUTHOR
Wilk i kowal (?)	1) *Saint Stanislaw and the Wolf* (rS) 2) *The Wolf and the Blacksmith* (rS)	Kędzierski, C.
Wilkołaki	*Men-Wolves* (S)	Wóycicki, K. W.
Wiosna	*Spring* *	Żeromski, S.
Witaj dostojny gościu!	*Welcome Our Distinguished Guest*	Pietrkiewicz, J.
Wniebowstąpienie	1) *Ascent to Heaven* 2) *Raisa's Ascent to Heaven*	Rudnicki, A.
Woda, woda, woda . . .	*Water, Water Everywhere* *	Fiedler, A.
Wołanie	*The Mother (the Call)*	Reymont, W. St.
Wróble	*Sparrows* (P)	Gwiżdż, F.
Wspaniały kapitan i niezłomny statek	*A Gallant Captain and a Dauntless Ship* *	Fiedler, A.
Wspomnienie z Mariposy	*Memories of Mariposa*	Sienkiewicz, H.
Wybraniec losu	*A Stroke of Luck*	Perzyński, W.
Wycieczka do Aten	1) *An Excursion to Athens* * 2) *A Journey to Athens* *	Sienkiewicz, H.
Wykład profesora Tutki	*Professor Tutka's Lecture* (P)	Szaniawski, J.
Wypadek w Krasnymstawie	*The Accident at Krasnystaw*	Putrament, J.
Wyrok	*The Sentence*	Bandrowski, J. Kaden
Wyrok Zeusa	1) *The Decision of Zeus* 2) *The Verdict*	Sienkiewicz, H.
Wyspa Ostatniej Nadziei	*The Island of Last Hope* *	Meissner, J.
Wzorowe małżeństwo	*The Exemplary Couple* (P)	Różewicz, T.
Z ciemności	*Written in the Darkness* (P)	Mrożek, S.

ORIGINAL TITLE	ENGLISH VERSION	AUTHOR
Z legend dawnego Egiptu	1) *From Legends of Ancient Egypt* 2) *From the Legends of Ancient Egypt*	Prus, B.
Z pamiętnika poznań-skiego nauczyciela	1) *From the Diary of a Tutor in Poznan* 2) *Paul*	Sienkiewicz, H.
Za chlebem	1) *After Bread* 2) *For Bread* 3) *For Daily Bread* 4) *Her Tragic Fate* 5) *In the New Promised Land* 6) *Peasants in Exile*	Sienkiewicz, H.
Za mąż	*The Dowry*	Niedźwiecki, Z.
Za Wolność Naszą i Waszą	*For Our Freedom and Yours* *	Żeromski, S.
Żaba	*The Frog* (S)	Gliński, K.
Zabawa myszek	*The Mice Give a Ball* (S)	Szelburg-Zarembina, E.
Żądło Genowefy	*"Genevieve's" Sting* *	Meissner, J.
Zajęcze serce	*The Hare's Heart* (S)	Wóycicki, K. W.
Żałosny żywot djabła Hejdasza	*The Sad History of Heydasz the Devil* (P)	Bunikiewicz, W.
Zasadzka	*Ambush*	Wierzyński, K.
Zbrodnia z premedy-tacją	*Premeditated Crime*	Gombrowicz, W.
Zemsta (?)	*Vengeance*	Goetel, F.
Zemsta jest moja . . .	*The Birches*	Żeromski, S.
Zestrzelili nas nad Francją	*Just Prejudice* *	Meissner, J.
Zimowe panny albo o Maćku, który przepadł w górach	*The Winter Maidens*	Tetmajer, K. Przerwa
Złe przeczucie	*Forebodings;* [the first of] *Two Sketches*	Żeromski, S.
Złote okna	*Golden Windows* *	Rudnicki, A.
Zmierzch	*Twilight*	Żeromski, S.
Znów padają deszcze	*More Rain* *	Fiedler, A.

451

ORIGINAL TITLE	ENGLISH VERSION	AUTHOR
Żołnierska dola	*A Soldier's Lot* (P)	Żeromski, S.
Żurawie	*The Cranes*	Sienkiewicz, H.
Zwycięstwo	*Victory*	Filipowicz, K.
Żywila	*Zevila*	Mickiewicz, A.
Żywot pijaka	*Life of a Drunkard*	Lisiewicz, M. J.
Żywe i martwe morze	*The Dead and the Living Sea*	Rudnicki, A.
Żywy telegraf	*The Human Telegraph*	Prus, B.

A Comparative Analysis of Translations
into English of Sienkiewicz's Za chlebem

Henryk Sienkiewicz's *Za chlebem* has appeared in English translation in six different versions. This makes it possible to compare the translations and draw some conclusions. The opening paragraphs of the first chapter of the story have served this compiler as a basis for the comparison. The original Polish text comes first, followed by the compiler's literal translations of the text, prepared for the benefit of the readers who do not know Polish. This is followed by six different translations in alphabetical order by the name of the translator. Finally, the compiler has ventured into some comments and observations of his own.

Polish.   *Za chlebem*

Na szerokich falach oceanu kołysał się niemiecki statek "Blücher," płynący z Hamburga do New Yorku.

Od czterech dni był już w drodze, a od dwóch minął zielone brzegi Irlandii i wydostał się na pełnię. Z pokładu, jak okiem dojrzeć, widać było tylko zieloną i szarą równinę, pooraną w bruzdy i zagony, rozkołysaną ciężko, miejscami zapienioną, w dali coraz ciemniejszą i zlewającą się z widnokręgiem, pokrytym białymi chmurami.

Blask tych chmur padał miejscami i na wodę, a na tym tle perłowym odrzynał się wyraźnie czarny kadłub statku. Kadłub ten, zwrócony dziobem ku zachodowi, to wspinał się pracowicie na fale, to zapadał w głąb, jakby tonął; czasem wzniesiony na grzbiecie bałwanu wynurzył się tak, że aż dno było mu widać, a szedł naprzód. Fala płynęła ku niemu, a on ku fali—i rozcinał ją piersią. Za nim, jakby olbrzymi wąż, gonił biały gościniec spienionej wody; kilka mew leciało za sterem, przewracając kozły w powietrzu i kwiląc, jakby polskie czajki.

Literal translation.   *After Bread*

On the broad waves of the ocean the German steamer "Blücher" was rocking, sailing from Hamburg to New York.

It was already at sea four days; two days ago it had passed the green shores of Ireland and had come out on the open ocean. From the deck, so far as the eye could reach, there was to be seen only the green and gray plain, ploughed into furrows and ridges, swaying heavily, in places foaming, growing darker in the distance and blending with the horizon, covered with white clouds.

The light of these clouds also fell in places on the water, and against that pearly background the black body of the vessel stood out sharply. Turned with its prow to the west, that body now laboriously rose on the waves, now it plunged into the depth, as if it were sinking; at times it vanished from the eye, then, lifted on the back of a billow, it would emerge so that one could see its bottom; but it went forward. The wave moved toward it, and it moved toward the wave—and it cut it with its breast. Behind it, like a giant serpent, chased a white road of foaming water; a few seagulls flew behind the rudder, turning somersaults in the air and shrieking like Polish lapwings.

Her Tragic Fate.   Translated by J. Christian Bay.

"Blucher," the German emigrant steamship running between Hamburg and New York, was rocking across the waters of the Atlantic ocean.

It was on the fourth day of the voyage. Two days ago it had passed beyond the view of Ireland's green borders, and now found itself on high sea. From the deck nothing was visible, so far as the view extended, save the even desert of green and gray, furrowed and streaked in all directions, moving slowly and incessantly, here and there with patches of foam; farther away becoming darker and more and more shrouded, and finally merging into the cloudy horizon.

Here and there these bright masses of clouds were reflected in the surface of the water, and from this pearly foundation the ship's dark body rose majestically. This massive-looking hull, facing toward the west, would ascend one wave, climbing swiftly upward, whereupon it plunged into the depths beyond, as if rushing away, never again to be seen. Now entirely invisible, now riding high upon the back of the foamy waves—now carried so far into the air that one might almost see the whole of its bottom, it was speeding onward, safely and steadily. One wave after another rose up against it; the ship cut into them, drove them aside, one by one, and pursued its steady course. And in its trail was a long furrow of foam not unlike a gigantic serpent. Over and about the stern followed a flock of gulls.

For Bread. Translated by Jeremiah Curtin.

On the broad waves of the ocean the German steamer Blücher was rocking as it sailed to New York from Hamburg.

That was its fourth day on the voyage; two days before it had passed the green shores of Ireland, and had come out on the open ocean. From the deck, as far as the eye could see, nothing was visible save the green and gray plain, ploughed into furrows and ridges, swaying heavily, in places foaming, in the distance darker and darker and blending with the horizon, which was covered with white clouds.

The light of these clouds fell in places on the water too, and on that pearly background the black body of the vessel was outlined distinctly. The prow of that body was turned to the west; now it rose on a wave with great labor, now it plunged into the depth, as if drowning; at moments it vanished from the eye; at moments, lifted on the back of a billow, it rose so high that the bottom of it was visible, but the steamer went forward. The sea moved toward it, and it toward the sea, cleaving the water with its breast. Behind it, like a giant serpent, chased a white road of foaming water; sea-gulls flew after the rudder, turning somersaults in the air and piping like Polish lapwings.

After Bread. Translated by Vatslaf A. Hlasko and Thomas H. Bullick.

On the waves of the wide ocean rode the German steamer Blucher, on its passage from Hamburg to New York.

It had been on its way four days. Two days ago it had passed the green coast of Ireland and reached the broad Atlantic. From the deck, as far as the eye could reach, could be seen the gray and green surface, plowed up in furrows and hollows, rocking heavily, foaming in places, in the distance more dark, where the water joined the sky in a white, cloudy mist.

The reflection from the clouds fell sometimes upon the water, and upon this pearly background was drawn with sharp outlines the figure of the steamer. The ship, with its bow pointing to the west, climbed to the crest of the billows, and then, as if going to drown itself, sank in the trough of the sea; sometimes it disappeared from view, sometimes it was lifted so high on the top of the waves that part of its keel could be seen—still pressed steadily onward. The waves rolled toward it, and it rushed toward the waves and cut them with its prow. Behind it chased, like a gigantic snake, a wide strip of foaming water; several sea-gulls followed in its wake, circling in the air with their wild cries.

Peasants in Exile. Translated by C. O'Conor-Eccles.

The German emigrant vessel Blucher labored heavily through the Atlantic on her way from Hamburg to New York. She had already been four days on her voyage, and it was now forty-eight hours since she had passed the green shores of Ireland and gained the open sea.

From the deck nothing was visible as far as the eye could reach save grey-green water, furrowed like a ploughed field, foaming here and there, and melting gradually into the mist as it reached the distant, hazy horizon. A shimmer from the clouds lay on the water.

Against the pearly background the dark hull of the vessel stood out clearly,—rising as with an effort, sinking as if exhausted; now disappearing from sight; now rising on the crest of a wave; but moving steadily onward the while. The waves at times seemed rushing to meet it, again it rushed to meet them, and cut through them with its prow. Behind it, like a giant snake, curled a track of foam. A flock of gulls circled overhead, turned somersaults in the air, and shrieked fiercely.

In the New Promised Land. Translated by S. C. de Soissons.

On the waves of the Atlantic rode the German steamer "Blucher," on its passage from Hamburg to New York.

It had been four days at sea. Two days since, it had passed the green coast of Ireland and reached the great ocean. As far as the eye could reach stretched the greyish-green surface, ploughed into furrows and hollows, rocking heavily, and foaming, and gleaming darker in the distance.

Sometimes the reflection from the clouds fell on the water, and on this pearly background the outlines of the steamer showed sharply. The ship, with its bow pointing to the west, climbed to the crest of the billows, and then, as though intending to drown itself, sank in the trough of the sea. Sometimes it disappeared from view, sometimes it was lifted so high on the summit of the waves that part of its keel could be seen—but pressing steadily onward. The waves rolled towards it, and it rushed towards the waves, and cut them with its prow. Behind it, like a gigantic snake, coiled a strip of foaming water; sea-gulls followed in its wake, circling in the air with wild cries.

For Daily Bread. Translated by Iza Young.

A German steamer, the "Blücher," from Hamburg, was on her way to America.

It was the fourth day of her voyage and the second since she had left the green shores of Ireland behind and was on the open sea. From her deck, as far as the eye could reach, nothing was to be seen but an expanse of greyish-green water, ploughed into deep, foam-crested furrows, getting darker in the distance and melting into the horizon covered with fleecy clouds.

The reflection of the clouds lent here and there a pearly tint to the water, on the background of which the black hull stood out in sharp distinct lines. Her head was toward the West and she rose and fell

456

steadily with the waves; at times she seemed to disappear altogether and then again rose almost clean out of the water. Waves went to meet her and she went towards the waves cutting them in two with her bow. A long streak of churning, milky water trailed like a serpent behind and a few seagulls followed screaming in her wake.

It may be of interest to take the count of words first. No definite or indefinite articles were counted. The literal translation has 192 words. Then in the same order: Bay—222, Curtin—196, Hlasko and Bullick—188, O'Conor-Eccles—158, Soissons—165 (the Polish text, by the way, happens to have 165 words, too), and finally Young—154.

The longest is the text of J. Christian Bay, the shortest—that of Iza Young. The significant fact is—and here, perhaps, may lie the value of the count—that the most literal translation of the six, that of Jeremiah Curtin, shows almost the same number of words as the literal translation prepared by this compiler. O'Conor-Eccles, Soissons and Young make cuts in their texts, omitting whole sentences. J. Christian Bay, in order to be explicit, offers some additions. It is interesting to note that, despite his 222 words, Bay omits the final clause about the shrieking lapwings which both C. O'Conor-Eccles and Iza Young have retained.

All the translators, with the exception of O'Conor-Eccles, have followed the pattern of the paragraph arrangement of the Polish text. O'Conor-Eccles transferred one sentence from the second paragraph to the first. Her decision seems justified. The sentence falls logically in place, smoothly rounds up the first paragraph, and gives the additional advantage of making the length of the three paragraphs a little more even.

There are two places in the text (and this was partly a reason for its selection) which may serve as illustrations of some of the difficulties of rendering a Polish literary text into English. At the beginning of the third paragraph we read in the Polish text that *blask tych chmur padał miejscami i na wodę* (the light of these clouds fell in places on the water). Obviously clouds are not the source of light; what Sienkiewicz has in mind here is the light reflected from the clouds. This understandable lack of linguistic precision is not striking in the Polish text, but it becomes evident in the English translation. In another place, at the end of the same paragraph, when referring to the foam behind the ship, the author applies a double comparison: road—serpent. In Polish this is nothing more than an old cliché, and was used by Sienkiewicz as such. In English, however, this double comparison suffers from conflict between the stationary object (white road) and the object in motion (giant serpent chasing the boat). What do our translators do?

Curtin follows the author slavishly, and says just as the Polish text does that "the light of these clouds fell in places on the water." Referring to the foam, he also repeats the two images exactly as they appear in Polish, producing in English an oddity such as: "Behind it, like a giant serpent, chased a white road of foaming water . . ."

J. Christian Bay clearly saw both pitfalls, and did not fall into either one. Here are the two passages: "Here and there these bright masses of clouds were reflected in the surface of the water . . ." (the noun "light" seems to be consciously omitted) and ". . . in its trail was a long furrow of foam not unlike a gigantic serpent."

Vatslaf A. Hlasko and Thomas H. Bullick see the problem too. They find a good solution in the first sentence, when they speak of "the reflection from the clouds" which "fell sometimes upon the water." Their second passage is unfortunately as deplorable as that of Curtin: "Behind it chased, like a gigantic snake, a wide strip of foaming water . . ."

O'Conor-Eccles does not try to untie the first knot, and omits entirely the matter of "light of the clouds." Here is her solution of the dilemma presented by the second passage: "Behind it, like a giant snake, curled a track of foam."

The same right solution of the first dilemma is offered by S. C. de Soissons: "Sometimes the reflection from the clouds fell upon the water." In the second phrase, "Behind it, like a gigantic snake, coiled a strip of foaming water," the verb "to coil" is probably not the most appropriate one to use, but at least the translator gets away from the nonsense of the road chasing something.

Iza Young departs from the Polish text fully aware, it seems, of the difficulty: "The reflection of the clouds lent here and there a pearly tint to the water . . ." Her other sentence does not offend one's common sense, although it is still fairly close to the original. "A long streak of churning, milky water trailed like a serpent behind . . ."

Summing up, although many solutions show at least the translators' awareness of the problem, they seem to stay too close to the original text, when a legitimate reason to depart from it undoubtedly exists.

Obviously Jeremiah Curtin's translation seems to show too much respect for the words rather than the thoughts of the author. It closely resembles the non-artistic literal translation of this compiler. O'Conor-Eccles does not seem to be afraid of taking liberties with the Polish text. Although some of her changes are well justified and have a sound foundation, there are also cases when she departs from the original text with no good reason for departing, and stays close to the text when she should not.

J. Christian Bay sometimes plunges into verbiage that is unnecessary. The translations of Hlasko and Bullick and of Iza Young can be rated as fairly good, while slightly rising above them is the work of S. C. de Soissons. One cannot escape the conclusion that no translation stands out in excellence. None could be used as an example to follow.

Glossary of Polish Given Names

Explanatory remarks.

The glossary is restricted to the first names appearing in the stories sum-marized. Most of the names of foreign origin which have the same form in Polish and in English have been omitted. The Polish name is followed by its English equivalent (whenever there is one), then by its diminutive forms in Polish only.

For the benefit of the readers who do not know Polish, a brief descrip-tion of the sounds represented by letters which do not appear in the English alphabet is offered below:

VOWELS

ó—as in book

ę—as in French *un* (nasal e)

ą—as in French *on* (nasal o)

CONSONANTS

ń—a very soft, palatalized *n* (the nearest sound in English is the first *n* in onion)

ś—a very soft palatalized, hissing *s*

ć—combination *t+s* pronounced in rapid succession as a single sound

ź—a very soft, palatalized, hissing *z*

ż—as the sound of *s* in measure

There are also sounds which exist in English, but are indicated in Polish by a different letter or a combination of letters, e.g.

w—pronounced like the English *v*

ł—generally pronounced in Polish like the English *w*

j—like the sound for *y* in yield

sz—almost like the English *sh*

rz—the same pronunciation as the Polish *ż* (see above)

cz—almost like the English *ch* in church

dż—like the English *j* in jungle

ch—also spelled *h,* like the *ch* in the Scottish pronunciation of loch

c—combination *t+s,* pronounced in quick succession; very much like *tz* in Switzerland

dz—combination of *d+z,* articulated as Polish *c,* but voiced.[1]

NAMES OF MEN

	Diminutive forms
Aleksander[2] = Alexander	Olek, Oleś
Andrzej or Jędrzej = Andrew	Jędrek, Jędruś
Antoni = Anthony or Antony	Antek, Antoś, Tolek, Tosiek
Bartłomiej or Bartosz = Bartholo-mew	Bartek
Bolesław	Bolcio, Bolek
Bronisław	Bronek
Czesław[3]	Czesiek, Czesio
Feliks = Felix	Felek, Feluś
Ferdynand = Ferdinand	Ferdek
Filip = Philip	Filipek
Florian	Florek
Franciszek = Francis	Franek, Franio, Franuś
Gustaw = Gustavus[4]	Gucio
Henryk = Henry	Heniek, Henio, Heniuś

---

[1] The above is not offered as the rules for the pronunciation of Polish. It may, however, help to explain why the name Janek is often given in the English translation as Yanek, Jaś as Yas, etc. The description of the Polish sounds has been based on M. Corbridge-Patkaniowska, TEACH YOURSELF POLISH Rev. and enl. (London: English Universities Press, 1964).

[2] Not the same as Aleksy which would correspond to Alexis. Alexander and Alexis stem from different roots.

[3] Czesław has no English equivalent, although it is usually rendered as Chester. (The English form Chester comes from a surname.)

[4] The German form "Gustav" has been used in the translation of Różewicz's *Beer.*

461

Ignacy = Ignatius[5]	Ignaś
Jacek = Hyacinthus (?)	Jacuś
Jakub or Kuba = James or Jacob	Kubuś
Jan[6] = John	Janek, Janko, Jaś, Jasiek, Jasio, Jaśko
Jędrzej, *see* Andrzej	
Jerzy = George	Jerzyk, Jurek
Józef = Joseph	Józek, Józiek, Józio, Ziutek
Juliusz = Julius	Julek
Karol = Charles	Karolek
Kaspar or Kasper = Caspar, Casper, or Jasper	Kasperek
Kazimierz = Casimir	Kazik, Kazio
Klemens = Clement	
Kuba, *see* Jakub	
Maciej = Matthias	Maciek, Maciuś
Marcin = Martin	Marcinek
Mateusz = Matthew	
Michał = Michael	Michałek, Michałko, Michaś
Mieczysław	Miecio, Mietek
Mikołaj = Nicholas or Nicolas	Mikołajek
Paweł = Paul	Pawełek
Piotr = Peter	Pietrek, Piotruś
Stanisław = Stanislaus[7]	Stach, Staś, Stasiek, Staszek, Staszko
Stefan = Stephen or Steven	Stefcio, Stefek
Szymon = Simon or Simeon	Szymek
Tadeusz = Thaddeus	Tadek, Tadzik, Tadzio
Tomasz = Thomas	Tomcio, Tomek
Walenty = Valentine	Walek
Wawrzyniec or Wawrzon[8] = Lawrence or Laurence	Wawrzek

---

[5] In some stories, e.g. Gombrowicz's *Premeditated Crime*, the French form "Ignace" has been used.
[6] Given in some stories in the anglicized form as Yan, Yanek, Yanko, Yas, Yasiek, Yasio, Yasko.
[7] The form Stanley comes from a surname.
[8] Given also in the anglicized form as Vavron.

Wincenty = Vincent   Wicek, Wicuś
Władysław = Ladislas or Ladislaus   Władek, Władzio
Wojciech = Adelbert   Wojtek,[9] Wojtuś
Zbigniew   Zbyszek, Zbyszko

NAMES OF WOMEN

Agnieszka = Agnes

Aleksandra = Alexandra (feminine of Alexander)   Ola, Oleńka, Olga, Olka

Aniela = Angela, Angelica, or Angelina   Anielka

Antonina = Antonia (feminine of Anthony)   Antosia, Tola, Tosia

Augustyna = Augusta (feminine of Augustus)   Augustynka or Jagustynka[10]

Elżbieta = Elizabeth, Elisabeth, or Eliza   Ela, Elżbietka, Elżunia

Ewa — Eve or Eva   Ewunia, Ewusia

Felicja = Felicia or Felice   Fela, Felka

Franciszka = Frances   Frania, Franka

Hanna = Ann, Anne, or Anna   Haneczka, Hania, Hanka, Hanusia

Helena = Helen or Helena   Hela, Helcia, Helenka

Jadwiga[11] = Hedwig   Jadwisia, Jadzia, Wisia

Janina = Jane, Jean, or Jeanne   Janeczka, Janka, Jasia,[12] Nina

Joanna = Joan, Joanna, or Johanna   Joasia

Józefina = Josepha or Josephine   Józia, Ziutka

Julia = Julia   Jula, Julcia, Julka

Katarzyna = Catherine, Catharine, Catherina, or Kathryn   Kasia

Klara = Clara or Clare

Krystyna = Christina or Christine   Krysia, Krystka, Krzysia

Magdalena = Madeline, Magdalen, or Magdalene   Madzia, Magda

---

9 Given also in the anglicized form as Voytek.
10 The form used in some peasants' dialects (cf. Reymont's *Tomek Baran*).
11 Given also in the anglicized form as Yadviga.
12 Given also in the anglicized form as Yaneczka, Yanka, or Yasia.

Maria[13] = Mary, Maria, or Marie	Mania, Mańka, Maryla, Marylka, Maryś, Marysia	
Monika = Monica		
Natalia = Natalia or Natalie[14]	Nacia, Nata, Natalka	
Stanisława = feminine of Stanislaus	Stasia, Staszka	
Wanda = Wanda	Wandka, Wandzia	
Weronika = Veronica	Werosia[15]	
Zofia = Sophia or Sophie	Zocha, Zosia, Zośka	
Zuzanna = Susan, Susanna, or Susannah	Zuzia	

---

[13] Maryna and Marianna stem from the same root as Maria.
[14] Translated in Grubiński's *Daimonion Bib* as Nathalie.
[15] Given also in the anglicized form as Verosia.

BIBLIOGRAPHY[1]

List of Bibliographies

Coleman, Marion Moore. ADAM MICKIEWICZ IN ENGLISH. Cambridge Springs, Penna.: Alliance College, 1954.

"East European Languages and Literatures: Annual Bibliography . . ." Usually in the May issue of the PMLA: Publications of the Modern Language Association of America (Menasha, Wis.). Annual, 1886–88; quarterly, 1889–

Hahn, Wiktor. BIBLIOGRAFIA BIBLIOGRAFIJ POLSKICH [The Bibliography of Polish Bibliographies.]. Wyd. drugie znacznie rozszerzone. Wrocław: Zakład imienia Ossolińskich, 1956.

INDEX TRANSLATIONUM. Repertoire international des traductions. International Bibliography of Translations. Paris: International Institute of Intellectual Cooperation, 1932–1940; n.s. 1948–
   Suspended publication 1941–1947. New series published by the United Nations Educational, Scientific and Cultural Organization. Annual.

Keckówna, Janina. "Literatura polska i o Polsce za granicą" [Polish Literature and Materials about Poland Abroad]. In ROCZNIK LITERACKI 1956. Warszawa. pp. 579–599.

Keckówna, Janina, and Łasiewicka, Alina (comps.). POLONICA ZAGRANICZNE; BIBLIOGRAFIA, 1956 [Polonica Abroad; a Bibliography, 1956]. (Na prawach rękopisu.) Warszawa: Biblioteka Narodowa, Instytut Bibliograficzny, 1960.

Koczorowski, St. P. (comp.). "Literatura polska w przekładach" [Polish literature in translation]. In ROCZNIK LITERACKI 1955. Warszawa. pp. 612–616.

Ledbetter, Eleanor E. THE POLISH IMMIGRANT AND HIS READING. Chicago: American Library Association, 1924.

---

[1] The inclusion of all the works in Polish consulted either to establish the Polish title of a story, or to compare the English translation with the Polish text, would make this bibliography very long and repetitious. Many such titles appear in the text. For these reasons the bulk of the Polish source material has been omitted.

————. POLISH LITERATURE IN ENGLISH TRANSLATION; a Bibliography with a List of Books about Poland and the Poles. New York: The H. W. Wilson Company, 1932.

Lipska, Helena, and Dembowska, Maria (comps.). BIBLIOGRAFIA BIBLIO-GRAFII I NAUKI O KSIĄŻCE. Bibliographia Poloniae Bibliographica. Rok 1947. Łódź: Państwowy Instytut Książki, 1947–1949.

Lipska, Helena, and Małachowska-Staszelis, Maria (comps.). BIBLIOGRAFIA BIBLIOGRAFII I NAUKI O KSIĄŻCE. Bibliographia Poloniae Bibliograph-ica. Rok 1945–1946. Warszawa: Państwowy Instytut Książki, 1955.

Ordon, Edmund. "A Tentative Bibliography of the Polish Short Story in English Translation," in The Polish Review; a quarterly published by the Polish Institute of Arts and Sciences in America (New York), I (Nos. 2–3, 1956), pp. [167]–176.

Sawoniak, Henryk (comp.). BIBLIOGRAFIA BIBLIOGRAFII I NAUKI O KSIĄŻCE. Bibliographia Poloniae Bibliographica Rok 1957. Warszawa: Pań-stwowy Instytut Książki, 1959

Shaw, Joseph T. (ed.). THE AMERICAN BIBLIOGRAPHY OF SLAVIC AND EAST EUROPEAN STUDIES FOR 1957. Bloomington, Indiana: University Pub-lications, 1958.

————. (ed.). THE AMERICAN BIBLIOGRAPHY OF SLAVIC AND EAST EUROPEAN STUDIES FOR 1958. Bloomington, Indiana: University Publications, 1959.

————. (ed.). THE AMERICAN BIBLIOGRAPHY OF SLAVIC AND EAST EUROPEAN STUDIES IN LANGUAGE, LITERATURE, FOLKLORE, AND PEDAGOGY. Bloom-ington, Indiana: University Publications, 1957.

Shaw, Joseph T., and Djaparidze, David (eds.). THE AMERICAN BIBLIOG-RAPHY OF SLAVIC AND EAST EUROPEAN STUDIES FOR 1959. Bloomington, Indiana: University Publications, 1960.

Turek, Victor. POLONICA CANADIANA; a Bibliographical List of the Canadian Polish Imprints, 1848–1957. (Polish Research Institute in Canada: Studies 2.) Toronto: Canadian Polish Congress, 1958.

Whitfield, Francis J. "Polish Literature; Bibliography," in Strakhovsky, Leonid I. A HANDBOOK OF SLAVIC STUDIES. Cambridge, Mass.: Harvard University Press, 1949. pp. 476–483.

Wolanin, Alphonse S. POLONICA AMERICANA; Annotated Catalogue of the Archives and Museum of the Polish Roman Catholic Union. Chi-cago: Polish Roman Catholic Union of America, Archives and Museum, 1950.

————. POLONICA IN ENGLISH; Annotated Catalogue of the Archives and Museum of the Polish Roman Catholic Union. Chicago: Polish Roman Catholic Union of America, Archives and Museum, 1945.

Zabielska, Janina. BIBLIOGRAPHY OF BOOKS IN POLISH OR RELATING TO

POLAND, PUBLISHED OUTSIDE POLAND SINCE SEPTEMBER 1ST, 1939. 3 vols. London: The Polish Library, 1954–1966.

v.1, 1939–1951; v.2, 1952–1957; v.3, continued and supplemented by Maria L. Danilewicz and Halina Choynacka, 1958–1963. Supplements to 1939–1957 (Nr. 1–4120).

Theoretical and Critical Material

Albright, Evelyn May. THE SHORT-STORY, ITS PRINCIPLES AND STRUCTURES. New York, London: Macmillan, 1924.

Amos, Flora Ross. EARLY THEORIES OF TRANSLATION. New York: Columbia University Press, 1920.

Atkinson, W. Patterson. THE SHORT-STORY. (The Academy classics.) Boston: Allyn and Bacon, 1923.

Bates, Ernest Stuart. INTERTRAFFIC; STUDIES IN TRANSLATION. London: J. Cape [1943].

————. MODERN TRANSLATION. London: Oxford University Press, H. Milford, 1936.

Bates, Herbert Ernest. THE MODERN SHORT STORY; a Critical Survey. London, New York: T. Nelson and sons, 1941.

Belloc, Hilaire. ON TRANSLATION; the Taylorian Lecture, 1931. Oxford: At the Clarendon Press, 1931.

Bowen, Elizabeth. "Introduction: The short story," in her THE FABER BOOK OF MODERN STORIES . . . London: Faber and Faber, 1937. pp. 7–19.

Brower, Reuben A. (ed.). ON TRANSLATION. Cambridge, Mass.: Harvard University Press, 1959.
   Contains an up-to-date, selective, and very well presented "A critical bibliography of works on translation," by Bayard Quincy Morgan. pp. [271]–293. It covers the period 46 B.C.–1958.

Brückner, Aleksander. DZIEJE LITERATURY POLSKIEJ W ZARYSIE [An Outline of the History of Polish Literature]. 2 vols. Warszawa: Instytut Wydawniczy "Biblioteka Polska," 1921.

Canby, Henry Seidel. THE SHORT STORY IN ENGLISH. New York: Henry Holt, 1909.

Canby, Henry Seidel, and Dashiell, Alfred. A STUDY OF THE SHORT STORY. Rev. ed. New York: Henry Holt, 1935.

Chlebowski, Bronisław. LITERATURA POLSKA 1795–1905, jako główny wyraz życia narodu po utracie niepodległości [Polish Literature 1795–1905, as the Main Expression of the Life of the Nation after the Loss of Its Independence]. Z rękopisu wydał i przedmową poprzedził Manfred Kridl. Lwów: Zakład Narodowy imienia Ossolińskich, 1923.

Conn, Edwin, and Kornstein, Max. TRANSLATION; a Handbook with Special Emphasis on English, French, German, Italian and Spanish. New York: Capital Publishing Institute, c1941.

Czachowski, Kazimierz. OBRAZ WSPÓŁCZESNEJ LITERATURY POLSKIEJ, 1884–1933 [Outline of the Polish Contemporary Literature, 1884–1933]. 2 vols. Lwów: Państwowe Wydawnictwo Książek Szkolnych, 1934.

———. OBRAZ WSPÓŁCZESNEJ LITERATURY POLSKIEJ, 1884–1934 [Outline of the Polish Contemporary Literature, 1884–1934]. vol. 3. Warszawa, Lwów: Państwowe Wydawnictwo Książek Szkolnych, 1936.

Dryden, John. "Essay on translation," in his ESSAYS . . . selected and edited with introduction and notes by C. D. Yonge. London, New York: Macmillan, 1903. pp. 111–128.

———. "Preface to Ovid's Epistles," in THE POETICAL WORKS OF DRYDEN; a new ed. rev. by George R. Noyes. (Cambridge ed.) Boston: Houghton, Mifflin Company, 1950. pp. 88–92.

Eichenbaum, Boris Mikhaĭlovich. "O. Genri [i.e. O. Henry] i teoriiã novelly." In his LITERATURA: TEORIIA, KRITIKA, POLEMIKA. Leningrad: "Priboĭ" [1927].

Erné, Giovanni Bruno. KUNST DER NOVELLE [von] Nino Erné [pseud.] [2nd ed.] Wiesbaden: Limes [1961].

Feldman, Wilhelm. WSPÓŁCZESNA LITERATURA POLSKA [Contemporary Polish Literature]. Okresem 1919–1930 uzupełnił Stefan Kołaczkowski. Wyd. ósme. Kraków: Krakowska Spółka Wydawnicza, 1930.

Frost, William. DRYDEN AND THE ART OF TRANSLATION. New Haven: Yale University Press; London: Geoffrey Cumberlege, Oxford University Press, 1955.

Gillon, Adam, and Krzyżanowski, Ludwik. INTRODUCTION TO MODERN POLISH LITERATURE; an Anthology of Fiction and Poetry. New York, Twayne Publishers [1964].[2]

Hamilton, Clayton. "The novel, the novelette, and the short-story," in his MATERIALS AND METHODS OF FICTION. New York: The Baker and Taylor Company, 1908. pp. 168–183.

———. "The structure of the short-story," in his MATERIALS AND METHODS OF FICTION. New York, The Baker and Taylor Company, 1908. pp. 184–200.

Harrison, Frederic. "The art of translation," in his DE SENECTUTE, MORE LAST WORDS. New York: D. Appleton, 1923. pp. 103–120.

Knox, R. A. ON ENGLISH TRANSLATION; the Romanes lecture delivered in

---

[2] Neither this anthology nor M. Kuncewiczowa's THE MODERN POLISH MIND are listed in Appendix I because the terminal date in the main body of this compilation is the end of 1960.

the Sheldonian Theatre 11 June 1957. Oxford: At the Clarendon Press, 1957.

Kridl, Manfred. LITERATURA POLSKA (na tle rozwoju kultury) [Polish Literature Against the Background of Its Cultural Development]. New York: Roy Publishers, 1945.

Krzyżanowski, Julian (ed.). DZIEŁA SIENKIEWICZA W PRZEKŁADACH [The works of Sienkiewicz in Translation]. Vol. 59 of Sienkiewicz, Henryk. DZIEŁA [Works]. Wydanie zbiorowe pod redakcją Juliana Krzyżanowskiego. Warszawa: Państwowy Instytut Wydawniczy, 1953.

——. KALENDARZ ŻYCIA I TWÓRCZOŚCI HENRYKA SIENKIEWICZA [The calendar of life and works of Henryk Sienkiewicz]. Vol. 57 of Sienkiewicz, Henryk. DZIEŁA [Works]. Wydanie zbiorowe pod redakcją Juliana Krzyżanowskiego. Warszawa: Państwowy Instytut Wydawniczy, 1954.

Kuncewiczowa, Maria, ed. Introduction to her THE MODERN POLISH MIND; an Anthology. London: Secker and Warburg [1963, c1962]. p.[3]–10.[3]

Matthews, Brander. "The philosophy of the Short-story," in his PEN AND INK. 3rd ed., rev. and enl. New York: Charles Scribner's Sons, 1902. pp. [73]–106.
      Also as a separate publication with imprint New York: Longmans, Green, and company, 1912.

Matuszewski, Ryszard. CONTEMPORARY POLISH WRITERS. [Cover title: Portraits of contemporary Polish writers.] Warsaw: Polonia Publishing House, 1959.

Notestein, Lucy Lilian, and Dunn, Waldo Hilary. THE MODERN SHORT-STORY; a Study of the Form, Its Plot, Structure, Development and Other Requirements. New York: The A. S. Barnes Company, 1914.

Ordon, Edmund. "The Reception of the Polish short story in English; reflections on a bibliography," in The Polish Review; a quarterly published by the Polish Institute of Arts and Sciences in America (New York), II (Nos. 2–3, 1957), pp. [125]–132.

Paull, Harry Major. "Translations," in his LITERARY ETHICS; a Study in the Growth of the Literary Conscience. New York: E. P. Dutton [1929]. pp. 299–312.

Peyre, Henri. INTRODUCTION TO CONTES MODERNES . . . by members of the Department of French, Yale University, rev. ed. New York: Harper, 1949. pp. xi–xxii.

Poe, Edgar Allan. "Hawthorne and the story-teller's art," in THE BOOK OF POE; Tales, Criticism, Poems, ed. Addison Hibbard. Garden City, N.Y.: Doubleday, Doran and company, 1929. pp. 116–126.

---

3 See footnote 2, p. 468.

————. "The philosophy of composition," in THE POEMS OF EDGAR ALLAN POE WITH A SELECTION OF ESSAYS. (Everyman's Library ed.) London, Toronto: J. M. Dent and sons; New York: Dutton and company, 1927. pp. 163–177.

Polish American Studies, Official Organ of the Polish American Historical Association; a Journal Devoted to Polish American Life and History. Published twice a year by the Polish American Historical Association of the Polish Institute of Arts and Sciences in America. Orchard Lake, Mich.: St. Mary's College, 1944–

Ransome, Arthur. A HISTORY OF STORY-TELLING; Studies in the Development of Narrative. London: T. C. and E. C. Jack, 1909.

Rusinek, Michał (ed.). O SZTUCE TŁUMACZENIA (The Art of Translating). Wrocław: Zakład imienia Ossolińskich, 1955.

————. (ed.). P.E.N.; BULLETIN DU CENTRE POLONAIS. Première Rencontre Internationale des Traducteurs Littéraires à Varsovie. Warsaw, 1959.

Savory, Theodore. THE ART OF TRANSLATION. London: Jonathan Cape, 1959.

Scherer-Virski, Olga. THE MODERN POLISH SHORT STORY. 's-Gravenhage, Mouton and company, 1955.

Spielhagen, Friedrich. BEITRÄGE ZUR THEORIE UND TECHNIK DES ROMANS. Leipzig: L. Staackman, 1883.

Upham, Alfred H. "The short story; an introduction to the historical and critical study of English literature for college classes," in his THE TYPICAL FORMS OF ENGLISH LITERATURE. New York, London: Oxford University Press, 1917. pp. 191–210.

Ward, Alfred Charles. "The short story," in his FOUNDATIONS OF ENGLISH PROSE. London: G. Bell and sons, 1931. pp. 119–134.

Warren, Thomas Herbert. "The art of translation," in his ESSAYS OF POETS AND POETRY ANCIENT AND MODERN. London: John Murray, 1909. pp. [85]–133.

Wojciechowski, Konstanty. DZIEJE LITERATURY POLSKIEJ [History of Polish Literature]. Wydanie trzecie przygotowane pod redakcją dr. J. Balickiego; wstępem poprzedzone przez Ign. Chrzanowskiego. Lwów, Warszawa: Książnica—Atlas, 1930.

Wojtasiewicz, Olgierd. WSTĘP DO TEORII TŁUMACZENIA [Introduction to the Theory of Translation]. Wrocław, Warszawa: Zakład imienia Ossolińskich, 1957.

Woodhouselee, Alexander Fraser Tytler. ESSAY ON THE PRINCIPLES OF TRANSLATION. (Everyman's Library.) London: J. M. Dent; New York: E. P. Dutton [1907].

Index of Authors

This index refers only to the main body of the bibliography and the Supplement. It does not include the Introduction.

No bio-bibliographic notes have been offered for the authors marked with an asterisk, i.e. the authors whose stories in translation have appeared in periodicals only or who are represented solely by fragments from their novels rather than stricto sensu *short stories*. There are no such notes in the Supplement. The reader is reminded that there is no connection between the length of a bio-bibliographic note or its absence and the importance of an author. (*See Explanatory Notes, p. 55.*)

471

Jerzy J. Maciuszko was born in Poland and received his M.A. in English from the University of Warsaw. He came to the United States in 1951 and received Masters and Ph.D. degrees in Library Science from Western Reserve University, Cleveland, Ohio. He is currently Head of the John G. White Department, Cleveland Public Library and Lecturer in Polish Language and Literature at Case Western Reserve University.

The manuscript was edited by Sandra Shapiro. The book was designed by Sylvia Winter. The type face for both the text and display in Baskerville based on original types cut by John Martin for John Baskerville about 1750.

The book is printed on S. D. Warren's Olde Style Antique paper and bound in Bancroft's Linen Finish cloth over boards. Manufactured in the United States of America.